SB
Shojo Beat

Kaze HIKARU

18

Story & Art by
Taeko Watanabe

Contents

Story Thus Far

It is the end of the Bakufu era, the third year of Bunkyu (1863) in Kyoto. The Shinsengumi is a band of warriors formed to protect the shogun.

Tominaga Sei, the daughter of a former Bakufu *bushi*, joined the Shinsengumi disguised as a boy by the name of Kamiya Seizaburo to avenge her father and brother. She has continued her training under the only person in the Shinsengumi who knows her true identity, Okita Soji, and she aspires to become a true *bushi*.

Acts of violence at the hands of the captain of the Seventh Troop, Tani Sanjuro, stationed in Osaka, have invited the hostility of the city's residents. With the First Troop, Kondo mobilizes to regain the troop's honor.

Tani has a hard past that has left him fighting demons of suspicion. Kondo wants to forgive him, but the situation has deteriorated to the point where the townsmen join forces with roshi to attack the Shinsengumi. Kondo decides to withdraw from the Osaka post.

Characters

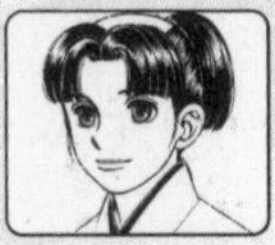

Tominaga Sei
She disguises herself as a boy to enter the Mibu-Roshi. She trains under Soji, aspiring to become a true *bushi*. But secretly, she is in love with Soji.

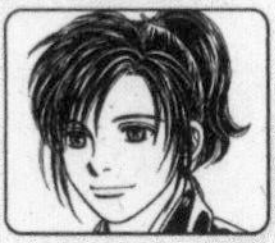

Okita Soji
Assistant vice captain of the Shinsengumi and licensed master of the Ten'nen Rishin-Ryu. He supports the troop alongside Kondo and Hijikata and guides Seizaburo with a kind yet firm hand.

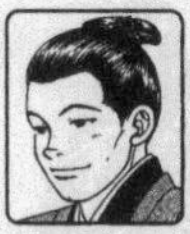

Kondo Isami
Captain of the Shinsengumi and fourth grandmaster of the Ten'nen Rishin-ryu. A passionate, warm and well-respected leader.

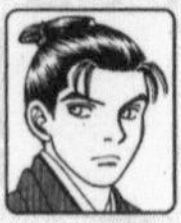

Hijikata Toshizo
Vice captain of the Shinsengumi. He commands both the group and himself with a rigid strictness. He is also known as the "Oni vice captain."

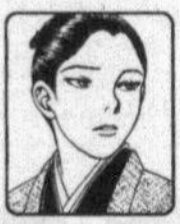

Ito Kashitaro
Councillor of the Shinsengumi. A skilled swordsman yet also an academic with anti-Bakufu sentiments, he plots to sway the direction of the troop.

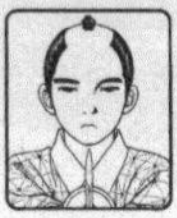

Saito Hajime
Assistant vice captain. He was a friend of Sei's older brother. Sei is attached to him in place of her lost brother.

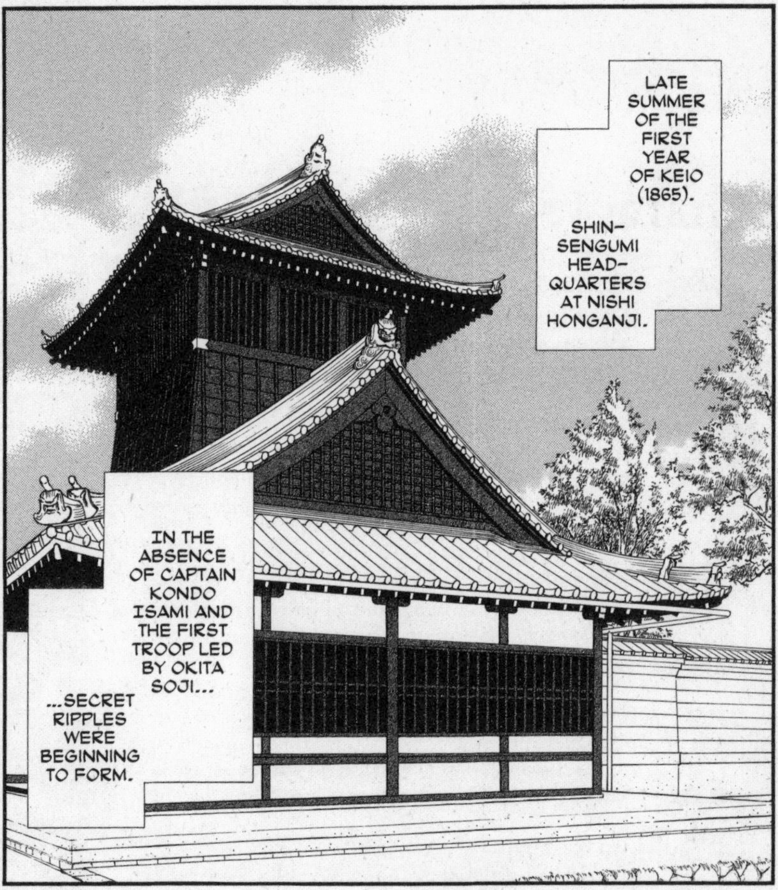
LATE SUMMER OF THE FIRST YEAR OF KEIO (1865).
SHIN-SENGUMI HEAD-QUARTERS AT NISHI HONGANJI.
IN THE ABSENCE OF CAPTAIN KONDO ISAMI AND THE FIRST TROOP LED BY OKITA SOJI...
...SECRET RIPPLES WERE BEGINNING TO FORM.

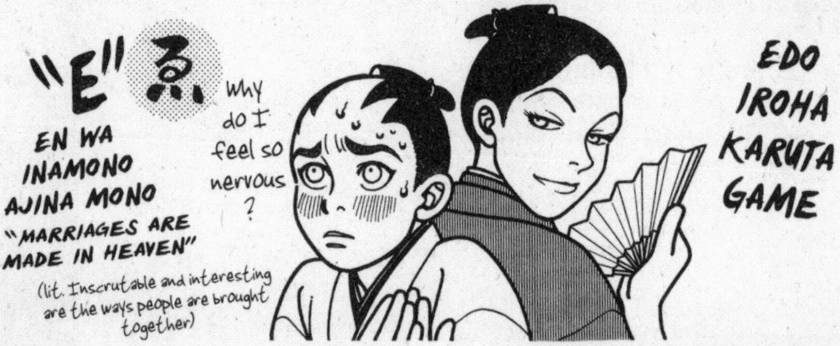
EDO IROHA KARUTA GAME
"E" ゑ
EN WA INAMONO AJINA MONO
"MARRIAGES ARE MADE IN HEAVEN"
(lit. Inscrutable and interesting are the ways people are brought together)
Why do I feel so nervous?

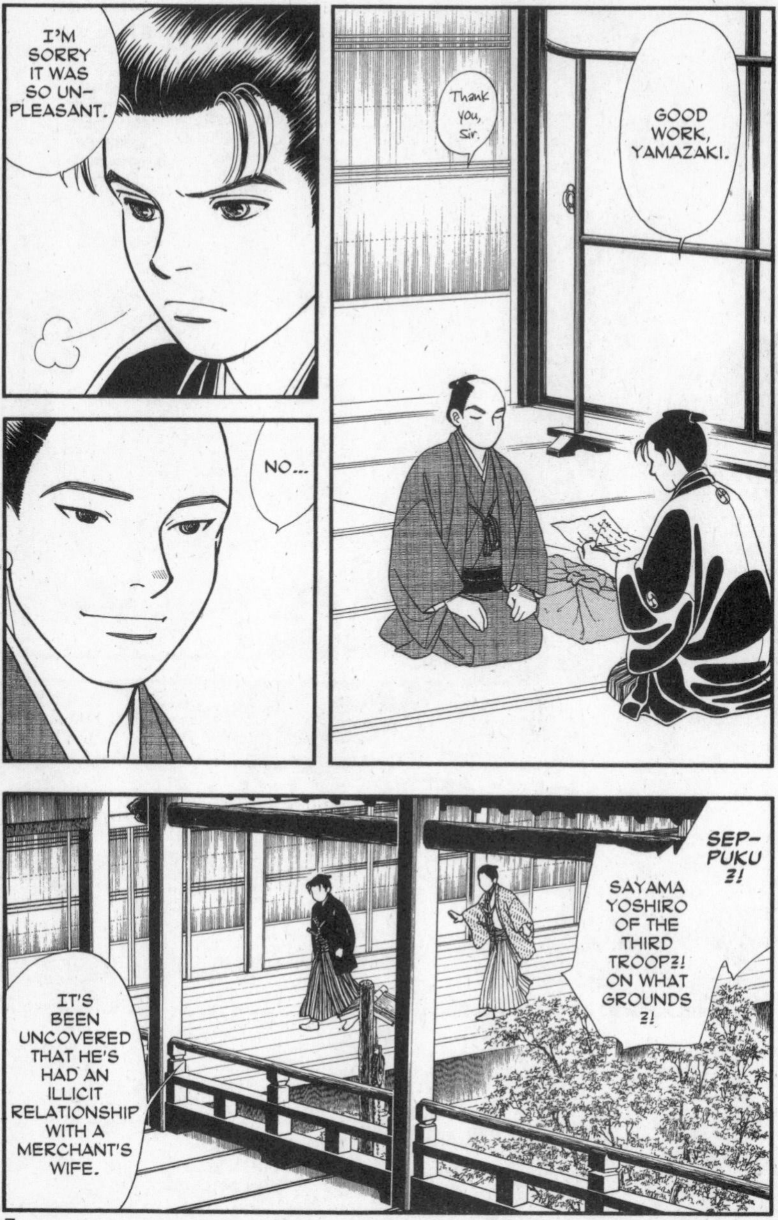
GOOD WORK, YAMAZAKI.
Thank you, Sir.
I'M SORRY IT WAS SO UN-PLEASANT.
NO...
SEP-PUKU?!
SAYAMA YOSHIRO OF THE THIRD TROOP?! ON WHAT GROUNDS?!
IT'S BEEN UNCOVERED THAT HE'S HAD AN ILLICIT RELATIONSHIP WITH A MERCHANT'S WIFE.

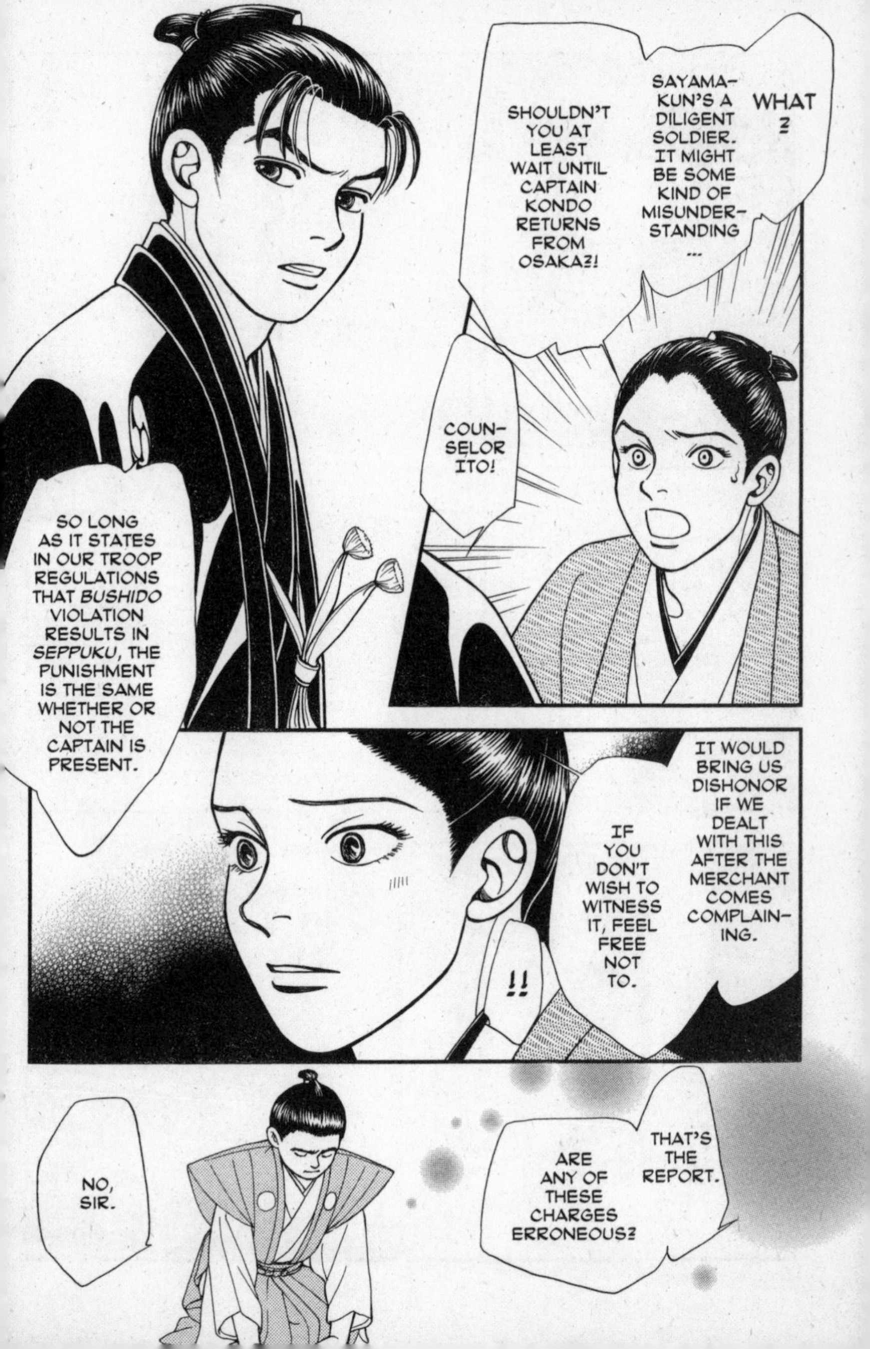
WHAT?
SAYAMA-KUN'S A DILIGENT SOLDIER. IT MIGHT BE SOME KIND OF MISUNDER-STANDING ...
SHOULDN'T YOU AT LEAST WAIT UNTIL CAPTAIN KONDO RETURNS FROM OSAKA?!
COUN-SELOR ITO!
SO LONG AS IT STATES IN OUR TROOP REGULATIONS THAT *BUSHIDO* VIOLATION RESULTS IN *SEPPUKU*, THE PUNISHMENT IS THE SAME WHETHER OR NOT THE CAPTAIN IS PRESENT.
IT WOULD BRING US DISHONOR IF WE DEALT WITH THIS AFTER THE MERCHANT COMES COMPLAIN-ING.
IF YOU DON'T WISH TO WITNESS IT, FEEL FREE NOT TO.
!!
THAT'S THE REPORT.
ARE ANY OF THESE CHARGES ERRONEOUS?
NO, SIR.

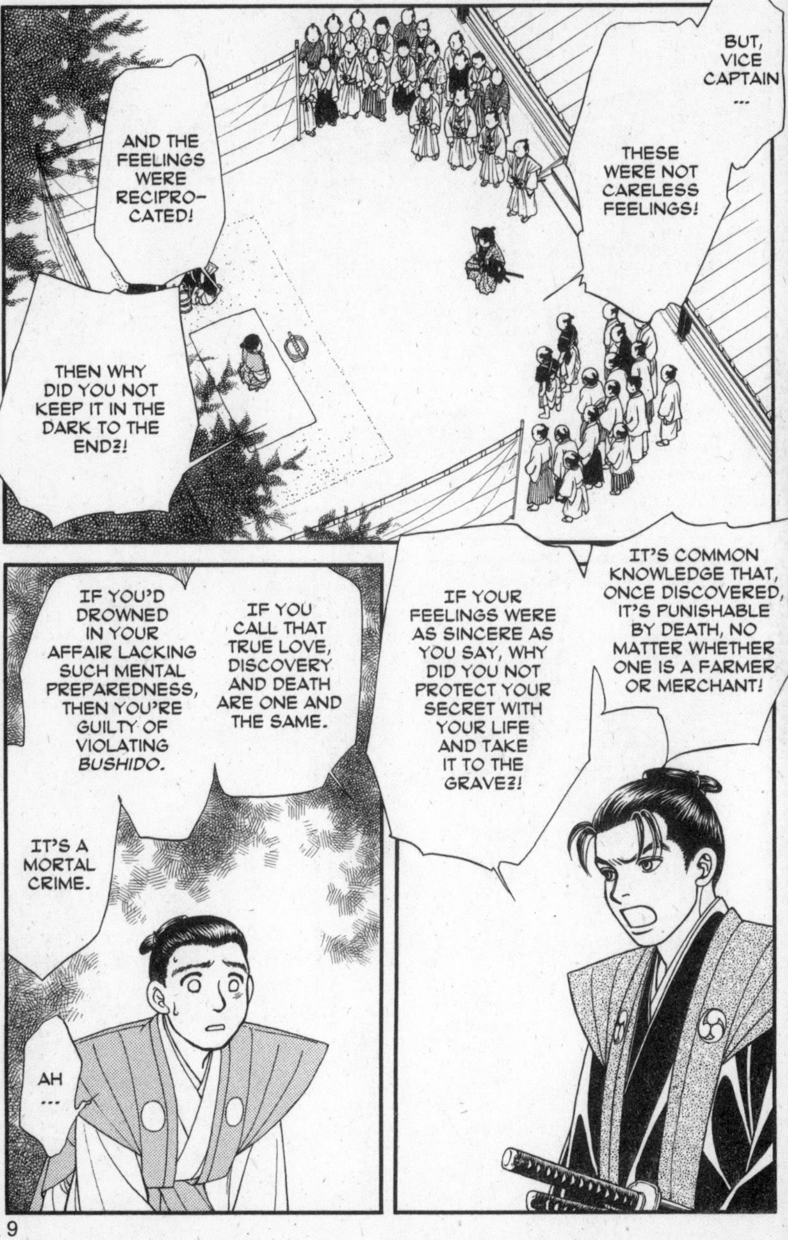
BUT, VICE CAPTAIN ...
THESE WERE NOT CARELESS FEELINGS!
AND THE FEELINGS WERE RECIPROCATED!
THEN WHY DID YOU NOT KEEP IT IN THE DARK TO THE END?!
IT'S COMMON KNOWLEDGE THAT, ONCE DISCOVERED, IT'S PUNISHABLE BY DEATH, NO MATTER WHETHER ONE IS A FARMER OR MERCHANT!
IF YOUR FEELINGS WERE AS SINCERE AS YOU SAY, WHY DID YOU NOT PROTECT YOUR SECRET WITH YOUR LIFE AND TAKE IT TO THE GRAVE?!
IF YOU CALL THAT TRUE LOVE, DISCOVERY AND DEATH ARE ONE AND THE SAME.
IF YOU'D DROWNED IN YOUR AFFAIR LACKING SUCH MENTAL PREPAREDNESS, THEN YOU'RE GUILTY OF VIOLATING *BUSHIDO*.
IT'S A MORTAL CRIME.
AH ...

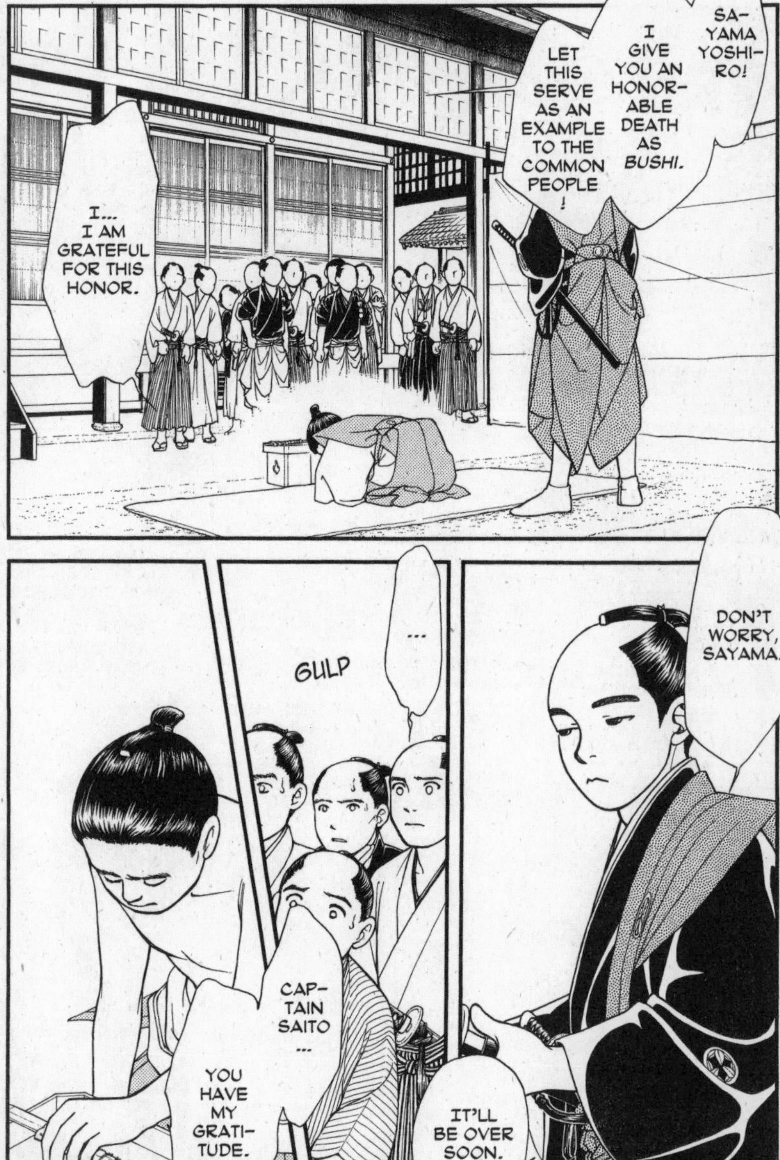
SAYAMA YOSHIRO!
I GIVE YOU AN HONORABLE DEATH AS *BUSHI*.
LET THIS SERVE AS AN EXAMPLE TO THE COMMON PEOPLE!
I... I AM GRATEFUL FOR THIS HONOR.
DON'T WORRY, SAYAMA.
IT'LL BE OVER SOON.
...
GULP
CAPTAIN SAITO...
YOU HAVE MY GRATITUDE.

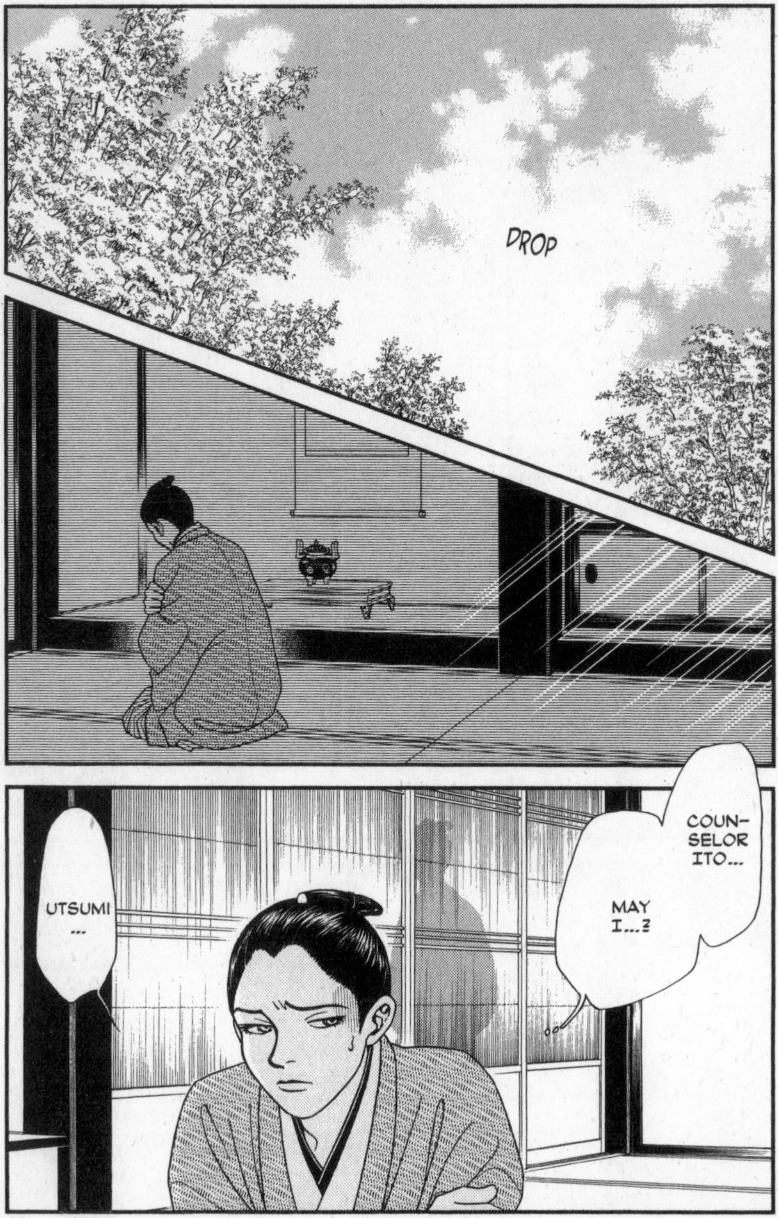
DROP
COUN-SELOR ITO...
MAY I...?
UTSUMI ...

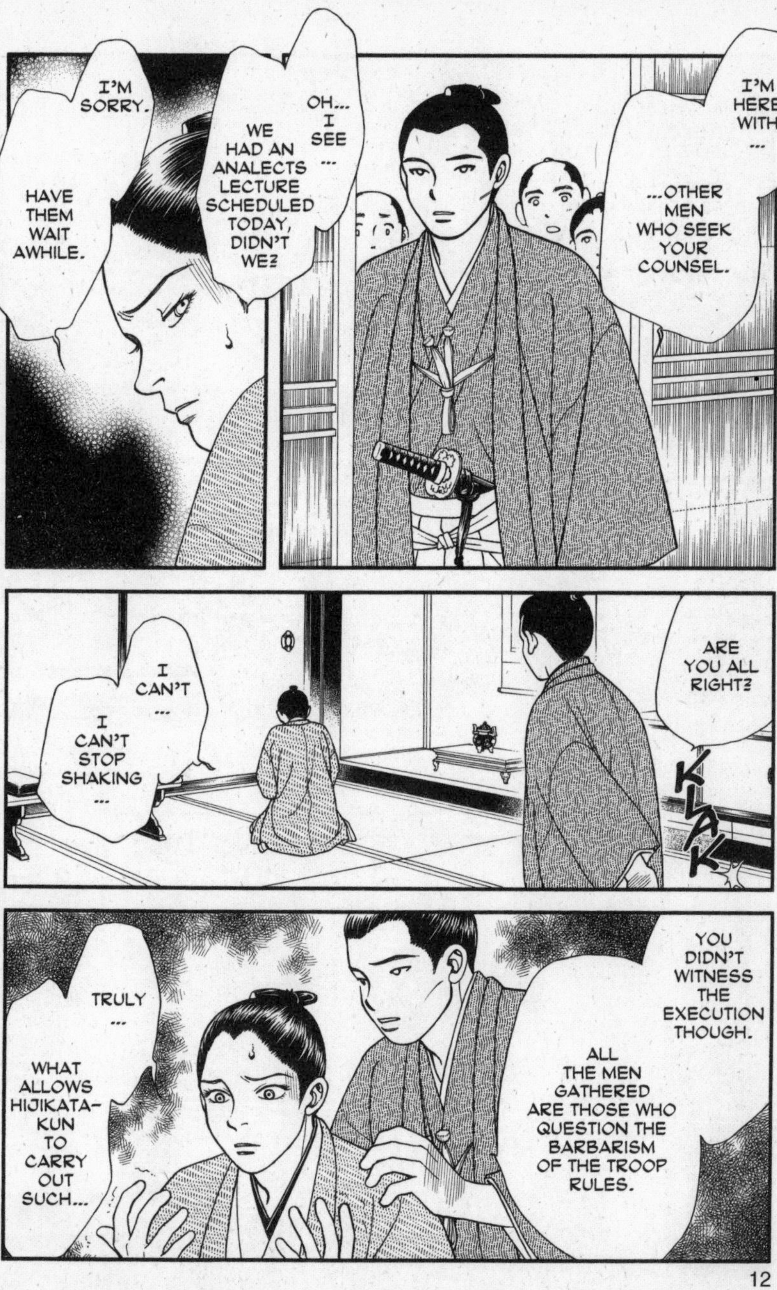

I'M HERE WITH ...
...OTHER MEN WHO SEEK YOUR COUNSEL.
OH... I SEE ...
WE HAD AN ANALECTS LECTURE SCHEDULED TODAY, DIDN'T WE?
I'M SORRY.
HAVE THEM WAIT AWHILE.
ARE YOU ALL RIGHT?
KLAK
I CAN'T ...
I CAN'T STOP SHAKING ...
YOU DIDN'T WITNESS THE EXECUTION THOUGH.
ALL THE MEN GATHERED ARE THOSE WHO QUESTION THE BARBARISM OF THE TROOP RULES.
TRULY ...
WHAT ALLOWS HIJIKATA-KUN TO CARRY OUT SUCH...

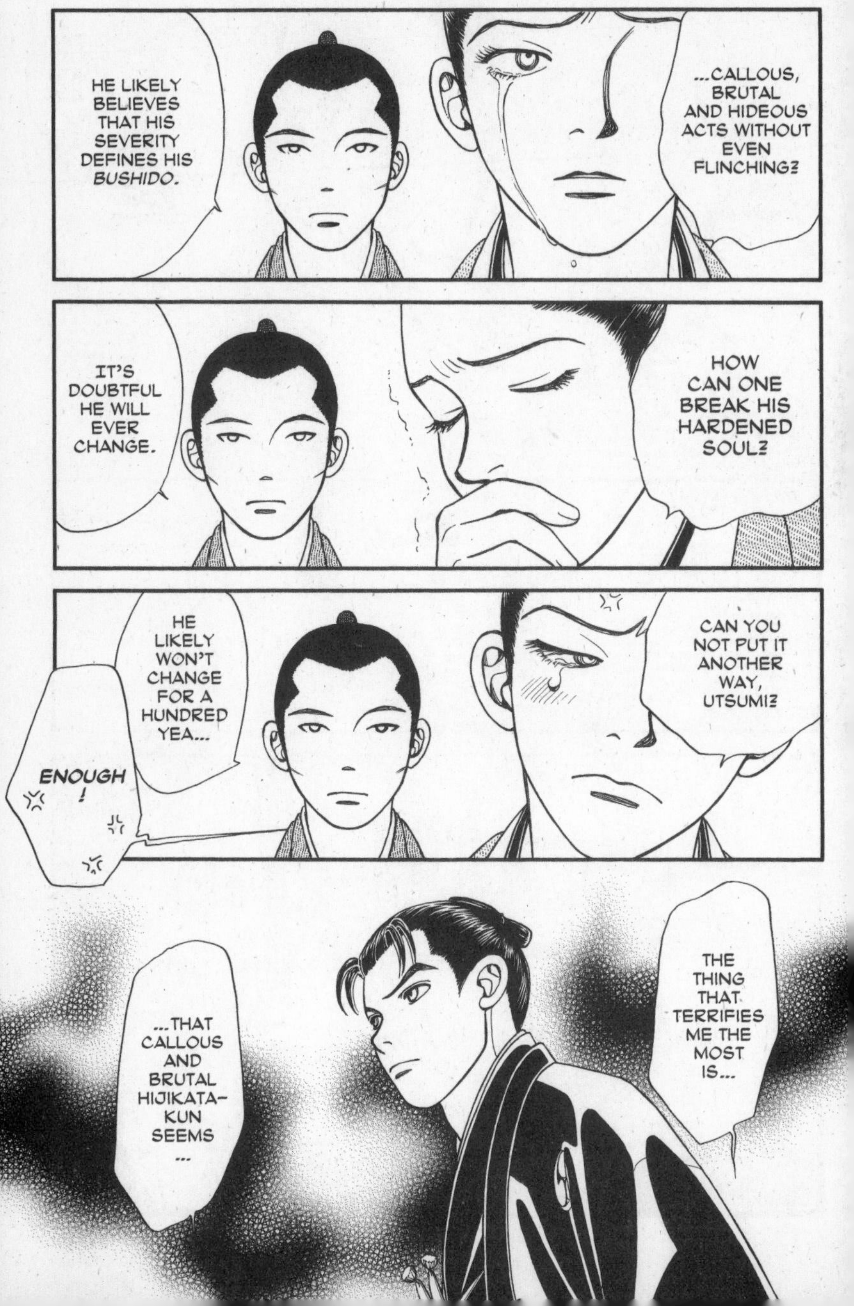
...CALLOUS, BRUTAL AND HIDEOUS ACTS WITHOUT EVEN FLINCHING?
HE LIKELY BELIEVES THAT HIS SEVERITY DEFINES HIS *BUSHIDO*.
HOW CAN ONE BREAK HIS HARDENED SOUL?
IT'S DOUBTFUL HE WILL EVER CHANGE.
CAN YOU NOT PUT IT ANOTHER WAY, UTSUMI?
HE LIKELY WON'T CHANGE FOR A HUNDRED YEA...
ENOUGH!
THE THING THAT TERRIFIES ME THE MOST IS...
...THAT CALLOUS AND BRUTAL HIJIKATA-KUN SEEMS...

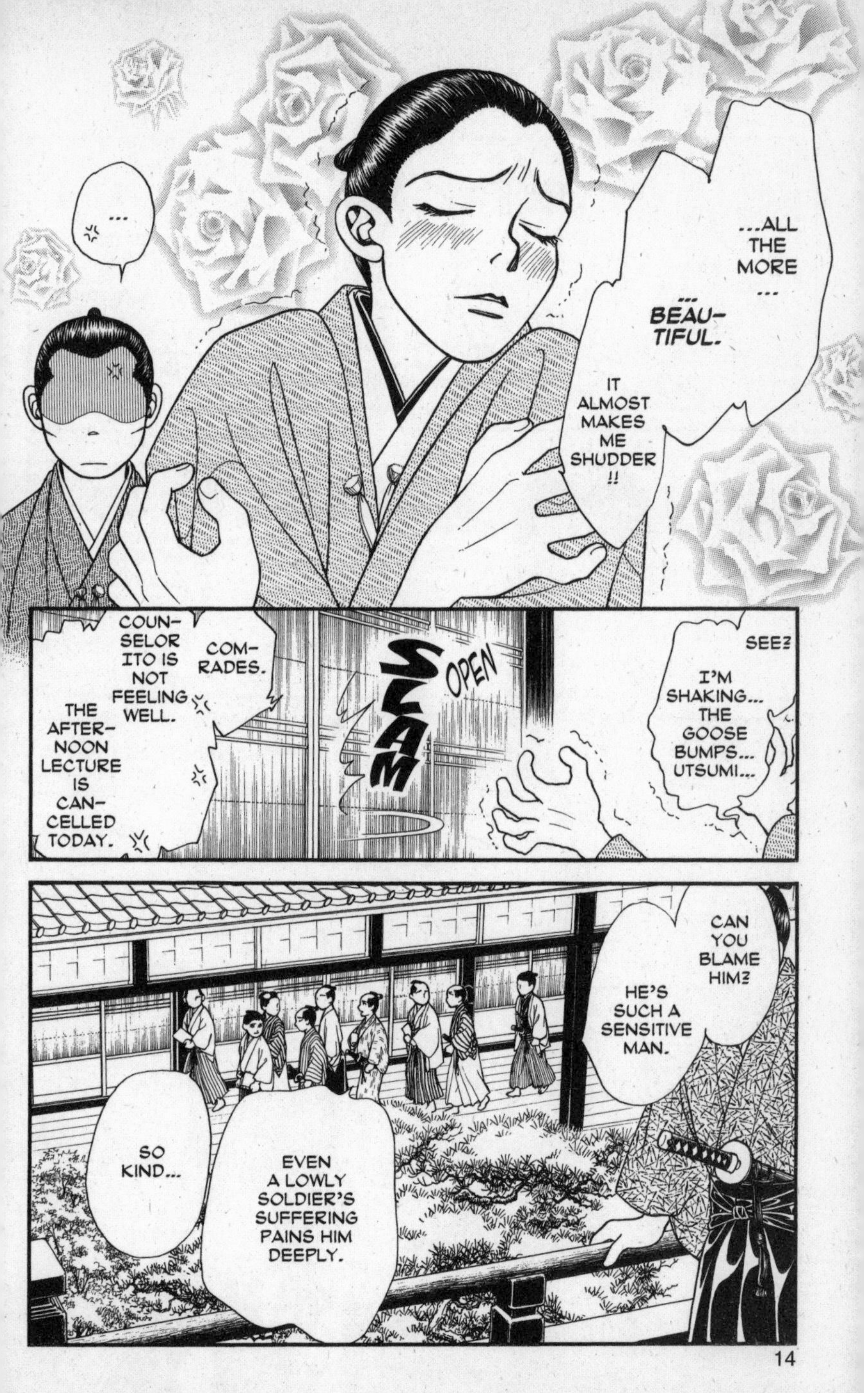
...ALL THE MORE ... ...BEAUTIFUL.
IT ALMOST MAKES ME SHUDDER!!
...
SEE? I'M SHAKING... THE GOOSE BUMPS... UTSUMI...
OPEN
SLAM
COMRADES.
COUNSELOR ITO IS NOT FEELING WELL.
THE AFTERNOON LECTURE IS CANCELLED TODAY.
CAN YOU BLAME HIM?
HE'S SUCH A SENSITIVE MAN.
EVEN A LOWLY SOLDIER'S SUFFERING PAINS HIM DEEPLY.
SO KIND...

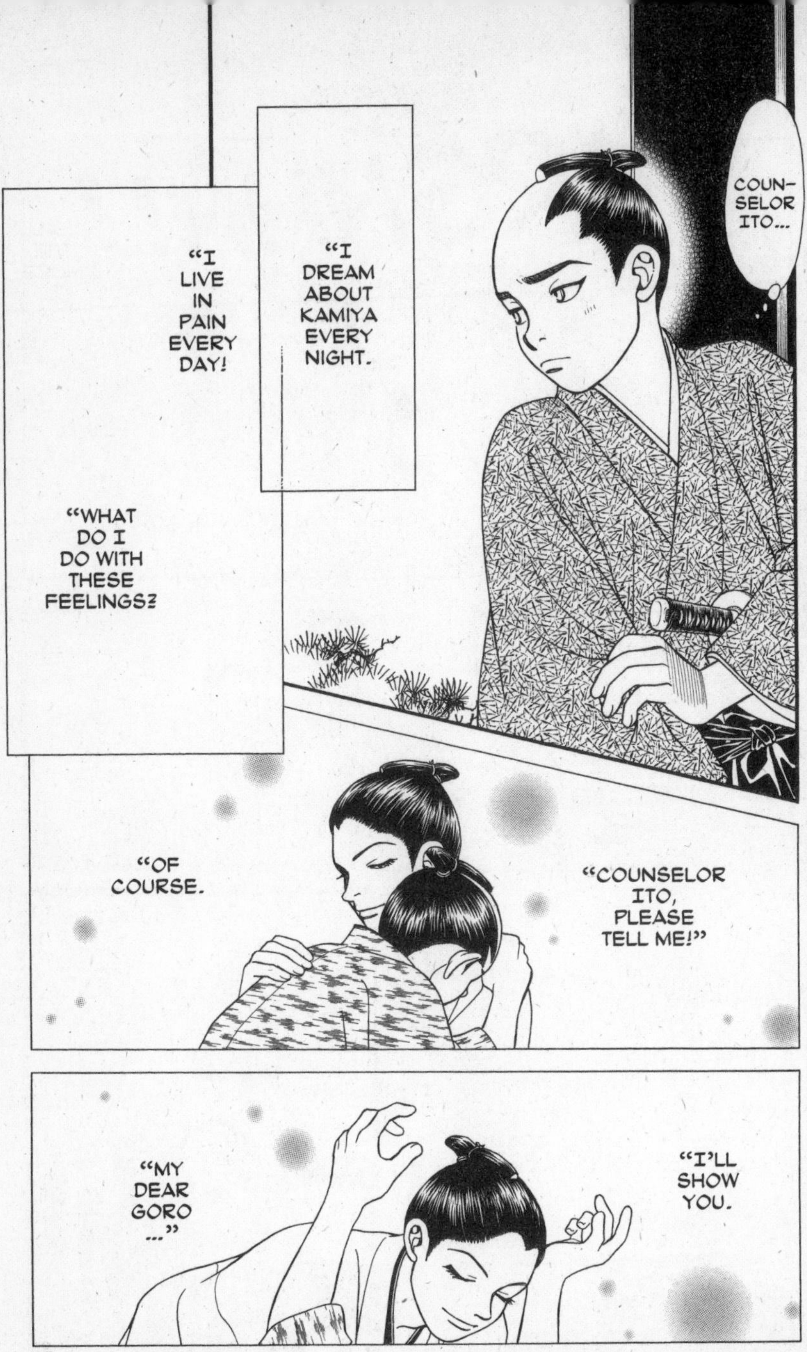
COUNSELOR ITO...
"I DREAM ABOUT KAMIYA EVERY NIGHT.
"I LIVE IN PAIN EVERY DAY!
"WHAT DO I DO WITH THESE FEELINGS?
"COUNSELOR ITO, PLEASE TELL ME!"
"OF COURSE.
"I'LL SHOW YOU.
"MY DEAR GORO..."

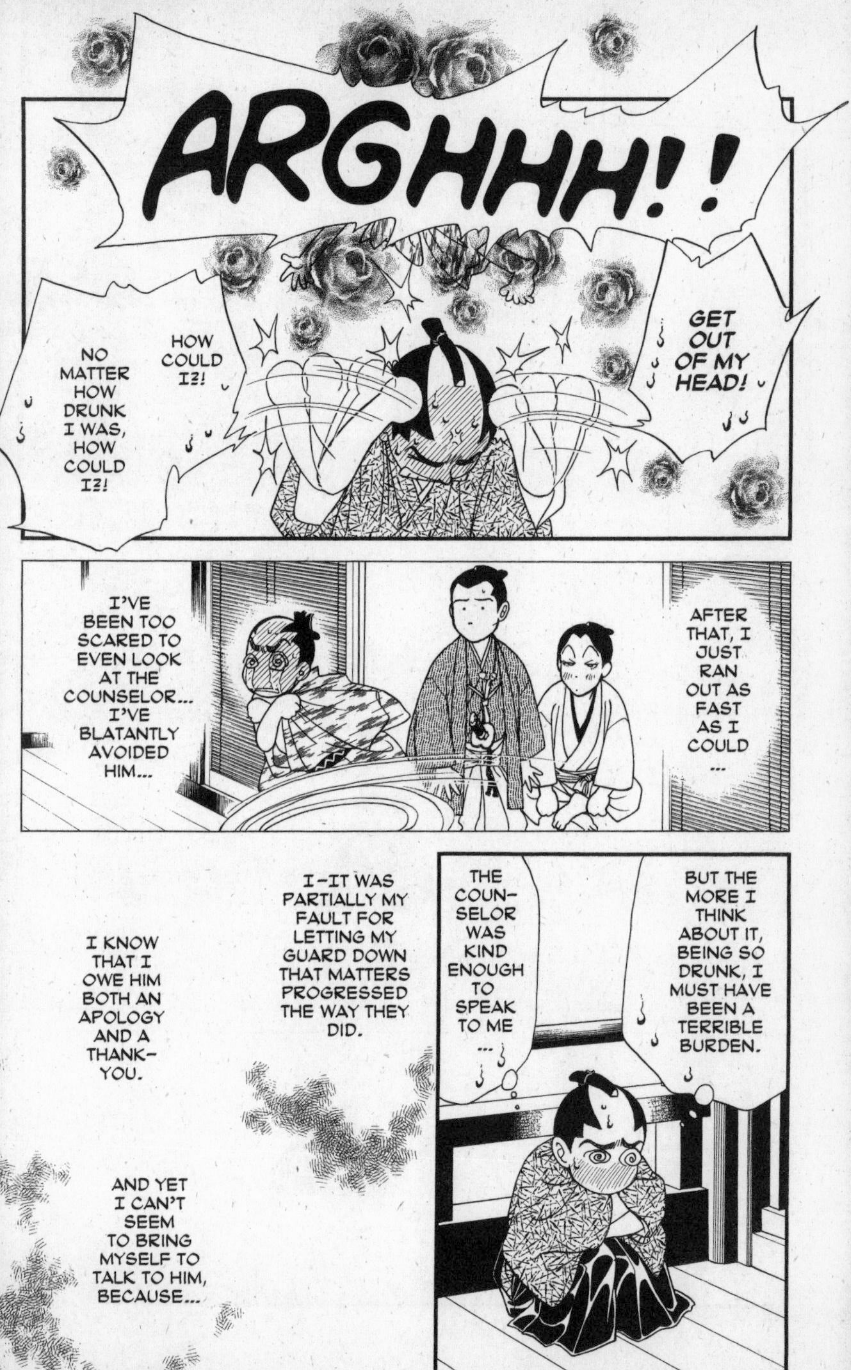
ARGHHH!!
GET OUT OF MY HEAD!
HOW COULD I?!
NO MATTER HOW DRUNK I WAS, HOW COULD I?!
AFTER THAT, I JUST RAN OUT AS FAST AS I COULD...
I'VE BEEN TOO SCARED TO EVEN LOOK AT THE COUNSELOR... I'VE BLATANTLY AVOIDED HIM...
BUT THE MORE I THINK ABOUT IT, BEING SO DRUNK, I MUST HAVE BEEN A TERRIBLE BURDEN.
THE COUNSELOR WAS KIND ENOUGH TO SPEAK TO ME...
I-IT WAS PARTIALLY MY FAULT FOR LETTING MY GUARD DOWN THAT MATTERS PROGRESSED THE WAY THEY DID.
I KNOW THAT I OWE HIM BOTH AN APOLOGY AND A THANK-YOU.
AND YET I CAN'T SEEM TO BRING MYSELF TO TALK TO HIM, BECAUSE...

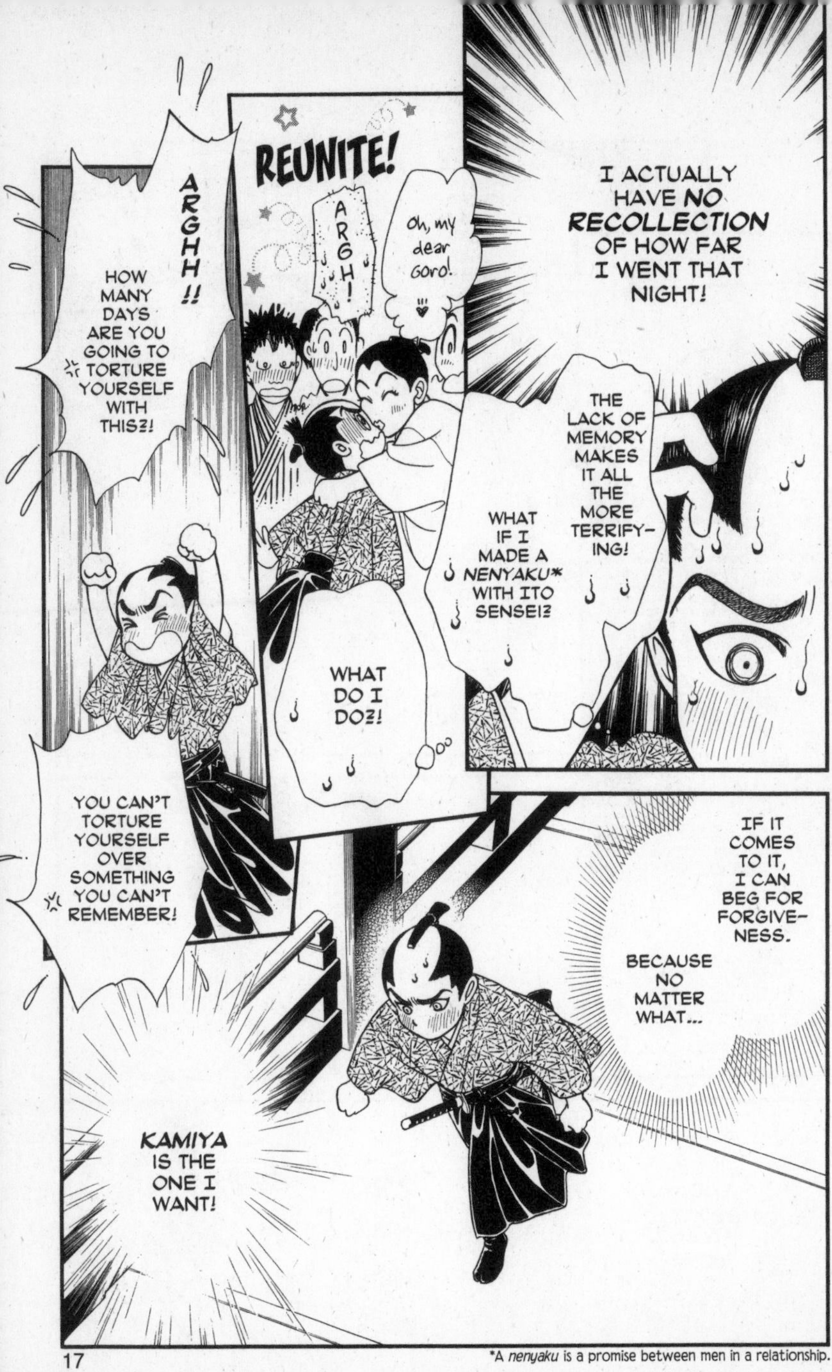
I ACTUALLY HAVE NO RECOLLECTION OF HOW FAR I WENT THAT NIGHT!
THE LACK OF MEMORY MAKES IT ALL THE MORE TERRIFYING!
WHAT IF I MADE A NENYAKU* WITH ITO SENSEI?!
REUNITE!
Oh, my dear Goro!
ARGH!
WHAT DO I DO?!
ARGHH!!
HOW MANY DAYS ARE YOU GOING TO TORTURE YOURSELF WITH THIS?!
YOU CAN'T TORTURE YOURSELF OVER SOMETHING YOU CAN'T REMEMBER!
IF IT COMES TO IT, I CAN BEG FOR FORGIVENESS.
BECAUSE NO MATTER WHAT...
KAMIYA IS THE ONE I WANT!

*A *nenyaku* is a promise between men in a relationship.

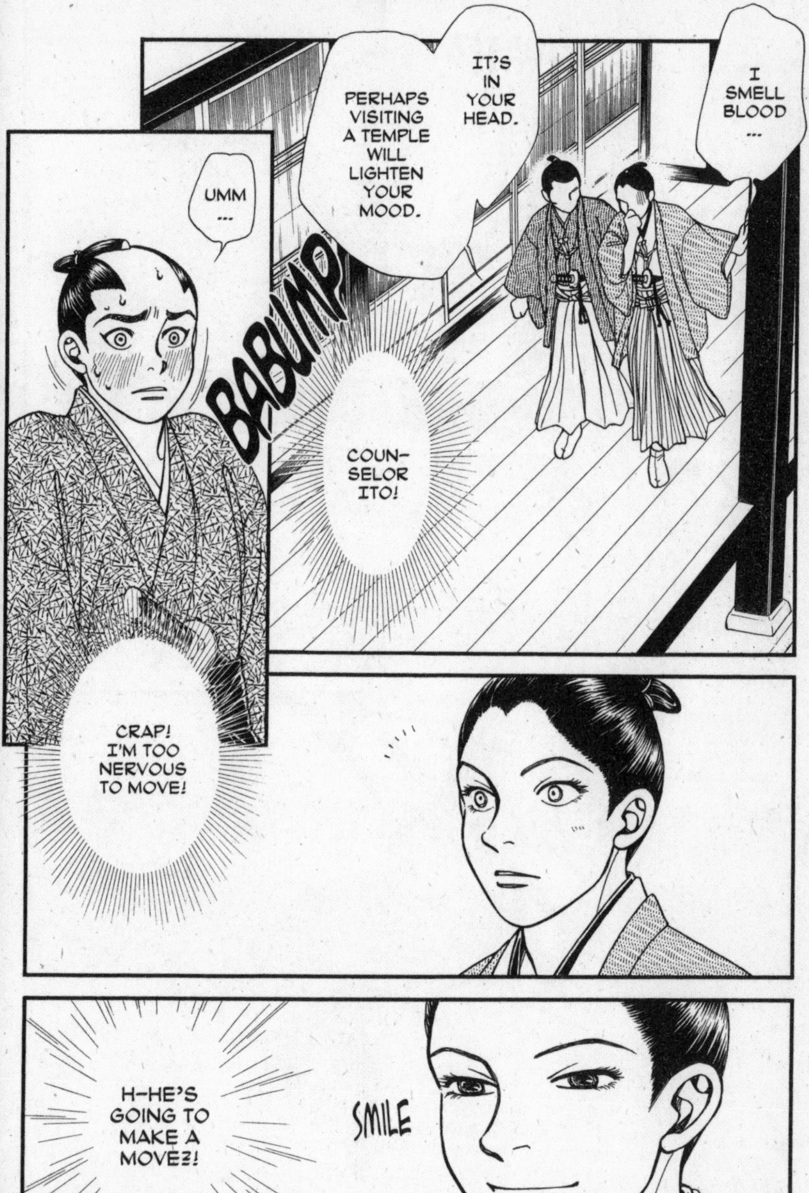
I SMELL BLOOD ...
IT'S IN YOUR HEAD.
PERHAPS VISITING A TEMPLE WILL LIGHTEN YOUR MOOD.
BABUMP
COUN-SELOR ITO!
UMM ...
CRAP! I'M TOO NERVOUS TO MOVE!
SMILE
H-HE'S GOING TO MAKE A MOVE?!

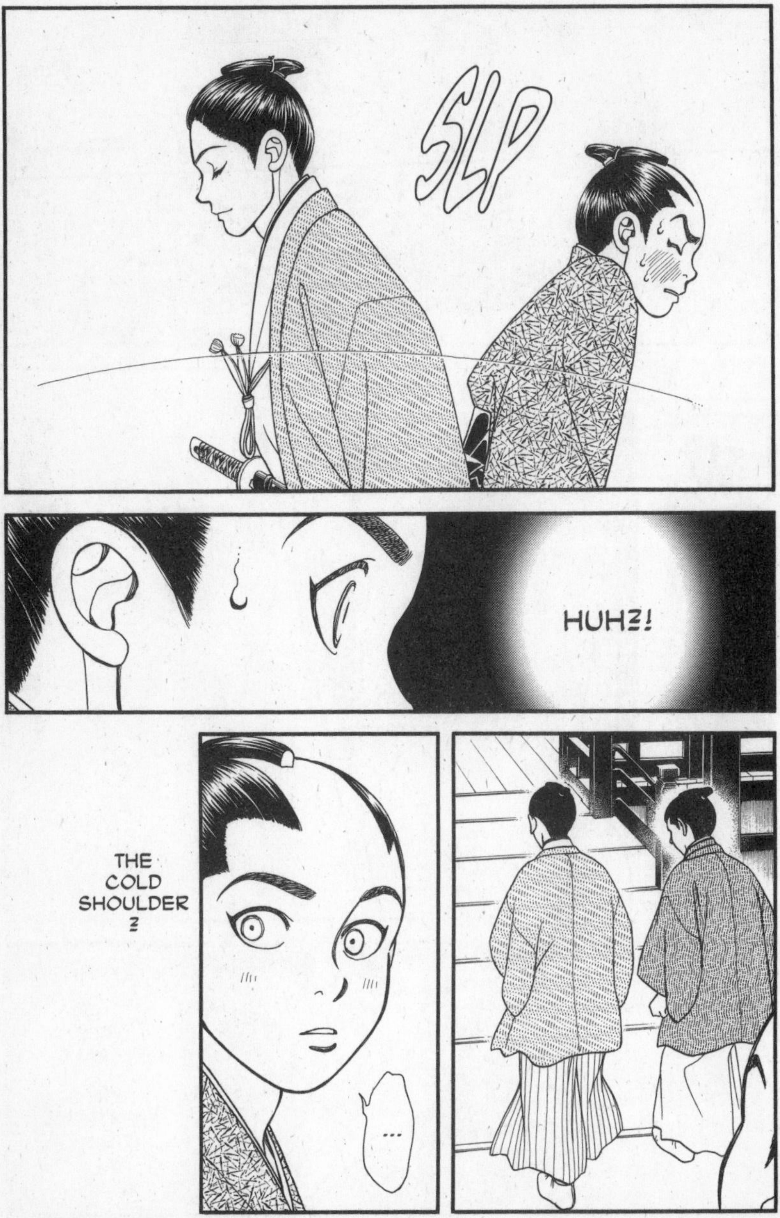
SLP
HUH?!
...
THE COLD SHOULDER?

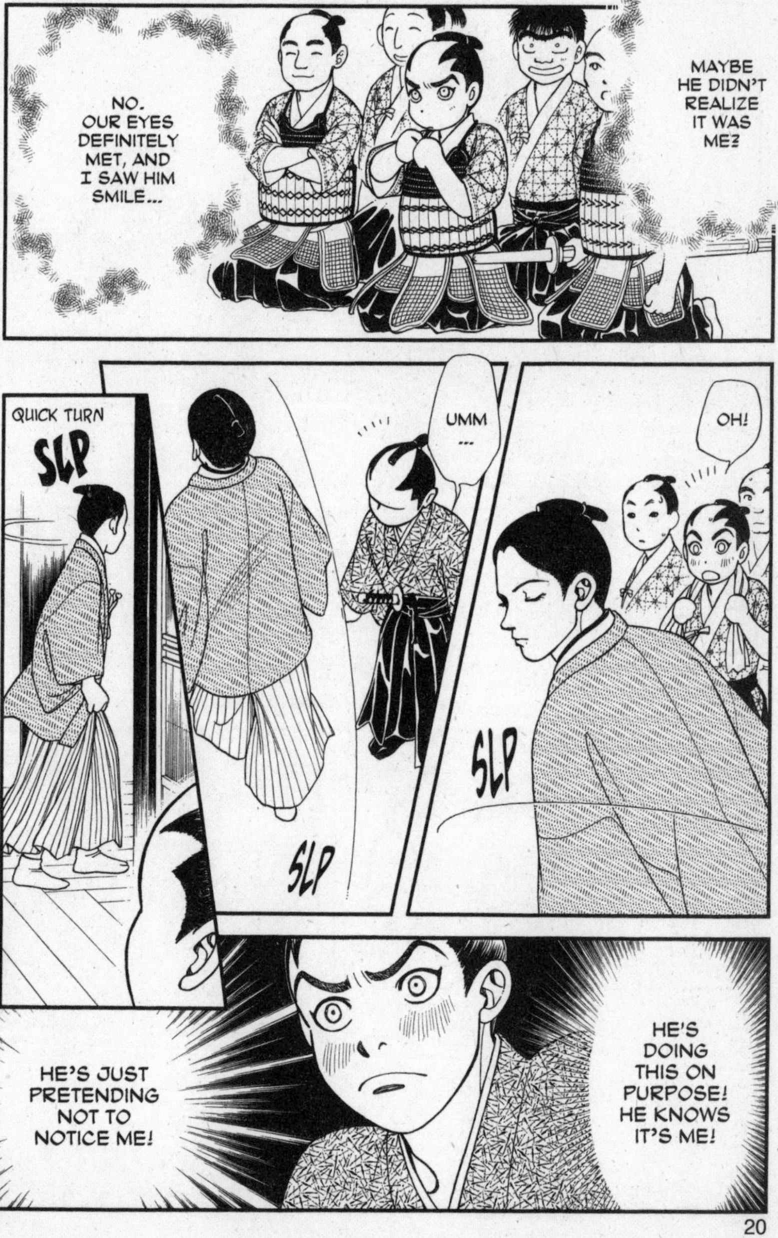
MAYBE HE DIDN'T REALIZE IT WAS ME?
NO. OUR EYES DEFINITELY MET, AND I SAW HIM SMILE...
OH!
SLP
UMM ...
SLP
QUICK TURN
SLP
HE'S DOING THIS ON PURPOSE! HE KNOWS IT'S ME!
HE'S JUST PRETENDING NOT TO NOTICE ME!

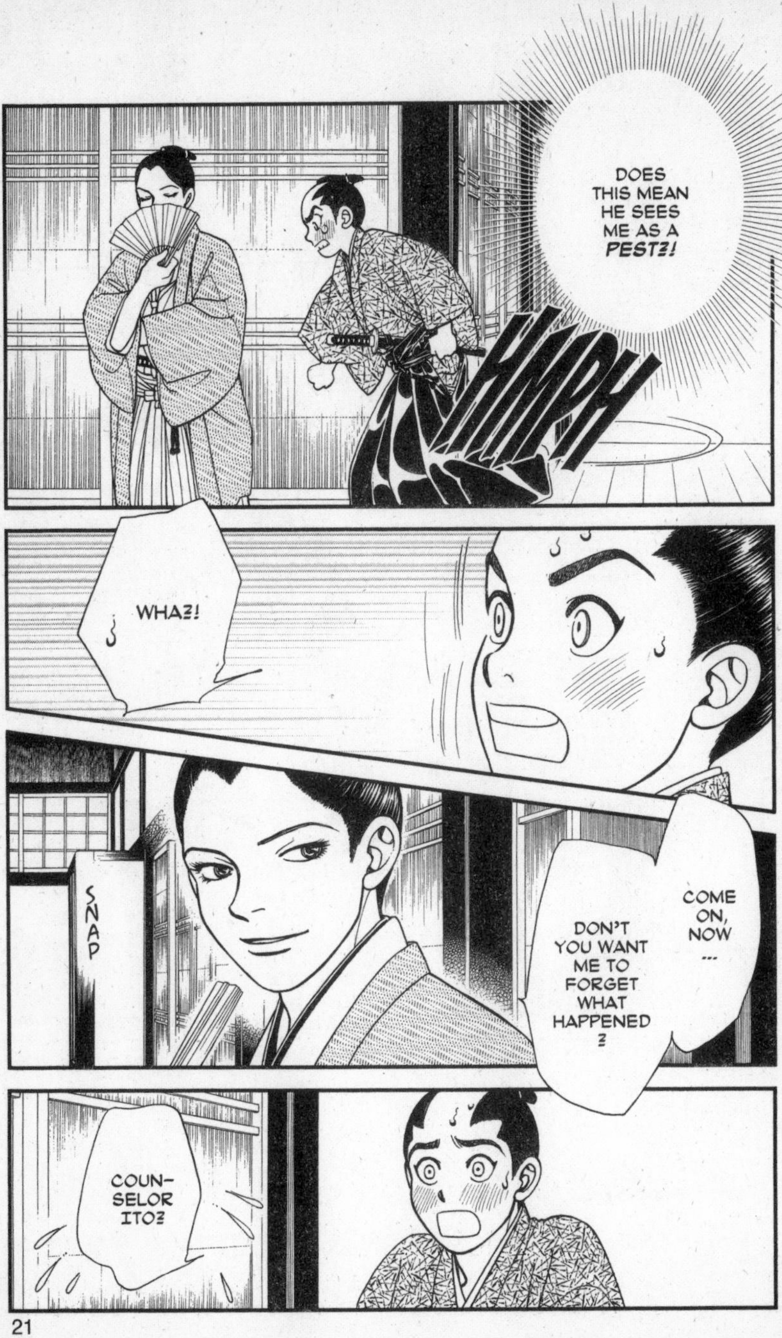

DOES THIS MEAN HE SEES ME AS A *PEST?!*
HMPH
WHA?!
COME ON, NOW...
DON'T YOU WANT ME TO FORGET WHAT HAPPENED?
SNAP
COUN-SELOR ITO?

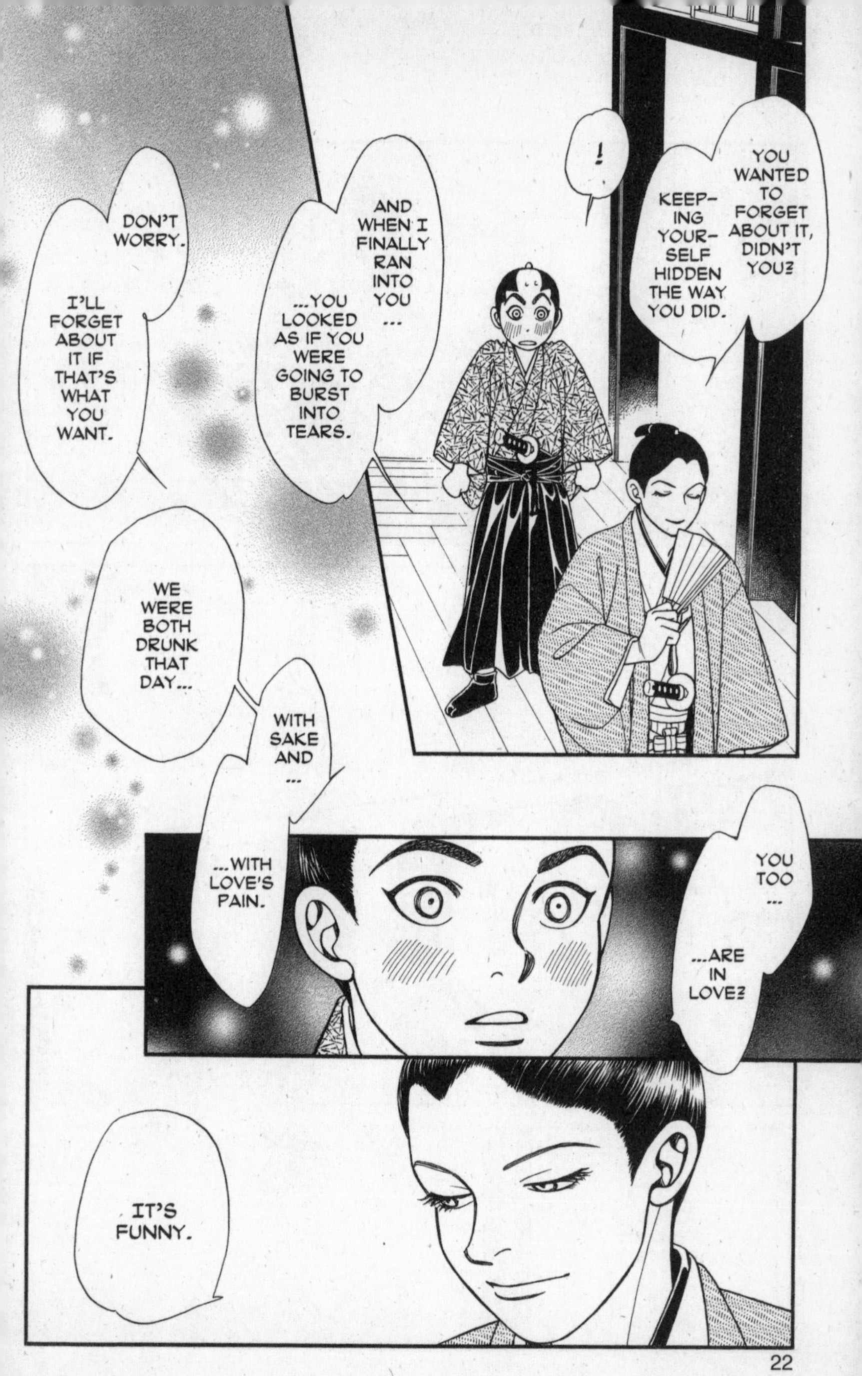
YOU WANTED TO FORGET ABOUT IT, DIDN'T YOU?
KEEPING YOURSELF HIDDEN THE WAY YOU DID.
!
AND WHEN I FINALLY RAN INTO YOU...
...YOU LOOKED AS IF YOU WERE GOING TO BURST INTO TEARS.
DON'T WORRY.
I'LL FORGET ABOUT IT IF THAT'S WHAT YOU WANT.
WE WERE BOTH DRUNK THAT DAY...
WITH SAKE AND...
...WITH LOVE'S PAIN.
YOU TOO...
...ARE IN LOVE?
IT'S FUNNY.

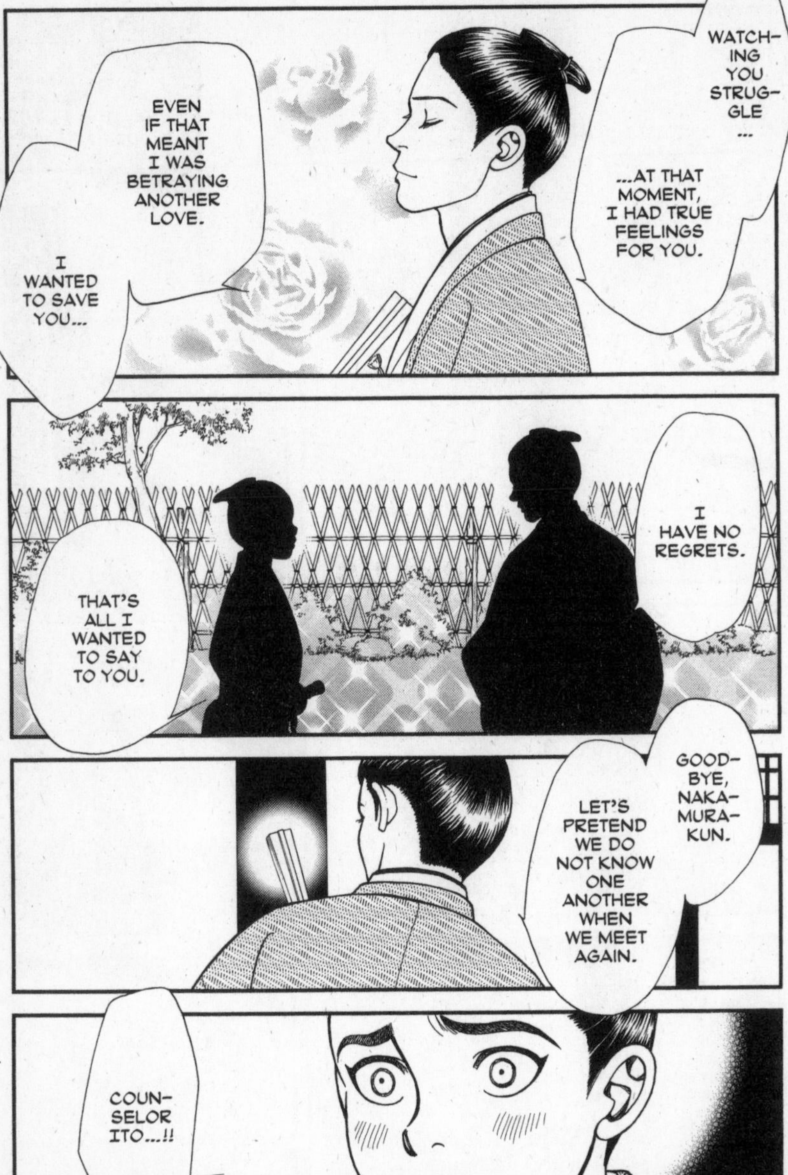
WATCHING YOU STRUGGLE...
...AT THAT MOMENT, I HAD TRUE FEELINGS FOR YOU.
EVEN IF THAT MEANT I WAS BETRAYING ANOTHER LOVE.
I WANTED TO SAVE YOU...
I HAVE NO REGRETS.
THAT'S ALL I WANTED TO SAY TO YOU.
GOODBYE, NAKAMURA-KUN.
LET'S PRETEND WE DO NOT KNOW ONE ANOTHER WHEN WE MEET AGAIN.
COUNSELOR ITO...!!

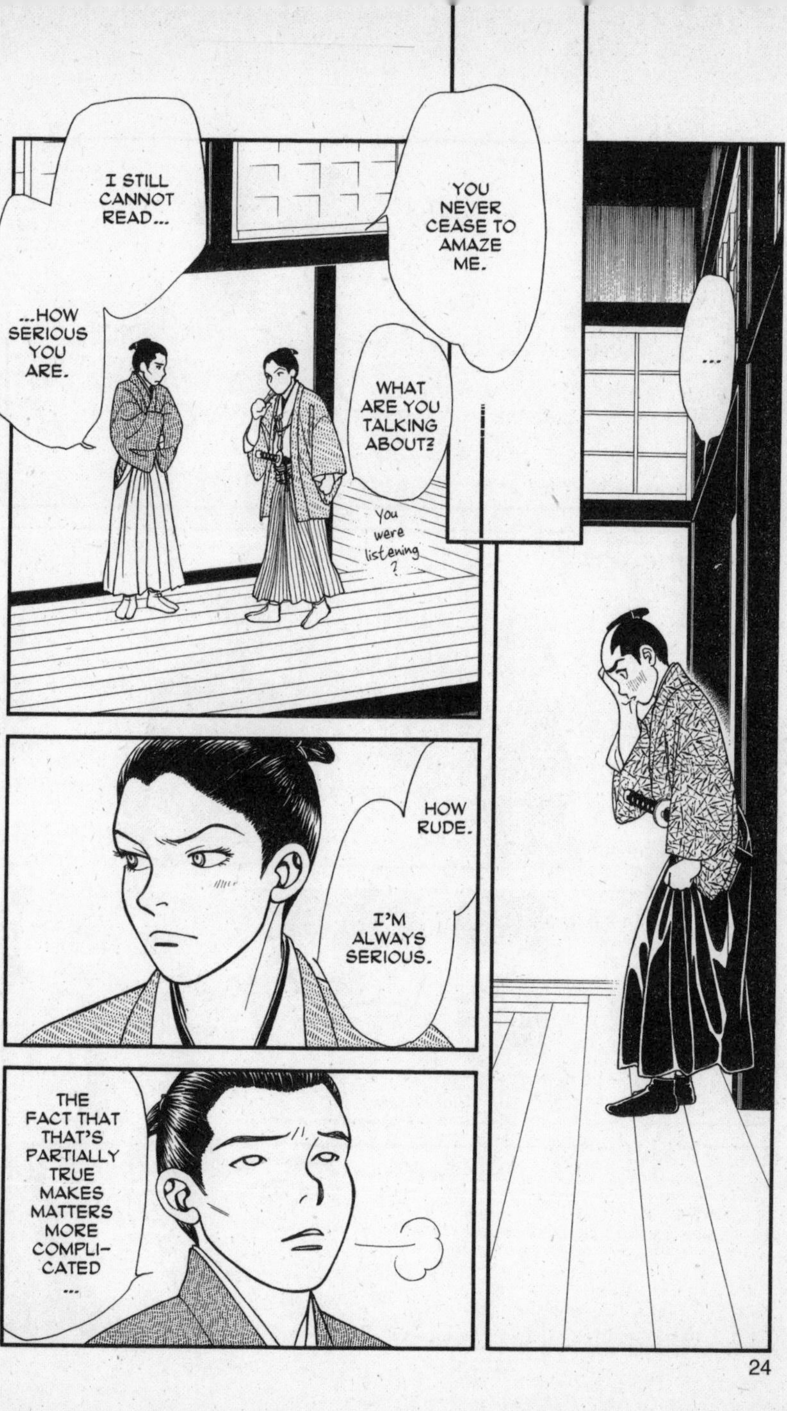
...
YOU NEVER CEASE TO AMAZE ME.
WHAT ARE YOU TALKING ABOUT?
You were listening?
I STILL CANNOT READ...
...HOW SERIOUS YOU ARE.
HOW RUDE.
I'M ALWAYS SERIOUS.
THE FACT THAT THAT'S PARTIALLY TRUE MAKES MATTERS MORE COMPLICATED ...

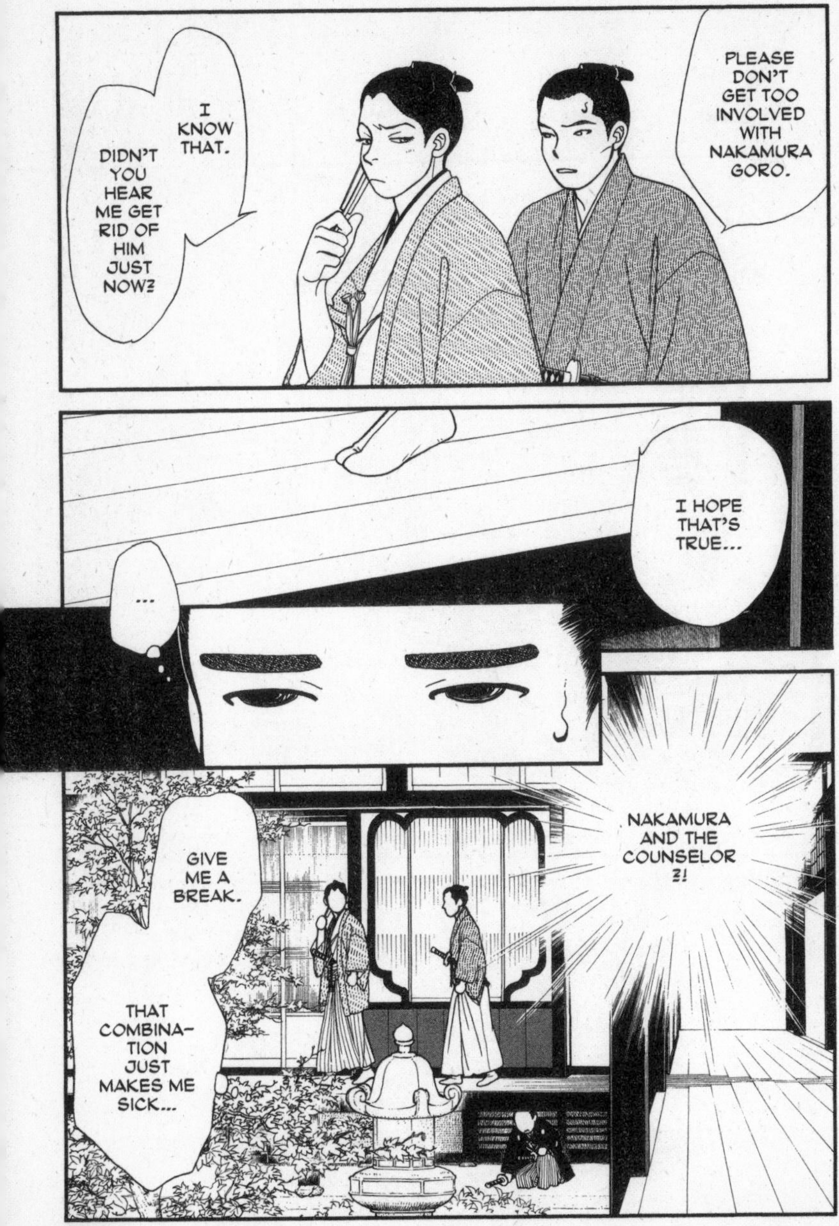
PLEASE DON'T GET TOO INVOLVED WITH NAKAMURA GORO.
I KNOW THAT.
DIDN'T YOU HEAR ME GET RID OF HIM JUST NOW?
I HOPE THAT'S TRUE...
...
NAKAMURA AND THE COUNSELOR ?!
GIVE ME A BREAK.
THAT COMBINA-TION JUST MAKES ME SICK...

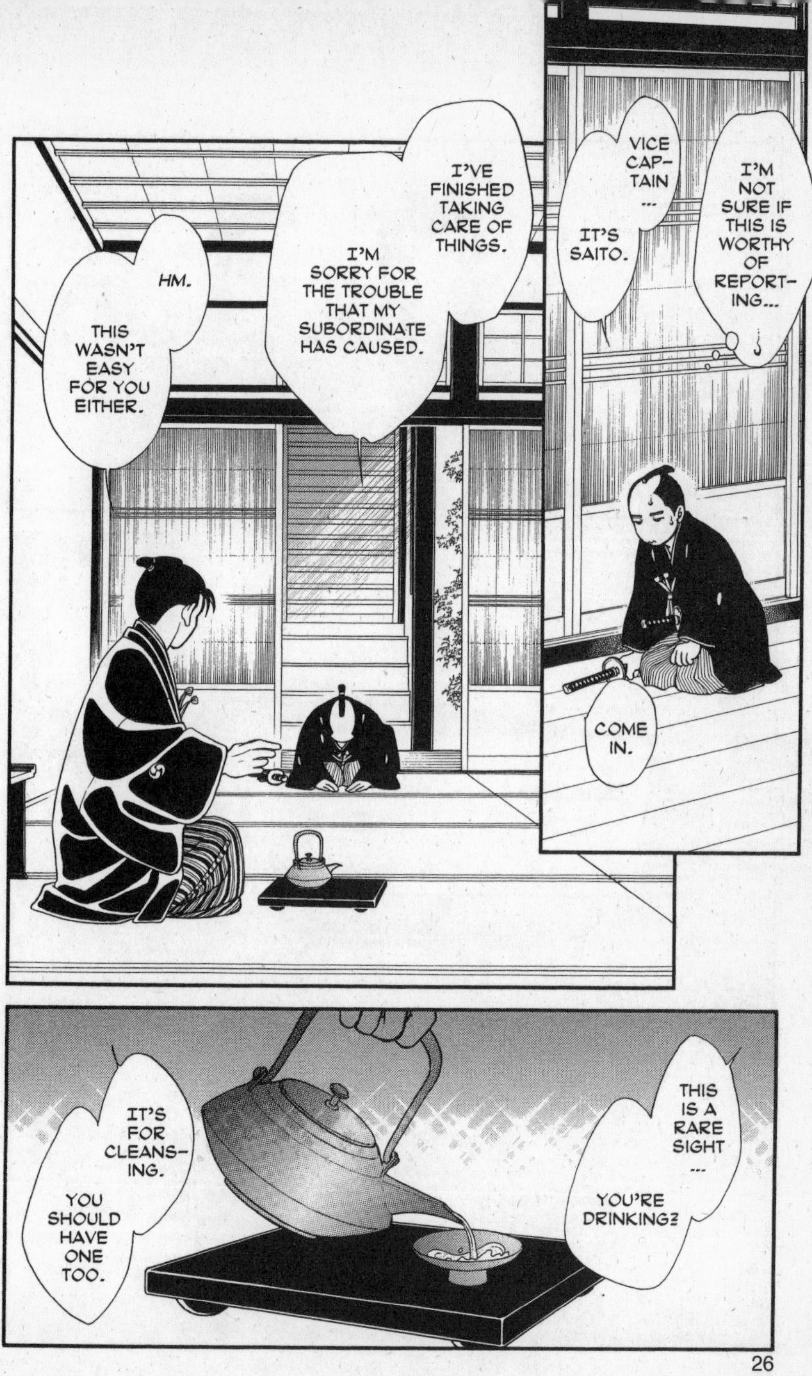
I'M NOT SURE IF THIS IS WORTHY OF REPORTING...
VICE CAPTAIN... IT'S SAITO.
COME IN.
I'VE FINISHED TAKING CARE OF THINGS.
I'M SORRY FOR THE TROUBLE THAT MY SUBORDINATE HAS CAUSED.
HM. THIS WASN'T EASY FOR YOU EITHER.
THIS IS A RARE SIGHT... YOU'RE DRINKING?
IT'S FOR CLEANSING. YOU SHOULD HAVE ONE TOO.

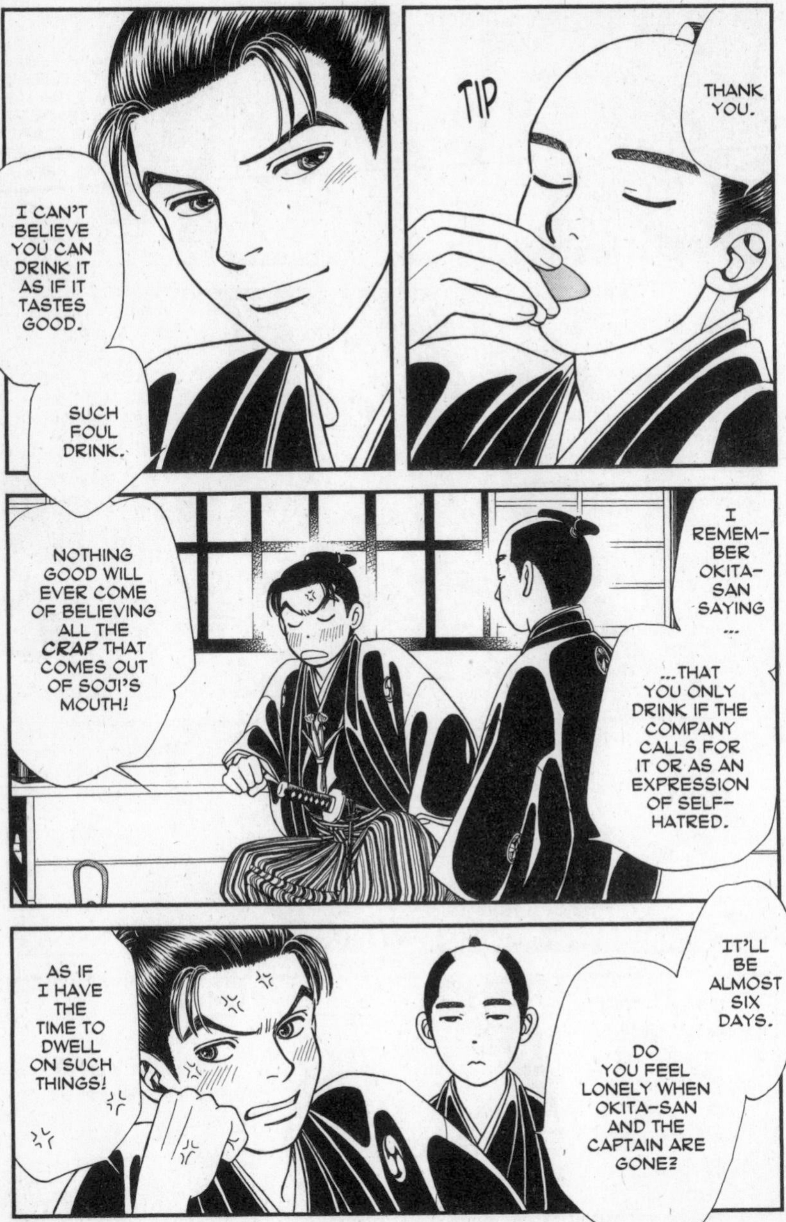
TIP
THANK YOU.
I CAN'T BELIEVE YOU CAN DRINK IT AS IF IT TASTES GOOD.
SUCH FOUL DRINK.
I REMEMBER OKITA-SAN SAYING ...
...THAT YOU ONLY DRINK IF THE COMPANY CALLS FOR IT OR AS AN EXPRESSION OF SELF-HATRED.
NOTHING GOOD WILL EVER COME OF BELIEVING ALL THE *CRAP* THAT COMES OUT OF SOJI'S MOUTH!
IT'LL BE ALMOST SIX DAYS.
DO YOU FEEL LONELY WHEN OKITA-SAN AND THE CAPTAIN ARE GONE?
AS IF I HAVE THE TIME TO DWELL ON SUCH THINGS!

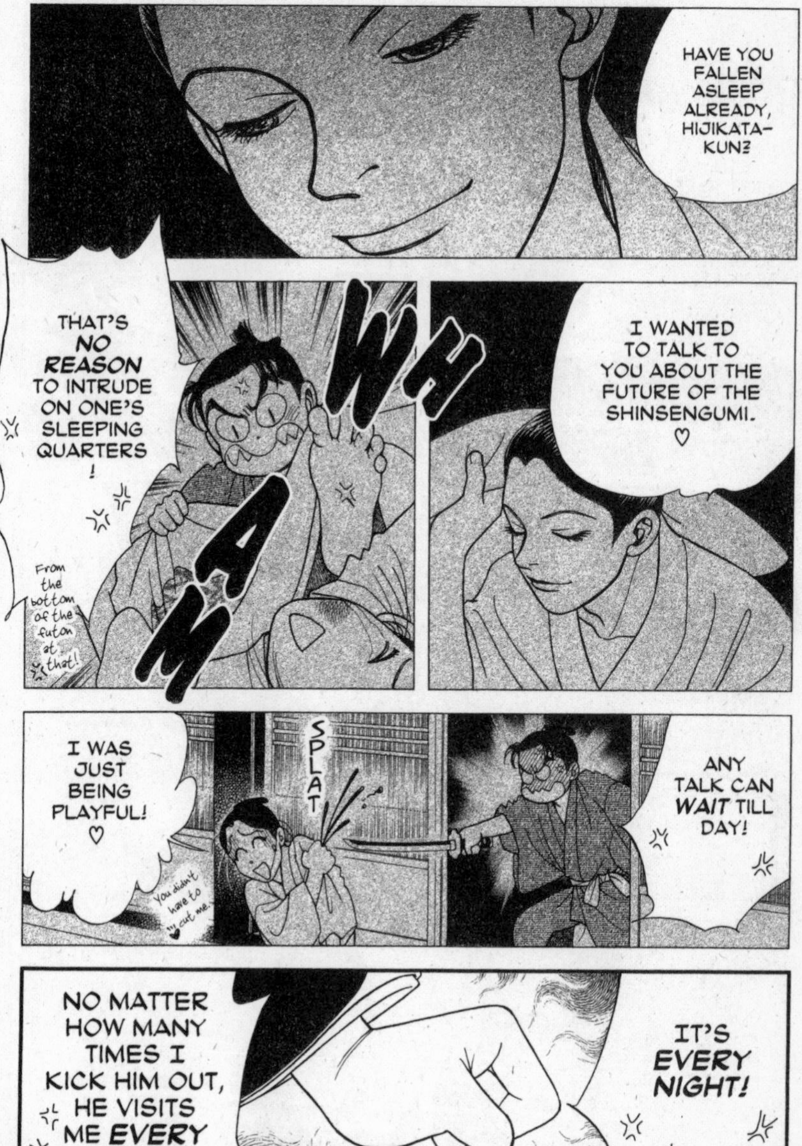
HAVE YOU FALLEN ASLEEP ALREADY, HIJIKATA-KUN?
I WANTED TO TALK TO YOU ABOUT THE FUTURE OF THE SHINSENGUMI. ♡
WHAM
THAT'S NO REASON TO INTRUDE ON ONE'S SLEEPING QUARTERS!
From the bottom of the futon at that!
ANY TALK CAN WAIT TILL DAY!
SPLAT
I WAS JUST BEING PLAYFUL! ♡
You didn't have to cut me. ♡
IT'S EVERY NIGHT!
NO MATTER HOW MANY TIMES I KICK HIM OUT, HE VISITS ME EVERY NIGHT!

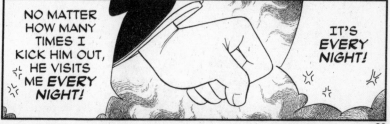

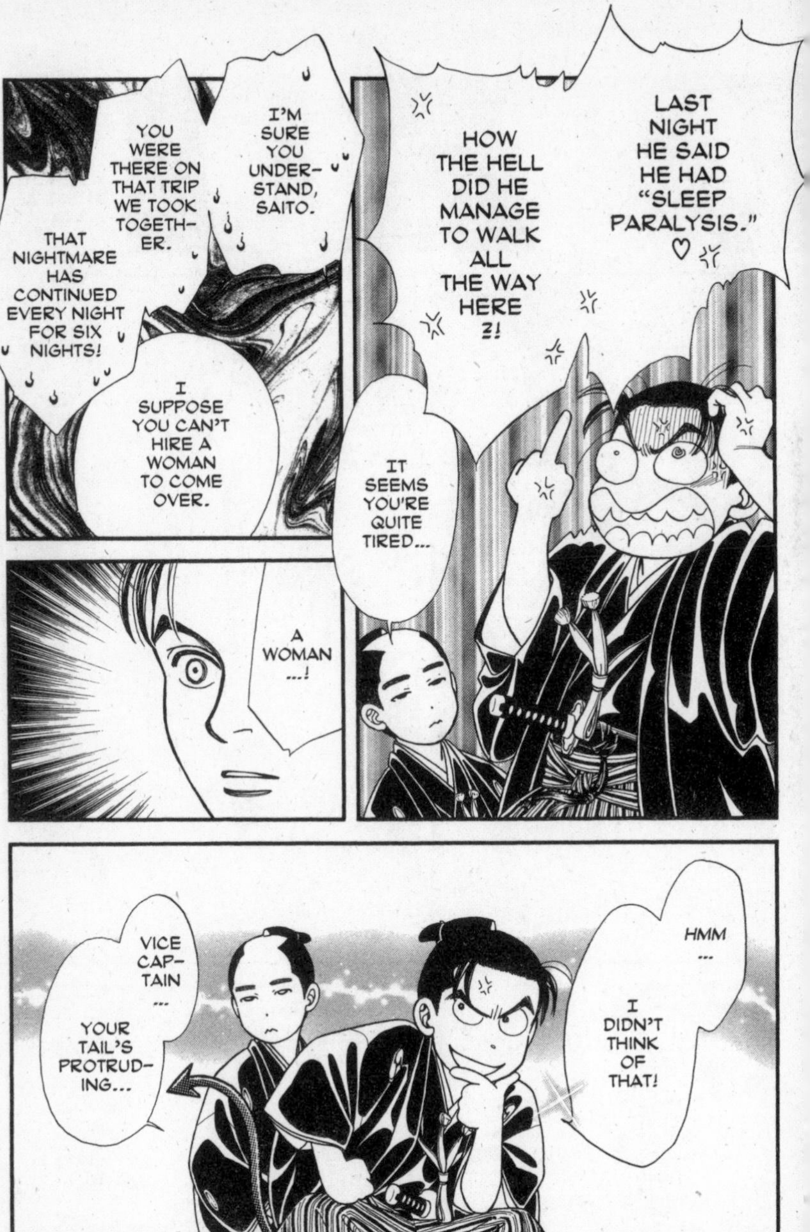
LAST NIGHT HE SAID HE HAD "SLEEP PARALYSIS." ♡
HOW THE HELL DID HE MANAGE TO WALK ALL THE WAY HERE ?!
IT SEEMS YOU'RE QUITE TIRED...
I'M SURE YOU UNDER-STAND, SAITO.
YOU WERE THERE ON THAT TRIP WE TOOK TOGETH-ER.
THAT NIGHTMARE HAS CONTINUED EVERY NIGHT FOR SIX NIGHTS!
I SUPPOSE YOU CAN'T HIRE A WOMAN TO COME OVER.
A WOMAN ...!
HMM ...
I DIDN'T THINK OF THAT!
VICE CAP-TAIN ...
YOUR TAIL'S PROTRUD-ING...

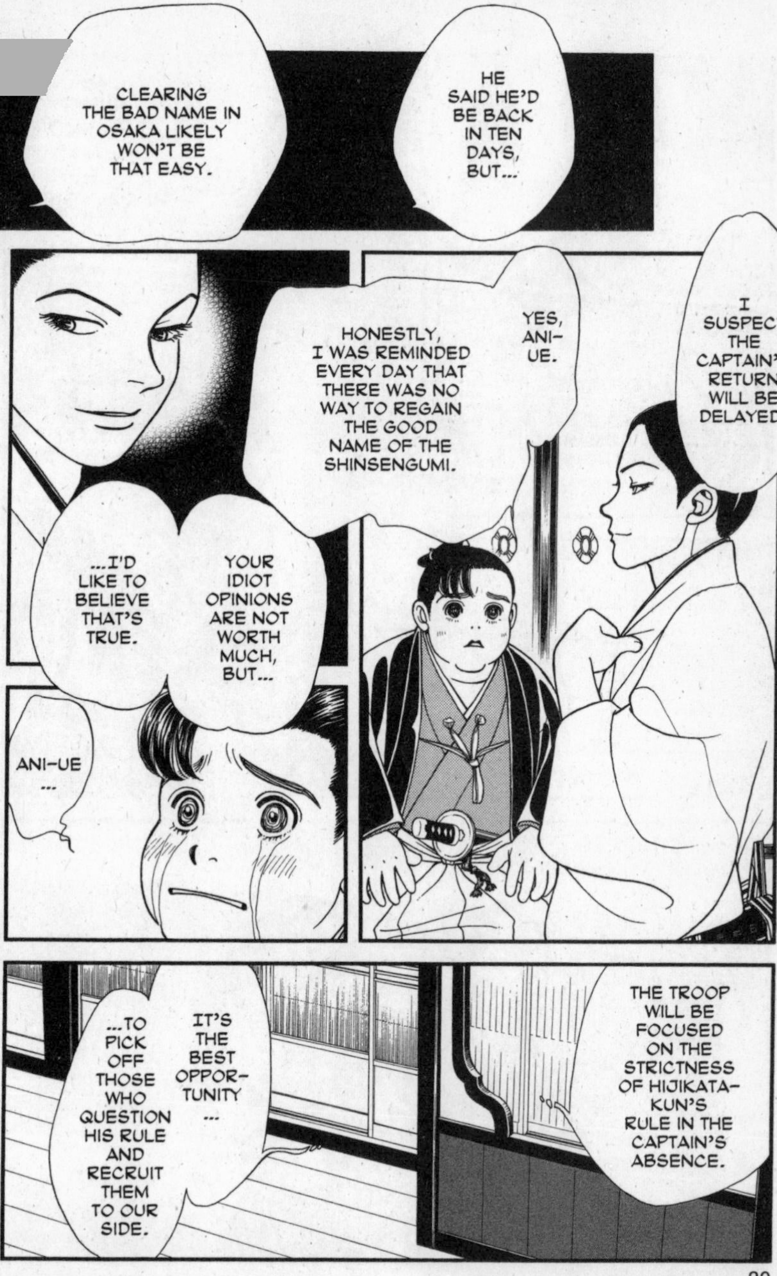
HE SAID HE'D BE BACK IN TEN DAYS, BUT...
CLEARING THE BAD NAME IN OSAKA LIKELY WON'T BE THAT EASY.
I SUSPECT THE CAPTAIN'S RETURN WILL BE DELAYED.
YES, ANI-UE.
HONESTLY, I WAS REMINDED EVERY DAY THAT THERE WAS NO WAY TO REGAIN THE GOOD NAME OF THE SHINSENGUMI.
YOUR IDIOT OPINIONS ARE NOT WORTH MUCH, BUT...
...I'D LIKE TO BELIEVE THAT'S TRUE.
ANI-UE ...
THE TROOP WILL BE FOCUSED ON THE STRICTNESS OF HIJIKATA-KUN'S RULE IN THE CAPTAIN'S ABSENCE.
IT'S THE BEST OPPORTUNITY ...
...TO PICK OFF THOSE WHO QUESTION HIS RULE AND RECRUIT THEM TO OUR SIDE.

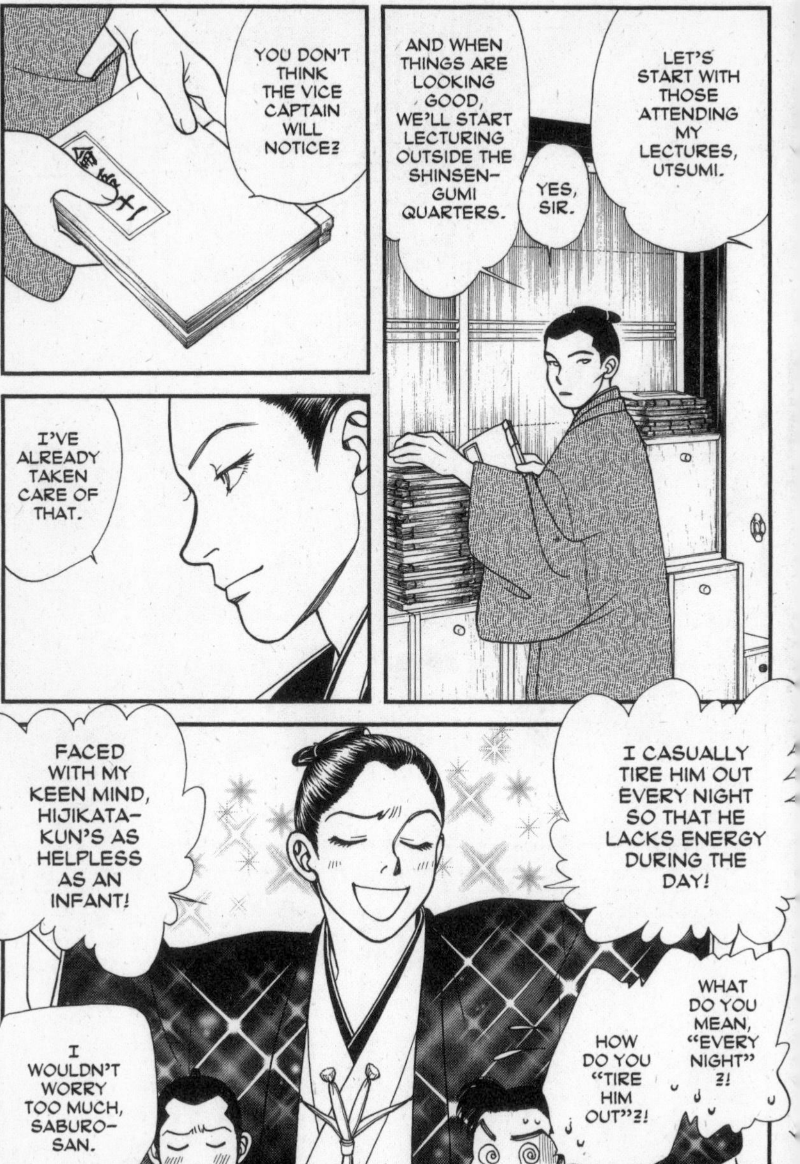
LET'S START WITH THOSE ATTENDING MY LECTURES, UTSUMI.
YES, SIR.
AND WHEN THINGS ARE LOOKING GOOD, WE'LL START LECTURING OUTSIDE THE SHINSEN-GUMI QUARTERS.
YOU DON'T THINK THE VICE CAPTAIN WILL NOTICE?
I'VE ALREADY TAKEN CARE OF THAT.
I CASUALLY TIRE HIM OUT EVERY NIGHT SO THAT HE LACKS ENERGY DURING THE DAY!
FACED WITH MY KEEN MIND, HIJIKATA-KUN'S AS HELPLESS AS AN INFANT!
WHAT DO YOU MEAN, "EVERY NIGHT"?!
HOW DO YOU "TIRE HIM OUT"?!
I WOULDN'T WORRY TOO MUCH, SABURO-SAN.

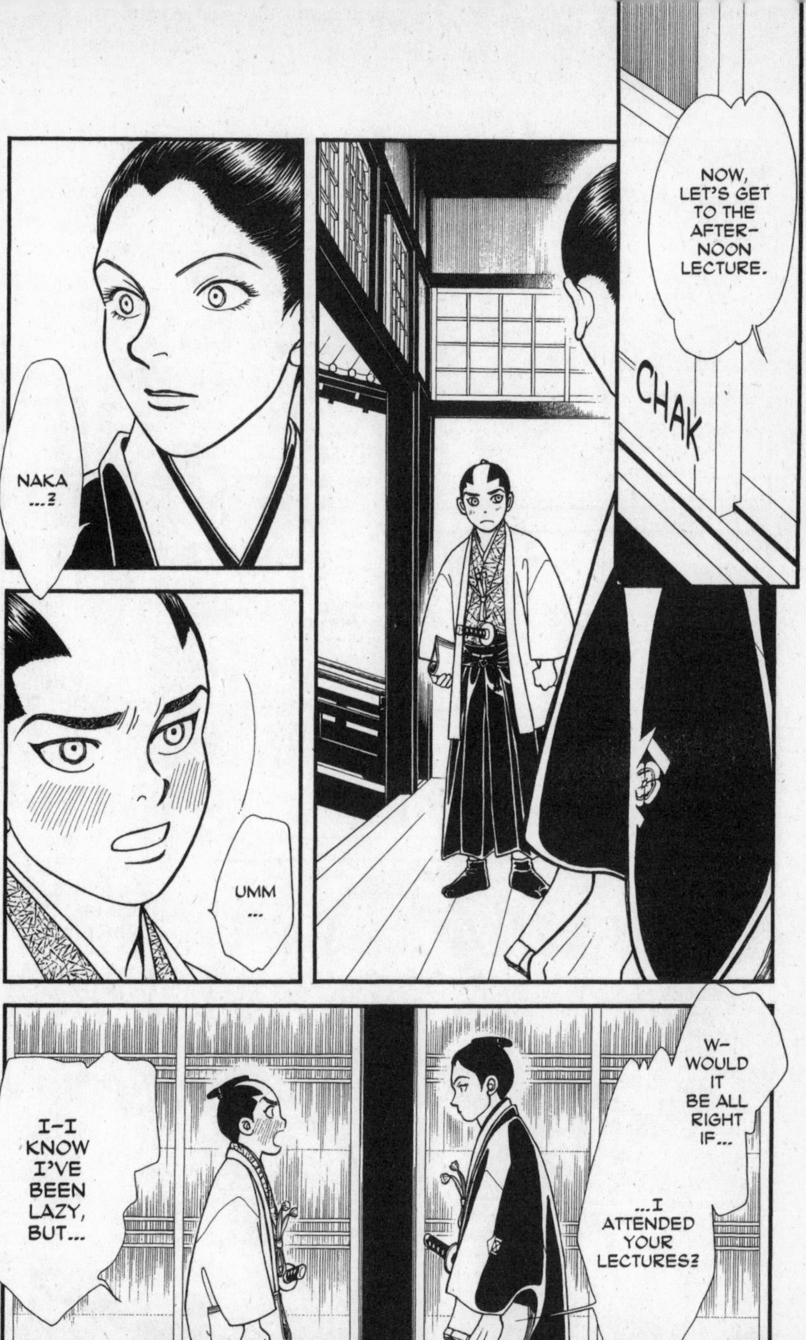
NOW, LET'S GET TO THE AFTER-NOON LECTURE.
CHAK
NAKA ...?
UMM ...
W-WOULD IT BE ALL RIGHT IF...
...I ATTENDED YOUR LECTURES?
I-I KNOW I'VE BEEN LAZY, BUT...

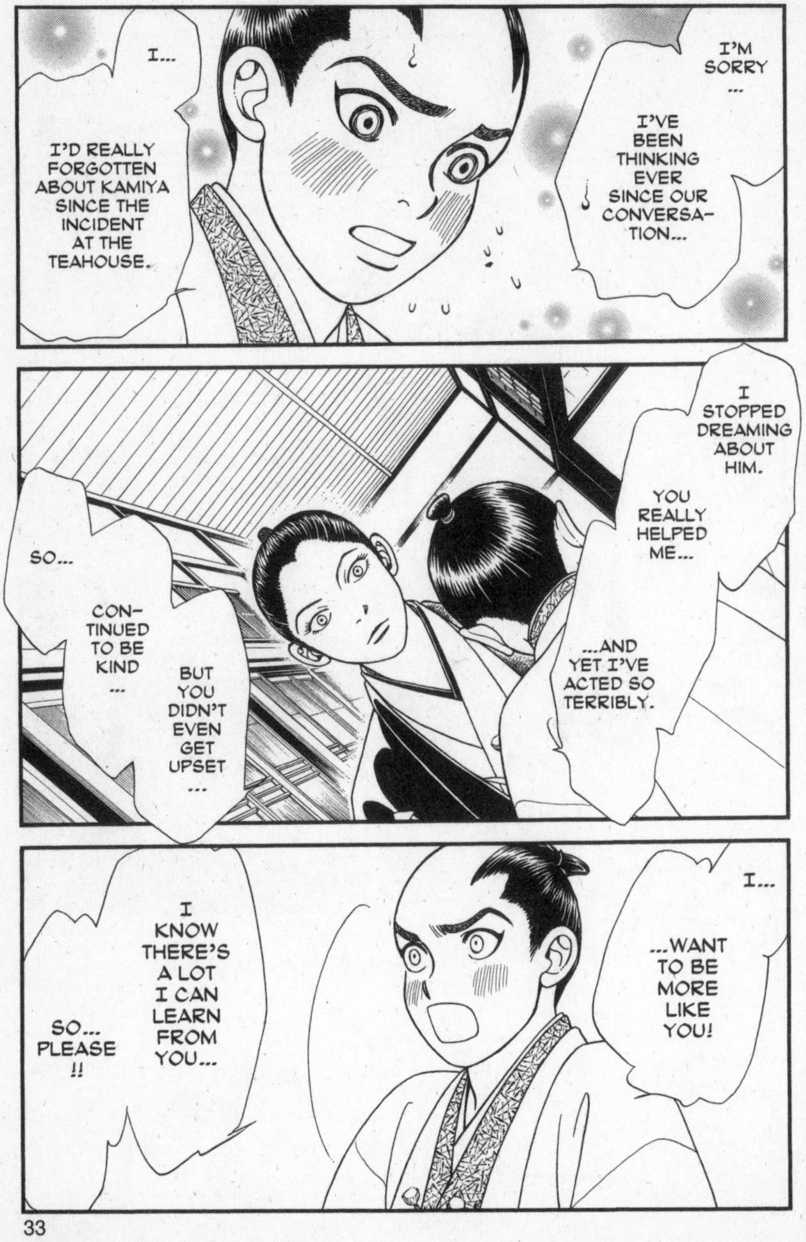
I'M SORRY ...
I'VE BEEN THINKING EVER SINCE OUR CONVERSA-TION...
I...
I'D REALLY FORGOTTEN ABOUT KAMIYA SINCE THE INCIDENT AT THE TEAHOUSE.
I STOPPED DREAMING ABOUT HIM.
YOU REALLY HELPED ME...
...AND YET I'VE ACTED SO TERRIBLY.
BUT YOU DIDN'T EVEN GET UPSET ...
CON-TINUED TO BE KIND ...
SO...
I...
...WANT TO BE MORE LIKE YOU!
I KNOW THERE'S A LOT I CAN LEARN FROM YOU...
SO... PLEASE !!

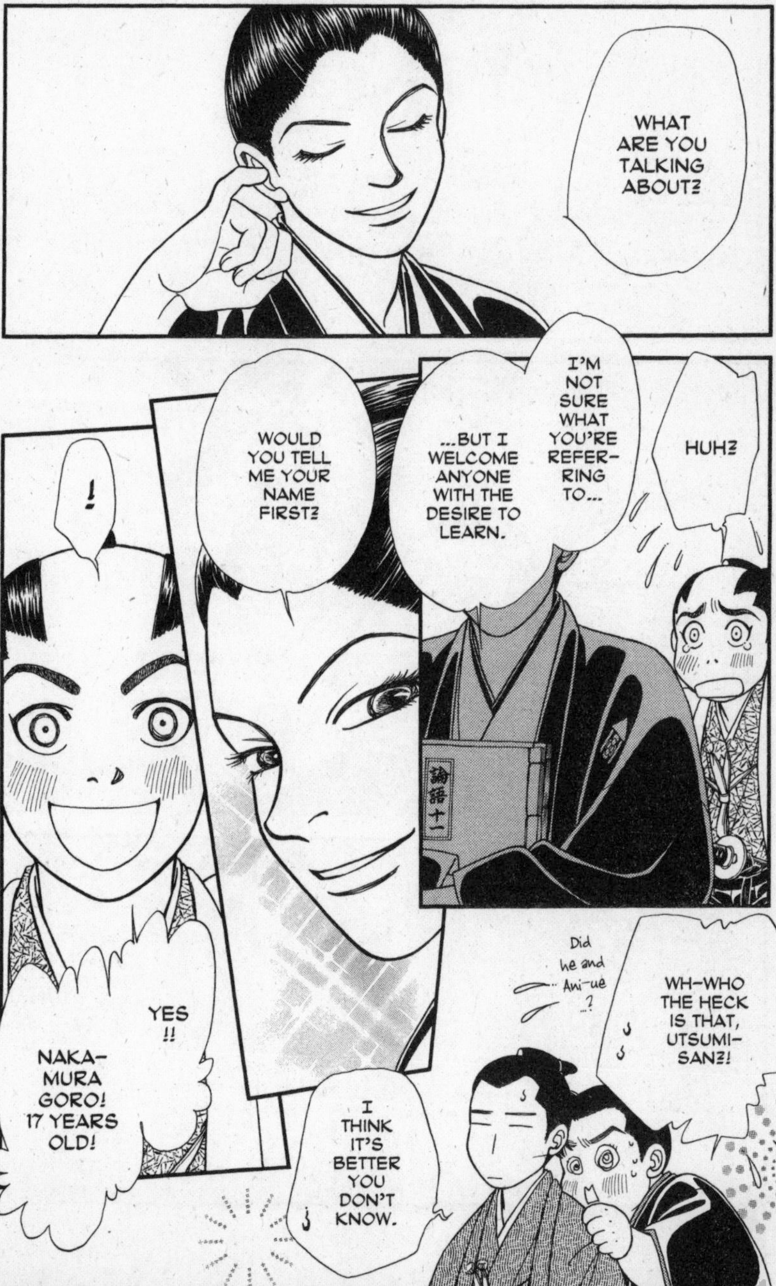
WHAT ARE YOU TALKING ABOUT?
I'M NOT SURE WHAT YOU'RE REFERRING TO...
...BUT I WELCOME ANYONE WITH THE DESIRE TO LEARN.
HUH?
WOULD YOU TELL ME YOUR NAME FIRST?
!
YES!!
NAKAMURA GORO! 17 YEARS OLD!
WH-WHO THE HECK IS THAT, UTSUMI-SAN?!
Did he and Ani-ue ...?
I THINK IT'S BETTER YOU DON'T KNOW.

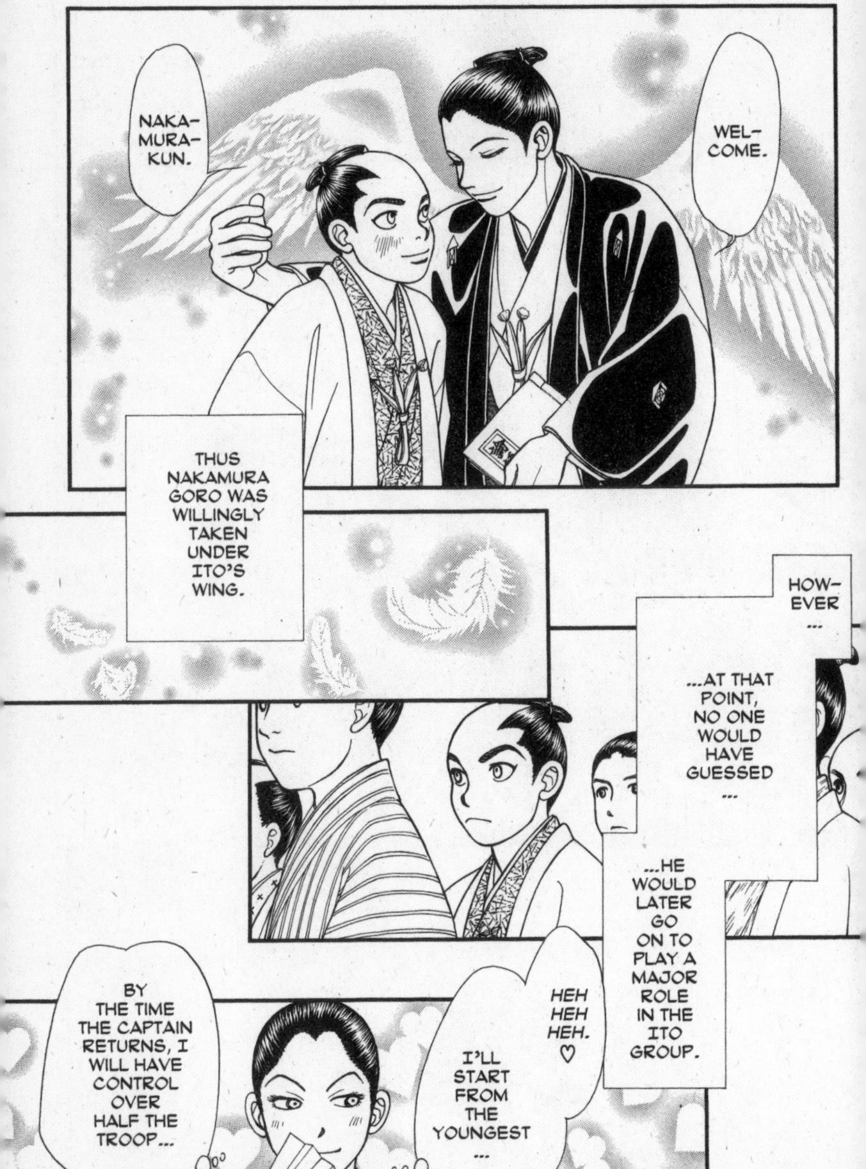
WEL-COME.
NAKA-MURA-KUN.
THUS NAKAMURA GORO WAS WILLINGLY TAKEN UNDER ITO'S WING.
HOW-EVER...
...AT THAT POINT, NO ONE WOULD HAVE GUESSED...
...HE WOULD LATER GO ON TO PLAY A MAJOR ROLE IN THE ITO GROUP.
HEH HEH HEH. ♡
I'LL START FROM THE YOUNGEST...
BY THE TIME THE CAPTAIN RETURNS, I WILL HAVE CONTROL OVER HALF THE TROOP...

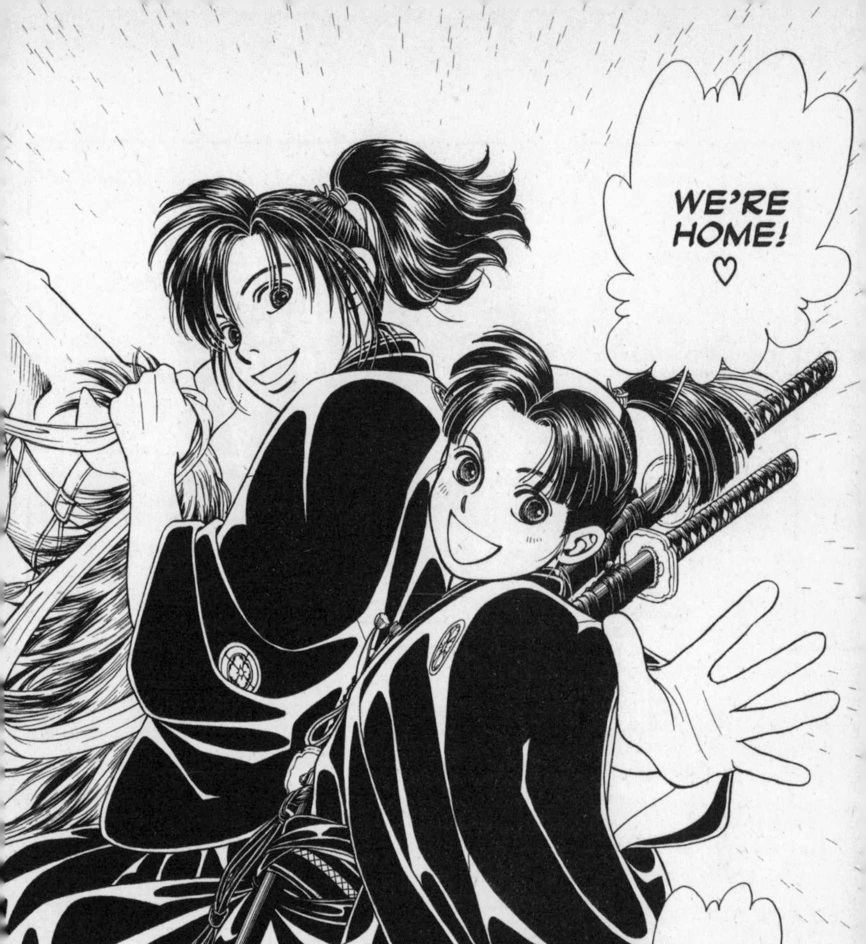
WE'RE HOME! ♡

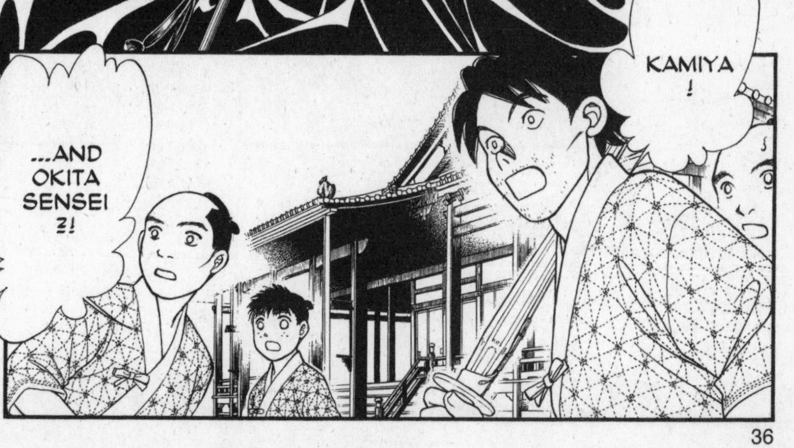
KAMIYA!
...AND OKITA SENSEI?!

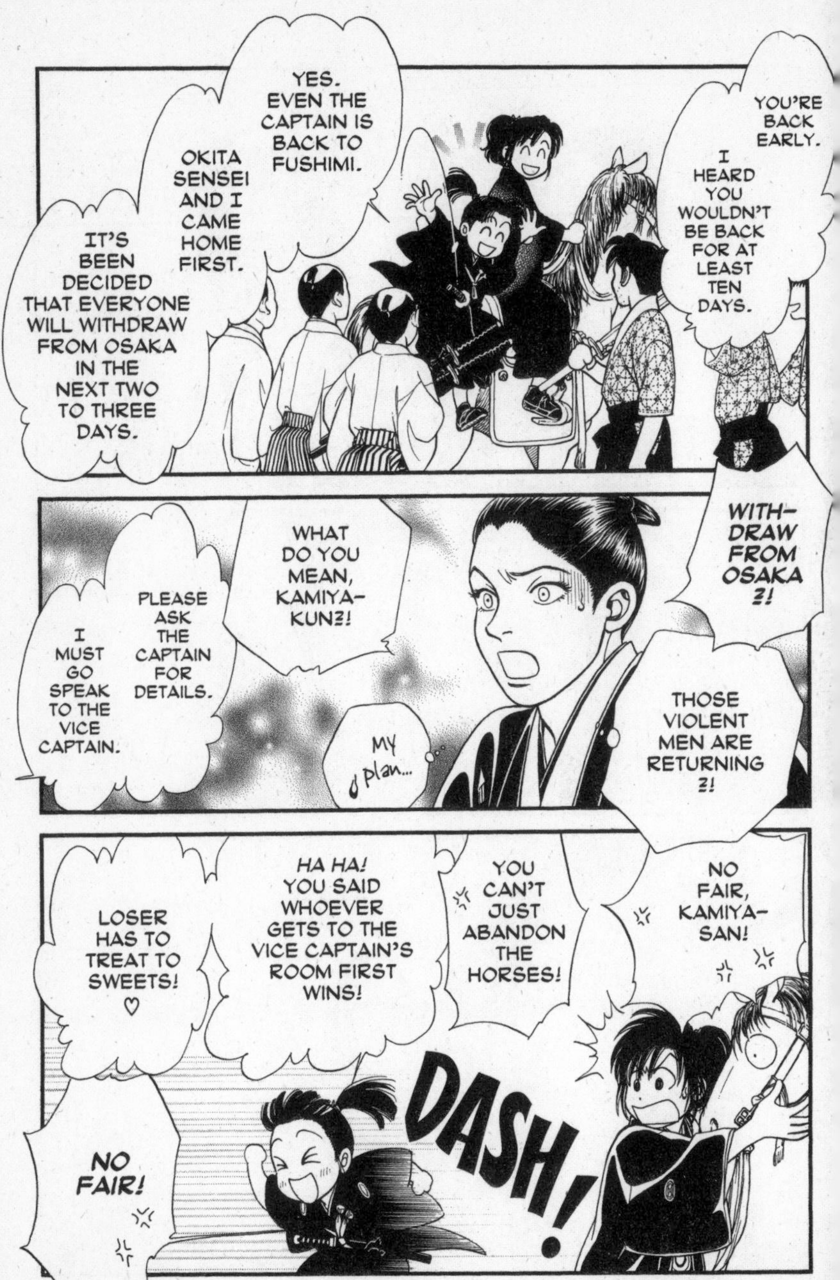
YOU'RE BACK EARLY.
I HEARD YOU WOULDN'T BE BACK FOR AT LEAST TEN DAYS.
YES. EVEN THE CAPTAIN IS BACK TO FUSHIMI.
OKITA SENSEI AND I CAME HOME FIRST.
IT'S BEEN DECIDED THAT EVERYONE WILL WITHDRAW FROM OSAKA IN THE NEXT TWO TO THREE DAYS.
WITHDRAW FROM OSAKA?!
THOSE VIOLENT MEN ARE RETURNING?!
WHAT DO YOU MEAN, KAMIYA-KUN?!
My plan...
PLEASE ASK THE CAPTAIN FOR DETAILS.
I MUST GO SPEAK TO THE VICE CAPTAIN.
NO FAIR, KAMIYA-SAN!
YOU CAN'T JUST ABANDON THE HORSES!
HA HA! YOU SAID WHOEVER GETS TO THE VICE CAPTAIN'S ROOM FIRST WINS!
LOSER HAS TO TREAT TO SWEETS! ♡
DASH!
NO FAIR!

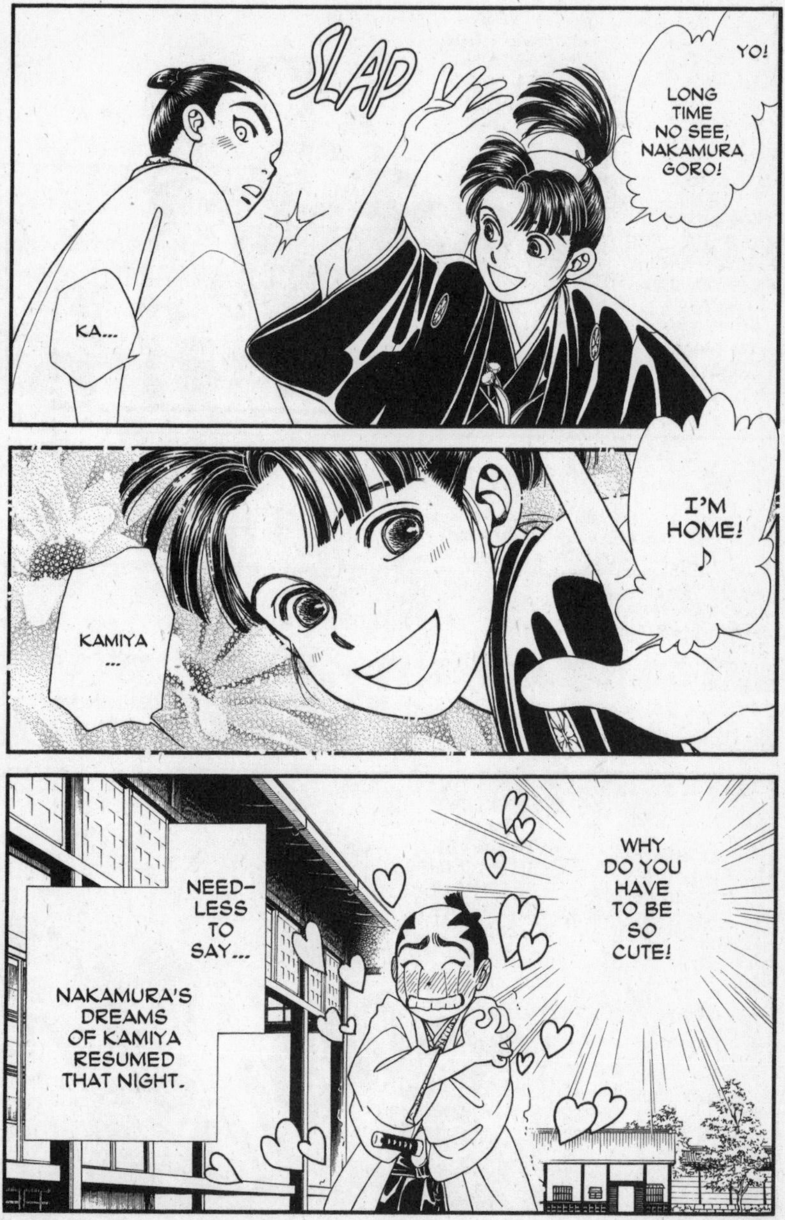
SLAP
YO!
LONG TIME NO SEE, NAKAMURA GORO!
KA...
I'M HOME! ♪
KAMIYA ...
WHY DO YOU HAVE TO BE SO CUTE!
NEED-LESS TO SAY...
NAKAMURA'S DREAMS OF KAMIYA RESUMED THAT NIGHT.

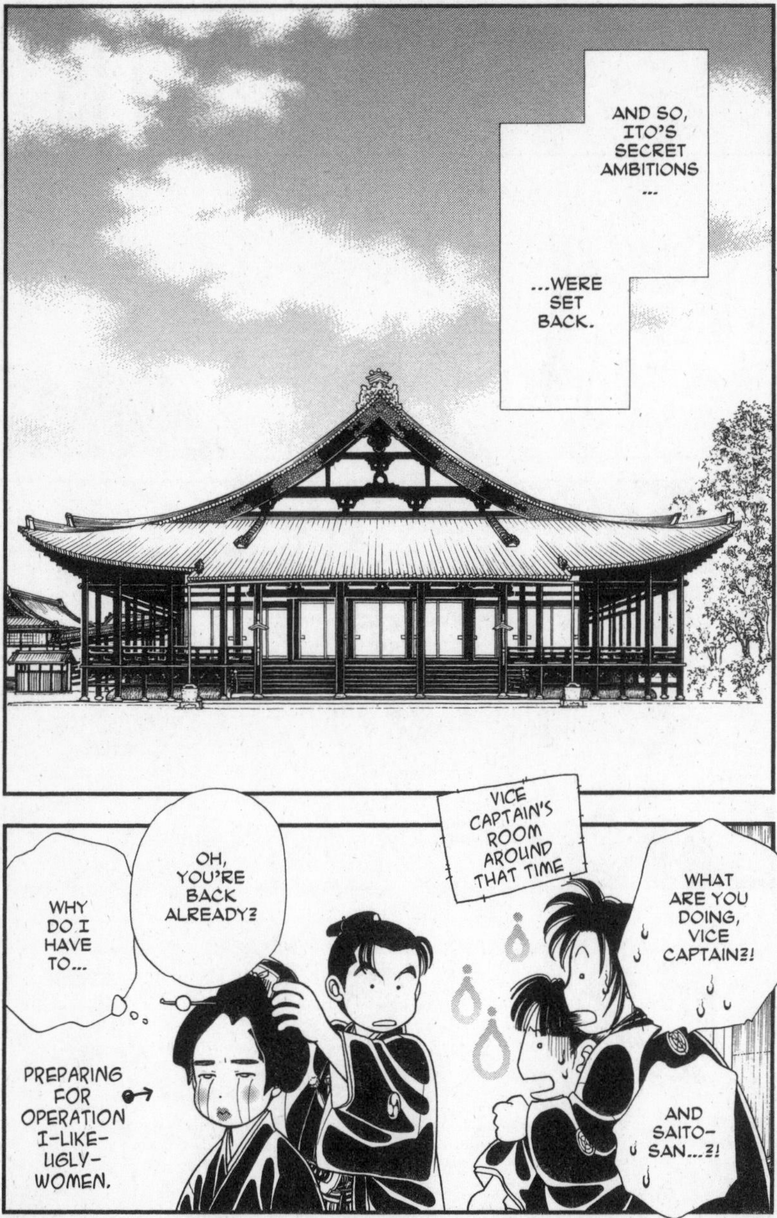
AND SO, ITO'S SECRET AMBITIONS...
...WERE SET BACK.
VICE CAPTAIN'S ROOM AROUND THAT TIME
WHAT ARE YOU DOING, VICE CAPTAIN?!
AND SAITO-SAN...?!
OH, YOU'RE BACK ALREADY?
WHY DO I HAVE TO...
PREPARING FOR OPERATION I-LIKE-UGLY-WOMEN.

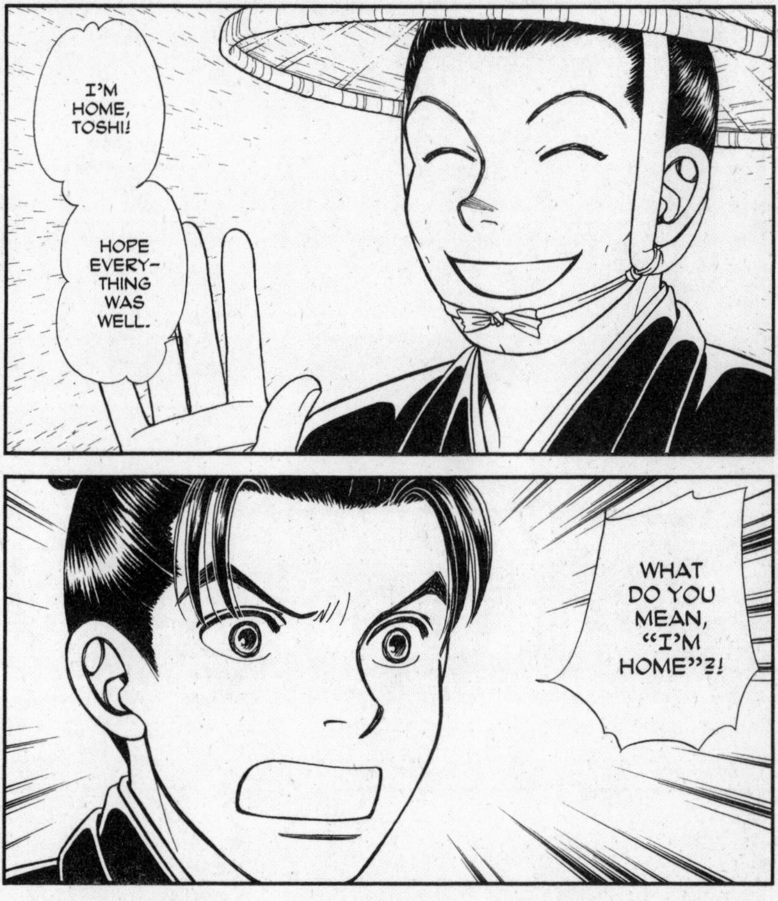
I'M HOME, TOSHI!
HOPE EVERYTHING WAS WELL.
WHAT DO YOU MEAN, "I'M HOME"?!

EDO IROHA KARUTA GAME

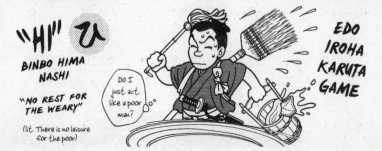

"HI" ひ

BINBO HIMA NASHI

"NO REST FOR THE WEARY"

(lit. There is no leisure for the poor)

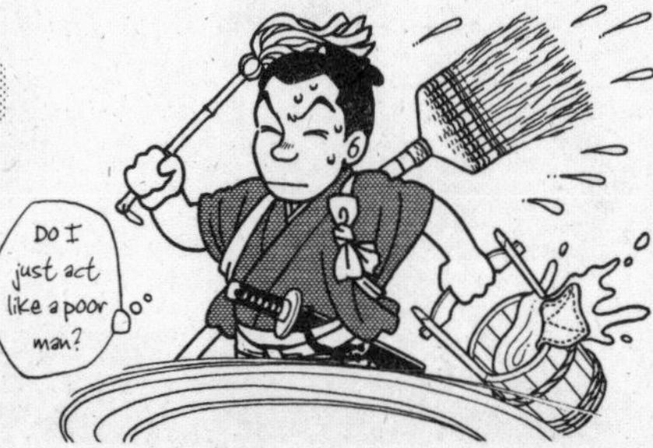
Do I just act like a poor man?

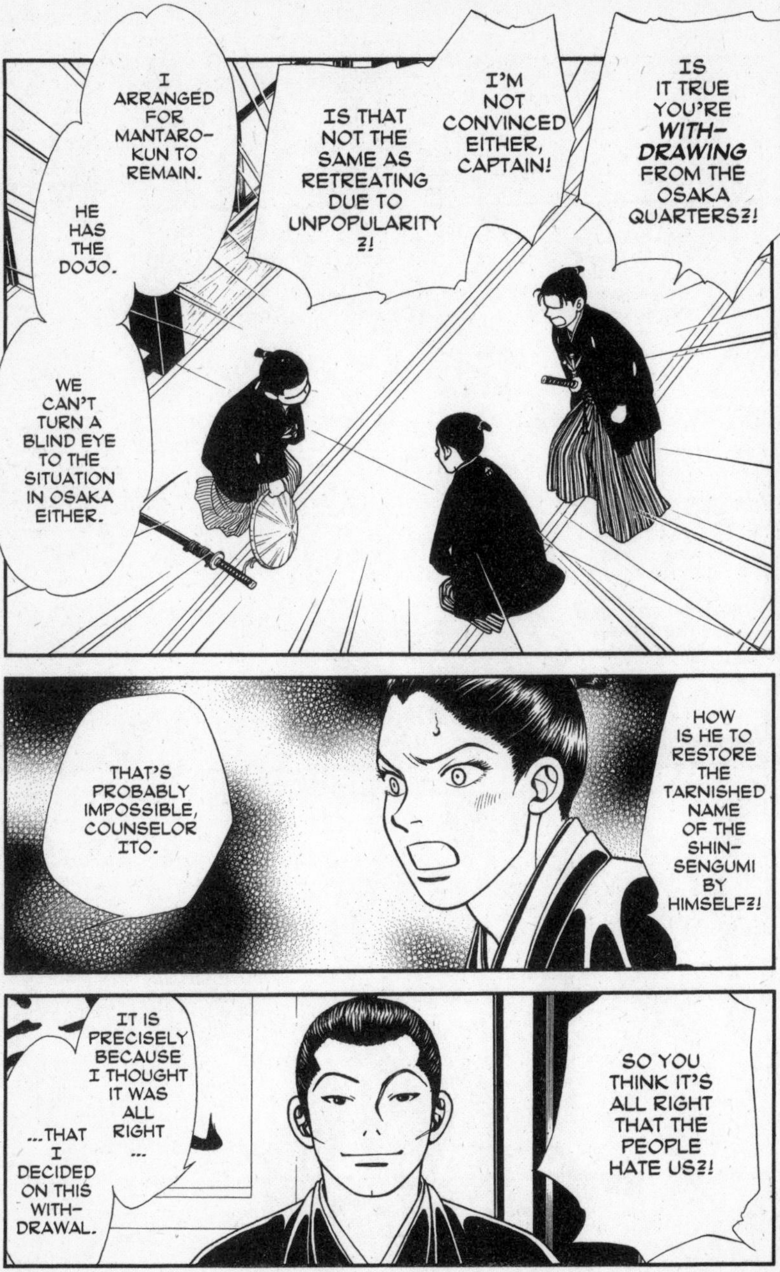
IS IT TRUE YOU'RE *WITHDRAWING* FROM THE OSAKA QUARTERS?!
I'M NOT CONVINCED EITHER, CAPTAIN!
IS THAT NOT THE SAME AS RETREATING DUE TO UNPOPULARITY?!
I ARRANGED FOR MANTARO-KUN TO REMAIN.
HE HAS THE DOJO.
WE CAN'T TURN A BLIND EYE TO THE SITUATION IN OSAKA EITHER.
HOW IS HE TO RESTORE THE TARNISHED NAME OF THE SHINSENGUMI BY HIMSELF?!
THAT'S PROBABLY IMPOSSIBLE, COUNSELOR ITO.
SO YOU THINK IT'S ALL RIGHT THAT THE PEOPLE HATE US?!
IT IS PRECISELY BECAUSE I THOUGHT IT WAS ALL RIGHT...
...THAT I DECIDED ON THIS WITHDRAWAL.

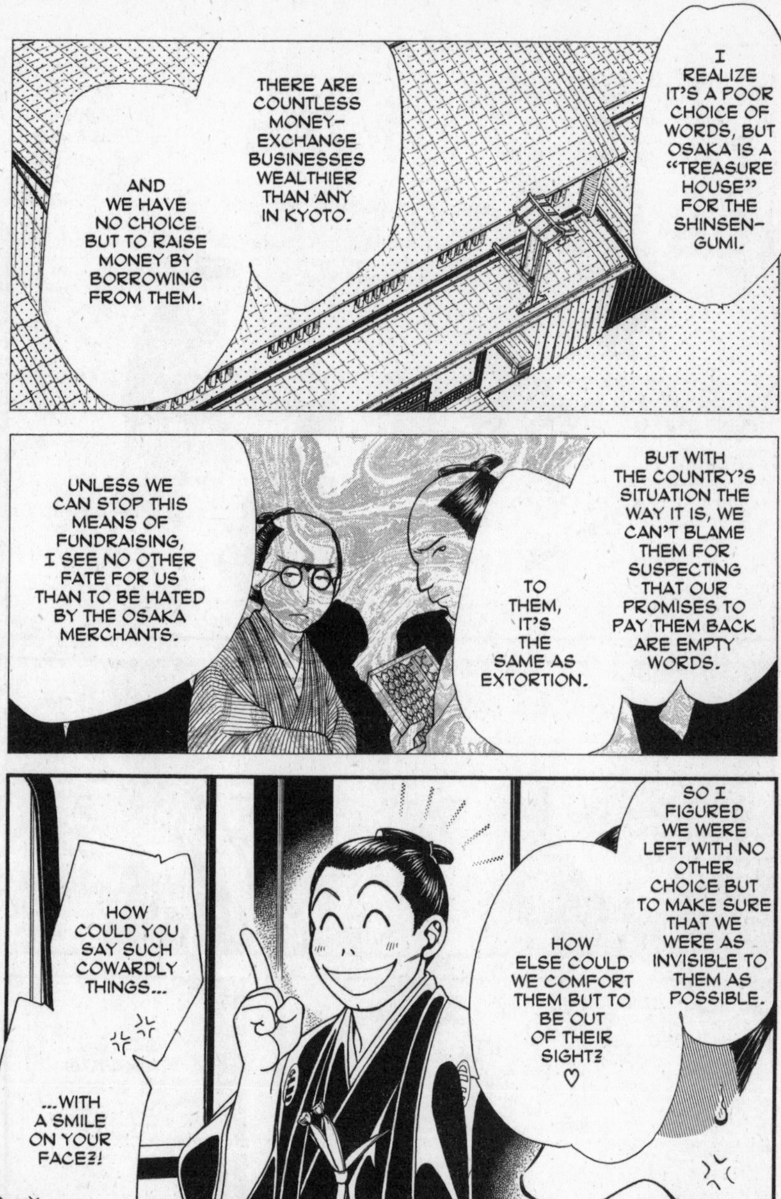
I REALIZE IT'S A POOR CHOICE OF WORDS, BUT OSAKA IS A "TREASURE HOUSE" FOR THE SHINSEN-GUMI.
THERE ARE COUNTLESS MONEY-EXCHANGE BUSINESSES WEALTHIER THAN ANY IN KYOTO.
AND WE HAVE NO CHOICE BUT TO RAISE MONEY BY BORROWING FROM THEM.
BUT WITH THE COUNTRY'S SITUATION THE WAY IT IS, WE CAN'T BLAME THEM FOR SUSPECTING THAT OUR PROMISES TO PAY THEM BACK ARE EMPTY WORDS.
TO THEM, IT'S THE SAME AS EXTORTION.
UNLESS WE CAN STOP THIS MEANS OF FUNDRAISING, I SEE NO OTHER FATE FOR US THAN TO BE HATED BY THE OSAKA MERCHANTS.
SO I FIGURED WE WERE LEFT WITH NO OTHER CHOICE BUT TO MAKE SURE THAT WE WERE AS INVISIBLE TO THEM AS POSSIBLE.
HOW ELSE COULD WE COMFORT THEM BUT TO BE OUT OF THEIR SIGHT? ♡
HOW COULD YOU SAY SUCH COWARDLY THINGS...
...WITH A SMILE ON YOUR FACE?!

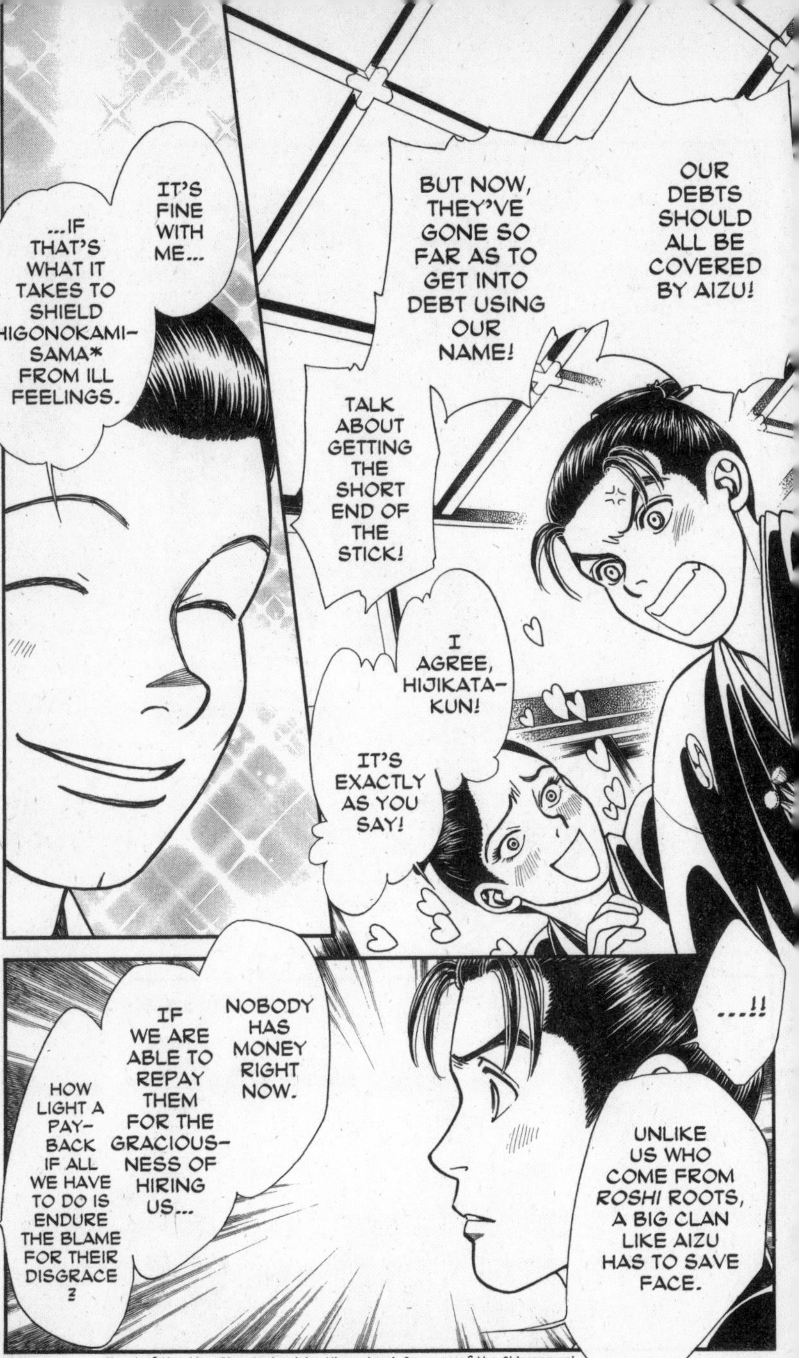
OUR DEBTS SHOULD ALL BE COVERED BY AIZU!
BUT NOW, THEY'VE GONE SO FAR AS TO GET INTO DEBT USING OUR NAME!
TALK ABOUT GETTING THE SHORT END OF THE STICK!
I AGREE, HIJIKATA-KUN!
IT'S EXACTLY AS YOU SAY!
IT'S FINE WITH ME...
...IF THAT'S WHAT IT TAKES TO SHIELD HIGONOKAMI-SAMA* FROM ILL FEELINGS.
...!!
UNLIKE US WHO COME FROM *ROSHI* ROOTS, A BIG CLAN LIKE AIZU HAS TO SAVE FACE.
NOBODY HAS MONEY RIGHT NOW.
IF WE ARE ABLE TO REPAY THEM FOR THE GRACIOUSNESS OF HIRING US...
HOW LIGHT A PAY-BACK IF ALL WE HAVE TO DO IS ENDURE THE BLAME FOR THEIR DISGRACE?

*Lord of the Aizu Clan, Matsudaira Higonokami. Sponsor of the Shinsengumi.

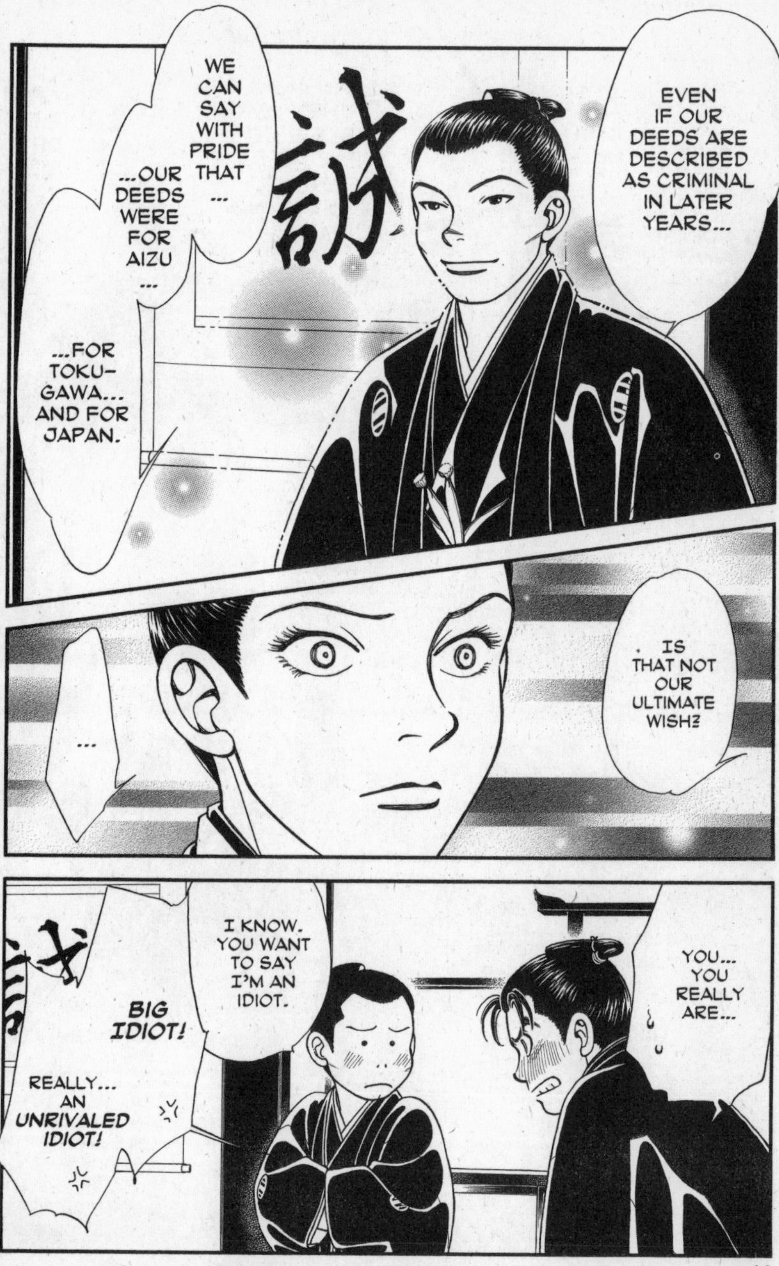
EVEN IF OUR DEEDS ARE DESCRIBED AS CRIMINAL IN LATER YEARS...
WE CAN SAY WITH PRIDE THAT...
...OUR DEEDS WERE FOR AIZU...
...FOR TOKUGAWA... AND FOR JAPAN.
IS THAT NOT OUR ULTIMATE WISH?
...
YOU... YOU REALLY ARE...
I KNOW. YOU WANT TO SAY I'M AN IDIOT.
BIG IDIOT!
REALLY... AN UNRIVALED IDIOT!

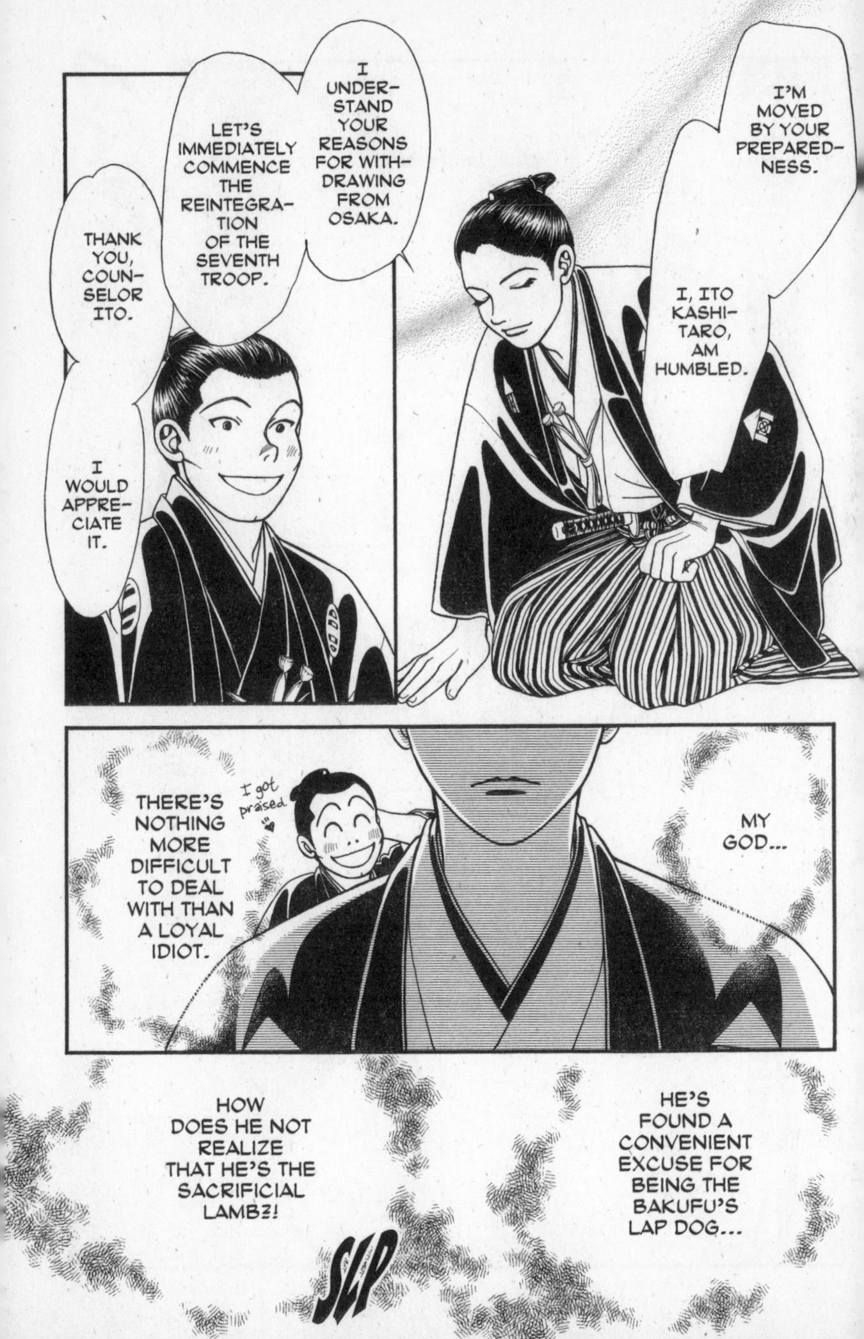
I'M MOVED BY YOUR PREPAREDNESS.
I, ITO KASHITARO, AM HUMBLED.
I UNDERSTAND YOUR REASONS FOR WITHDRAWING FROM OSAKA.
LET'S IMMEDIATELY COMMENCE THE REINTEGRATION OF THE SEVENTH TROOP.
THANK YOU, COUNSELOR ITO.
I WOULD APPRECIATE IT.
MY GOD...
I got praised.
THERE'S NOTHING MORE DIFFICULT TO DEAL WITH THAN A LOYAL IDIOT.
HE'S FOUND A CONVENIENT EXCUSE FOR BEING THE BAKUFU'S LAP DOG...
HOW DOES HE NOT REALIZE THAT HE'S THE SACRIFICIAL LAMB?!
SLIP

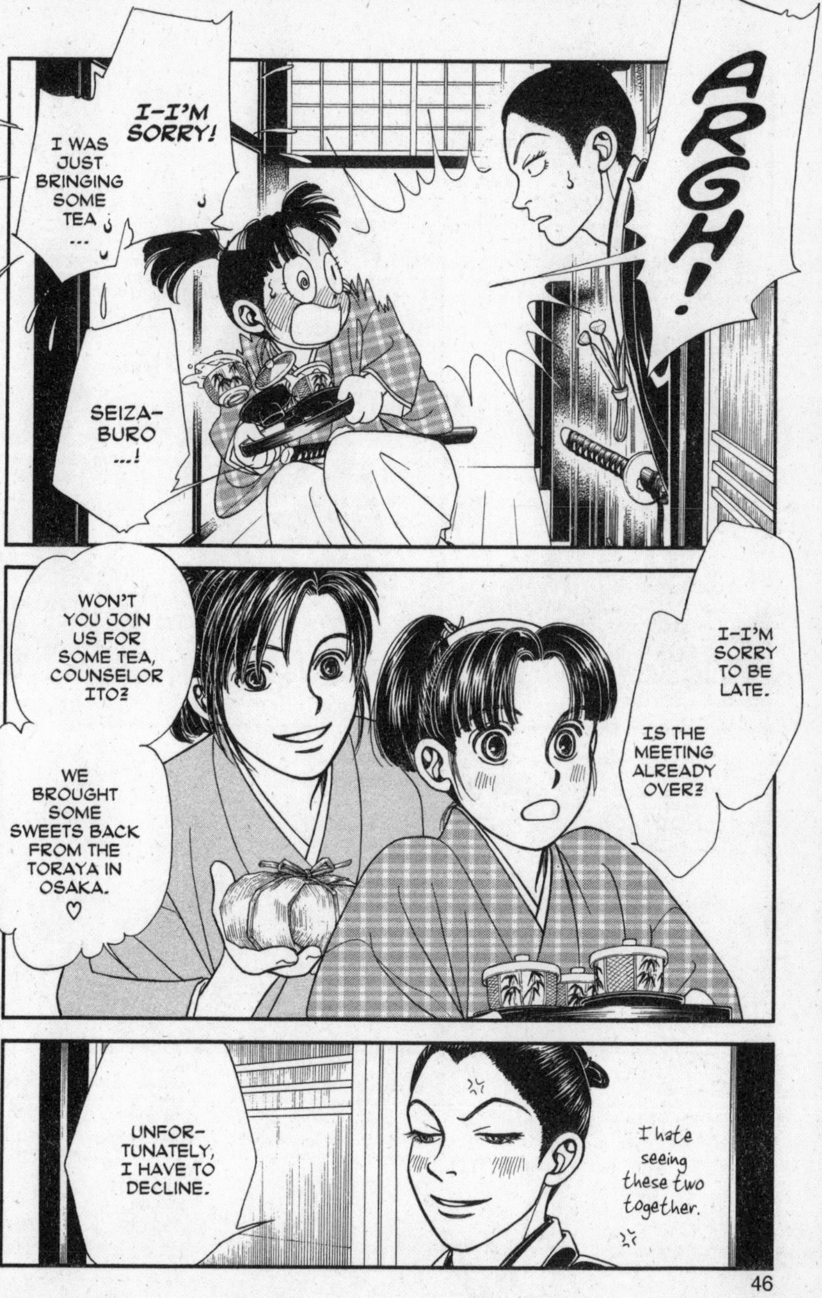
ARGH!
I-I'M SORRY!
I WAS JUST BRINGING SOME TEA ...
SEIZA-BURO ...!
I-I'M SORRY TO BE LATE.
IS THE MEETING ALREADY OVER?
WON'T YOU JOIN US FOR SOME TEA, COUNSELOR ITO?
WE BROUGHT SOME SWEETS BACK FROM THE TORAYA IN OSAKA. ♡
I hate seeing these two together.
UNFOR-TUNATELY, I HAVE TO DECLINE.

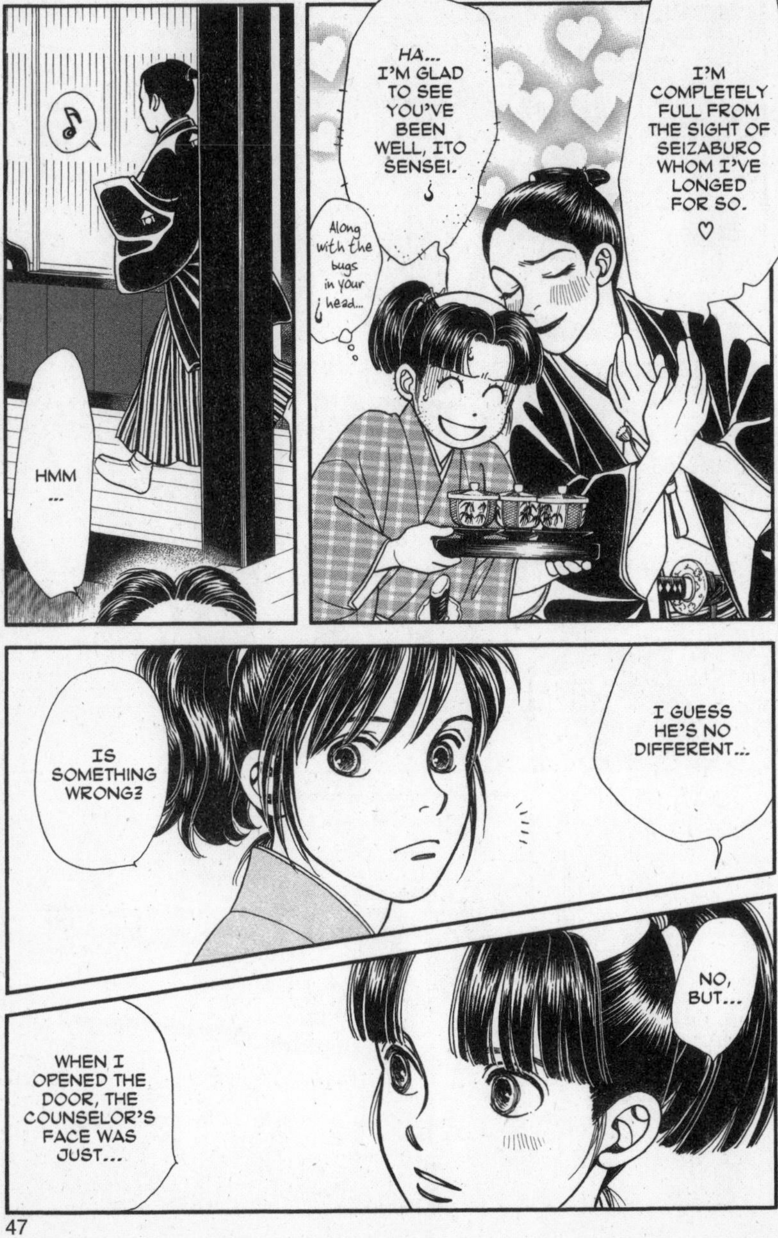
I'M COMPLETELY FULL FROM THE SIGHT OF SEIZABURO WHOM I'VE LONGED FOR SO. ♡
HA... I'M GLAD TO SEE YOU'VE BEEN WELL, ITO SENSEI.
Along with the bugs in your head...
HMM...
I GUESS HE'S NO DIFFERENT...
IS SOMETHING WRONG?
NO, BUT...
WHEN I OPENED THE DOOR, THE COUNSELOR'S FACE WAS JUST...

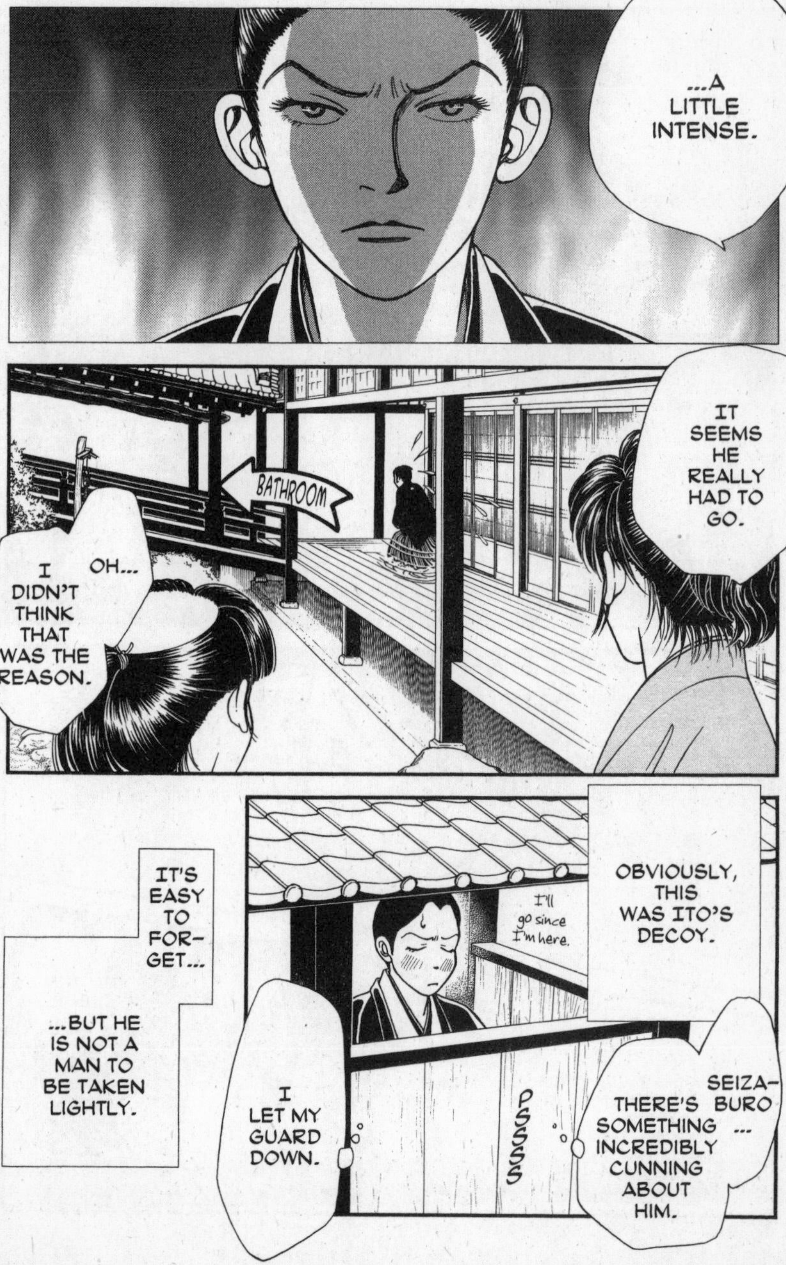
...A LITTLE INTENSE.
IT SEEMS HE REALLY HAD TO GO.
BATHROOM
OH... I DIDN'T THINK THAT WAS THE REASON.
OBVIOUSLY, THIS WAS ITO'S DECOY.
I'll go since I'm here.
SEIZABURO... THERE'S SOMETHING INCREDIBLY CUNNING ABOUT HIM.
PSSSS
I LET MY GUARD DOWN.
IT'S EASY TO FORGET...
...BUT HE IS NOT A MAN TO BE TAKEN LIGHTLY.

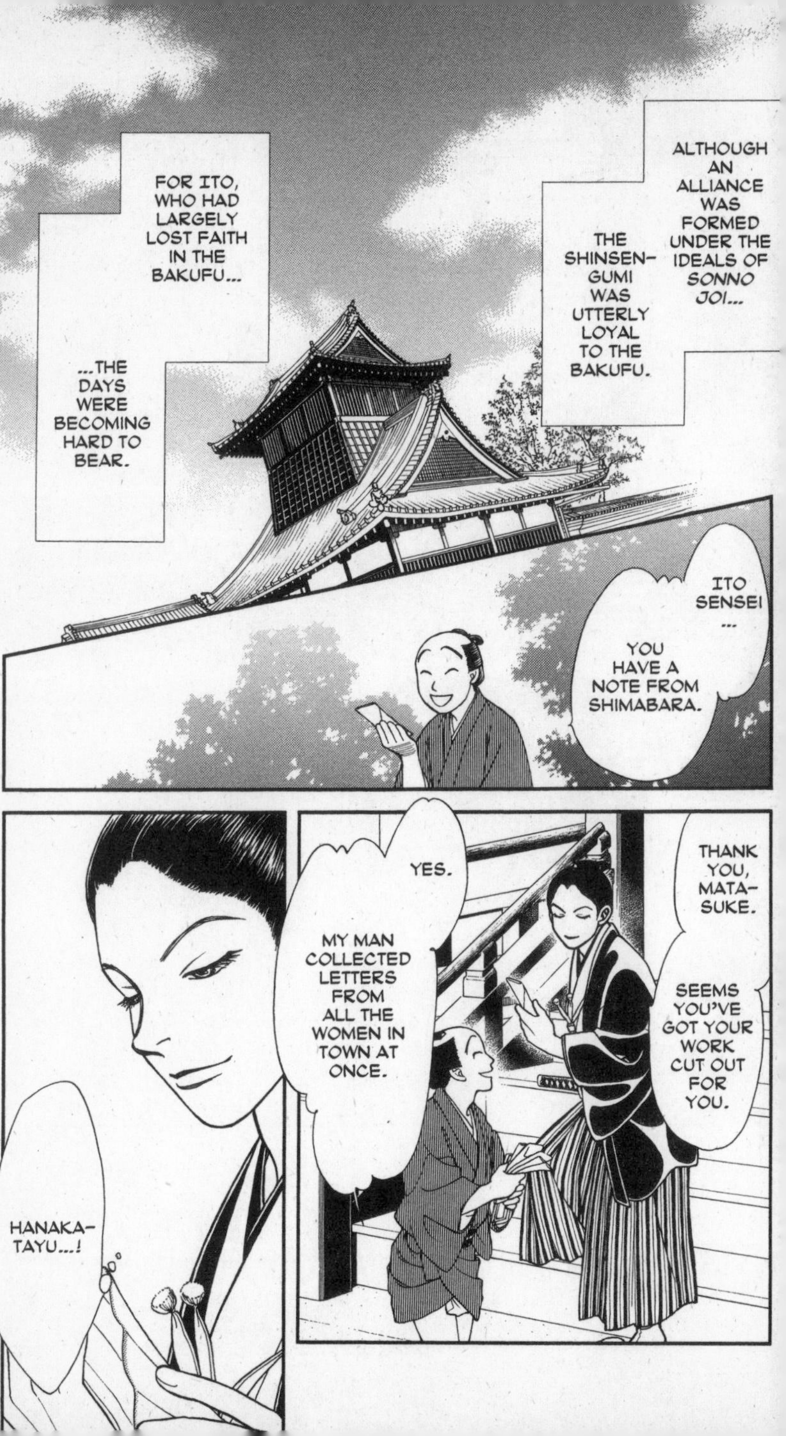

ALTHOUGH AN ALLIANCE WAS FORMED UNDER THE IDEALS OF SONNO JOI...
THE SHINSEN-GUMI WAS UTTERLY LOYAL TO THE BAKUFU.
FOR ITO, WHO HAD LARGELY LOST FAITH IN THE BAKUFU...
...THE DAYS WERE BECOMING HARD TO BEAR.
ITO SENSEI ...
YOU HAVE A NOTE FROM SHIMABARA.
THANK YOU, MATA-SUKE.
SEEMS YOU'VE GOT YOUR WORK CUT OUT FOR YOU.
YES.
MY MAN COLLECTED LETTERS FROM ALL THE WOMEN IN TOWN AT ONCE.
HANAKA-TAYU...!

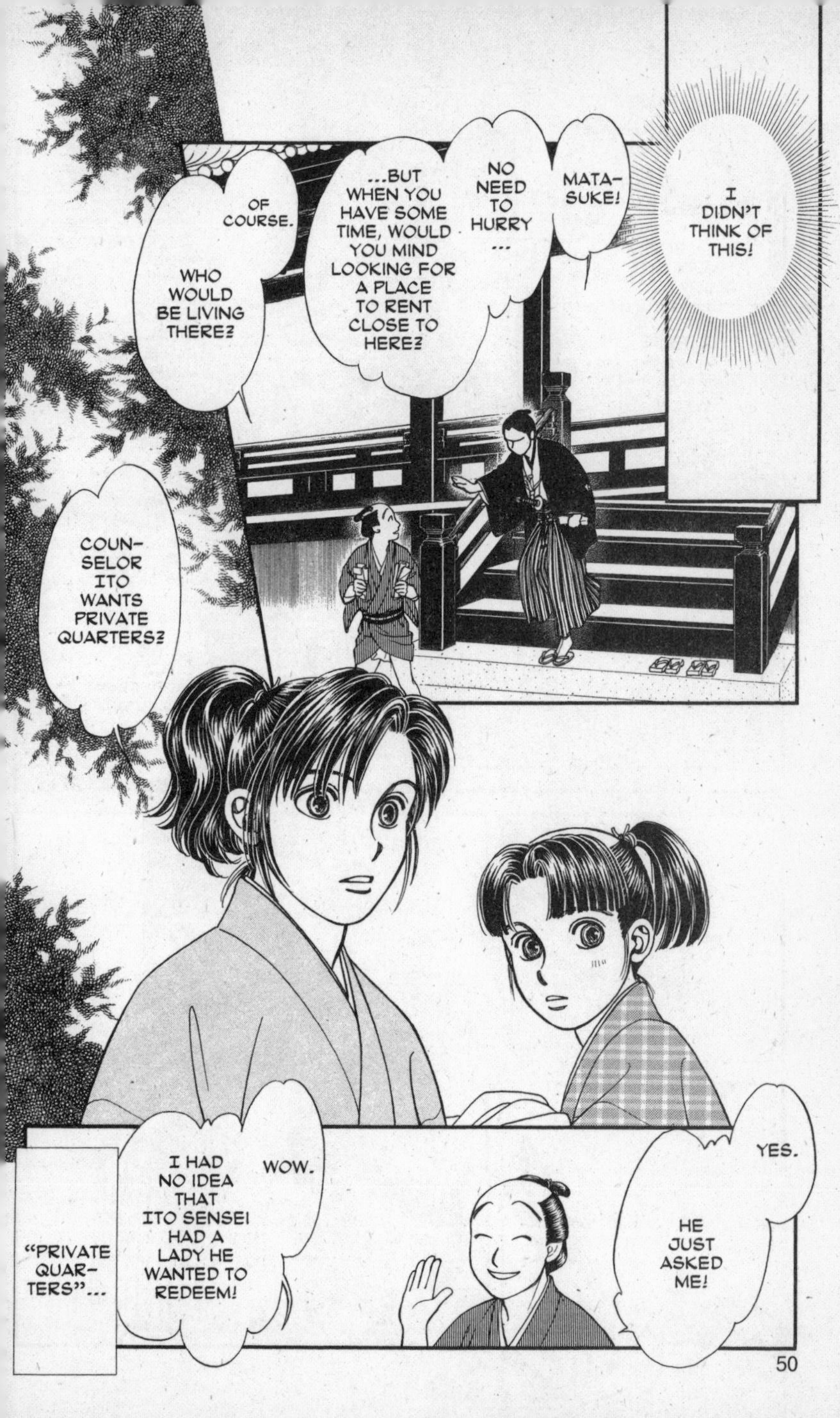

I DIDN'T THINK OF THIS!
MATA-SUKE!
NO NEED TO HURRY...
...BUT WHEN YOU HAVE SOME TIME, WOULD YOU MIND LOOKING FOR A PLACE TO RENT CLOSE TO HERE?
OF COURSE.
WHO WOULD BE LIVING THERE?
COUN-SELOR ITO WANTS PRIVATE QUARTERS?
YES.
HE JUST ASKED ME!
WOW.
I HAD NO IDEA THAT ITO SENSEI HAD A LADY HE WANTED TO REDEEM!
"PRIVATE QUAR-TERS"...

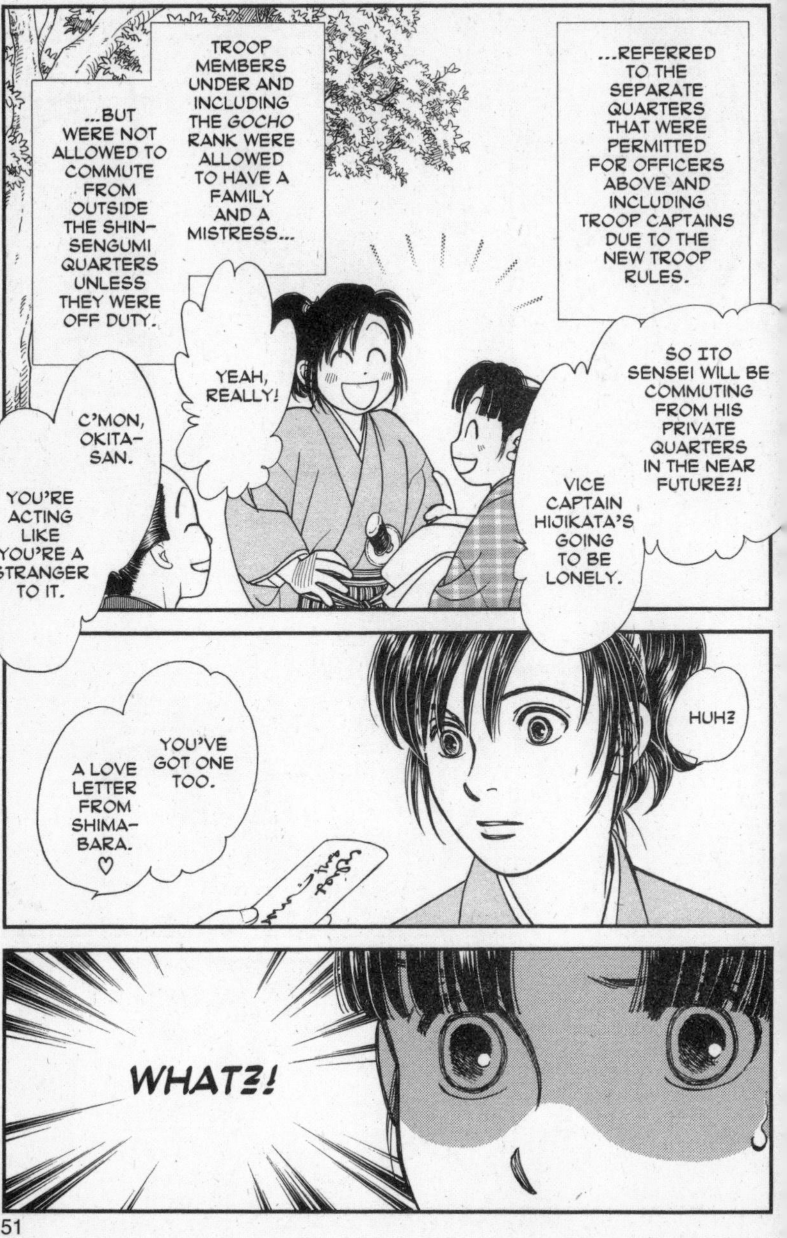
...REFERRED TO THE SEPARATE QUARTERS THAT WERE PERMITTED FOR OFFICERS ABOVE AND INCLUDING TROOP CAPTAINS DUE TO THE NEW TROOP RULES.
TROOP MEMBERS UNDER AND INCLUDING THE *GOCHO* RANK WERE ALLOWED TO HAVE A FAMILY AND A MISTRESS...
...BUT WERE NOT ALLOWED TO COMMUTE FROM OUTSIDE THE SHIN-SENGUMI QUARTERS UNLESS THEY WERE OFF DUTY.
SO ITO SENSEI WILL BE COMMUTING FROM HIS PRIVATE QUARTERS IN THE NEAR FUTURE?!
VICE CAPTAIN HIJIKATA'S GOING TO BE LONELY.
YEAH, REALLY!
C'MON, OKITA-SAN.
YOU'RE ACTING LIKE YOU'RE A STRANGER TO IT.
HUH?
YOU'VE GOT ONE TOO.
A LOVE LETTER FROM SHIMA-BARA. ♡
WHAT?!

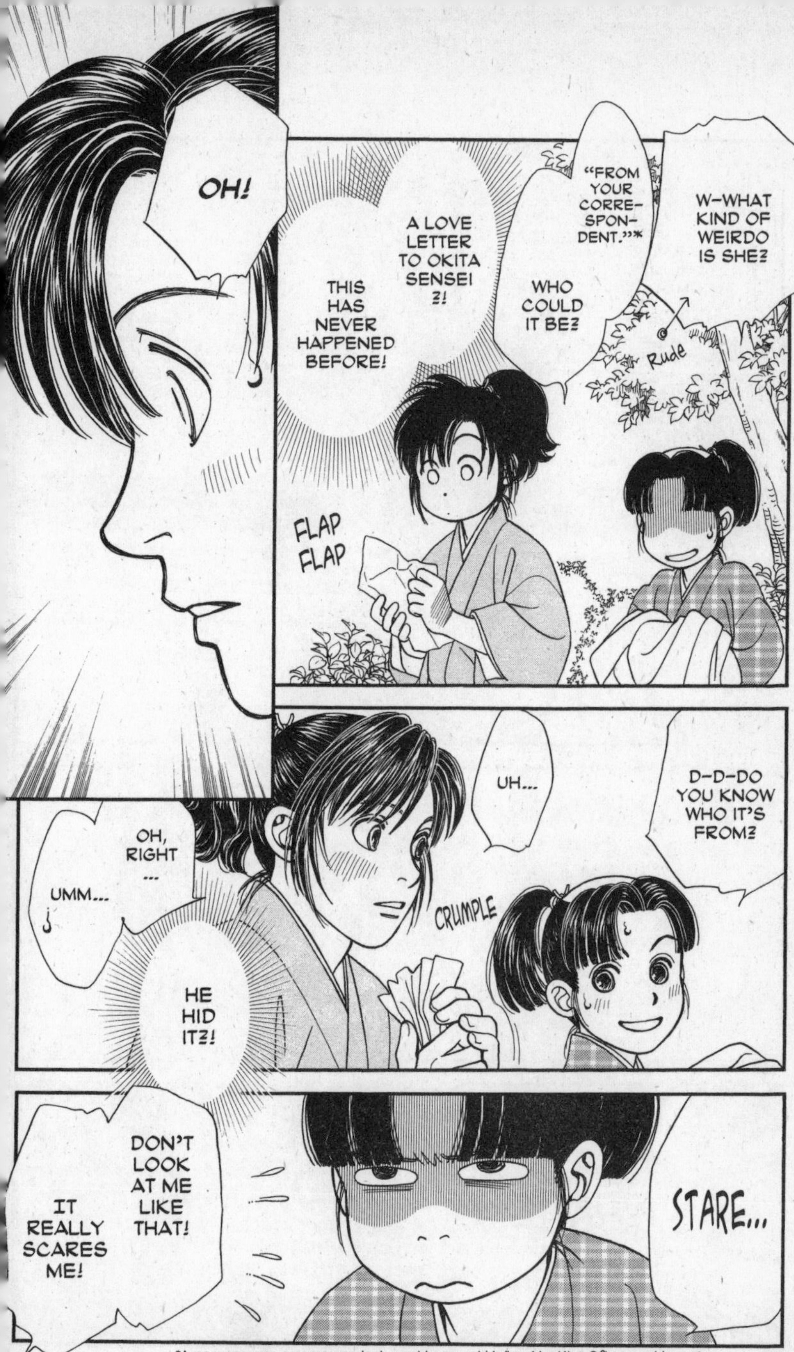
W–WHAT KIND OF WEIRDO IS SHE?
Rude
"FROM YOUR CORRE-SPON-DENT."*
WHO COULD IT BE?
A LOVE LETTER TO OKITA SENSEI ?!
THIS HAS NEVER HAPPENED BEFORE!
FLAP FLAP
OH!
D–D–DO YOU KNOW WHO IT'S FROM?
UH...
CRUMPLE
OH, RIGHT ...
UMM...
HE HID IT?!
STARE...
DON'T LOOK AT ME LIKE THAT!
IT REALLY SCARES ME!

*A common way a correspondent would conceal his/her identity. Often used by *yujo*.

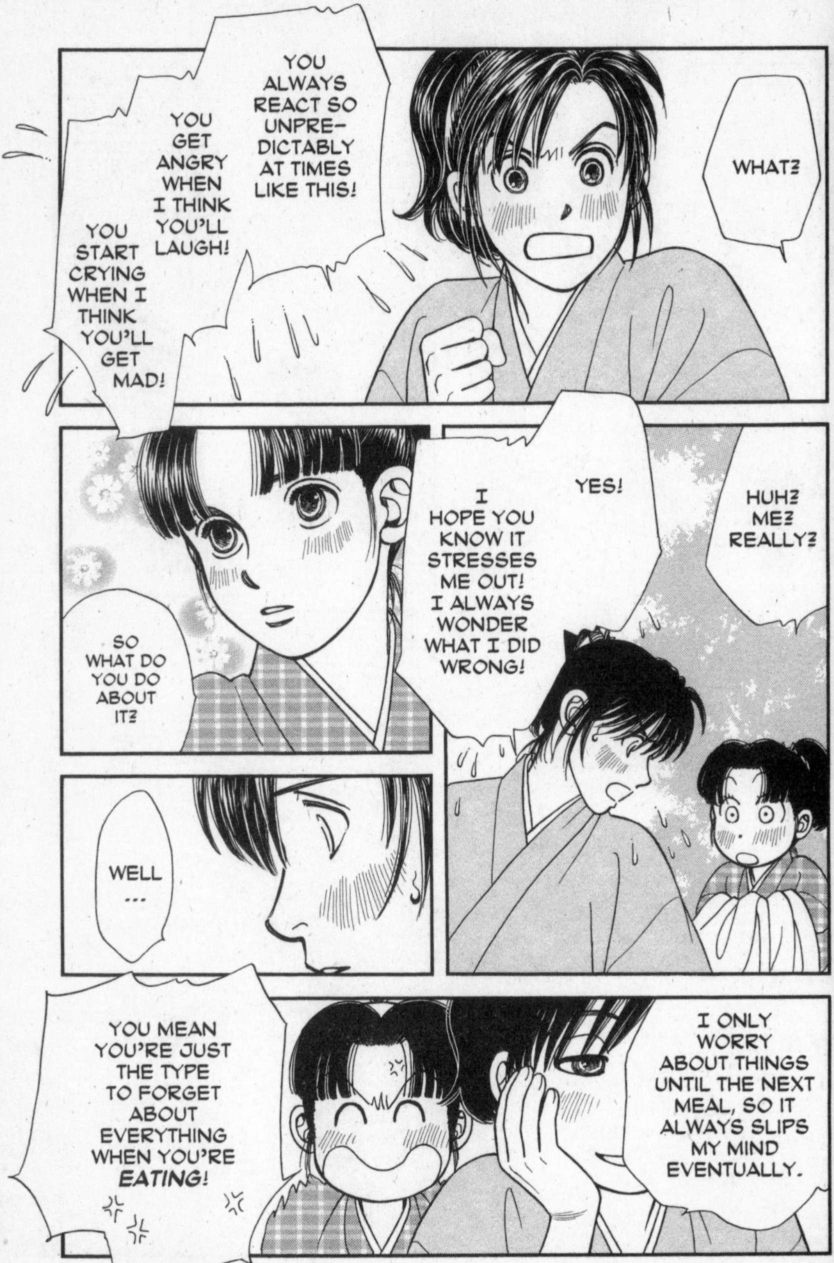
WHAT?
YOU ALWAYS REACT SO UNPRE-DICTABLY AT TIMES LIKE THIS!
YOU GET ANGRY WHEN I THINK YOU'LL LAUGH!
YOU START CRYING WHEN I THINK YOU'LL GET MAD!
HUH? ME? REALLY?
YES!
I HOPE YOU KNOW IT STRESSES ME OUT! I ALWAYS WONDER WHAT I DID WRONG!
SO WHAT DO YOU DO ABOUT IT?
WELL ...
I ONLY WORRY ABOUT THINGS UNTIL THE NEXT MEAL, SO IT ALWAYS SLIPS MY MIND EVENTUALLY.
YOU MEAN YOU'RE JUST THE TYPE TO FORGET ABOUT EVERYTHING WHEN YOU'RE *EATING*!

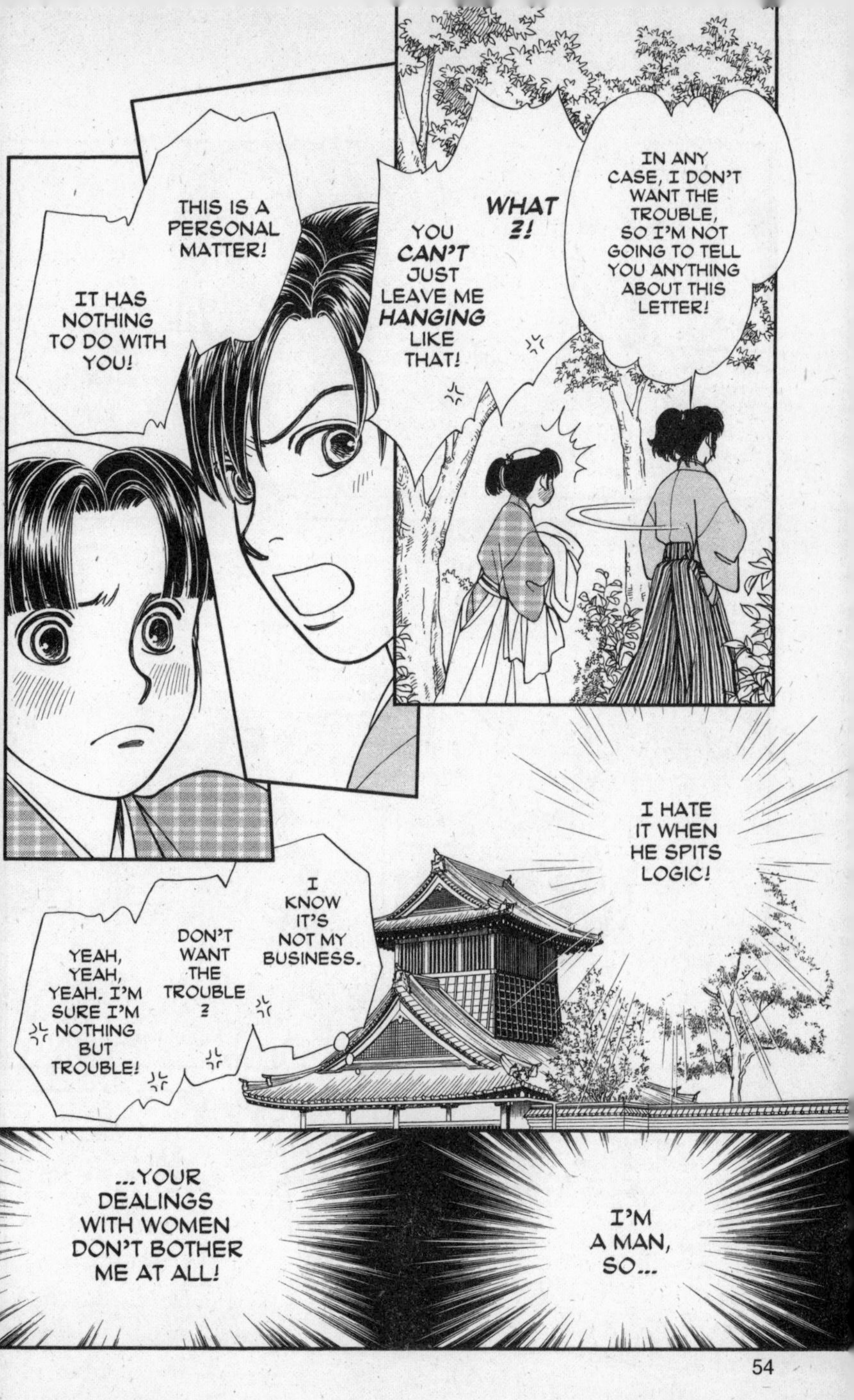
IN ANY CASE, I DON'T WANT THE TROUBLE, SO I'M NOT GOING TO TELL YOU ANYTHING ABOUT THIS LETTER!
WHAT?!
YOU CAN'T JUST LEAVE ME HANGING LIKE THAT!
THIS IS A PERSONAL MATTER!
IT HAS NOTHING TO DO WITH YOU!
I HATE IT WHEN HE SPITS LOGIC!
I KNOW IT'S NOT MY BUSINESS.
DON'T WANT THE TROUBLE?
YEAH, YEAH, YEAH. I'M SURE I'M NOTHING BUT TROUBLE!
I'M A MAN, SO...
...YOUR DEALINGS WITH WOMEN DON'T BOTHER ME AT ALL!

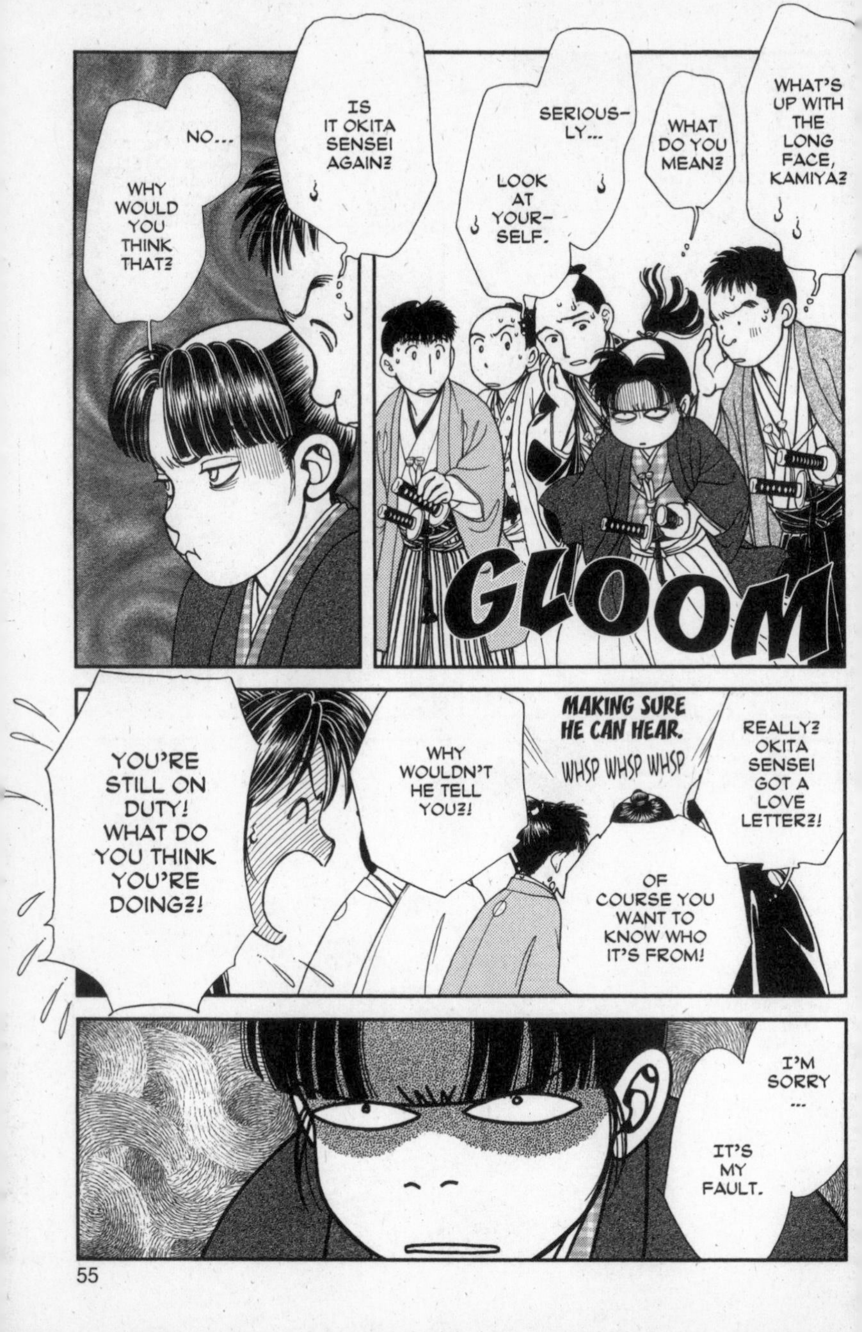
WHAT'S UP WITH THE LONG FACE, KAMIYA?
WHAT DO YOU MEAN?
SERIOUS-LY...
LOOK AT YOUR-SELF.
GLOOM
IS IT OKITA SENSEI AGAIN?
NO...
WHY WOULD YOU THINK THAT?
REALLY? OKITA SENSEI GOT A LOVE LETTER?!
MAKING SURE HE CAN HEAR.
WHSP WHSP WHSP
OF COURSE YOU WANT TO KNOW WHO IT'S FROM!
WHY WOULDN'T HE TELL YOU?!
YOU'RE STILL ON DUTY! WHAT DO YOU THINK YOU'RE DOING?!
I'M SORRY...
IT'S MY FAULT.

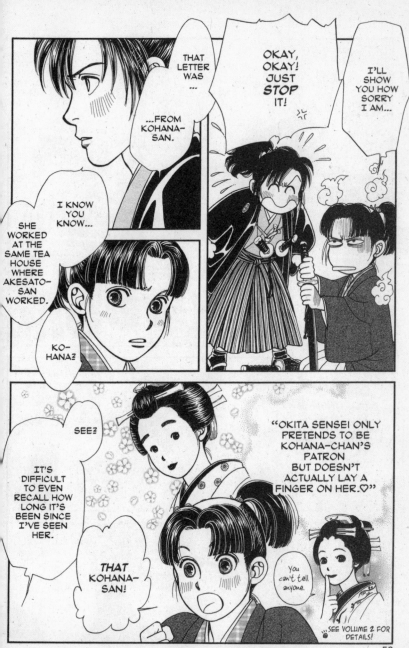

I'LL SHOW YOU HOW SORRY I AM...
OKAY, OKAY! JUST **STOP** IT!
THAT LETTER WAS ...
...FROM KOHANA-SAN.
I KNOW YOU KNOW...
SHE WORKED AT THE SAME TEA HOUSE WHERE AKESATO-SAN WORKED.
KO-HANA?
"OKITA SENSEI ONLY PRETENDS TO BE KOHANA-CHAN'S PATRON BUT DOESN'T ACTUALLY LAY A FINGER ON HER.♡"
You can't tell anyone.
SEE VOLUME 2 FOR DETAILS!
SEE?
IT'S DIFFICULT TO EVEN RECALL HOW LONG IT'S BEEN SINCE I'VE SEEN HER.
THAT KOHANA-SAN!

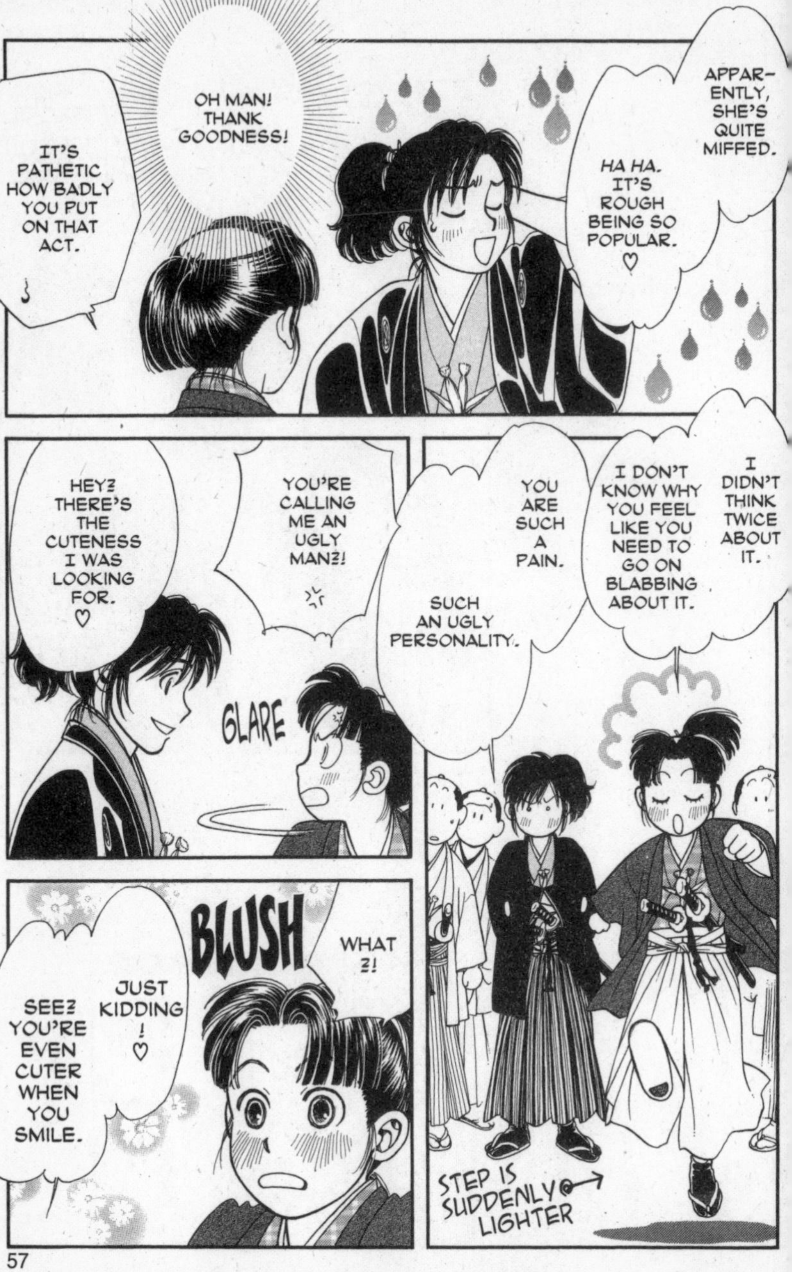
APPARENTLY, SHE'S QUITE MIFFED.
HA HA. IT'S ROUGH BEING SO POPULAR. ♡
OH MAN! THANK GOODNESS!
IT'S PATHETIC HOW BADLY YOU PUT ON THAT ACT.
I DIDN'T THINK TWICE ABOUT IT.
I DON'T KNOW WHY YOU FEEL LIKE YOU NEED TO GO ON BLABBING ABOUT IT.
YOU ARE SUCH A PAIN.
SUCH AN UGLY PERSONALITY.
STEP IS SUDDENLY LIGHTER
YOU'RE CALLING ME AN UGLY MAN?!
GLARE
HEY? THERE'S THE CUTENESS I WAS LOOKING FOR. ♡
WHAT?!
BLUSH
JUST KIDDING! ♡
SEE? YOU'RE EVEN CUTER WHEN YOU SMILE.

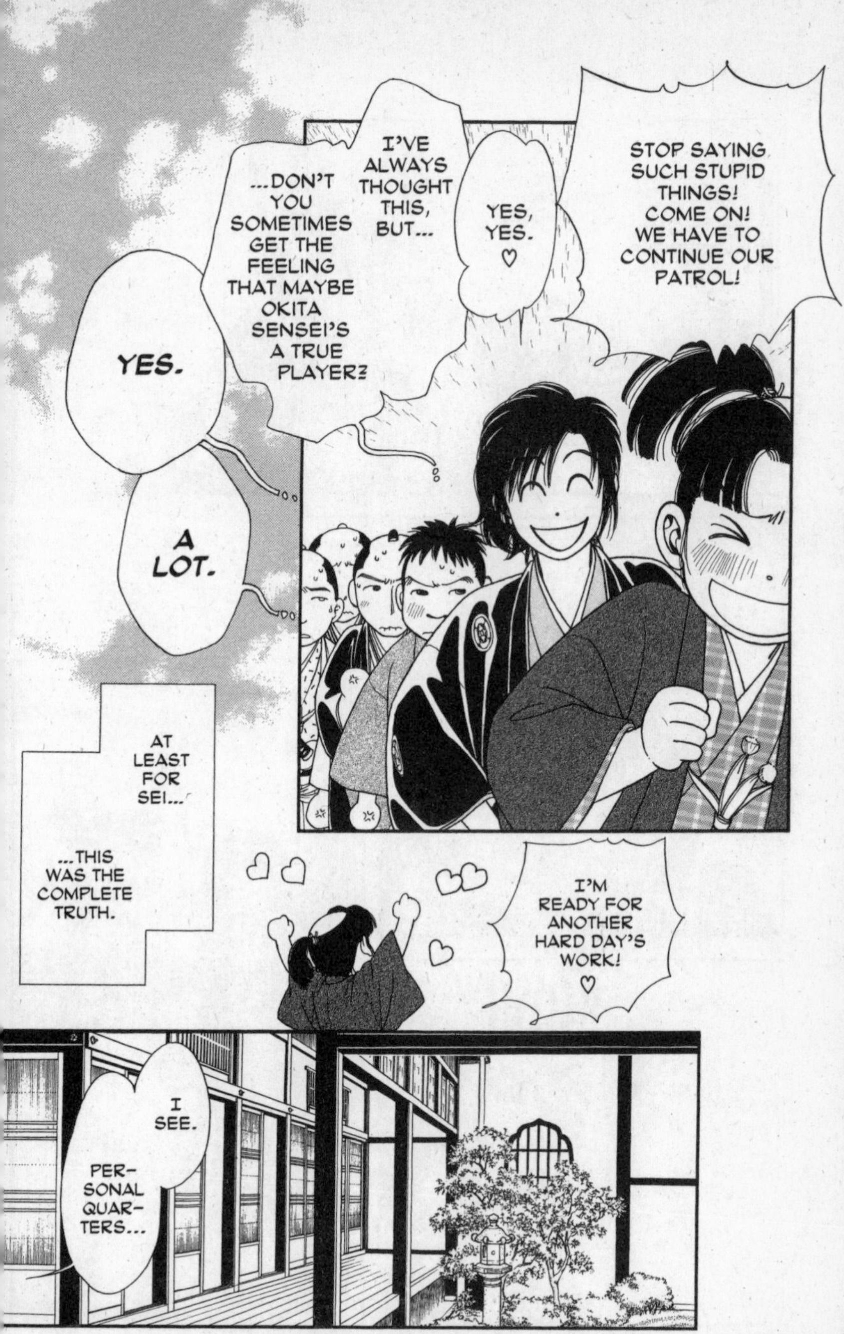
STOP SAYING SUCH STUPID THINGS! COME ON! WE HAVE TO CONTINUE OUR PATROL!
YES, YES. ♡
I'VE ALWAYS THOUGHT THIS, BUT...
...DON'T YOU SOMETIMES GET THE FEELING THAT MAYBE OKITA SENSEI'S A TRUE PLAYER?
YES.
A LOT.
I'M READY FOR ANOTHER HARD DAY'S WORK! ♡
AT LEAST FOR SEI...
...THIS WAS THE COMPLETE TRUTH.
I SEE.
PER-SONAL QUAR-TERS...

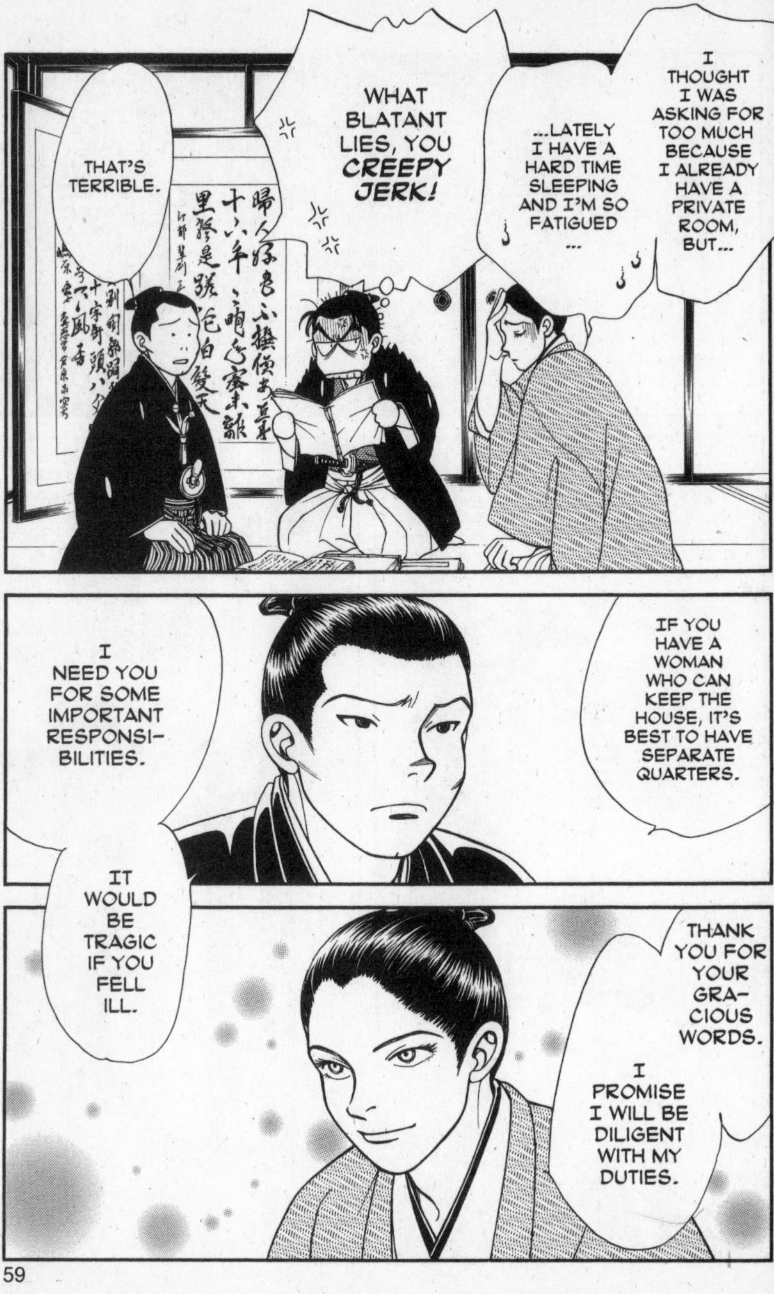

I THOUGHT I WAS ASKING FOR TOO MUCH BECAUSE I ALREADY HAVE A PRIVATE ROOM, BUT...
...LATELY I HAVE A HARD TIME SLEEPING AND I'M SO FATIGUED ...
WHAT BLATANT LIES, YOU *CREEPY JERK!*
THAT'S TERRIBLE.
IF YOU HAVE A WOMAN WHO CAN KEEP THE HOUSE, IT'S BEST TO HAVE SEPARATE QUARTERS.
I NEED YOU FOR SOME IMPORTANT RESPONSI-BILITIES.
IT WOULD BE TRAGIC IF YOU FELL ILL.
THANK YOU FOR YOUR GRA-CIOUS WORDS.
I PROMISE I WILL BE DILIGENT WITH MY DUTIES.

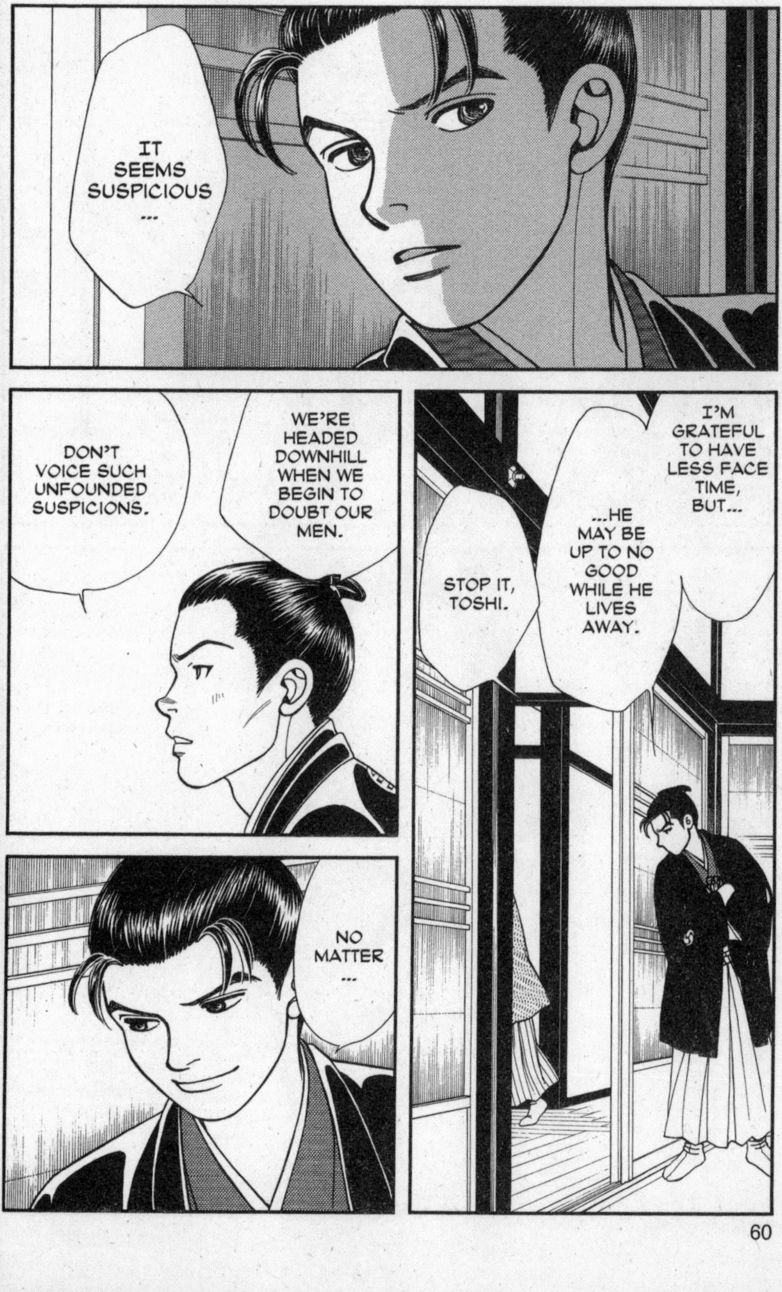
IT SEEMS SUSPICIOUS ...
I'M GRATEFUL TO HAVE LESS FACE TIME, BUT...
...HE MAY BE UP TO NO GOOD WHILE HE LIVES AWAY.
STOP IT, TOSHI.
WE'RE HEADED DOWNHILL WHEN WE BEGIN TO DOUBT OUR MEN.
DON'T VOICE SUCH UNFOUNDED SUSPICIONS.
NO MATTER ...

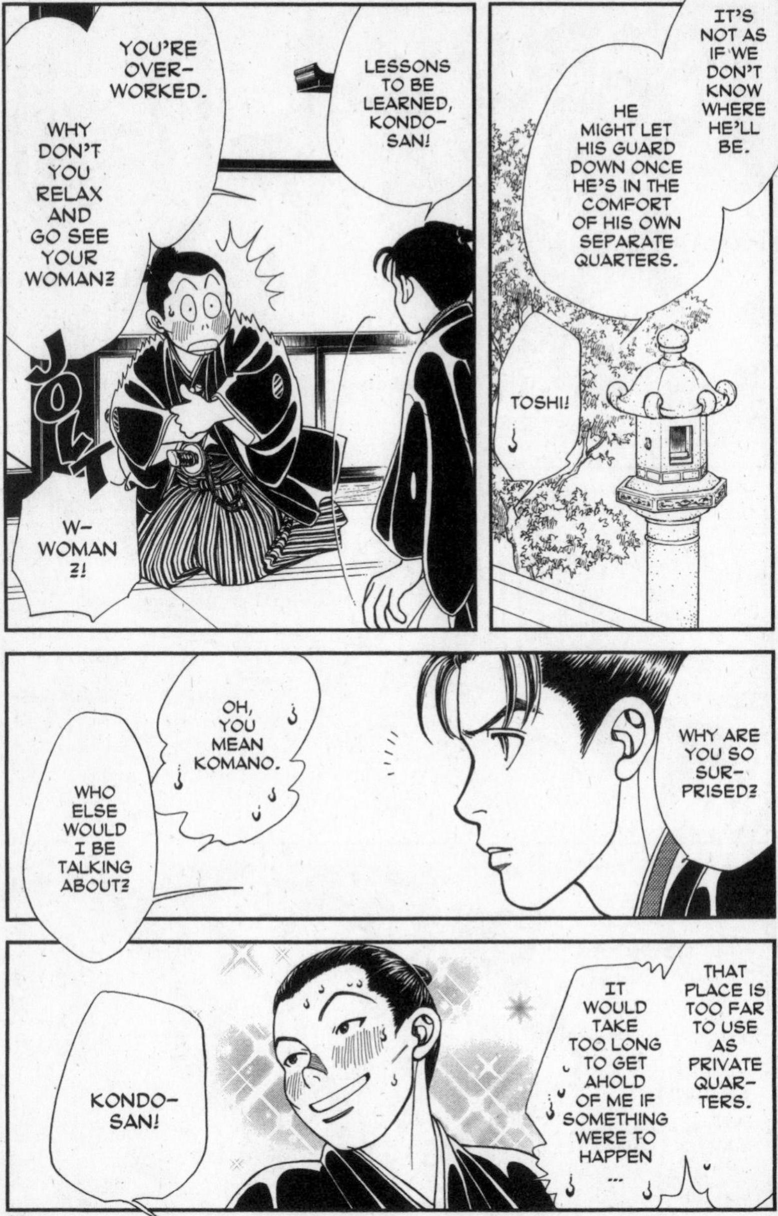
IT'S NOT AS IF WE DON'T KNOW WHERE HE'LL BE.
HE MIGHT LET HIS GUARD DOWN ONCE HE'S IN THE COMFORT OF HIS OWN SEPARATE QUARTERS.
TOSHI!
LESSONS TO BE LEARNED, KONDO-SAN!
YOU'RE OVER-WORKED.
WHY DON'T YOU RELAX AND GO SEE YOUR WOMAN?
JOLT
W-WOMAN?!
WHY ARE YOU SO SUR-PRISED?
OH, YOU MEAN KOMANO.
WHO ELSE WOULD I BE TALKING ABOUT?
THAT PLACE IS TOO FAR TO USE AS PRIVATE QUAR-TERS.
IT WOULD TAKE TOO LONG TO GET AHOLD OF ME IF SOMETHING WERE TO HAPPEN ...
KONDO-SAN!

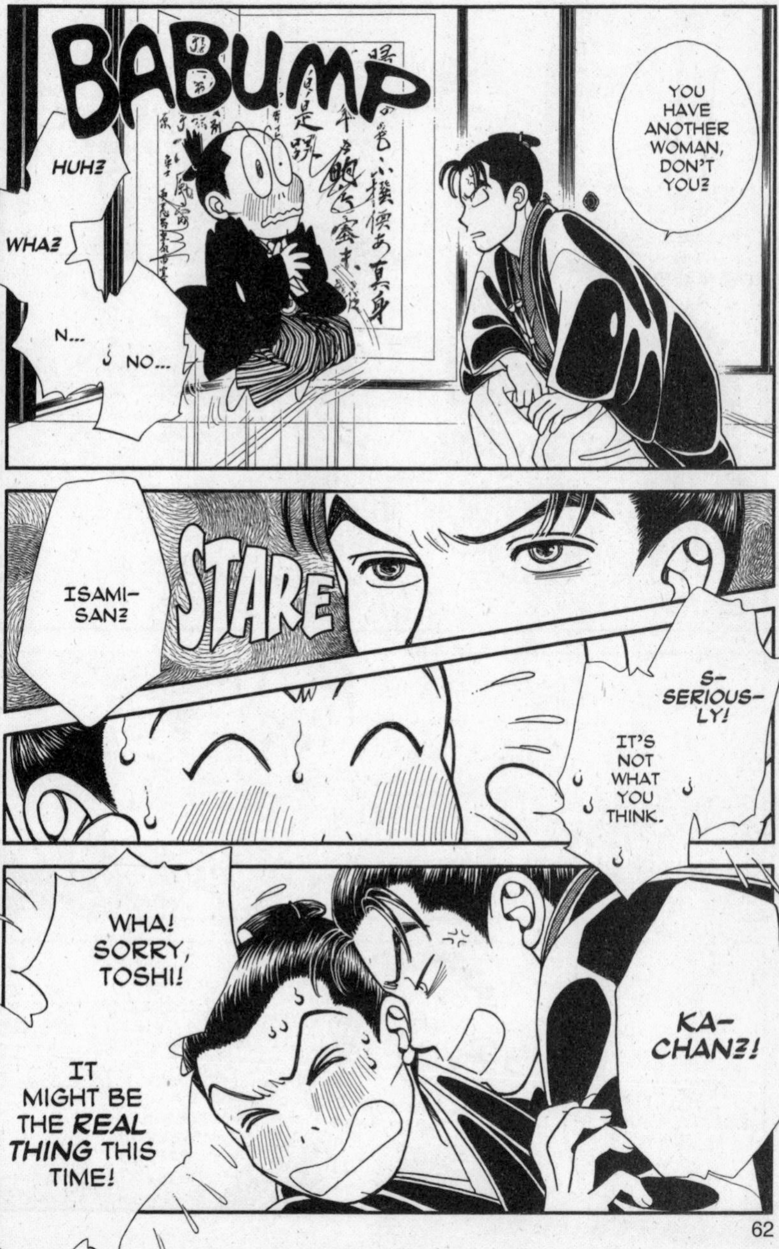
YOU HAVE ANOTHER WOMAN, DON'T YOU?
BABUMP
HUH?
WHA?
N... NO...
STARE
ISAMI-SAN?
S-SERIOUSLY!
IT'S NOT WHAT YOU THINK.
KA-CHAN?!
WHA! SORRY, TOSHI!
IT MIGHT BE THE REAL THING THIS TIME!

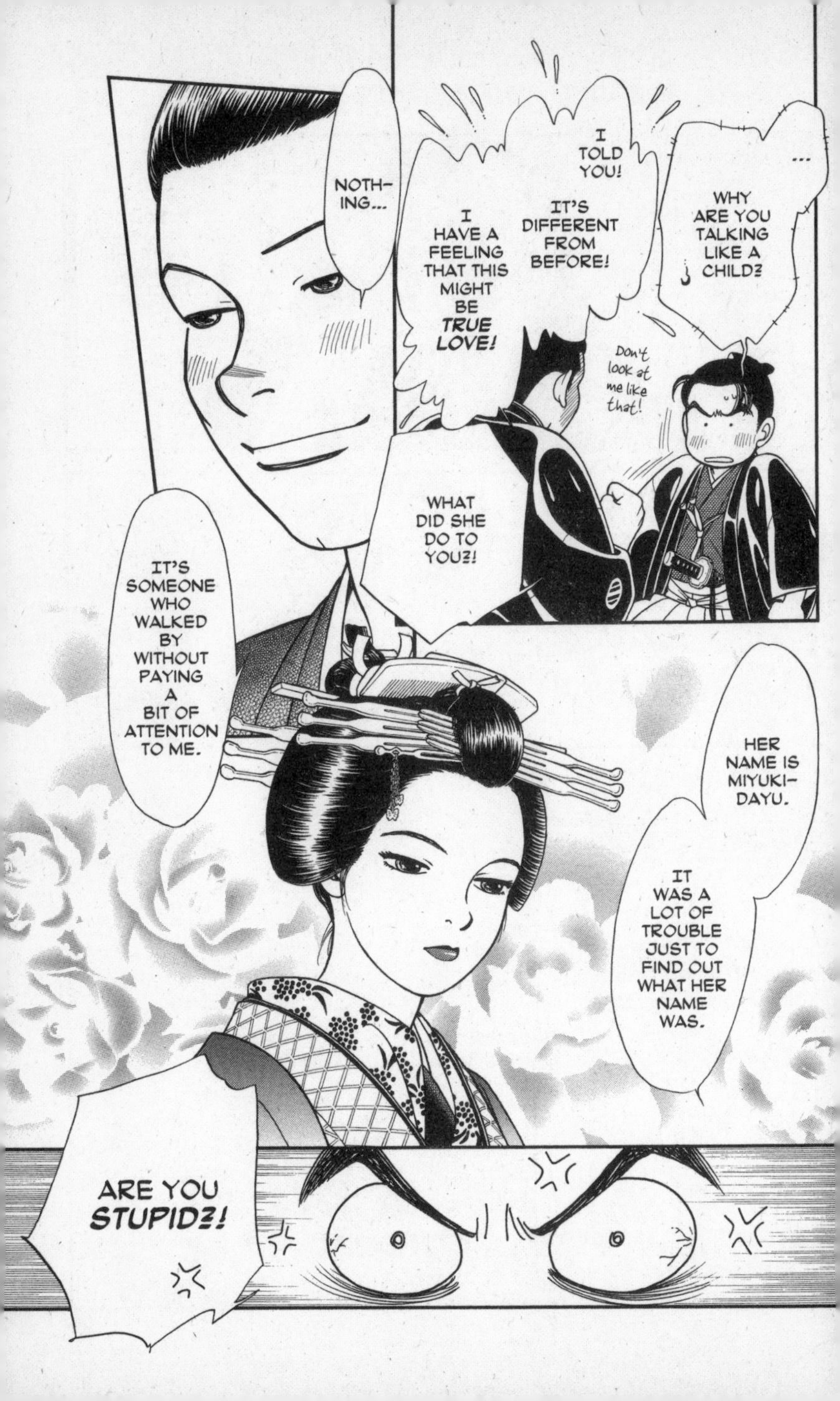
...
WHY ARE YOU TALKING LIKE A CHILD?
I TOLD YOU!
IT'S DIFFERENT FROM BEFORE!
I HAVE A FEELING THAT THIS MIGHT BE ***TRUE LOVE!***
Don't look at me like that!
WHAT DID SHE DO TO YOU?!
NOTHING...
IT'S SOMEONE WHO WALKED BY WITHOUT PAYING A BIT OF ATTENTION TO ME.
HER NAME IS MIYUKI-DAYU.
IT WAS A LOT OF TROUBLE JUST TO FIND OUT WHAT HER NAME WAS.
ARE YOU ***STUPID?!***

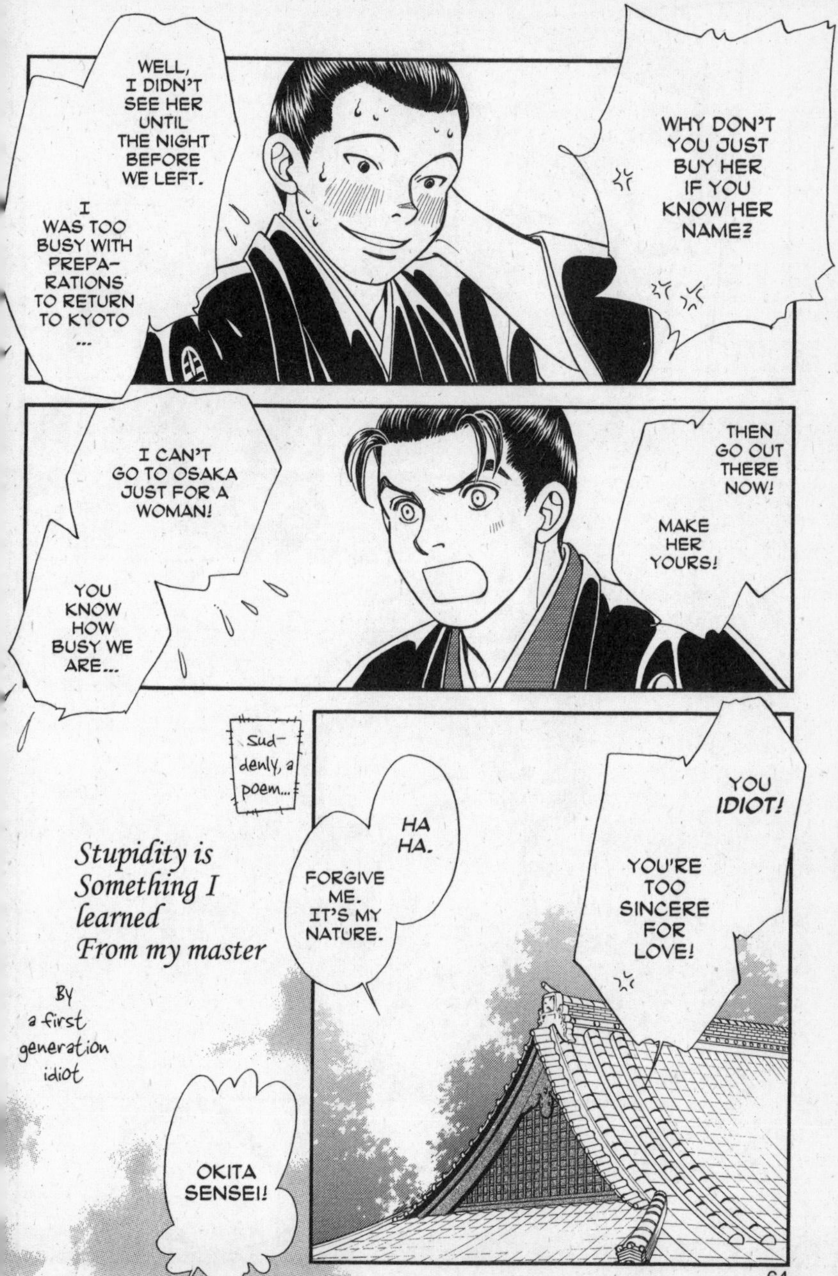
WHY DON'T YOU JUST BUY HER IF YOU KNOW HER NAME?
WELL, I DIDN'T SEE HER UNTIL THE NIGHT BEFORE WE LEFT.
I WAS TOO BUSY WITH PREPA-RATIONS TO RETURN TO KYOTO ...
THEN GO OUT THERE NOW!
MAKE HER YOURS!
I CAN'T GO TO OSAKA JUST FOR A WOMAN!
YOU KNOW HOW BUSY WE ARE...
YOU IDIOT!
YOU'RE TOO SINCERE FOR LOVE!
HA HA.
FORGIVE ME. IT'S MY NATURE.
Sud-denly, a poem...
Stupidity is Something I learned From my master
By a first generation idiot
OKITA SENSEI!

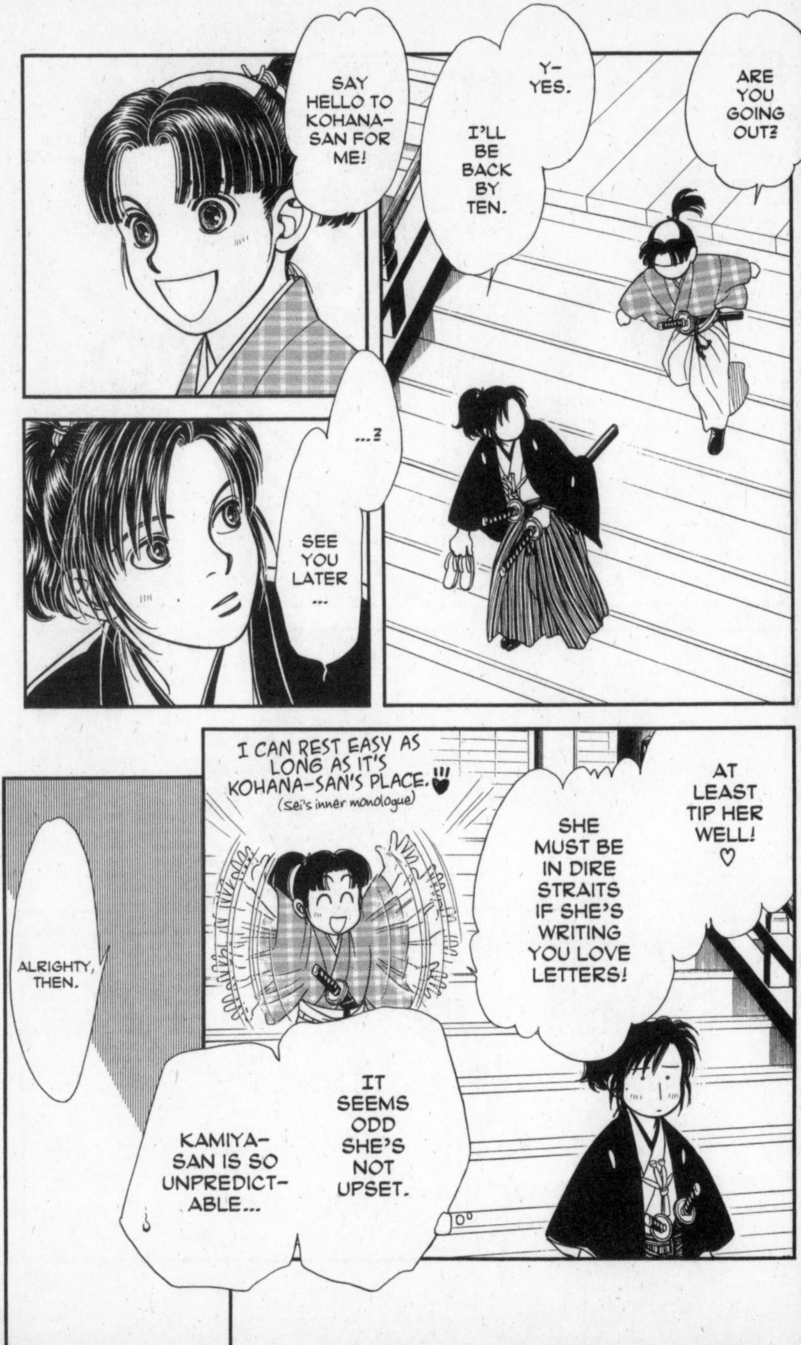
ARE YOU GOING OUT?
Y-YES.
I'LL BE BACK BY TEN.
SAY HELLO TO KOHANA-SAN FOR ME!
...? SEE YOU LATER...
AT LEAST TIP HER WELL! ♡
SHE MUST BE IN DIRE STRAITS IF SHE'S WRITING YOU LOVE LETTERS!
I CAN REST EASY AS LONG AS IT'S KOHANA-SAN'S PLACE.
(sei's inner monologue)
IT SEEMS ODD SHE'S NOT UPSET.
KAMIYA-SAN IS SO UNPREDICT-ABLE...
ALRIGHTY, THEN.

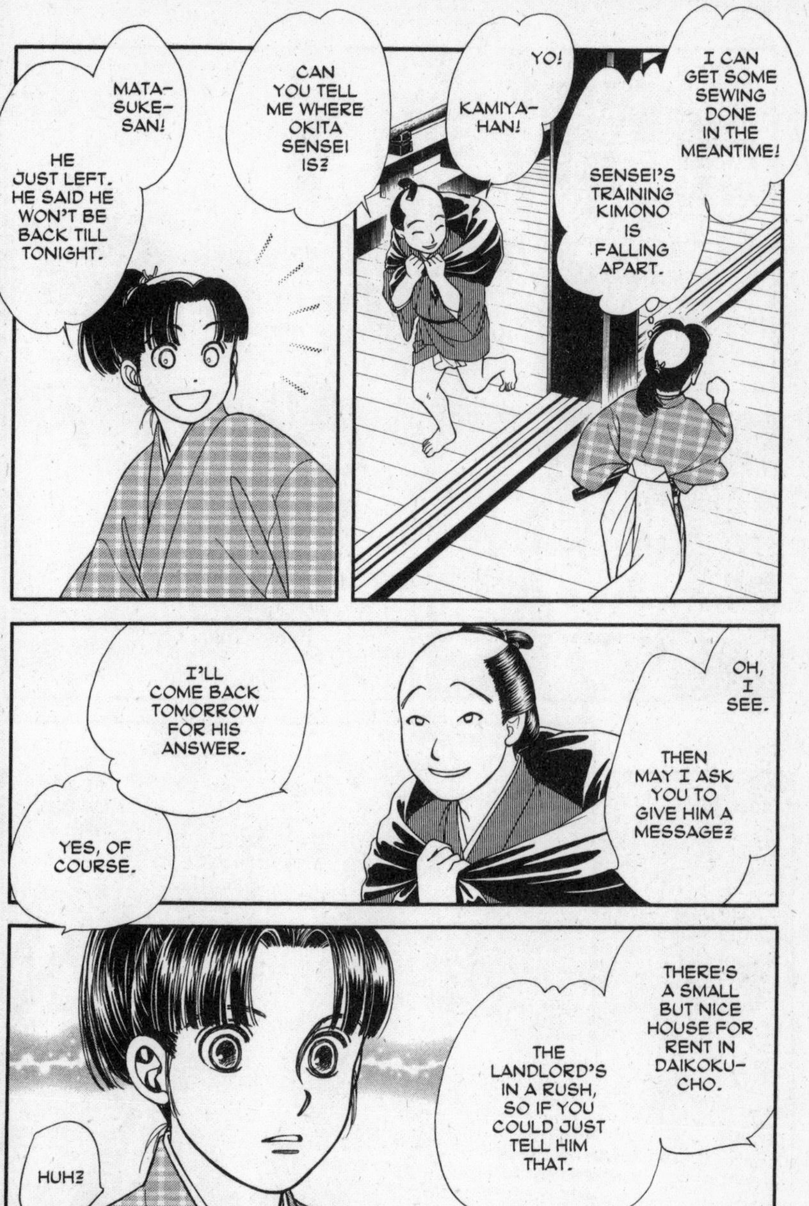
I CAN GET SOME SEWING DONE IN THE MEANTIME!
SENSEI'S TRAINING KIMONO IS FALLING APART.
YO! KAMIYA-HAN!
CAN YOU TELL ME WHERE OKITA SENSEI IS?
MATA-SUKE-SAN!
HE JUST LEFT. HE SAID HE WON'T BE BACK TILL TONIGHT.
OH, I SEE.
THEN MAY I ASK YOU TO GIVE HIM A MESSAGE?
I'LL COME BACK TOMORROW FOR HIS ANSWER.
YES, OF COURSE.
THERE'S A SMALL BUT NICE HOUSE FOR RENT IN DAIKOKU-CHO.
THE LANDLORD'S IN A RUSH, SO IF YOU COULD JUST TELL HIM THAT.
HUH?

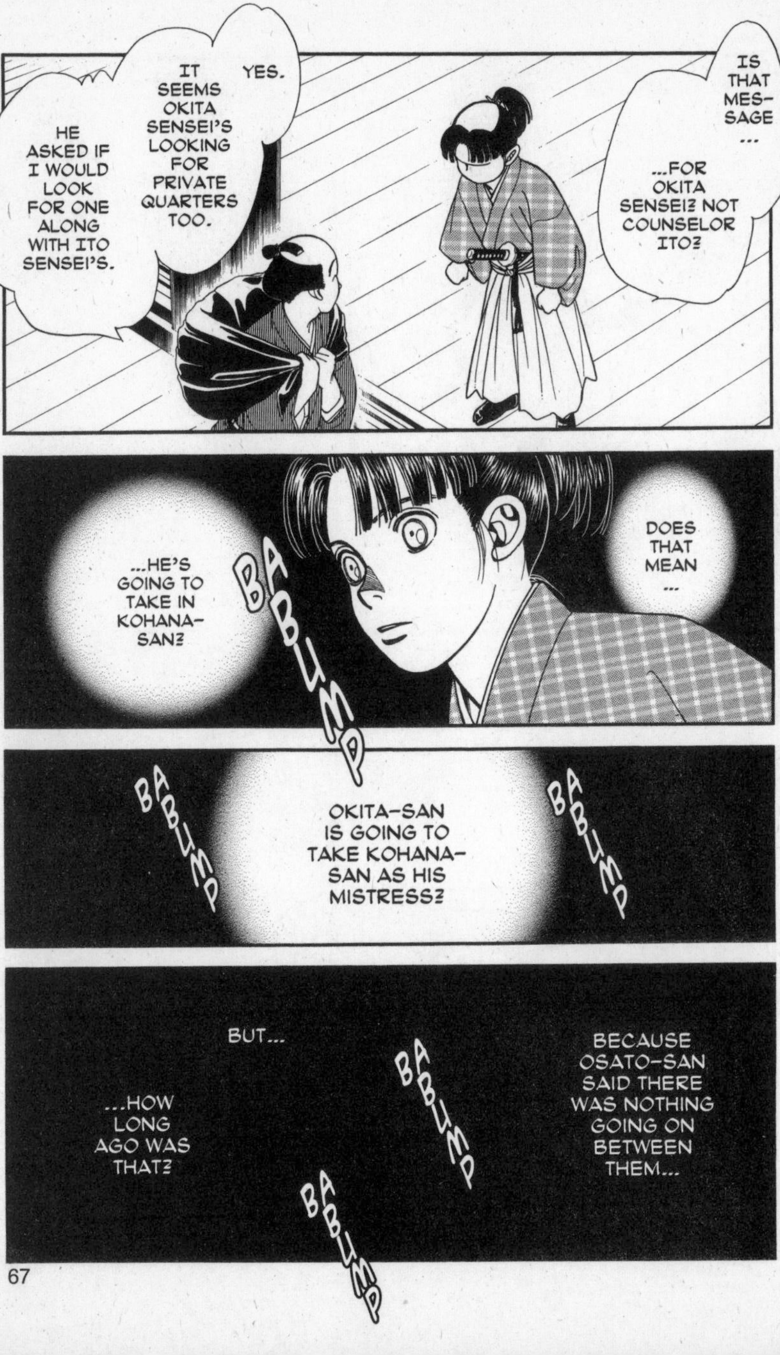
IS THAT MES-SAGE...
...FOR OKITA SENSEI? NOT COUNSELOR ITO?
YES.
IT SEEMS OKITA SENSEI'S LOOKING FOR PRIVATE QUARTERS TOO.
HE ASKED IF I WOULD LOOK FOR ONE ALONG WITH ITO SENSEI'S.
DOES THAT MEAN...
BABUMP
...HE'S GOING TO TAKE IN KOHANA-SAN?
BABUMP
OKITA-SAN IS GOING TO TAKE KOHANA-SAN AS HIS MISTRESS?
BABUMP
BECAUSE OSATO-SAN SAID THERE WAS NOTHING GOING ON BETWEEN THEM...
BABUMP
BUT...
...HOW LONG AGO WAS THAT?
BABUMP

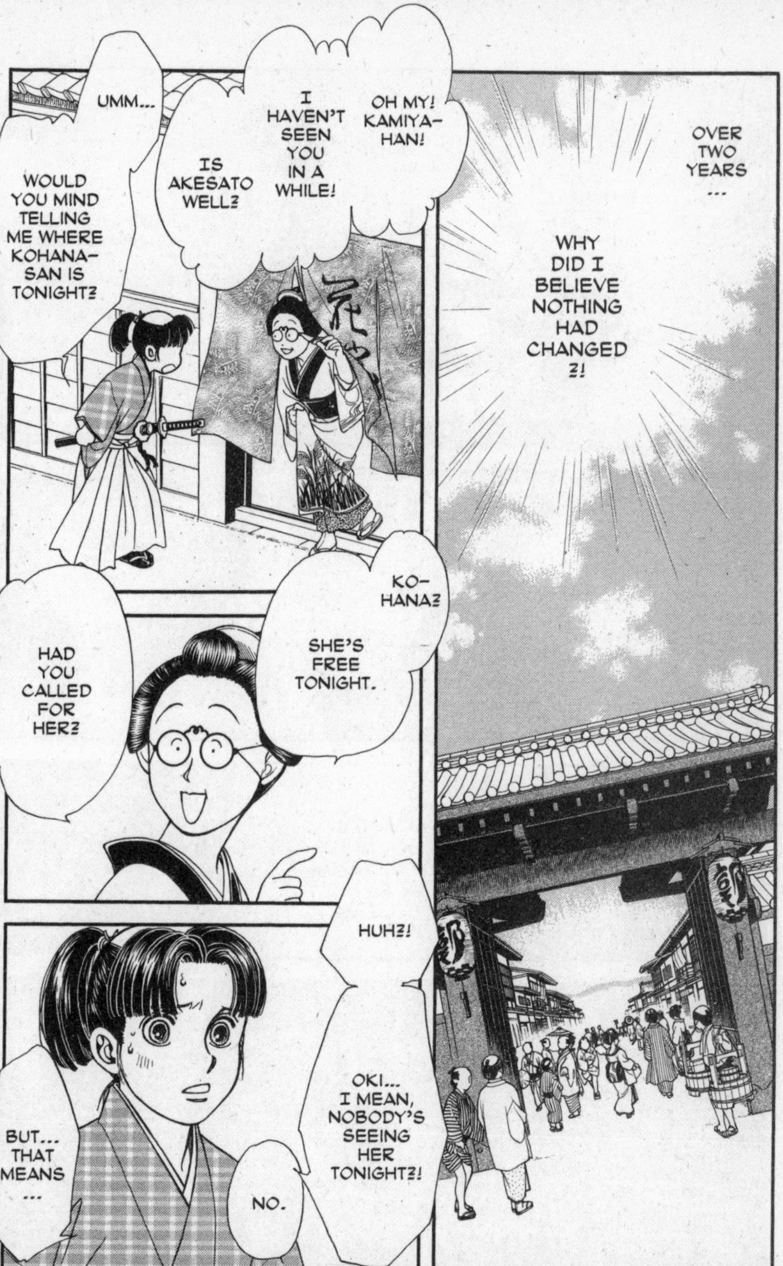
OVER TWO YEARS ...
WHY DID I BELIEVE NOTHING HAD CHANGED?!
OH MY! KAMIYA-HAN!
I HAVEN'T SEEN YOU IN A WHILE!
IS AKESATO WELL?
UMM...
WOULD YOU MIND TELLING ME WHERE KOHANA-SAN IS TONIGHT?
KO-HANA?
SHE'S FREE TONIGHT.
HAD YOU CALLED FOR HER?
HUH?!
OKI... I MEAN, NOBODY'S SEEING HER TONIGHT?!
NO.
BUT... THAT MEANS ...

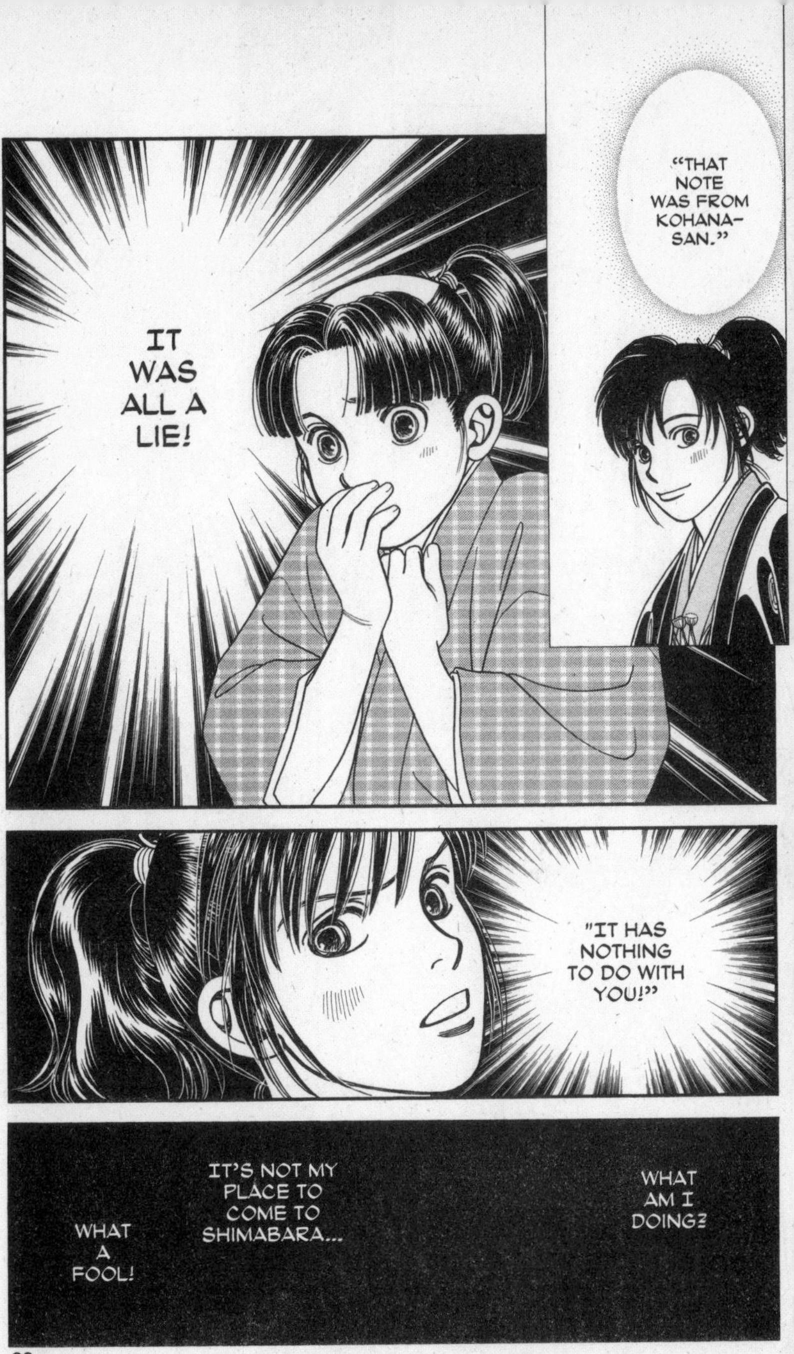
"THAT NOTE WAS FROM KOHANA-SAN."
IT WAS ALL A LIE!
"IT HAS NOTHING TO DO WITH YOU!"
WHAT AM I DOING?
IT'S NOT MY PLACE TO COME TO SHIMABARA...
WHAT A FOOL!

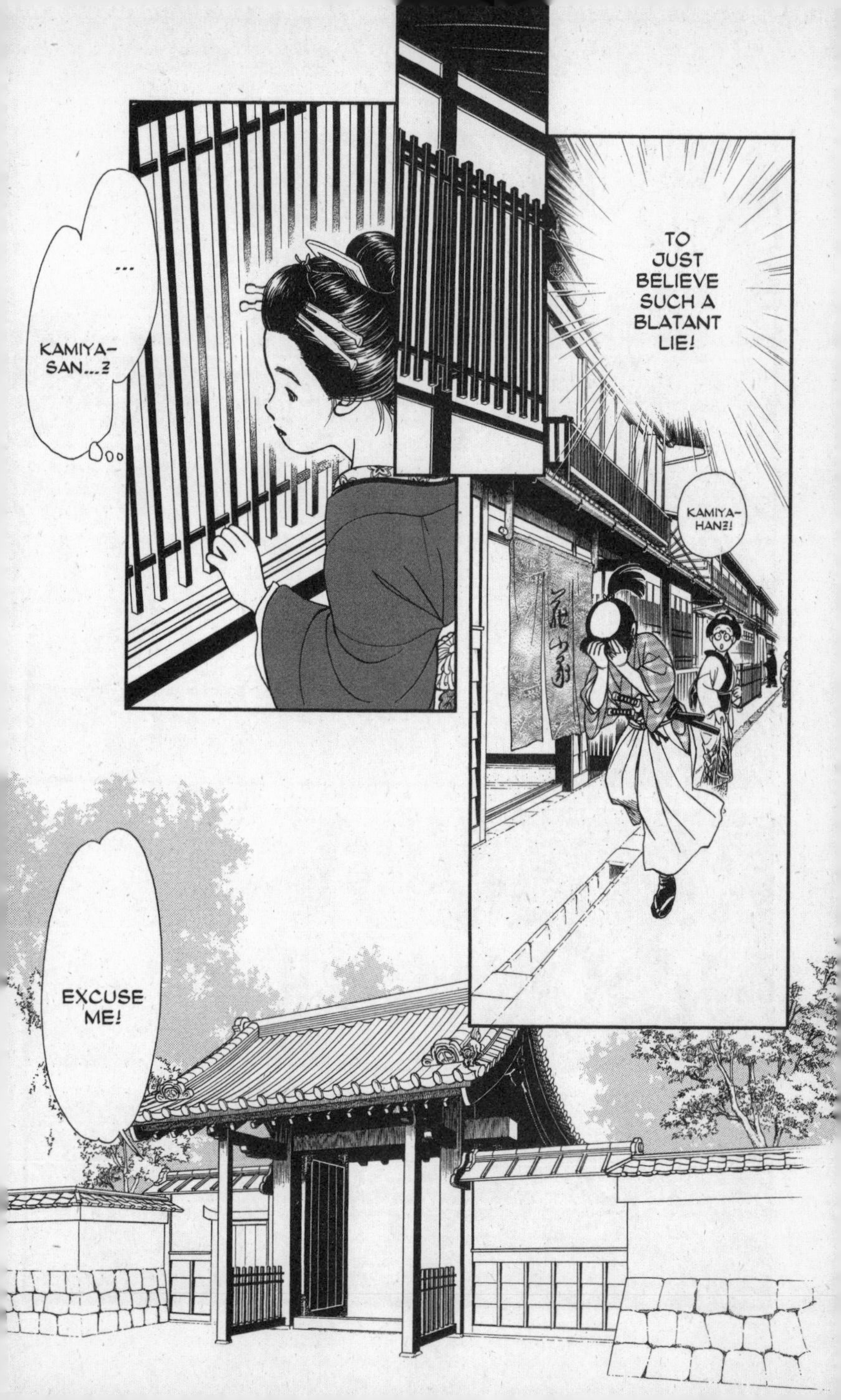
TO JUST BELIEVE SUCH A BLATANT LIE!
KAMIYA-HAN?!
...
KAMIYA-SAN...?
EXCUSE ME!

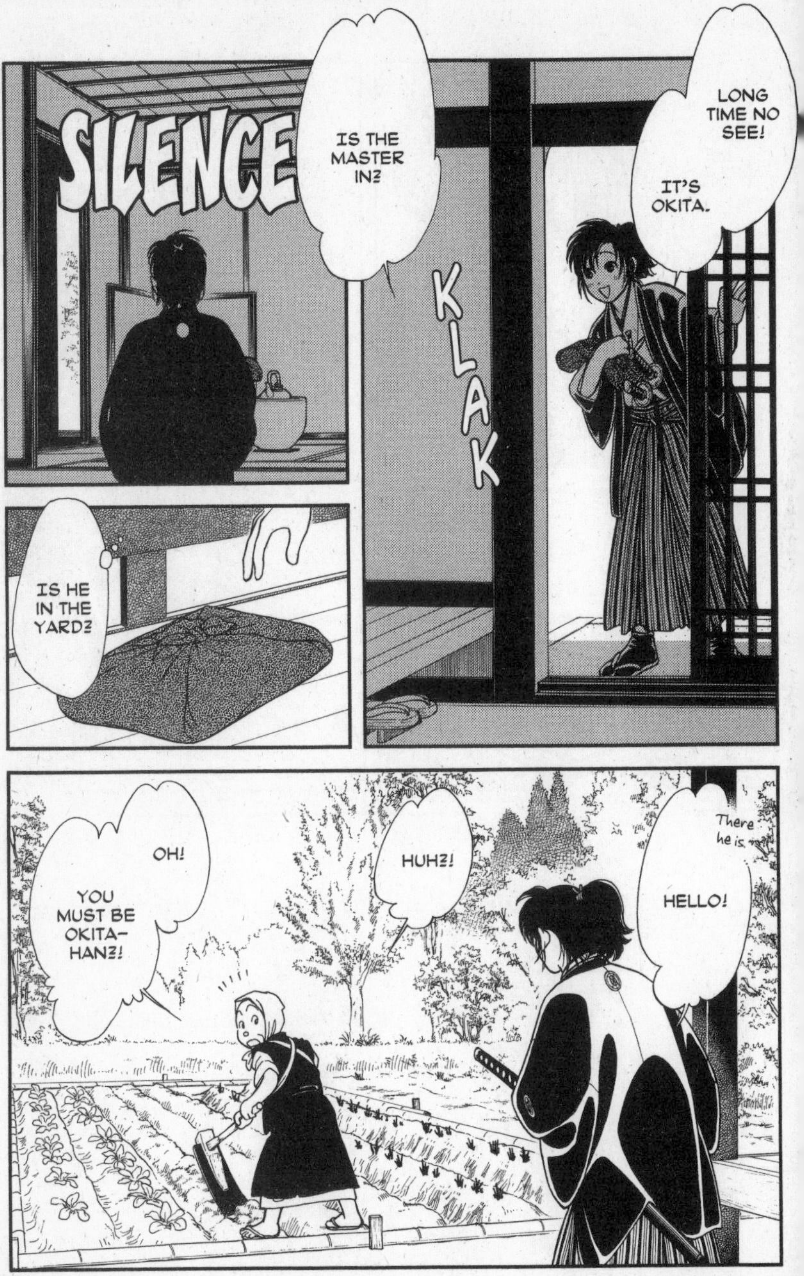
LONG TIME NO SEE!
IT'S OKITA.
IS THE MASTER IN?
KLAK
SILENCE
IS HE IN THE YARD?
There he is.
HELLO!
HUH?!
OH!
YOU MUST BE OKITA-HAN?!

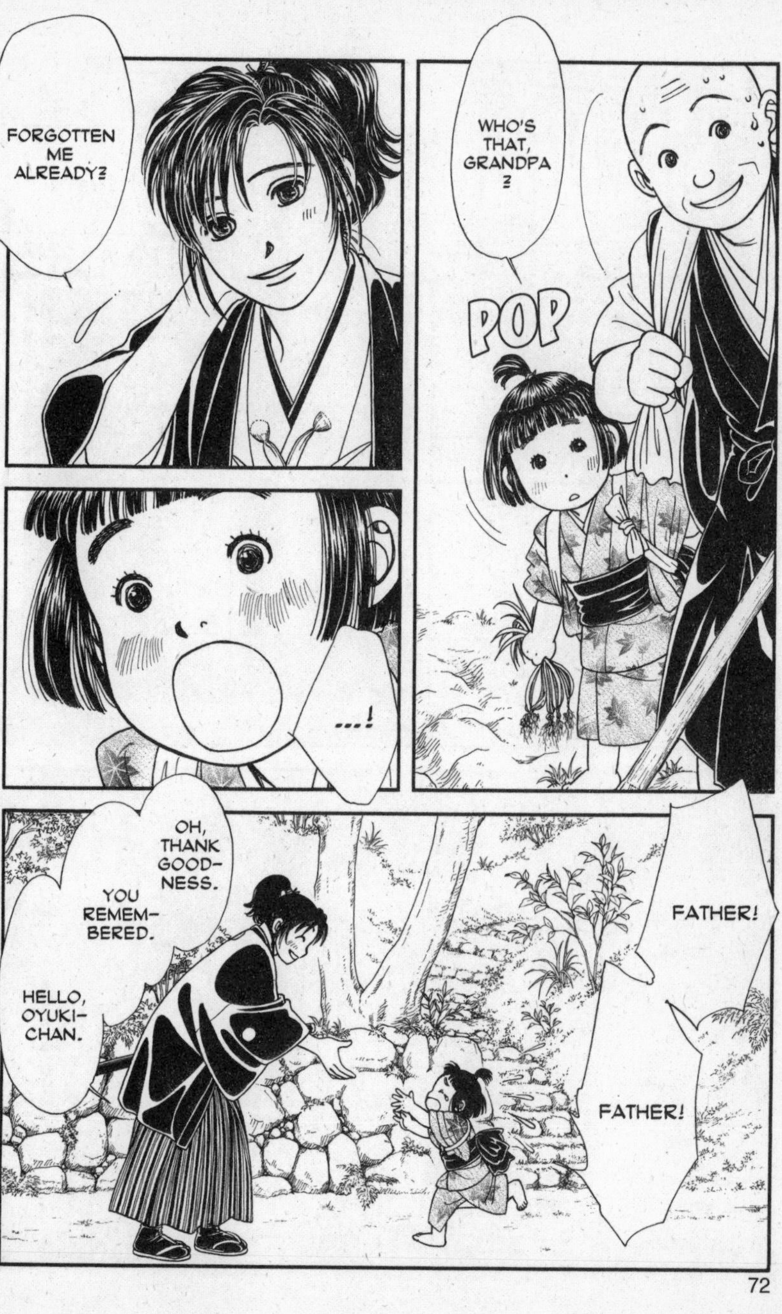
WHO'S THAT, GRANDPA?
POP
FORGOTTEN ME ALREADY?
...!
FATHER!
FATHER!
OH, THANK GOODNESS.
YOU REMEMBERED.
HELLO, OYUKI-CHAN.

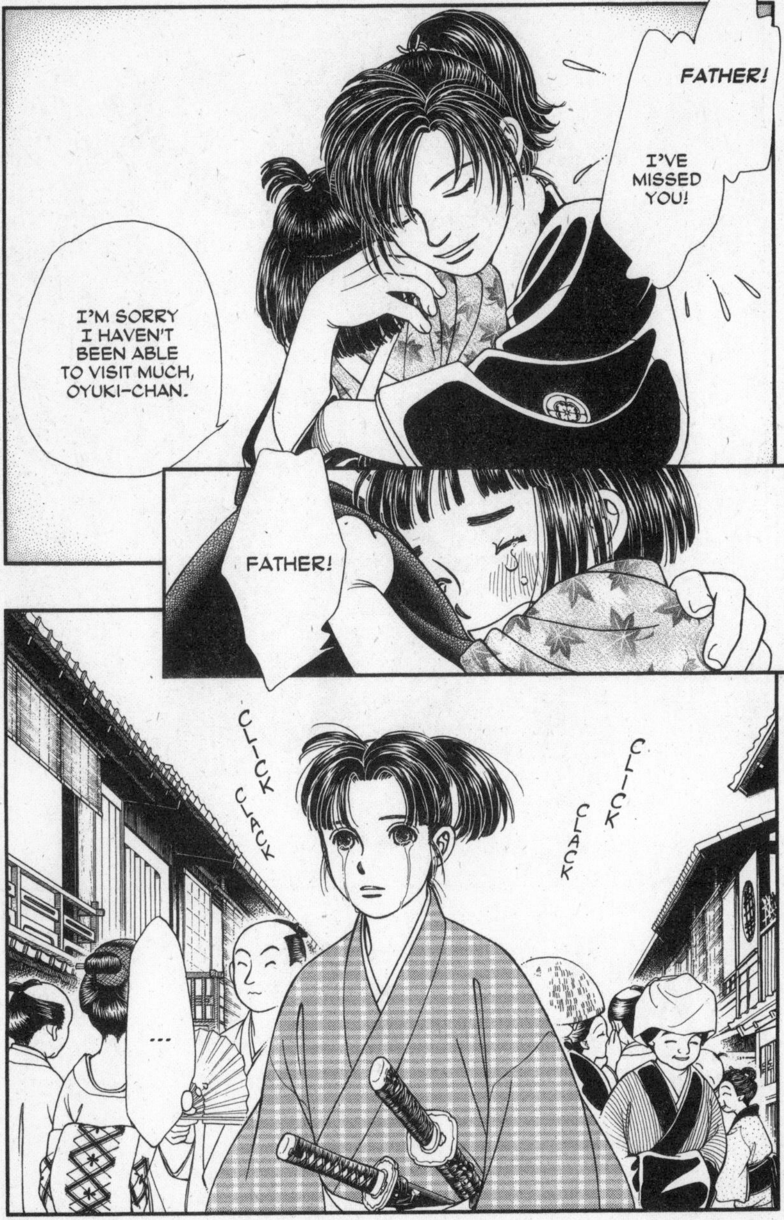
FATHER!
I'VE MISSED YOU!
I'M SORRY I HAVEN'T BEEN ABLE TO VISIT MUCH, OYUKI-CHAN.
FATHER!
CLICK CLACK
CLICK CLACK
...

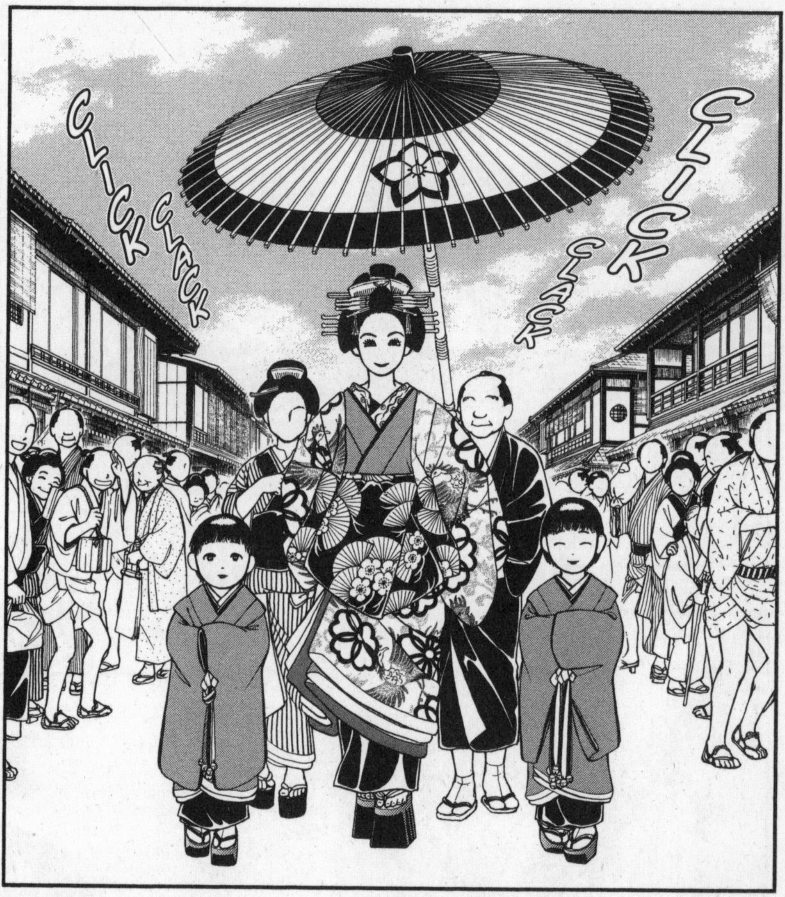
CLICK
CLACK
CLICK
CLACK

EDO IROHA KARUTA GAME

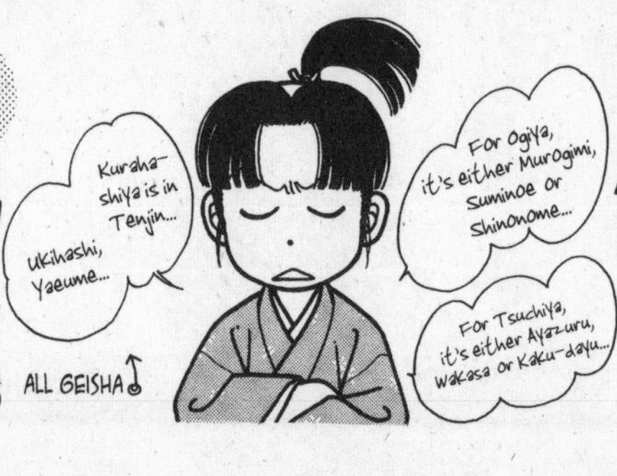
For Ogiya, it's either Murogimi, Suminoe or Shinonome...
For Tsuchiya, it's either Ayazuru, Wakasa or Kaku-dayu...
Kurahashiya is in Tenjin...
Ukihashi, Yaeume...
ALL GEISHA

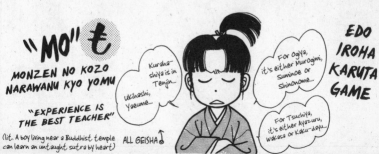

"MO" も

MONZEN NO KOZO NARAWANU KYO YOMU

"EXPERIENCE IS THE BEST TEACHER"

(lit. A boy living near a Buddhist temple can learn an untaught sutra by heart)

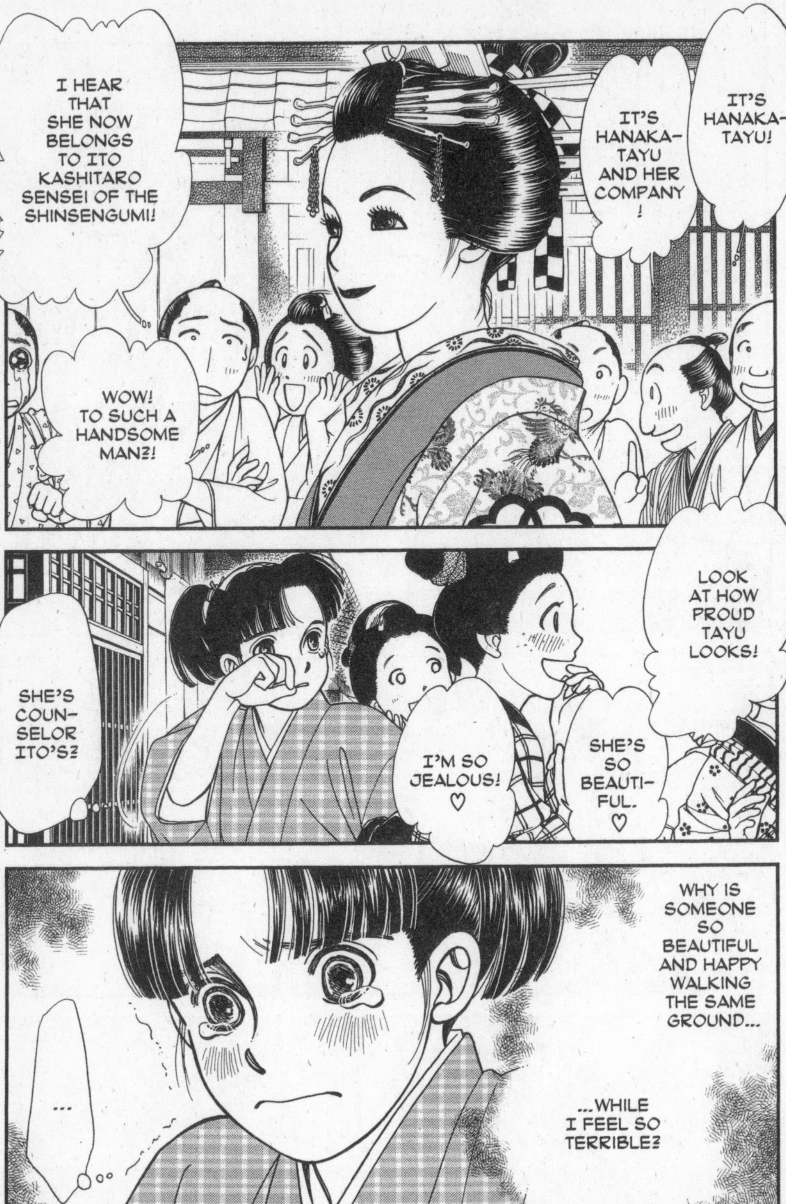
IT'S HANAKA-TAYU!
IT'S HANAKA-TAYU AND HER COMPANY!
I HEAR THAT SHE NOW BELONGS TO ITO KASHITARO SENSEI OF THE SHINSENGUMI!
WOW! TO SUCH A HANDSOME MAN?!
LOOK AT HOW PROUD TAYU LOOKS!
SHE'S SO BEAUTIFUL. ♡
I'M SO JEALOUS! ♡
SHE'S COUNSELOR ITO'S?!
WHY IS SOMEONE SO BEAUTIFUL AND HAPPY WALKING THE SAME GROUND...
...WHILE I FEEL SO TERRIBLE?!
...

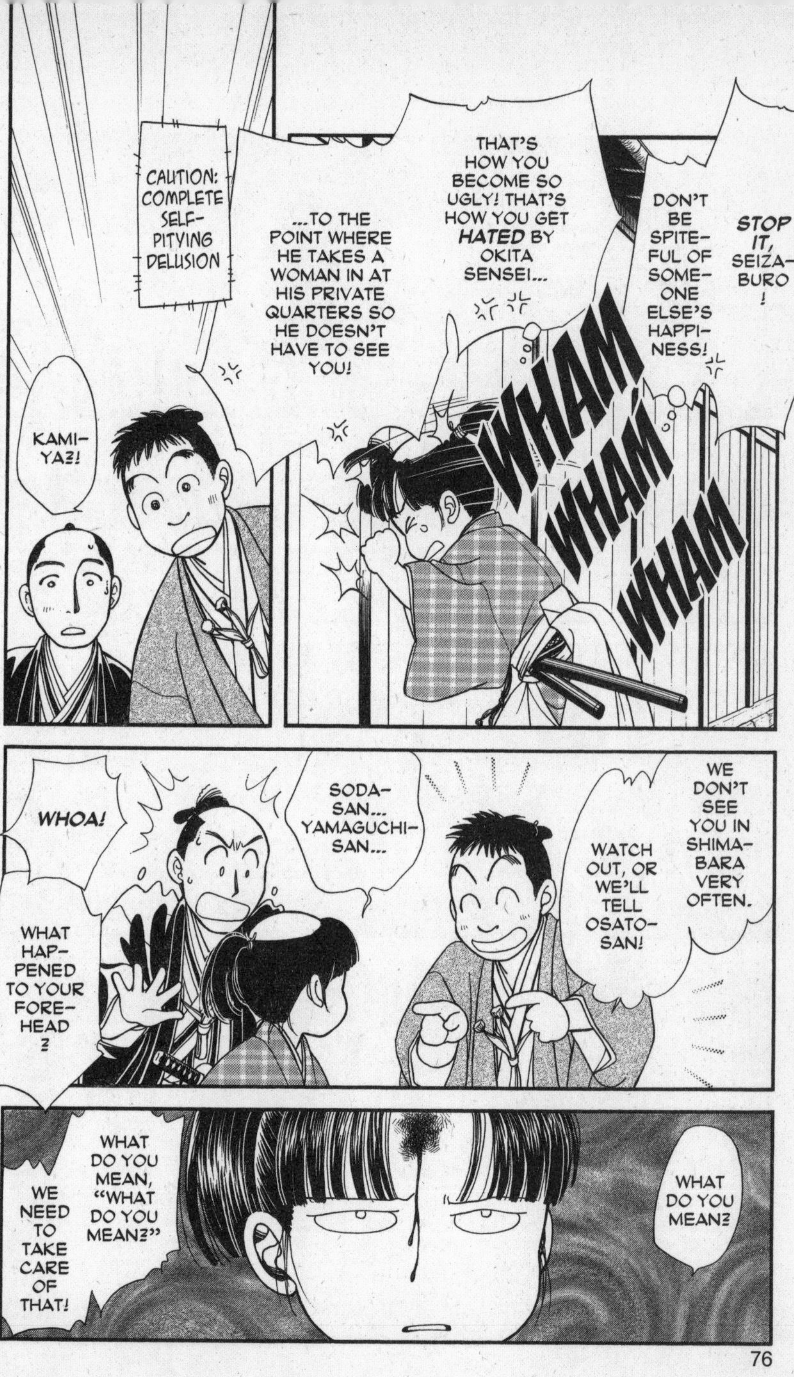
STOP IT, SEIZABURO!
DON'T BE SPITEFUL OF SOMEONE ELSE'S HAPPINESS!
THAT'S HOW YOU BECOME SO UGLY! THAT'S HOW YOU GET HATED BY OKITA SENSEI...
...TO THE POINT WHERE HE TAKES A WOMAN IN AT HIS PRIVATE QUARTERS SO HE DOESN'T HAVE TO SEE YOU!
WHAM WHAM WHAM
CAUTION: COMPLETE SELF-PITYING DELUSION
KAMIYA?!
WE DON'T SEE YOU IN SHIMABARA VERY OFTEN.
WATCH OUT, OR WE'LL TELL OSATO-SAN!
SODA-SAN... YAMAGUCHI-SAN...
WHOA!
WHAT HAPPENED TO YOUR FOREHEAD?
WHAT DO YOU MEAN?
WHAT DO YOU MEAN, "WHAT DO YOU MEAN?"
WE NEED TO TAKE CARE OF THAT!

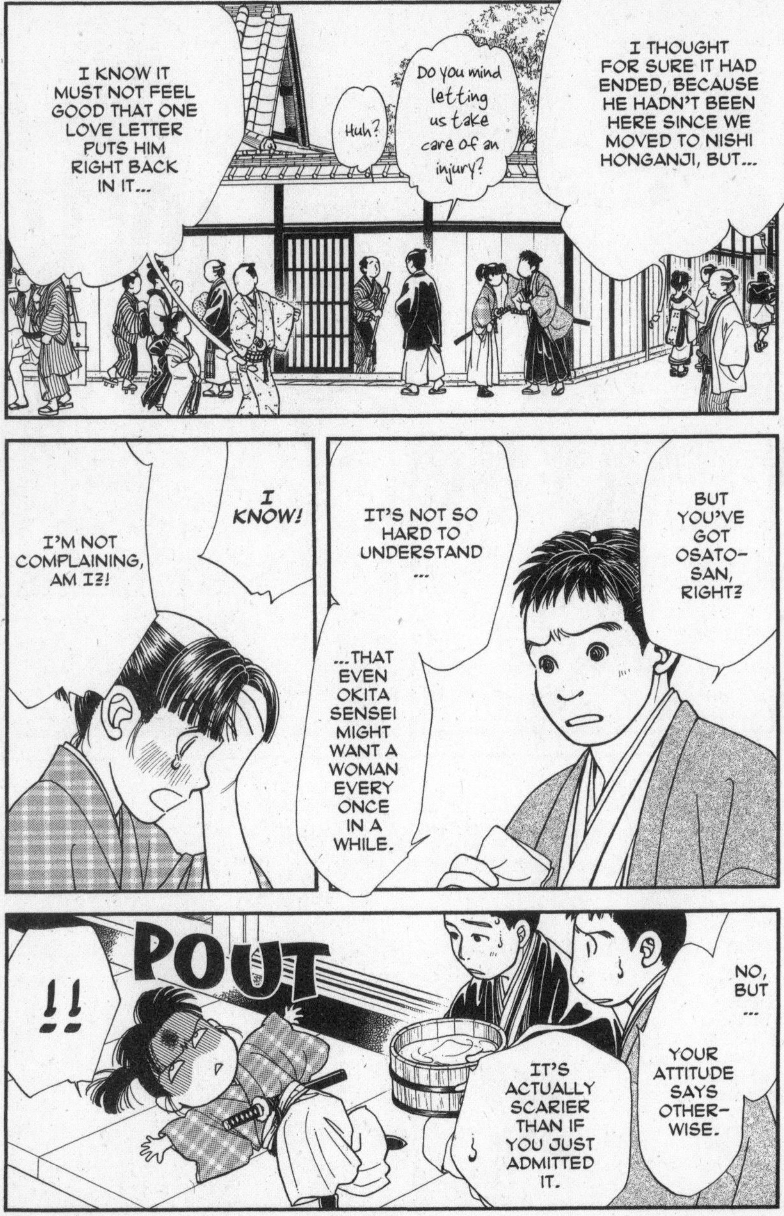
I THOUGHT FOR SURE IT HAD ENDED, BECAUSE HE HADN'T BEEN HERE SINCE WE MOVED TO NISHI HONGANJI, BUT...
Do you mind letting us take care of an injury?
Huh?
I KNOW IT MUST NOT FEEL GOOD THAT ONE LOVE LETTER PUTS HIM RIGHT BACK IN IT...
BUT YOU'VE GOT OSATO-SAN, RIGHT?
IT'S NOT SO HARD TO UNDERSTAND ...
...THAT EVEN OKITA SENSEI MIGHT WANT A WOMAN EVERY ONCE IN A WHILE.
I KNOW!
I'M NOT COMPLAINING, AM I?!
NO, BUT ...
YOUR ATTITUDE SAYS OTHER-WISE.
IT'S ACTUALLY SCARIER THAN IF YOU JUST ADMITTED IT.
POUT
!!

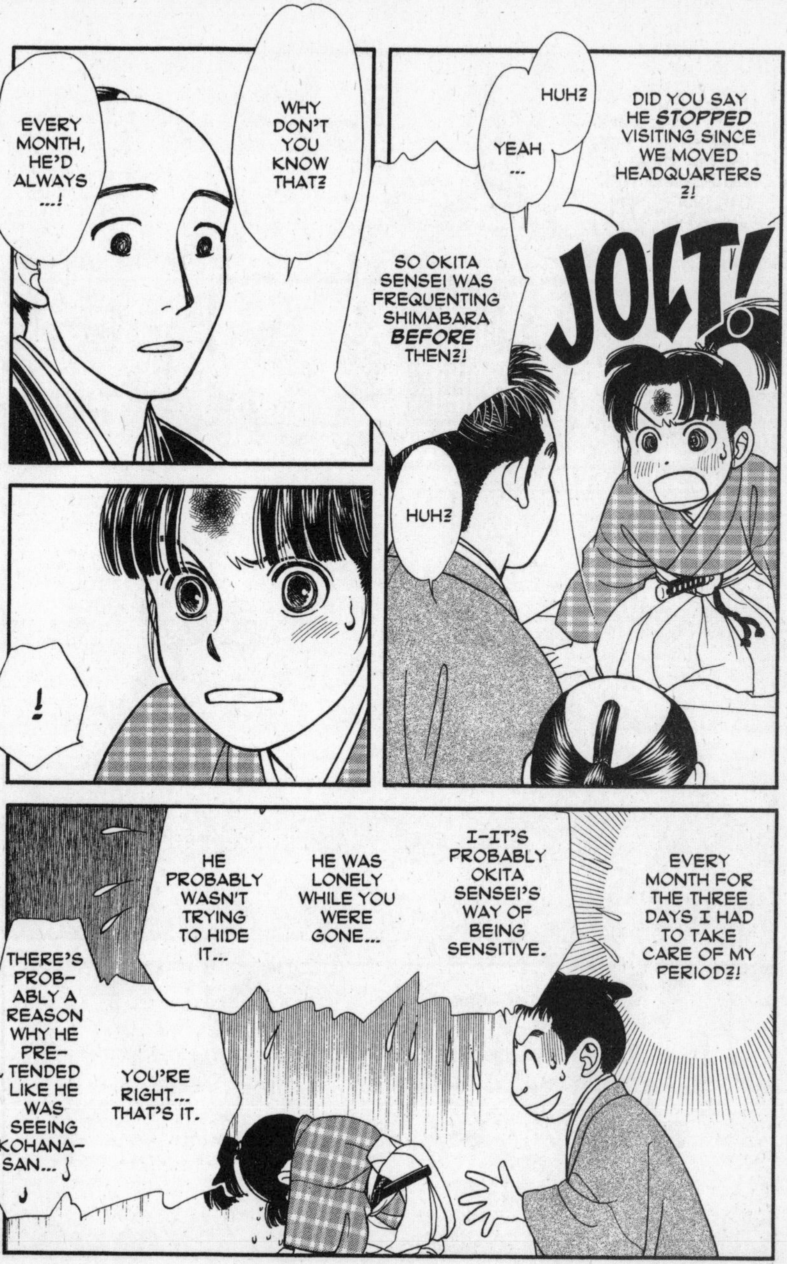
DID YOU SAY HE STOPPED VISITING SINCE WE MOVED HEADQUARTERS?!
HUH?
YEAH...
JOLT!
SO OKITA SENSEI WAS FREQUENTING SHIMABARA BEFORE THEN?!
HUH?
WHY DON'T YOU KNOW THAT?
EVERY MONTH, HE'D ALWAYS...!
!
EVERY MONTH FOR THE THREE DAYS I HAD TO TAKE CARE OF MY PERIOD?!
I-IT'S PROBABLY OKITA SENSEI'S WAY OF BEING SENSITIVE.
HE WAS LONELY WHILE YOU WERE GONE...
HE PROBABLY WASN'T TRYING TO HIDE IT...
THERE'S PROBABLY A REASON WHY HE PRETENDED LIKE HE WAS SEEING KOHANA-SAN...
YOU'RE RIGHT... THAT'S IT.

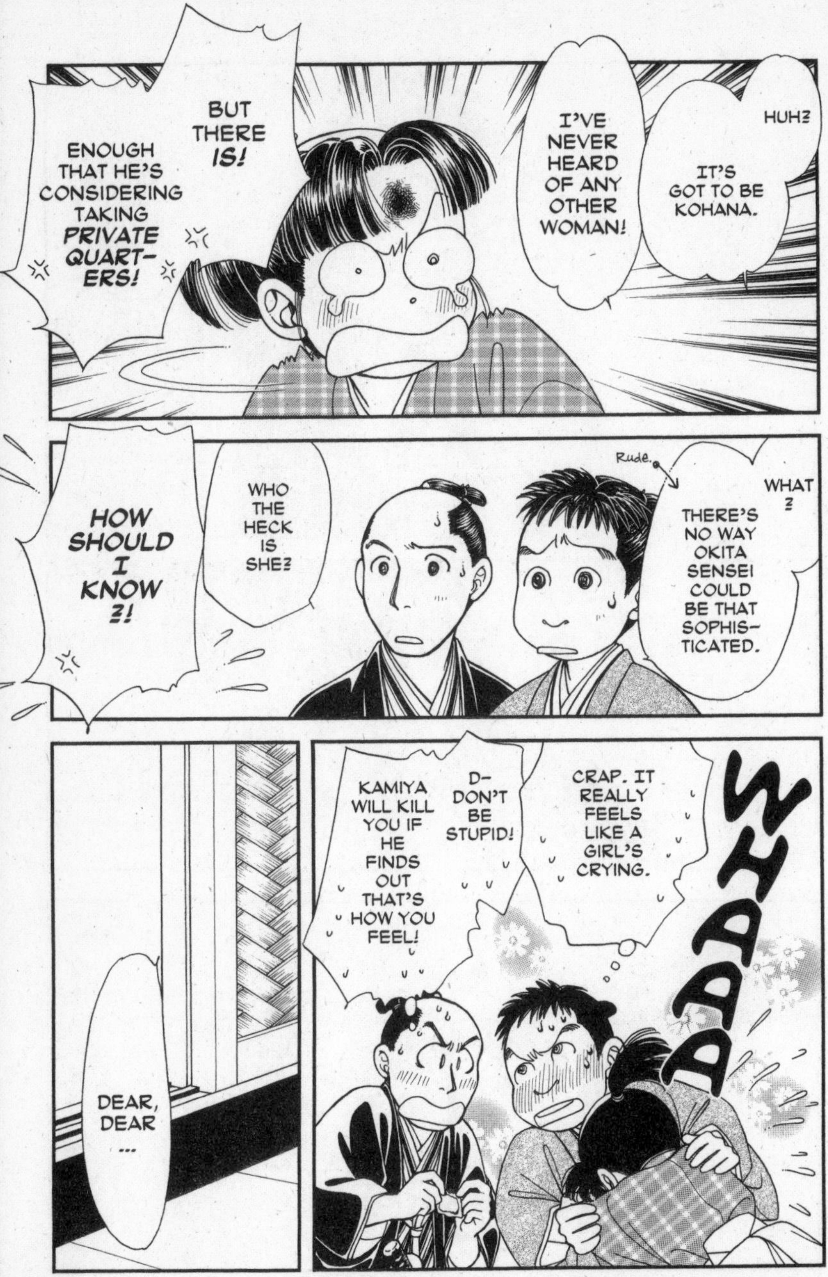
HUH?
IT'S GOT TO BE KOHANA.
I'VE NEVER HEARD OF ANY OTHER WOMAN!
BUT THERE *IS!*
ENOUGH THAT HE'S CONSIDERING TAKING *PRIVATE QUARTERS!*
Rude.
WHAT?
THERE'S NO WAY OKITA SENSEI COULD BE THAT SOPHISTICATED.
WHO THE HECK IS SHE?
HOW SHOULD I KNOW?!
WHAAAA
CRAP. IT REALLY FEELS LIKE A GIRL'S CRYING.
D-DON'T BE STUPID!
KAMIYA WILL KILL YOU IF HE FINDS OUT THAT'S HOW YOU FEEL!
DEAR, DEAR ...

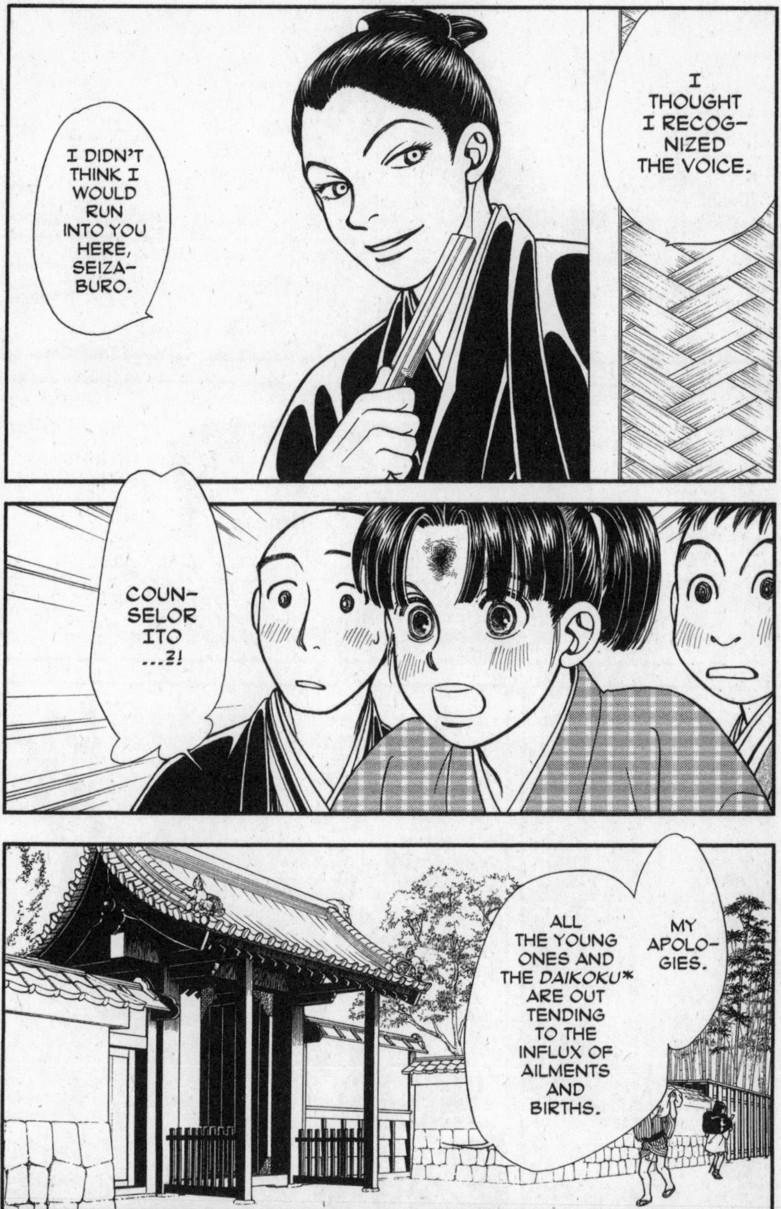
I THOUGHT I RECOGNIZED THE VOICE.
I DIDN'T THINK I WOULD RUN INTO YOU HERE, SEIZABURO.
COUNSELOR ITO ...?!
MY APOLOGIES.
ALL THE YOUNG ONES AND THE *DAIKOKU** ARE OUT TENDING TO THE INFLUX OF AILMENTS AND BIRTHS.

*A common way to refer to the head monk's wife. Many schools did not allow for marriage, so this was the common way to refer to her. It also became another way to refer to the wife who ruled the kitchen.

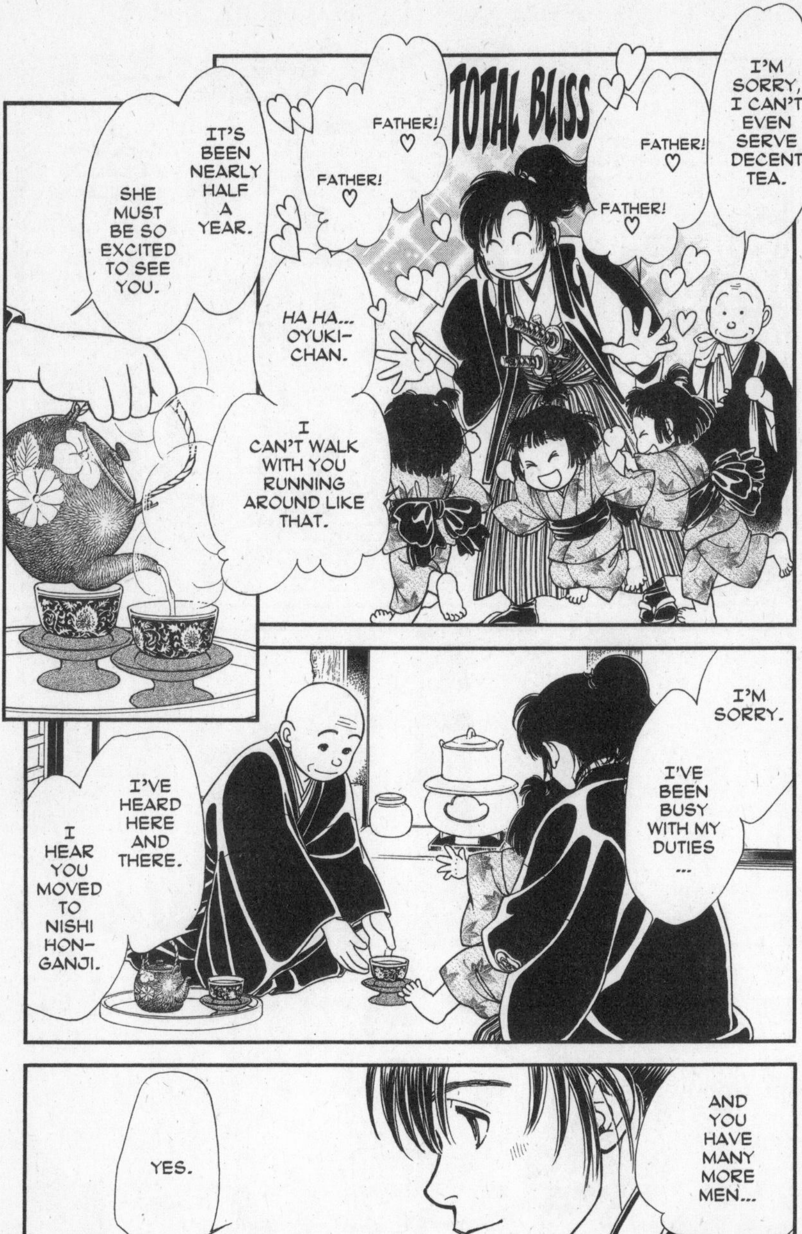
I'M SORRY, I CAN'T EVEN SERVE DECENT TEA.
TOTAL BLISS
FATHER! ♡
FATHER! ♡
FATHER! ♡
FATHER! ♡
HA HA... OYUKI-CHAN.
I CAN'T WALK WITH YOU RUNNING AROUND LIKE THAT.
IT'S BEEN NEARLY HALF A YEAR.
SHE MUST BE SO EXCITED TO SEE YOU.
I'M SORRY.
I'VE BEEN BUSY WITH MY DUTIES ...
I'VE HEARD HERE AND THERE.
I HEAR YOU MOVED TO NISHI HON-GANJI.
AND YOU HAVE MANY MORE MEN...
YES.

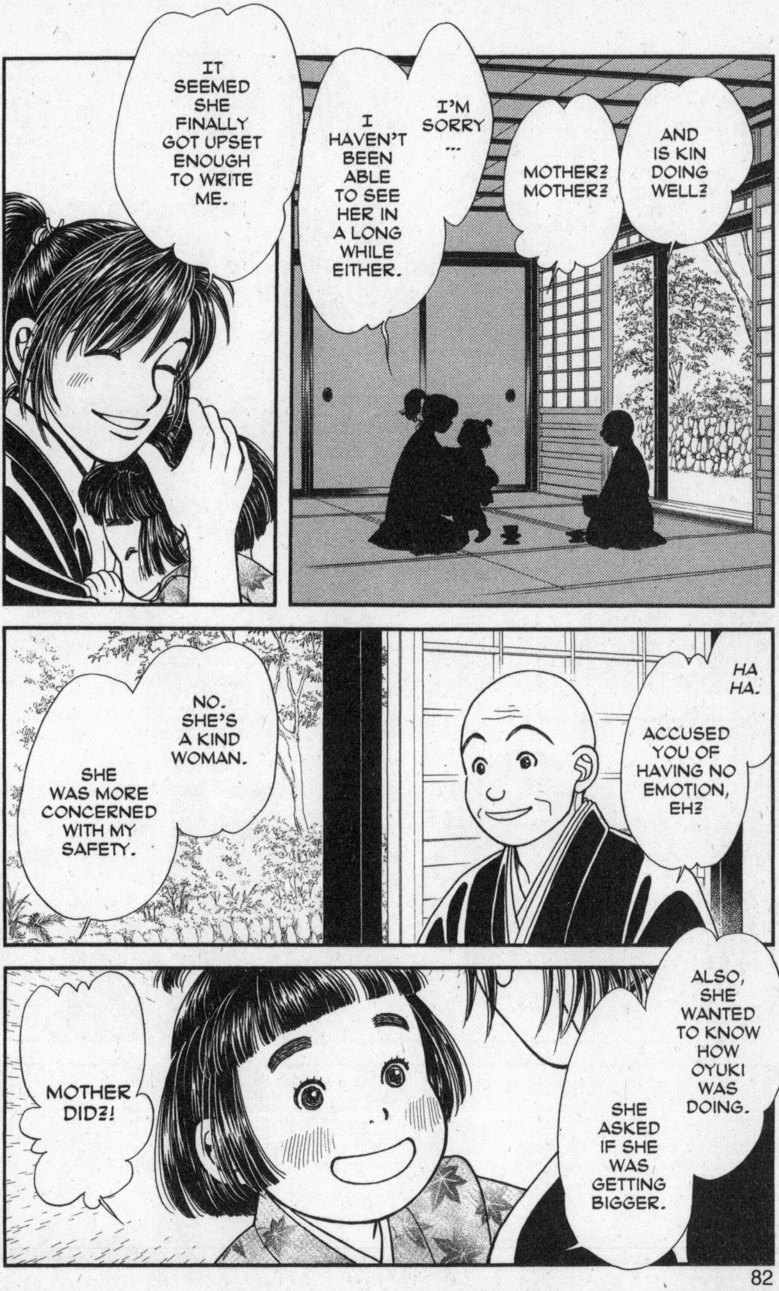
AND IS KIN DOING WELL?
MOTHER? MOTHER?
I'M SORRY ...
I HAVEN'T BEEN ABLE TO SEE HER IN A LONG WHILE EITHER.
IT SEEMED SHE FINALLY GOT UPSET ENOUGH TO WRITE ME.
HA HA.
ACCUSED YOU OF HAVING NO EMOTION, EH?
NO. SHE'S A KIND WOMAN.
SHE WAS MORE CONCERNED WITH MY SAFETY.
ALSO, SHE WANTED TO KNOW HOW OYUKI WAS DOING.
SHE ASKED IF SHE WAS GETTING BIGGER.
MOTHER DID?!

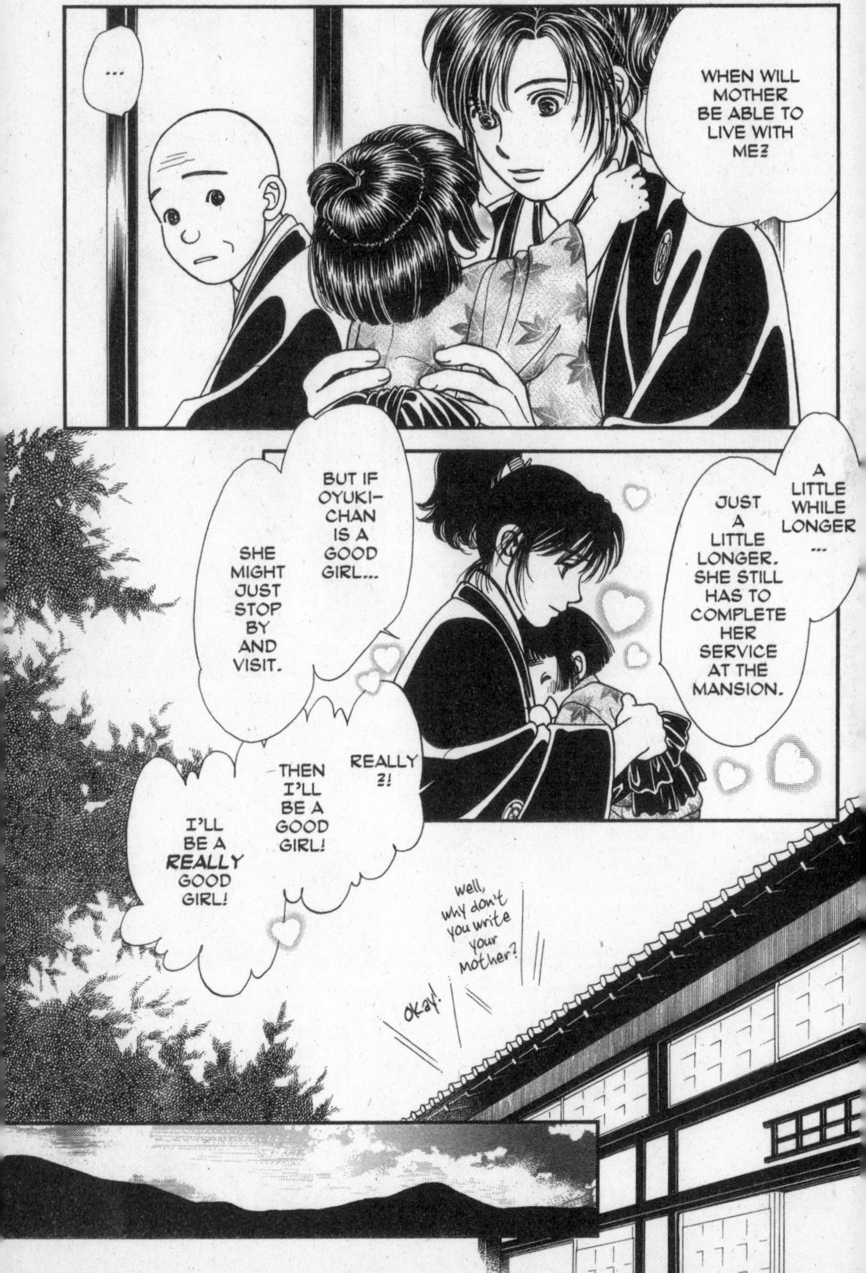
WHEN WILL MOTHER BE ABLE TO LIVE WITH ME?
...
A LITTLE WHILE LONGER...
JUST A LITTLE LONGER. SHE STILL HAS TO COMPLETE HER SERVICE AT THE MANSION.
BUT IF OYUKI-CHAN IS A GOOD GIRL...
SHE MIGHT JUST STOP BY AND VISIT.
REALLY?!
THEN I'LL BE A GOOD GIRL!
I'LL BE A REALLY GOOD GIRL!
Well, why don't you write your mother?
Okay!

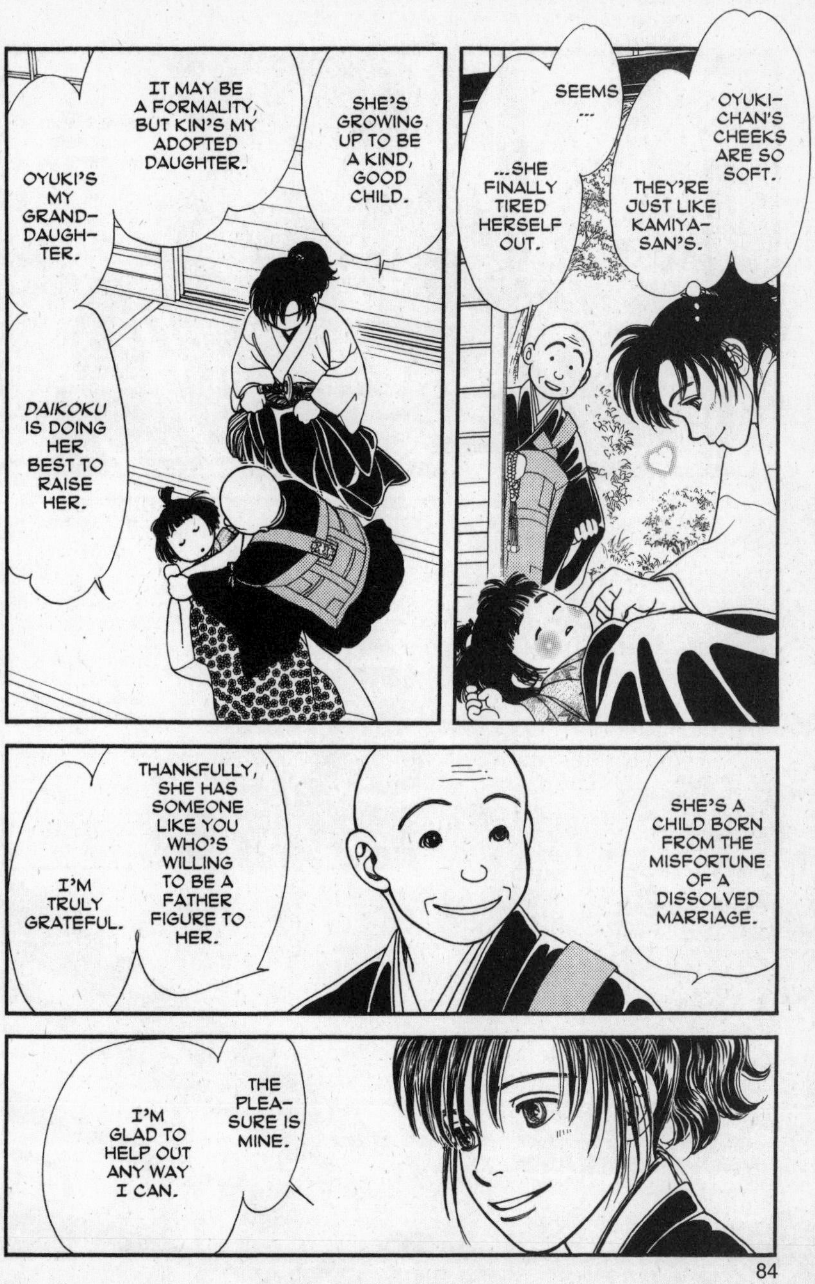
OYUKI-CHAN'S CHEEKS ARE SO SOFT.
THEY'RE JUST LIKE KAMIYA-SAN'S.
SEEMS...
...SHE FINALLY TIRED HERSELF OUT.
SHE'S GROWING UP TO BE A KIND, GOOD CHILD.
IT MAY BE A FORMALITY, BUT KIN'S MY ADOPTED DAUGHTER.
OYUKI'S MY GRAND-DAUGHTER.
DAIKOKU IS DOING HER BEST TO RAISE HER.
SHE'S A CHILD BORN FROM THE MISFORTUNE OF A DISSOLVED MARRIAGE.
THANKFULLY, SHE HAS SOMEONE LIKE YOU WHO'S WILLING TO BE A FATHER FIGURE TO HER.
I'M TRULY GRATEFUL.
THE PLEA-SURE IS MINE.
I'M GLAD TO HELP OUT ANY WAY I CAN.

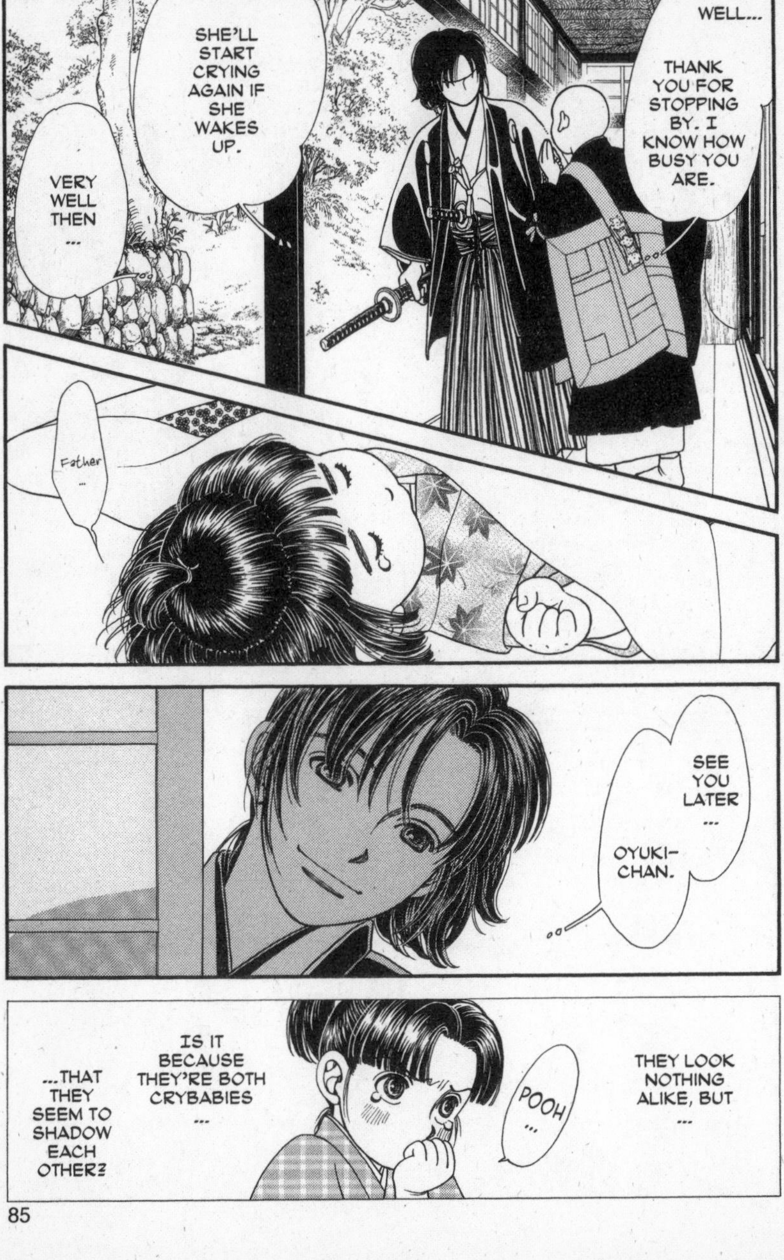
WELL...
THANK YOU FOR STOPPING BY. I KNOW HOW BUSY YOU ARE.
SHE'LL START CRYING AGAIN IF SHE WAKES UP.
VERY WELL THEN ...
Father ...
SEE YOU LATER ...
OYUKI-CHAN.
THEY LOOK NOTHING ALIKE, BUT ...
POOH ...
IS IT BECAUSE THEY'RE BOTH CRYBABIES ...
...THAT THEY SEEM TO SHADOW EACH OTHER?

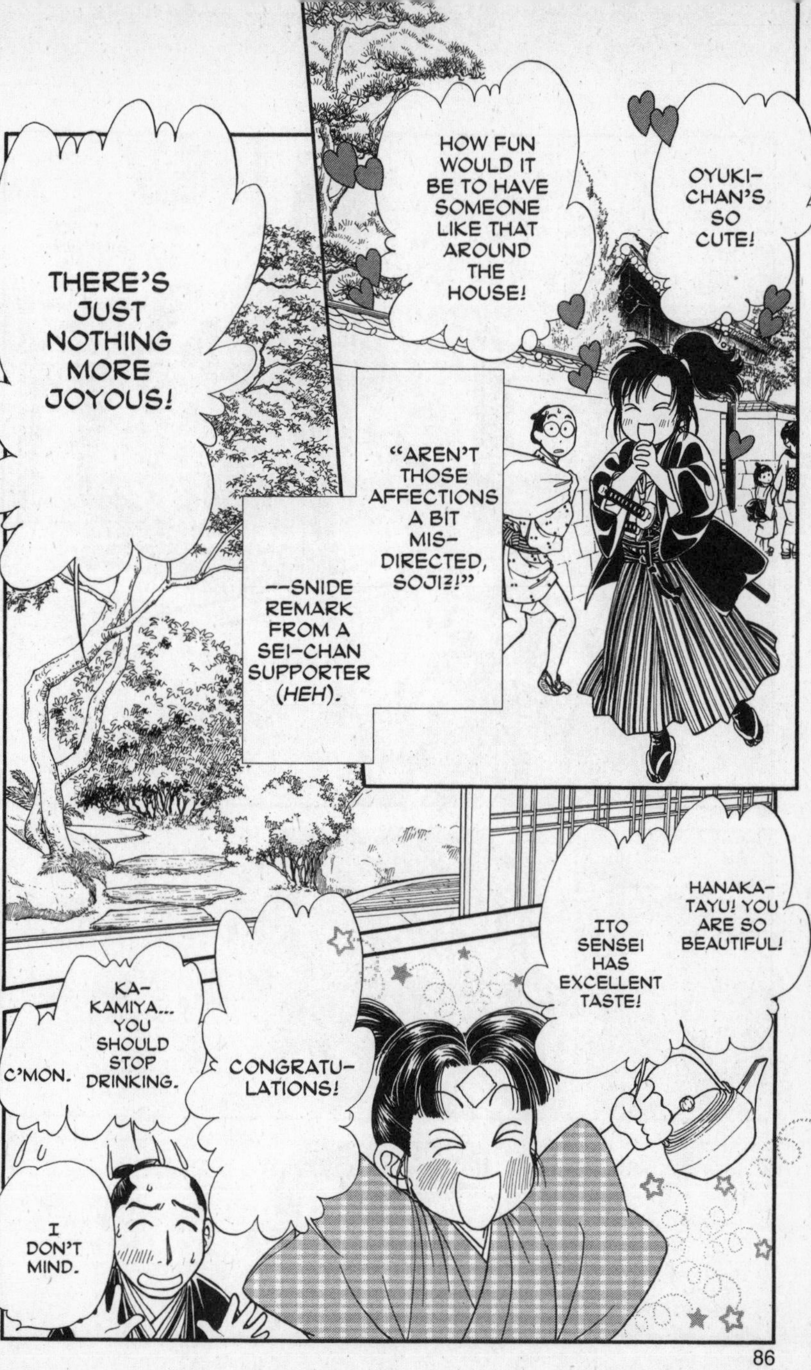
OYUKI-CHAN'S SO CUTE!
HOW FUN WOULD IT BE TO HAVE SOMEONE LIKE THAT AROUND THE HOUSE!
"AREN'T THOSE AFFECTIONS A BIT MIS-DIRECTED, SOJI?!"
--SNIDE REMARK FROM A SEI-CHAN SUPPORTER (*HEH*).
THERE'S JUST NOTHING MORE JOYOUS!
HANAKA-TAYU! YOU ARE SO BEAUTIFUL!
ITO SENSEI HAS EXCELLENT TASTE!
CONGRATU-LATIONS!
KA-KAMIYA... YOU SHOULD STOP DRINKING.
C'MON.
I DON'T MIND.

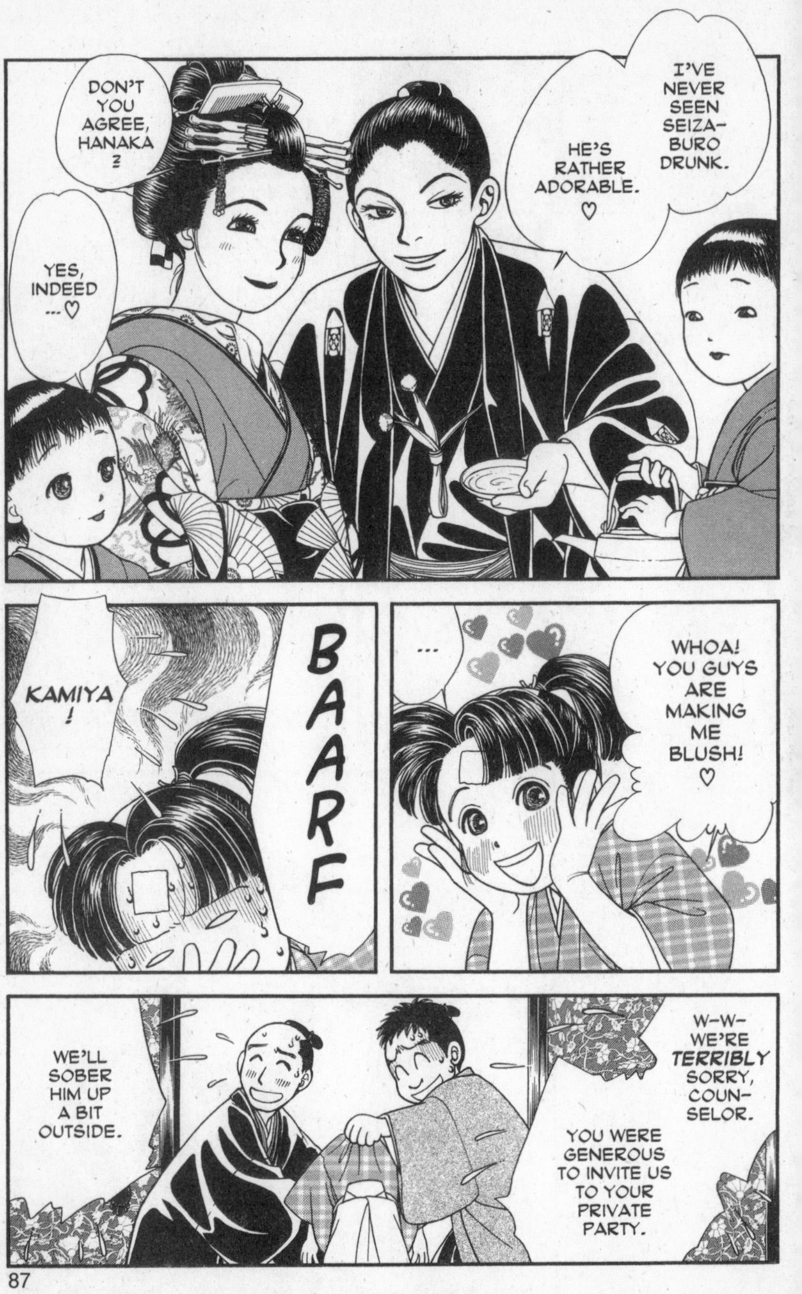
I'VE NEVER SEEN SEIZA-BURO DRUNK.
HE'S RATHER ADORABLE. ♡
DON'T YOU AGREE, HANAKA?
YES, INDEED ...♡
WHOA! YOU GUYS ARE MAKING ME BLUSH! ♡
...
BAARF
KAMIYA!
W-W-WE'RE *TERRIBLY* SORRY, COUN-SELOR.
YOU WERE GENEROUS TO INVITE US TO YOUR PRIVATE PARTY.
WE'LL SOBER HIM UP A BIT OUTSIDE.

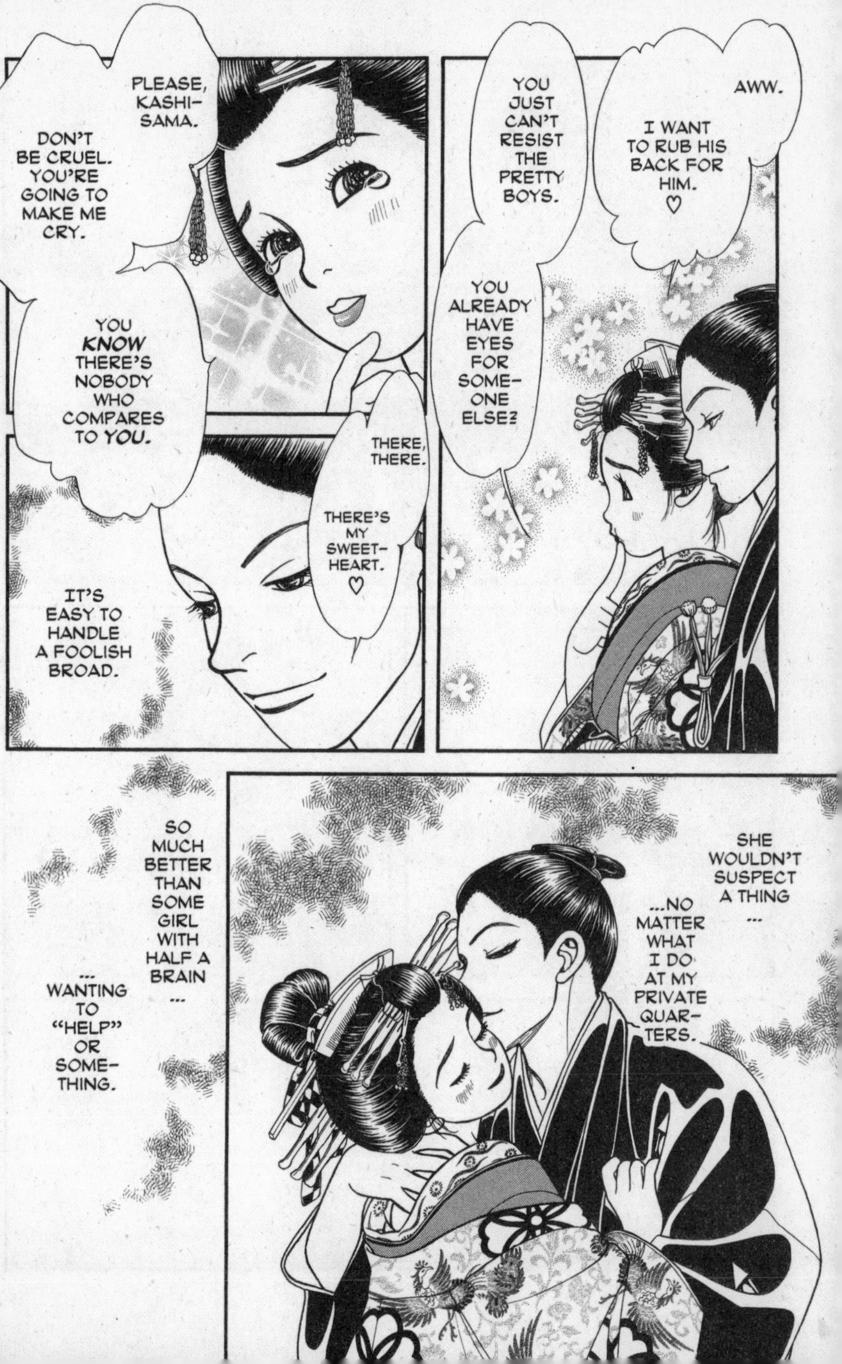
AWW.
I WANT TO RUB HIS BACK FOR HIM. ♡
YOU JUST CAN'T RESIST THE PRETTY BOYS.
YOU ALREADY HAVE EYES FOR SOME-ONE ELSE?
PLEASE, KASHI-SAMA.
DON'T BE CRUEL. YOU'RE GOING TO MAKE ME CRY.
YOU *KNOW* THERE'S NOBODY WHO COMPARES TO *YOU.*
THERE, THERE.
THERE'S MY SWEET-HEART. ♡
IT'S EASY TO HANDLE A FOOLISH BROAD.
SHE WOULDN'T SUSPECT A THING...
...NO MATTER WHAT I DO AT MY PRIVATE QUAR-TERS.
SO MUCH BETTER THAN SOME GIRL WITH HALF A BRAIN...
...WANTING TO "HELP" OR SOME-THING.

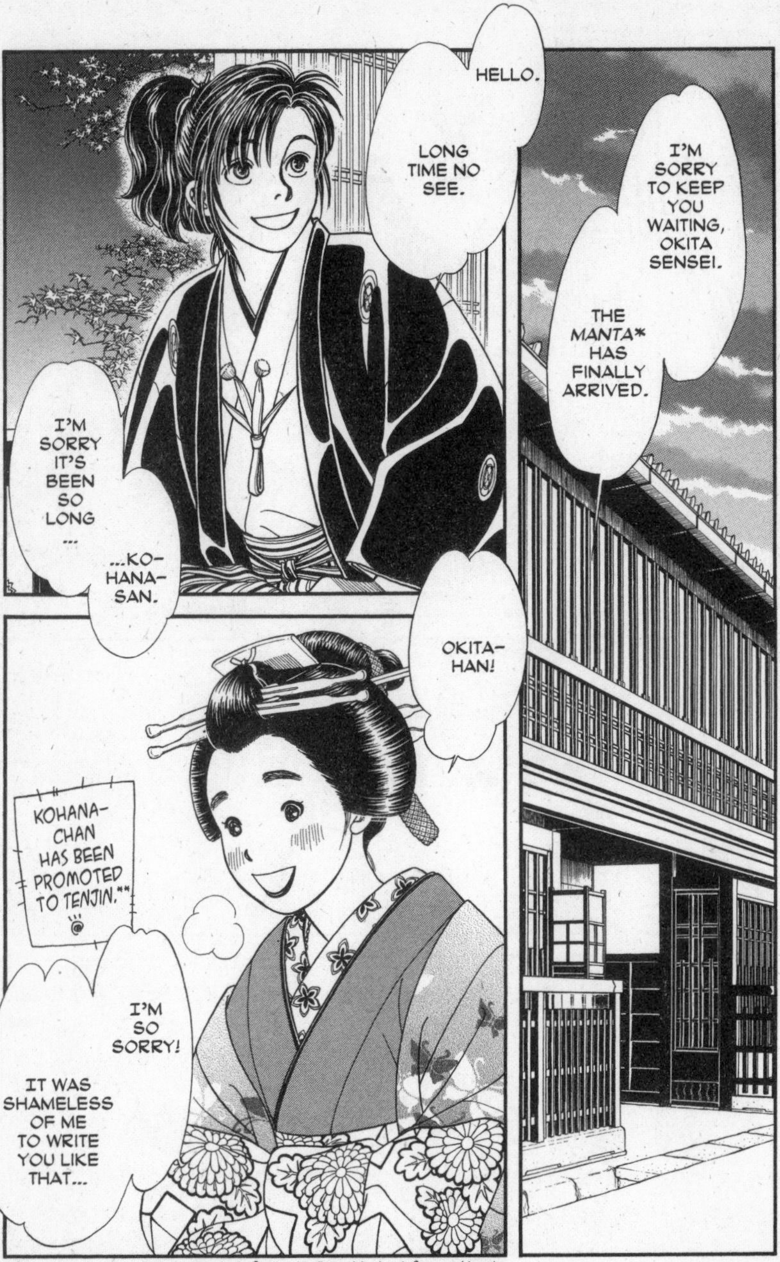
I'M SORRY TO KEEP YOU WAITING, OKITA SENSEI.
THE *MANTA** HAS FINALLY ARRIVED.
HELLO.
LONG TIME NO SEE.
I'M SORRY IT'S BEEN SO LONG ...
...KO-HANA-SAN.
OKITA-HAN!
KOHANA-CHAN HAS BEEN PROMOTED TO TENJIN.**
I'M SO SORRY!
IT WAS SHAMELESS OF ME TO WRITE YOU LIKE THAT...

**Manta* is a common way to refer to *tenjin* and is short for *moshianata*.

***Tenjin* is the second rank among *yujo*.

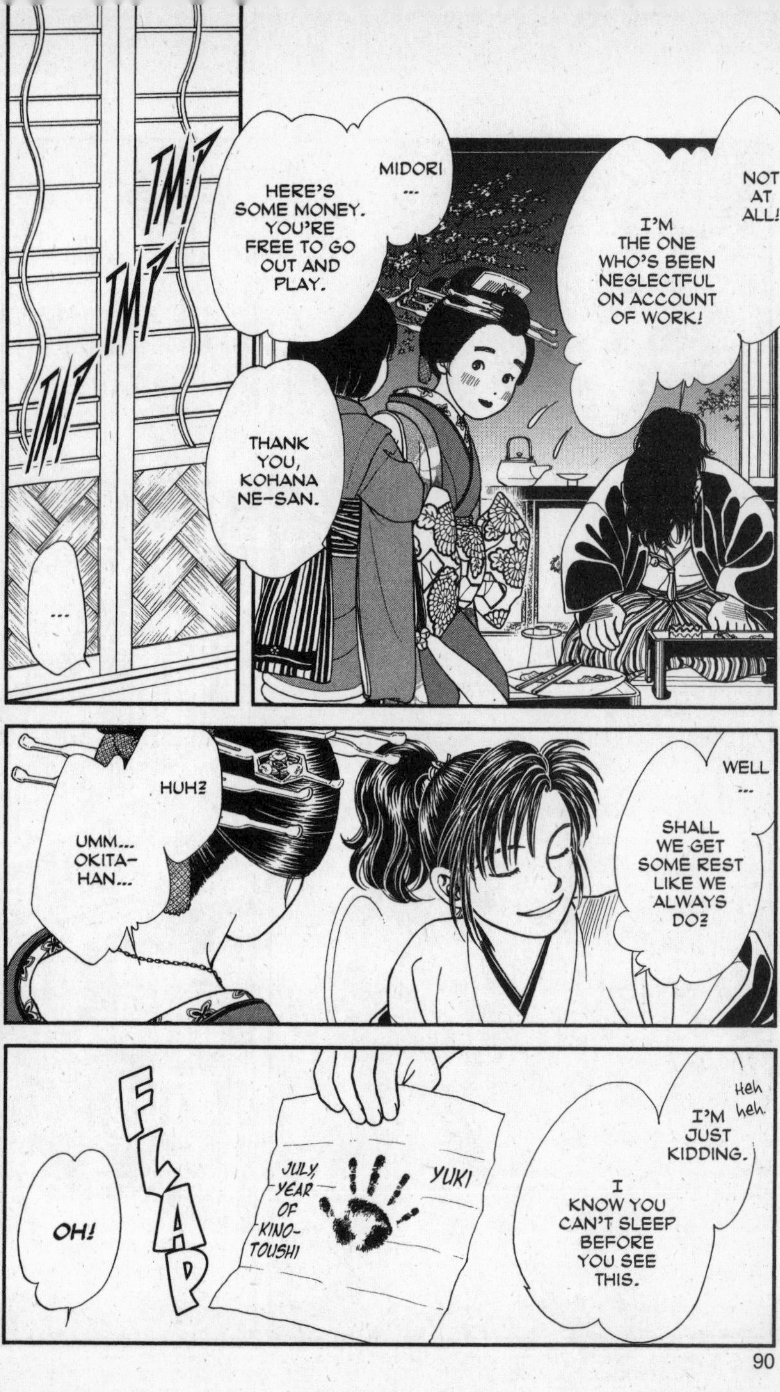
NOT AT ALL!
I'M THE ONE WHO'S BEEN NEGLECTFUL ON ACCOUNT OF WORK!
MIDORI ...
HERE'S SOME MONEY. YOU'RE FREE TO GO OUT AND PLAY.
THANK YOU, KOHANA NE-SAN.
TMP TMP TMP TMP
...
WELL ...
SHALL WE GET SOME REST LIKE WE ALWAYS DO?
HUH?
UMM... OKITA-HAN...
Heh heh.
I'M JUST KIDDING.
I KNOW YOU CAN'T SLEEP BEFORE YOU SEE THIS.
YUKI
JULY, YEAR OF KINOTOUSHI
FLAP
OH!

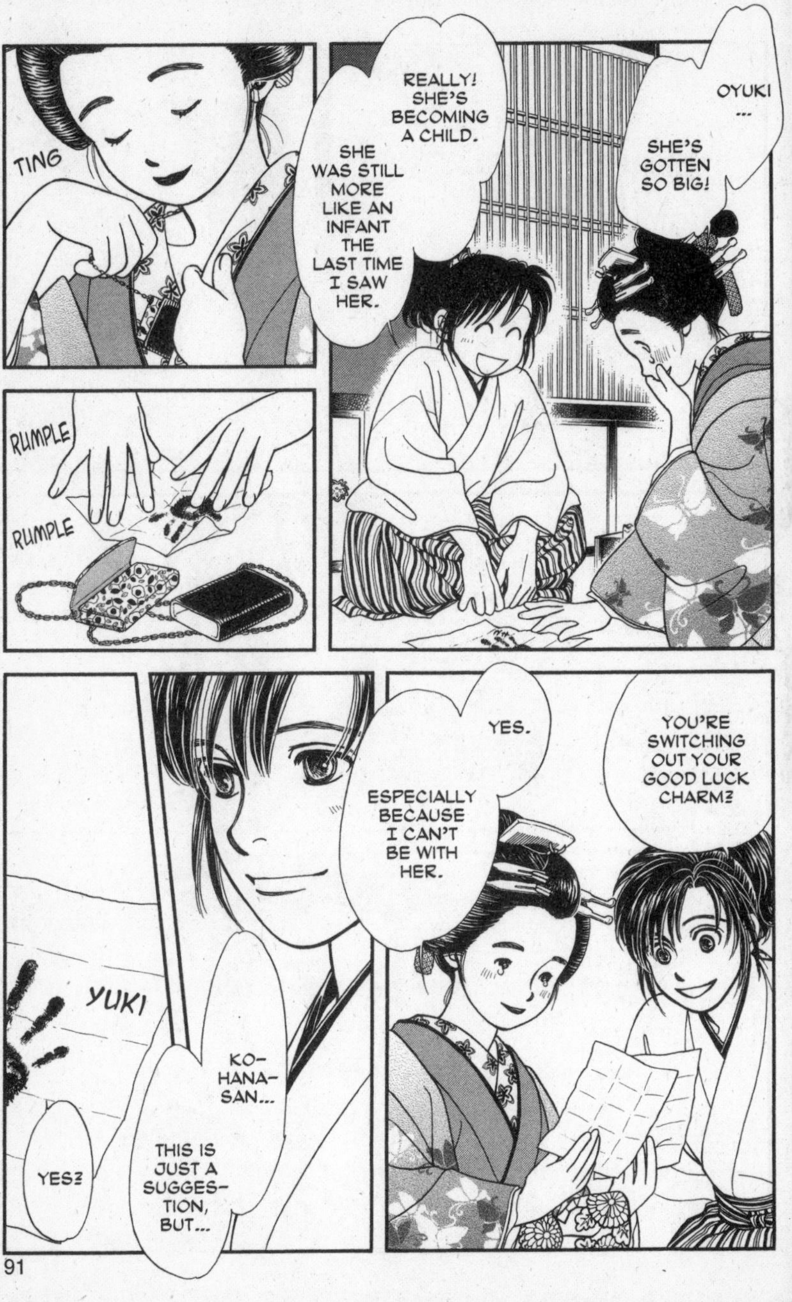
OYUKI ...
SHE'S GOTTEN SO BIG!
REALLY! SHE'S BECOMING A CHILD.
SHE WAS STILL MORE LIKE AN INFANT THE LAST TIME I SAW HER.
TING
RUMPLE
RUMPLE
YOU'RE SWITCHING OUT YOUR GOOD LUCK CHARM?
YES.
ESPECIALLY BECAUSE I CAN'T BE WITH HER.
KO-HANA-SAN...
THIS IS JUST A SUGGESTION, BUT...
YUKI
YES?

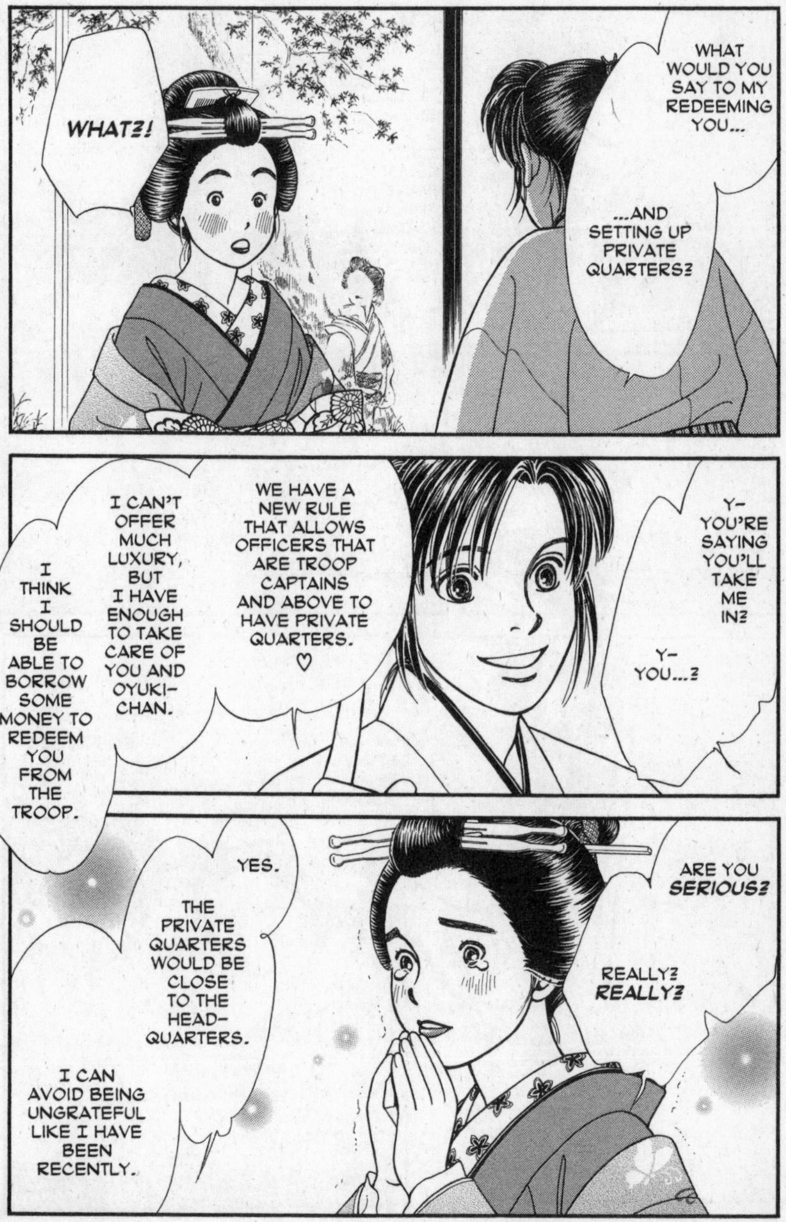
WHAT WOULD YOU SAY TO MY REDEEMING YOU...
...AND SETTING UP PRIVATE QUARTERS?
WHAT?!
Y- YOU'RE SAYING YOU'LL TAKE ME IN?
Y- YOU...?
WE HAVE A NEW RULE THAT ALLOWS OFFICERS THAT ARE TROOP CAPTAINS AND ABOVE TO HAVE PRIVATE QUARTERS. ♡
I CAN'T OFFER MUCH LUXURY, BUT I HAVE ENOUGH TO TAKE CARE OF YOU AND OYUKI-CHAN.
I THINK I SHOULD BE ABLE TO BORROW SOME MONEY TO REDEEM YOU FROM THE TROOP.
ARE YOU SERIOUS?
REALLY? REALLY?
YES.
THE PRIVATE QUARTERS WOULD BE CLOSE TO THE HEAD-QUARTERS.
I CAN AVOID BEING UNGRATEFUL LIKE I HAVE BEEN RECENTLY.

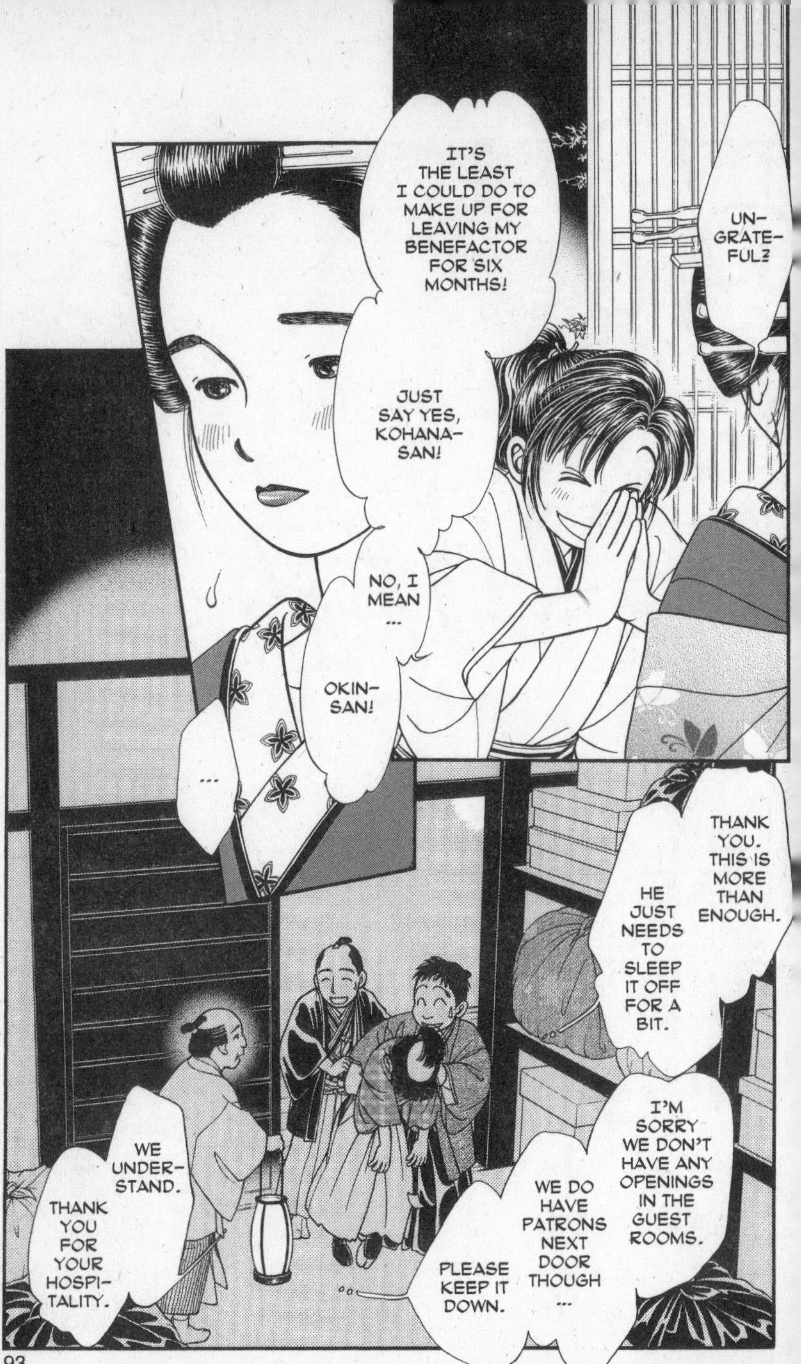
UN-GRATEFUL?
IT'S THE LEAST I COULD DO TO MAKE UP FOR LEAVING MY BENEFACTOR FOR SIX MONTHS!
JUST SAY YES, KOHANA-SAN!
NO, I MEAN ---
OKIN-SAN!
...
THANK YOU. THIS IS MORE THAN ENOUGH.
HE JUST NEEDS TO SLEEP IT OFF FOR A BIT.
I'M SORRY WE DON'T HAVE ANY OPENINGS IN THE GUEST ROOMS.
WE DO HAVE PATRONS NEXT DOOR THOUGH ---
PLEASE KEEP IT DOWN.
WE UNDERSTAND.
THANK YOU FOR YOUR HOSPITALITY.

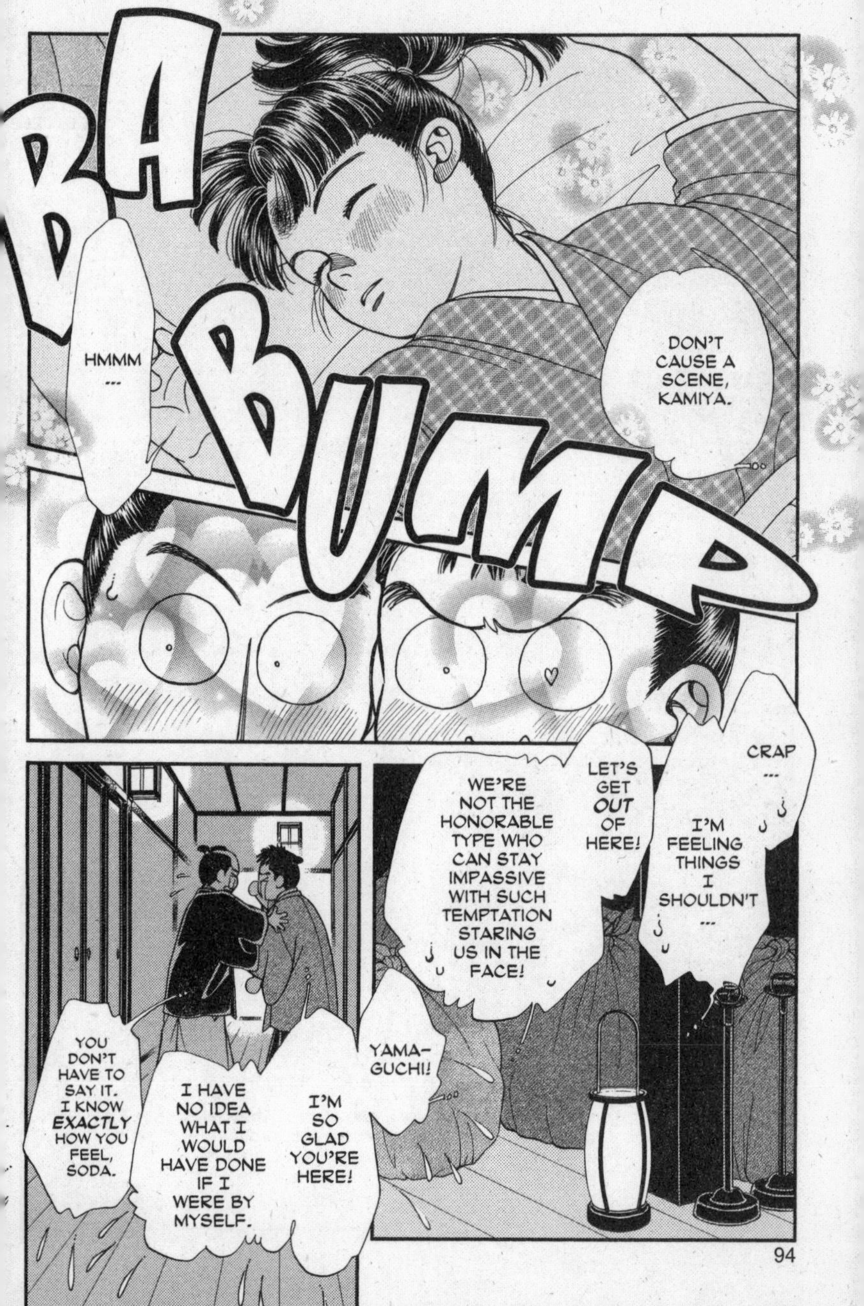
DON'T CAUSE A SCENE, KAMIYA.
HMMM ...
BA BUMP
CRAP ...
I'M FEELING THINGS I SHOULDN'T ...
LET'S GET OUT OF HERE!
WE'RE NOT THE HONORABLE TYPE WHO CAN STAY IMPASSIVE WITH SUCH TEMPTATION STARING US IN THE FACE!
YAMA-GUCHI!
I'M SO GLAD YOU'RE HERE!
I HAVE NO IDEA WHAT I WOULD HAVE DONE IF I WERE BY MYSELF.
YOU DON'T HAVE TO SAY IT. I KNOW EXACTLY HOW YOU FEEL, SODA.

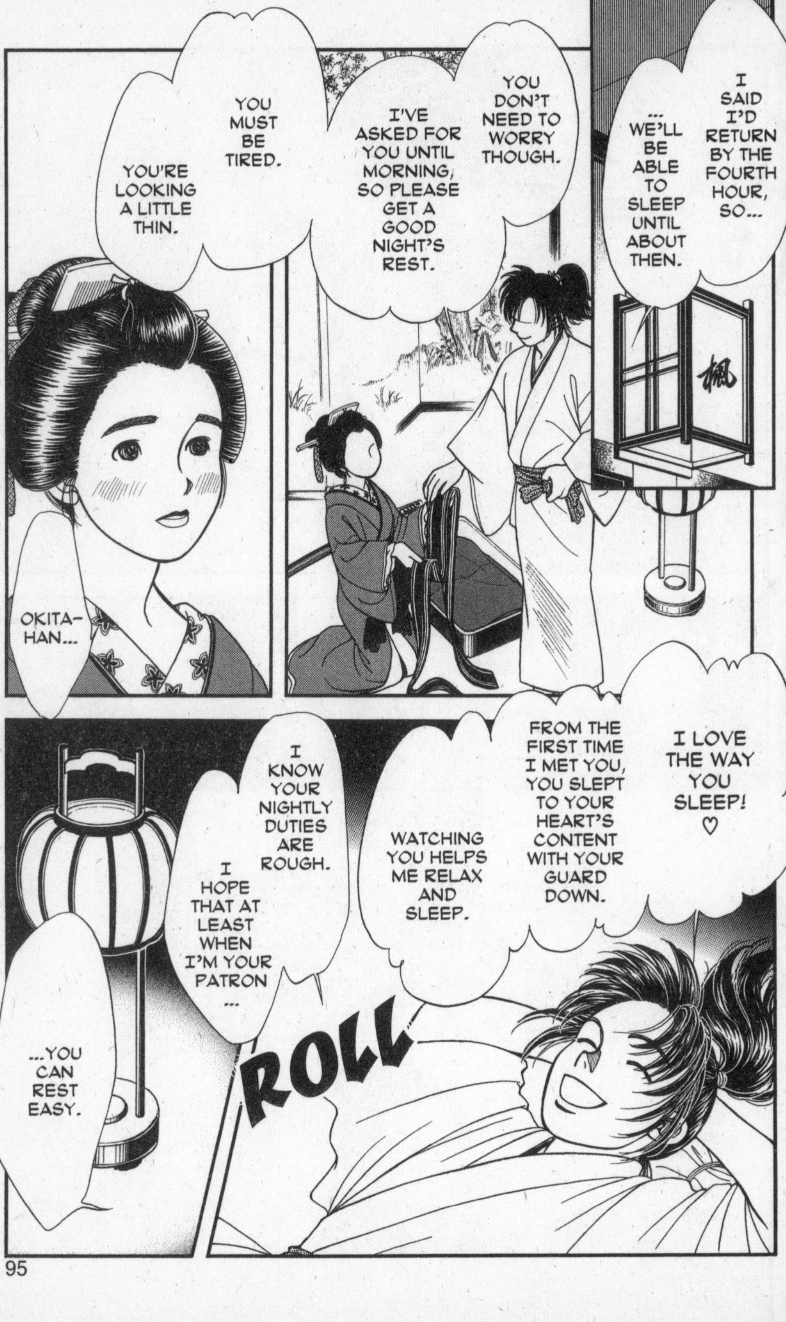
I SAID I'D RETURN BY THE FOURTH HOUR, SO...
...WE'LL BE ABLE TO SLEEP UNTIL ABOUT THEN.
YOU DON'T NEED TO WORRY THOUGH.
I'VE ASKED FOR YOU UNTIL MORNING, SO PLEASE GET A GOOD NIGHT'S REST.
YOU MUST BE TIRED.
YOU'RE LOOKING A LITTLE THIN.
OKITA-HAN...
I LOVE THE WAY YOU SLEEP! ♡
FROM THE FIRST TIME I MET YOU, YOU SLEPT TO YOUR HEART'S CONTENT WITH YOUR GUARD DOWN.
WATCHING YOU HELPS ME RELAX AND SLEEP.
I KNOW YOUR NIGHTLY DUTIES ARE ROUGH.
I HOPE THAT AT LEAST WHEN I'M YOUR PATRON...
ROLL
...YOU CAN REST EASY.

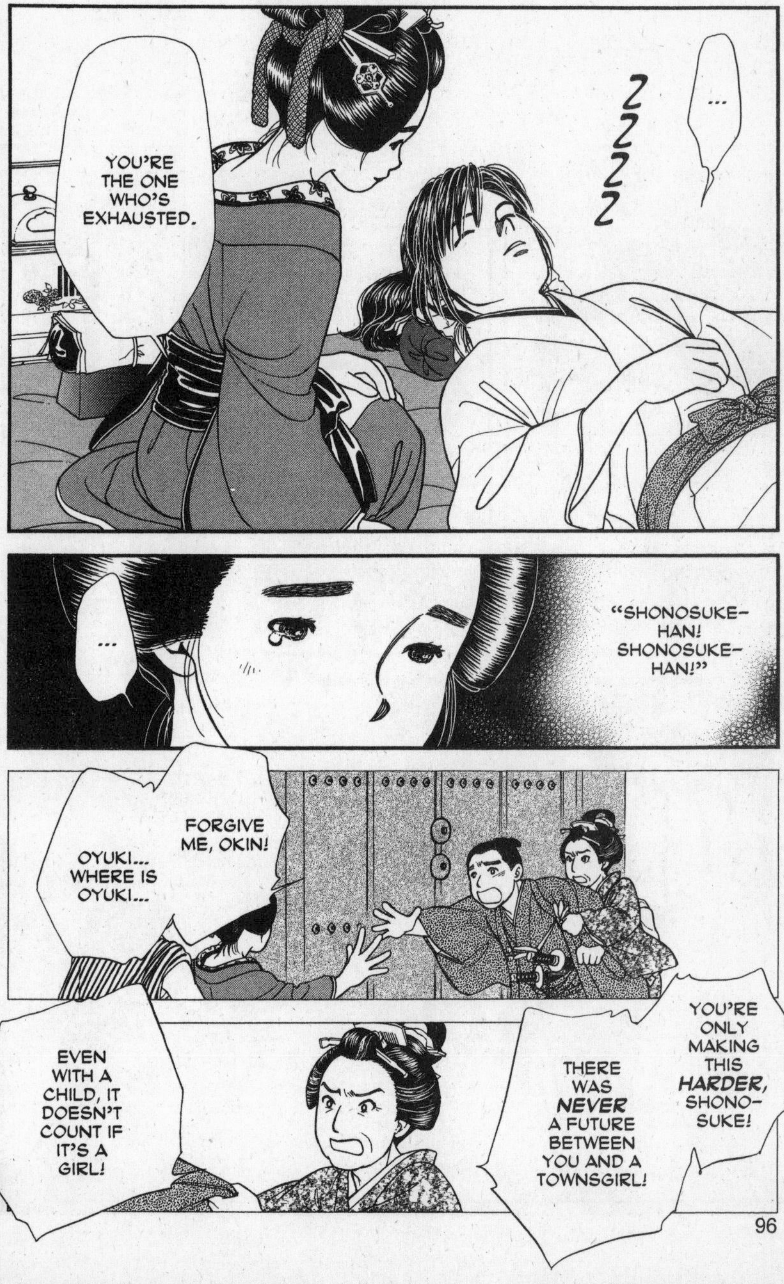
...
ZZZZ
YOU'RE THE ONE WHO'S EXHAUSTED.
"SHONOSUKE-HAN! SHONOSUKE-HAN!"
...
FORGIVE ME, OKIN!
OYUKI... WHERE IS OYUKI...
YOU'RE ONLY MAKING THIS *HARDER,* SHONOSUKE!
THERE WAS *NEVER* A FUTURE BETWEEN YOU AND A TOWNSGIRL!
EVEN WITH A CHILD, IT DOESN'T COUNT IF IT'S A GIRL!

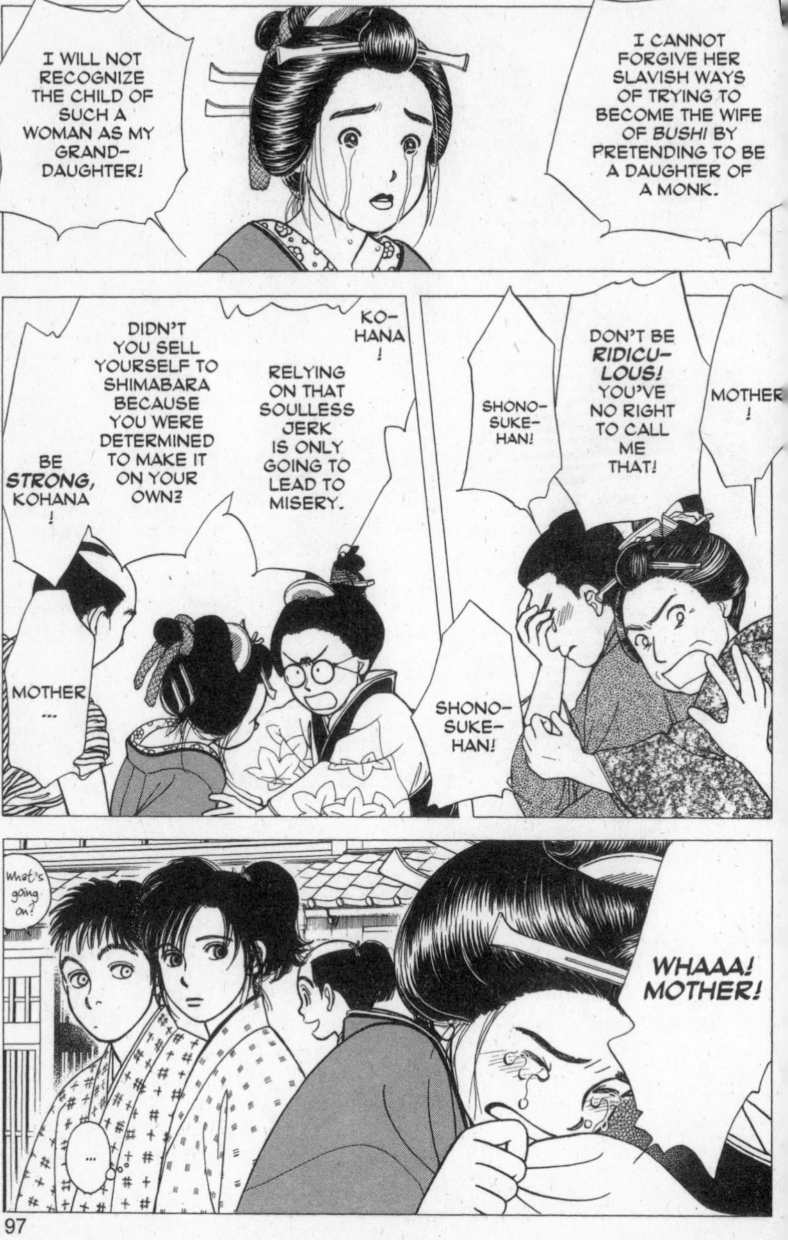
I CANNOT FORGIVE HER SLAVISH WAYS OF TRYING TO BECOME THE WIFE OF *BUSHI* BY PRETENDING TO BE A DAUGHTER OF A MONK.
I WILL NOT RECOGNIZE THE CHILD OF SUCH A WOMAN AS MY GRAND-DAUGHTER!
MOTHER!
DON'T BE ***RIDICULOUS!*** YOU'VE NO RIGHT TO CALL ME THAT!
SHONO-SUKE-HAN!
SHONO-SUKE-HAN!
KO-HANA!
RELYING ON THAT SOULLESS JERK IS ONLY GOING TO LEAD TO MISERY.
DIDN'T YOU SELL YOURSELF TO SHIMABARA BECAUSE YOU WERE DETERMINED TO MAKE IT ON YOUR OWN?
BE ***STRONG,*** KOHANA!
MOTHER...
WHAAA! MOTHER!
What's going on?
...

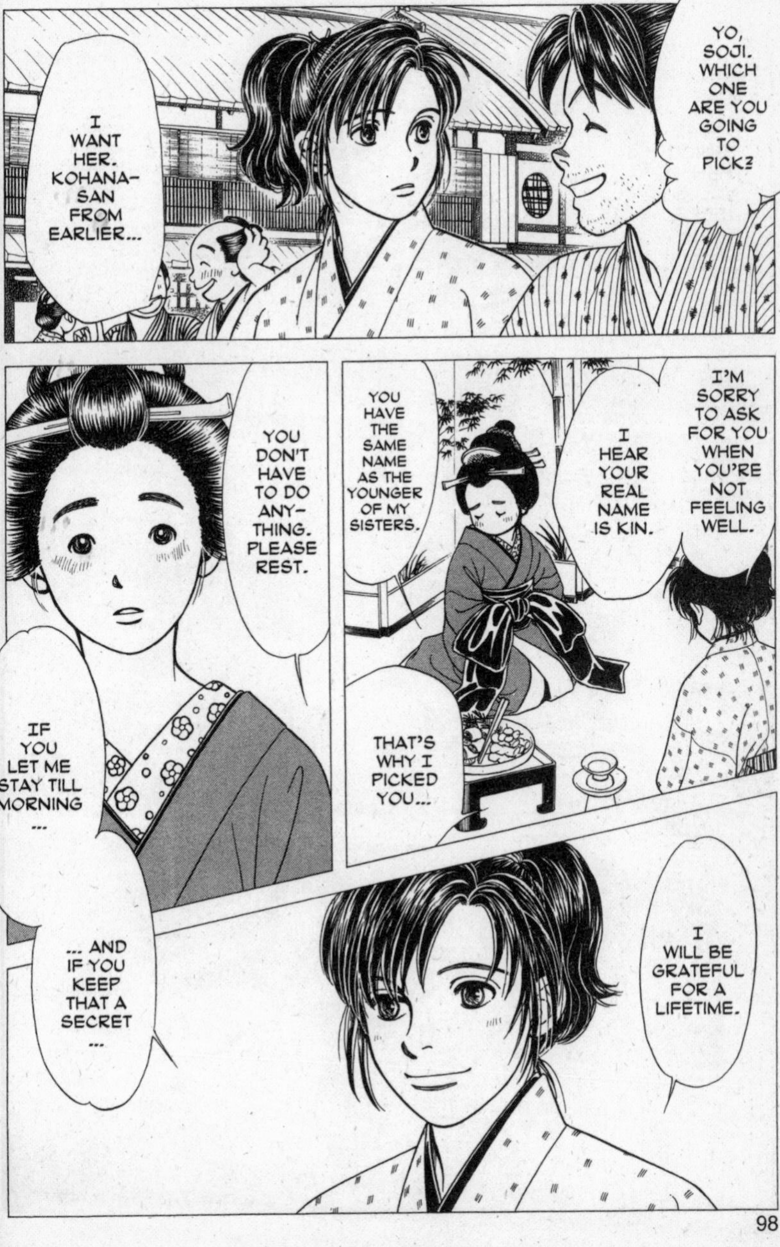
YO, SOJI. WHICH ONE ARE YOU GOING TO PICK?
I WANT HER. KOHANA-SAN FROM EARLIER...
I'M SORRY TO ASK FOR YOU WHEN YOU'RE NOT FEELING WELL.
I HEAR YOUR REAL NAME IS KIN.
YOU HAVE THE SAME NAME AS THE YOUNGER OF MY SISTERS.
THAT'S WHY I PICKED YOU...
YOU DON'T HAVE TO DO ANY-THING. PLEASE REST.
IF YOU LET ME STAY TILL MORNING ...
... AND IF YOU KEEP THAT A SECRET ...
I WILL BE GRATEFUL FOR A LIFETIME.

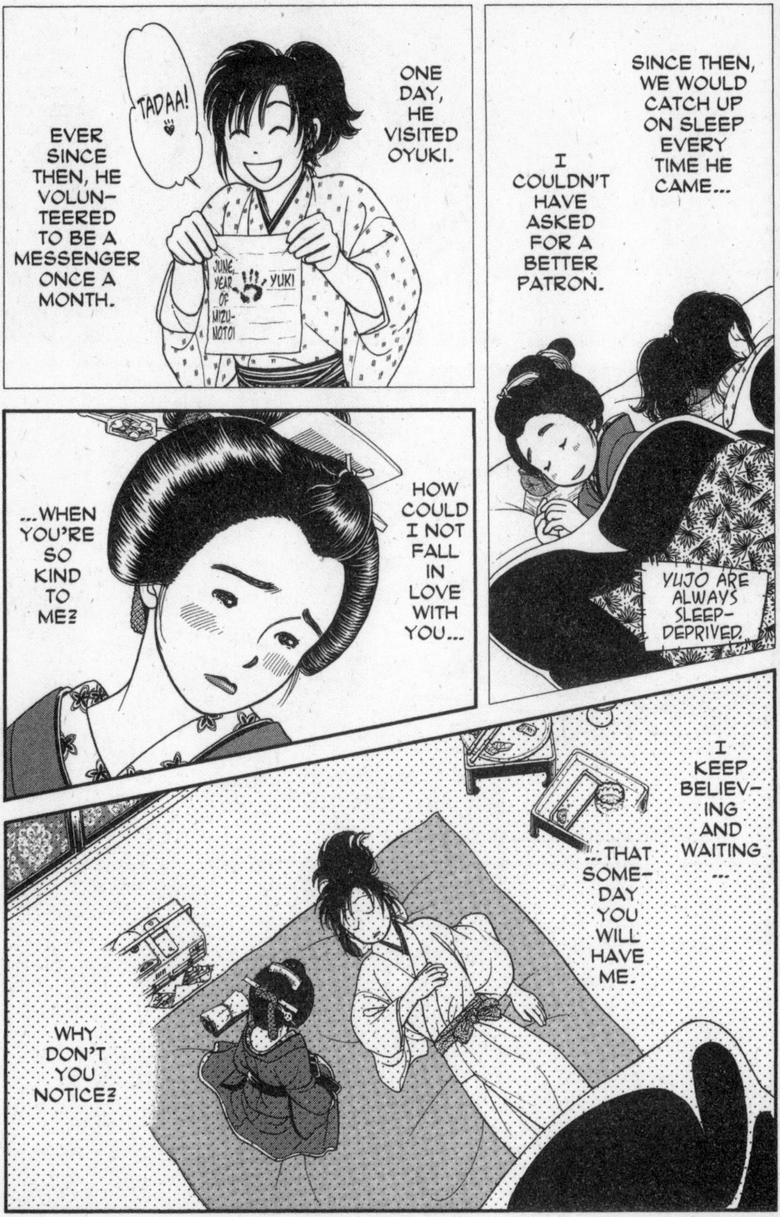
SINCE THEN, WE WOULD CATCH UP ON SLEEP EVERY TIME HE CAME...
I COULDN'T HAVE ASKED FOR A BETTER PATRON.
YUJO ARE ALWAYS SLEEP-DEPRIVED.
ONE DAY, HE VISITED OYUKI.
TADAA! ♥
JUNE, YEAR OF MIZUNOTOI
YUKI
EVER SINCE THEN, HE VOLUNTEERED TO BE A MESSENGER ONCE A MONTH.
HOW COULD I NOT FALL IN LOVE WITH YOU...
...WHEN YOU'RE SO KIND TO ME?
I KEEP BELIEVING AND WAITING...
...THAT SOMEDAY YOU WILL HAVE ME.
WHY DON'T YOU NOTICE?

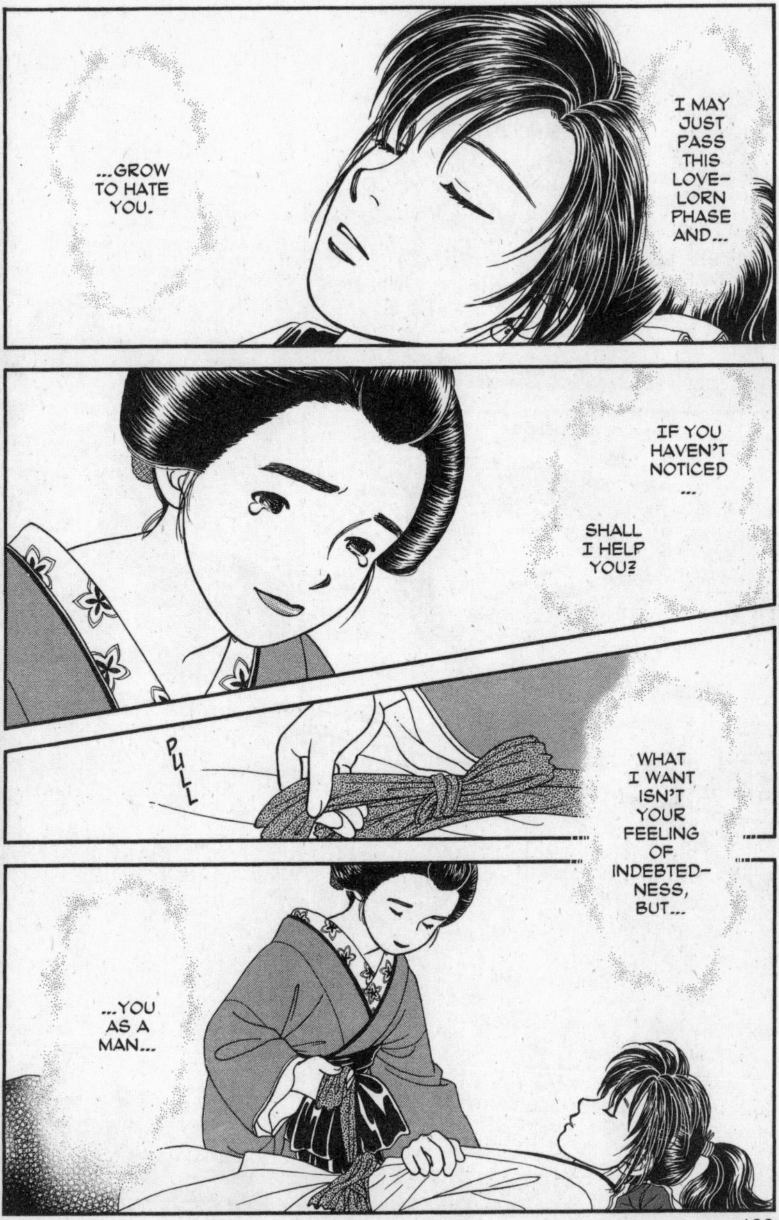
I MAY JUST PASS THIS LOVE-LORN PHASE AND...
...GROW TO HATE YOU.
IF YOU HAVEN'T NOTICED...
SHALL I HELP YOU?
PULL
WHAT I WANT ISN'T YOUR FEELING OF INDEBTED-NESS, BUT...
...YOU AS A MAN...

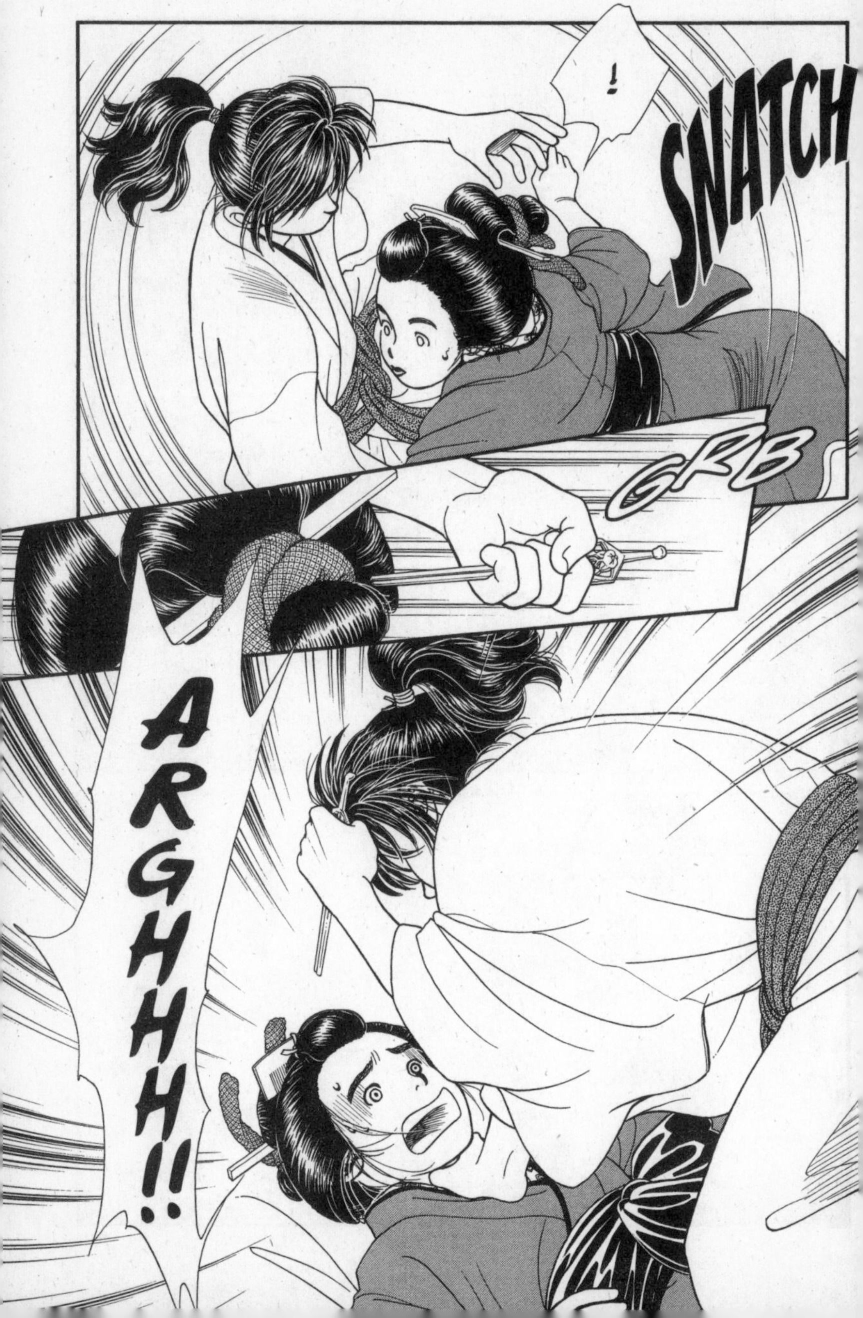
!
SNATCH
GRB
ARGHHH!!

OH....

IT'S YOU, KOHANA-SAN.

HUH?!

WHAT ?!

I'M SORRY.

I MUST HAVE BEEN DREAM-ING...

HUPP!

ACTUALLY IN THE NEXT ROOM. (HEH)

...

DROP

ZZZZZ

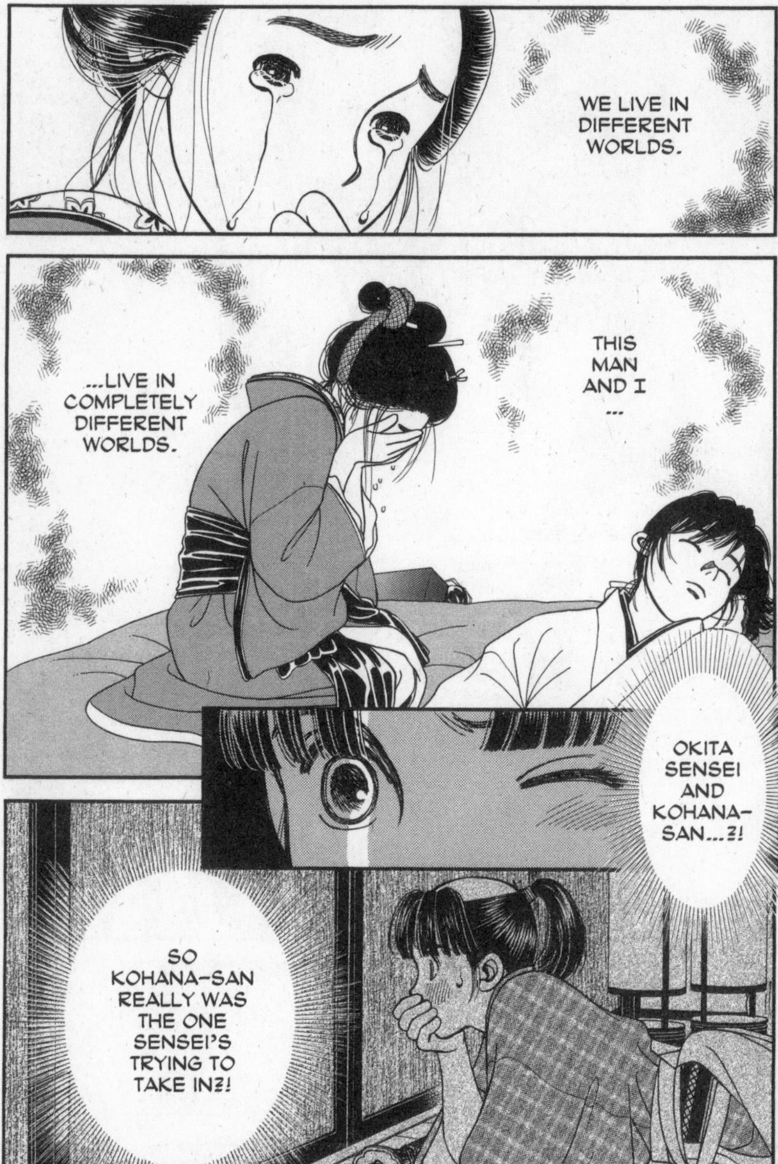
WE LIVE IN DIFFERENT WORLDS.
THIS MAN AND I ...
...LIVE IN COMPLETELY DIFFERENT WORLDS.
OKITA SENSEI AND KOHANA-SAN...?!
SO KOHANA-SAN REALLY WAS THE ONE SENSEI'S TRYING TO TAKE IN?!

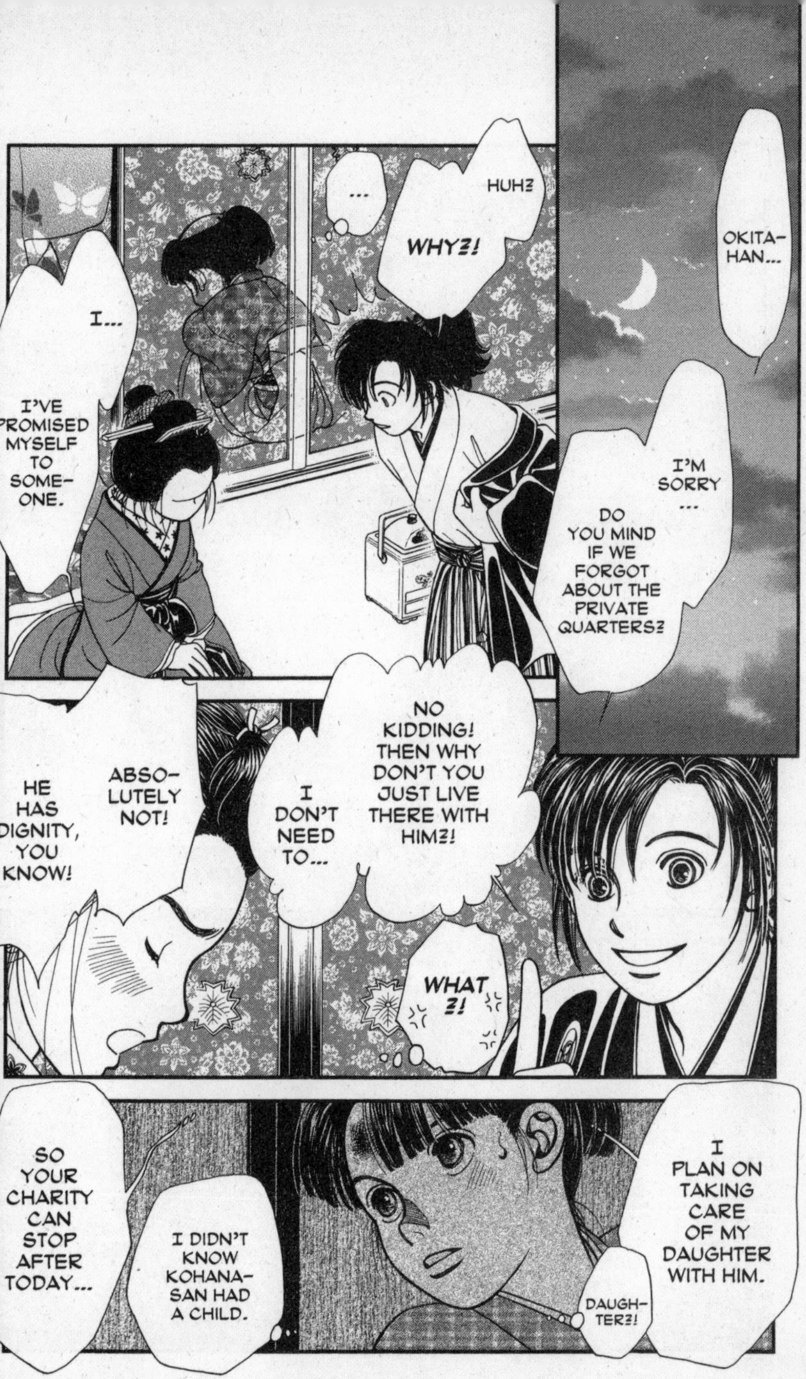
OKITA-HAN...
I'M SORRY...
DO YOU MIND IF WE FORGOT ABOUT THE PRIVATE QUARTERS?
HUH?
WHY?!
...
I...
I'VE PROMISED MYSELF TO SOMEONE.
NO KIDDING! THEN WHY DON'T YOU JUST LIVE THERE WITH HIM?!
WHAT?!
I DON'T NEED TO...
ABSOLUTELY NOT!
HE HAS DIGNITY, YOU KNOW!
I PLAN ON TAKING CARE OF MY DAUGHTER WITH HIM.
DAUGHTER?!
I DIDN'T KNOW KOHANA-SAN HAD A CHILD.
SO YOUR CHARITY CAN STOP AFTER TODAY...

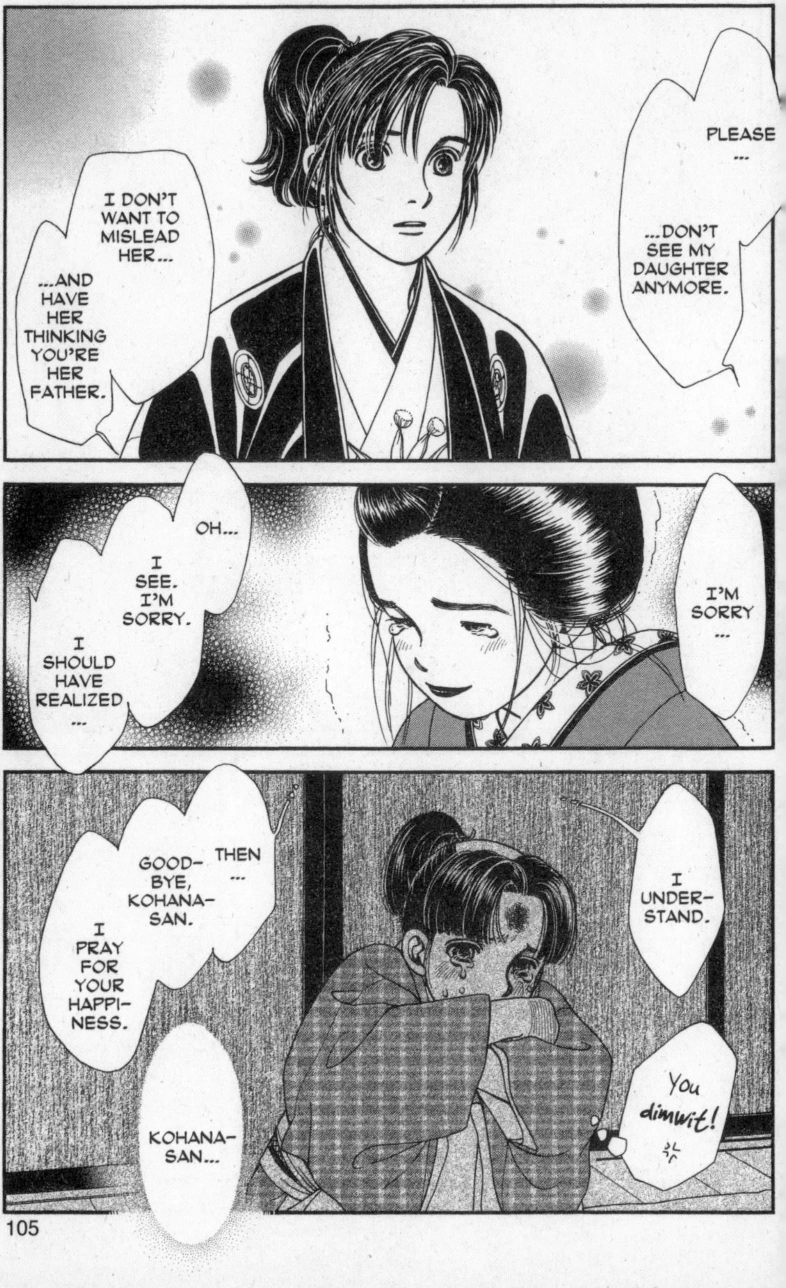
PLEASE ...
...DON'T SEE MY DAUGHTER ANYMORE.
I DON'T WANT TO MISLEAD HER...
...AND HAVE HER THINKING YOU'RE HER FATHER.
I'M SORRY ...
OH...
I SEE. I'M SORRY.
I SHOULD HAVE REALIZED ...
I UNDER-STAND.
You dimwit!
THEN ...
GOOD-BYE, KOHANA-SAN.
I PRAY FOR YOUR HAPPI-NESS.
KOHANA-SAN...

SHE REALLY LOVES...

...OKITA SENSEI.

SIGH

...

I'M SORRY.

MY SANDAL JUST FLEW OFF.

KAMIYA-SAN?!

OW!!

WHAM

106

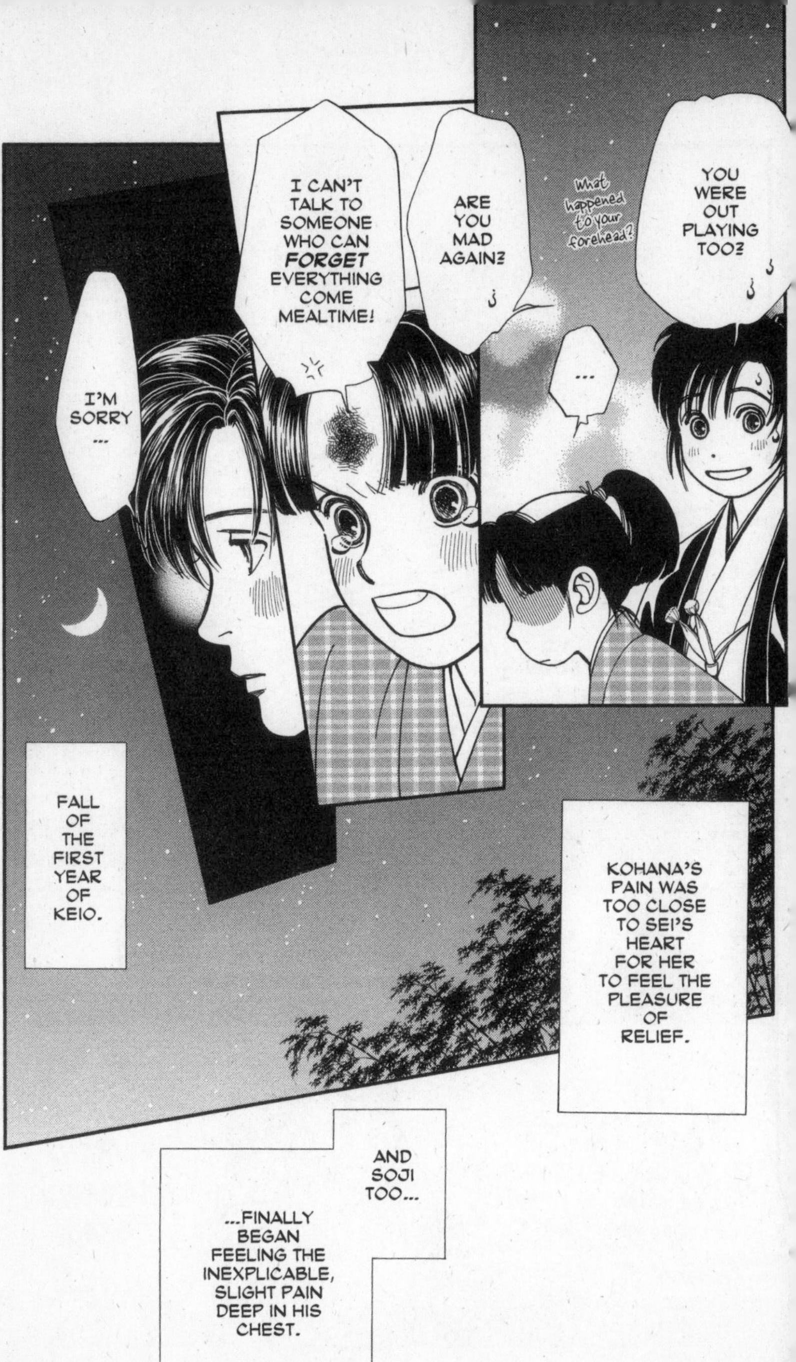
YOU WERE OUT PLAYING TOO?
What happened to your forehead?
...
ARE YOU MAD AGAIN?
I CAN'T TALK TO SOMEONE WHO CAN **FORGET** EVERYTHING COME MEALTIME!
I'M SORRY ...
KOHANA'S PAIN WAS TOO CLOSE TO SEI'S HEART FOR HER TO FEEL THE PLEASURE OF RELIEF.
FALL OF THE FIRST YEAR OF KEIO.
AND SOJI TOO...
...FINALLY BEGAN FEELING THE INEXPLICABLE, SLIGHT PAIN DEEP IN HIS CHEST.

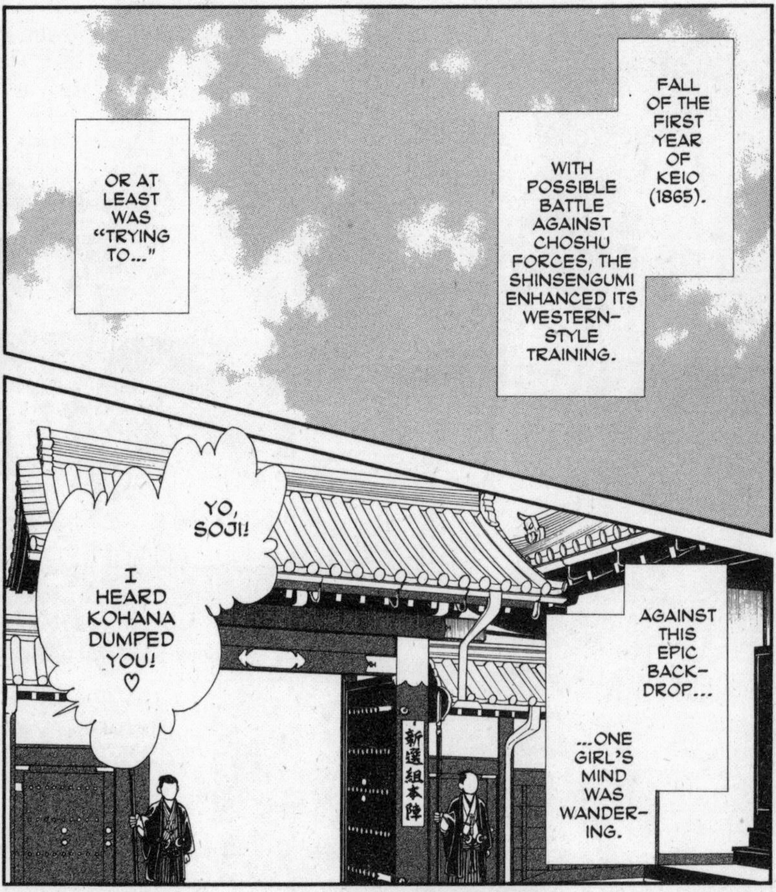
FALL OF THE FIRST YEAR OF KEIO (1865).
WITH POSSIBLE BATTLE AGAINST CHOSHU FORCES, THE SHINSENGUMI ENHANCED ITS WESTERN-STYLE TRAINING.
OR AT LEAST WAS "TRYING TO..."
AGAINST THIS EPIC BACK-DROP...
...ONE GIRL'S MIND WAS WANDER-ING.
新選組本陣
YO, SOJI!
I HEARD KOHANA DUMPED YOU! ♡

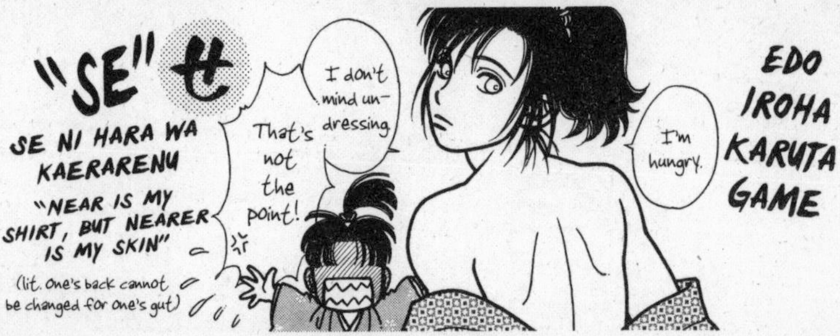
EDO IROHA KARUTA GAME
I'm hungry.
I don't mind un-dressing.
That's not the point!
"SE" せ
SE NI HARA WA KAERARENU
"NEAR IS MY SHIRT, BUT NEARER IS MY SKIN"
(lit. One's back cannot be changed for one's gut)

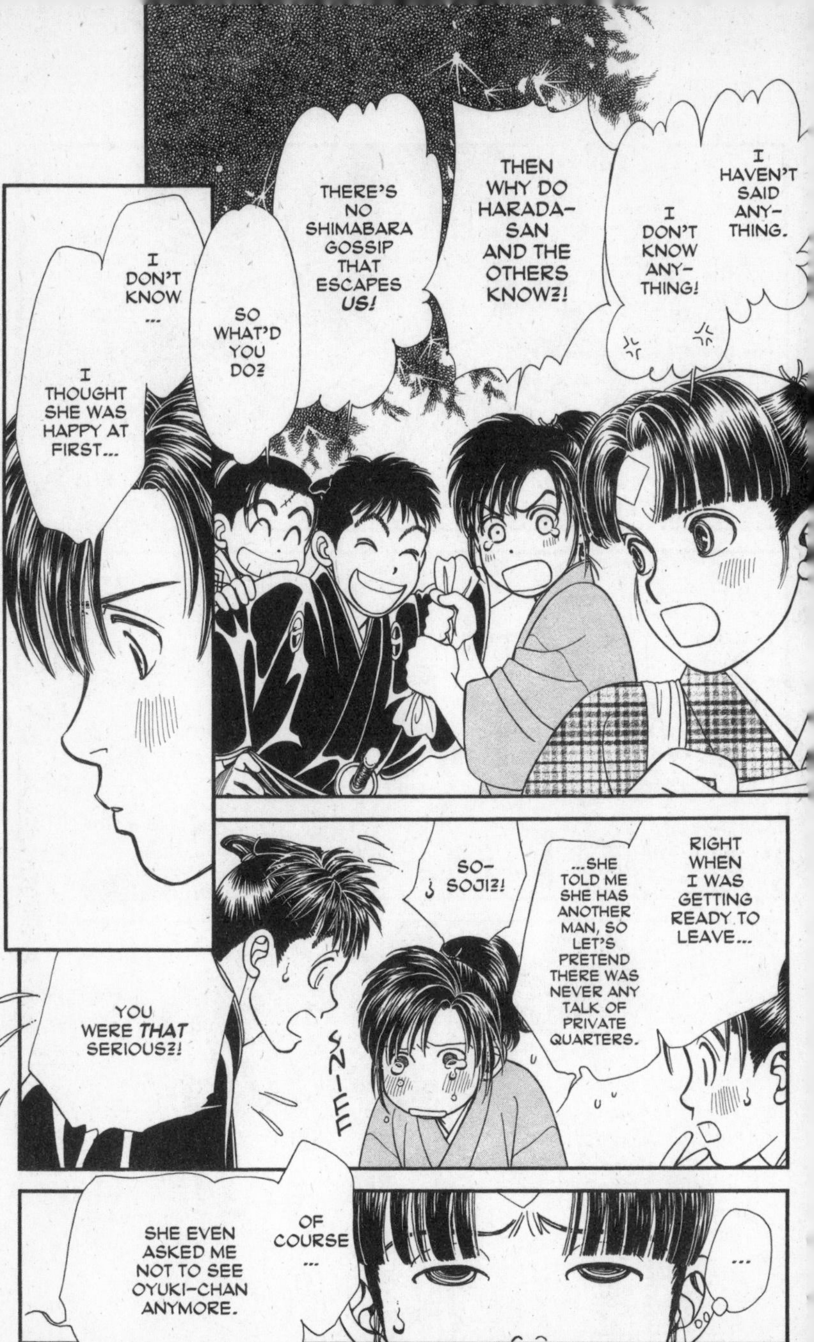
I HAVEN'T SAID ANYTHING.
I DON'T KNOW ANYTHING!
THEN WHY DO HARADA-SAN AND THE OTHERS KNOW?!
THERE'S NO SHIMABARA GOSSIP THAT ESCAPES *US!*
SO WHAT'D YOU DO?
I DON'T KNOW...
I THOUGHT SHE WAS HAPPY AT FIRST...
RIGHT WHEN I WAS GETTING READY TO LEAVE...
...SHE TOLD ME SHE HAS ANOTHER MAN, SO LET'S PRETEND THERE WAS NEVER ANY TALK OF PRIVATE QUARTERS.
SO-SOJI?!
SNIFF
YOU WERE *THAT* SERIOUS?!
...
OF COURSE...
SHE EVEN ASKED ME NOT TO SEE OYUKI-CHAN ANYMORE.

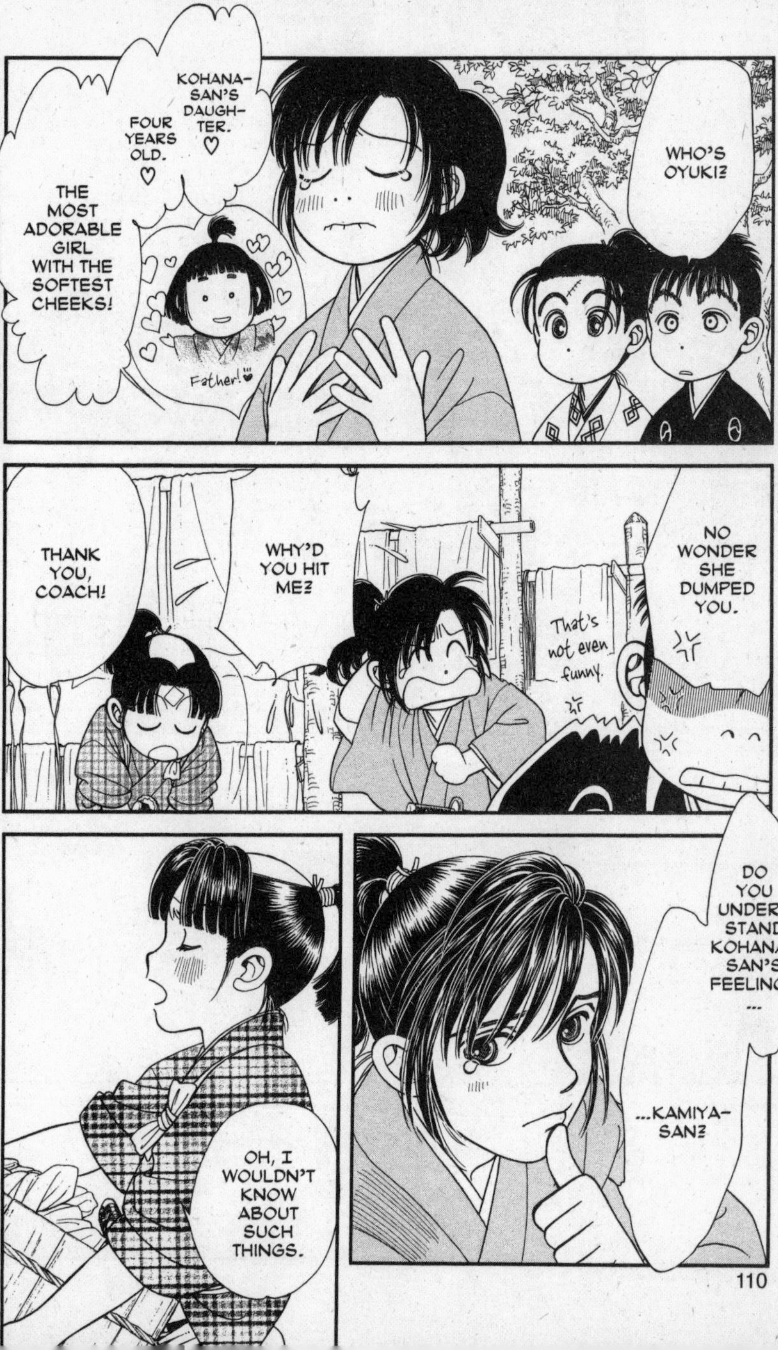

WHO'S OYUKI?
KOHANA-SAN'S DAUGH-TER. ♡
FOUR YEARS OLD. ♡
THE MOST ADORABLE GIRL WITH THE SOFTEST CHEEKS!
Father!
NO WONDER SHE DUMPED YOU.
That's not even funny.
WHY'D YOU HIT ME?
THANK YOU, COACH!
DO YOU UNDER-STAND KOHANA-SAN'S FEELINGS ...
...KAMIYA-SAN?
OH, I WOULDN'T KNOW ABOUT SUCH THINGS.

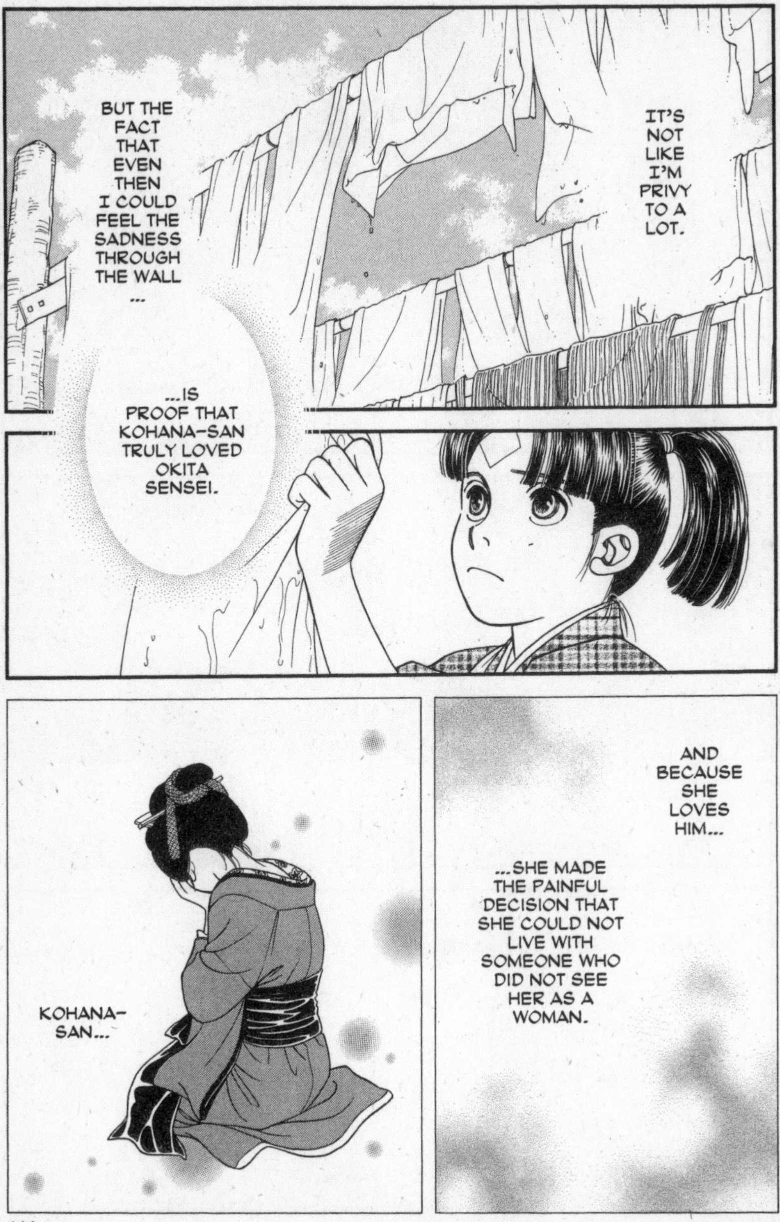
IT'S NOT LIKE I'M PRIVY TO A LOT.
BUT THE FACT THAT EVEN THEN I COULD FEEL THE SADNESS THROUGH THE WALL...
...IS PROOF THAT KOHANA-SAN TRULY LOVED OKITA SENSEI.
AND BECAUSE SHE LOVES HIM...
...SHE MADE THE PAINFUL DECISION THAT SHE COULD NOT LIVE WITH SOMEONE WHO DID NOT SEE HER AS A WOMAN.
KOHANA-SAN...

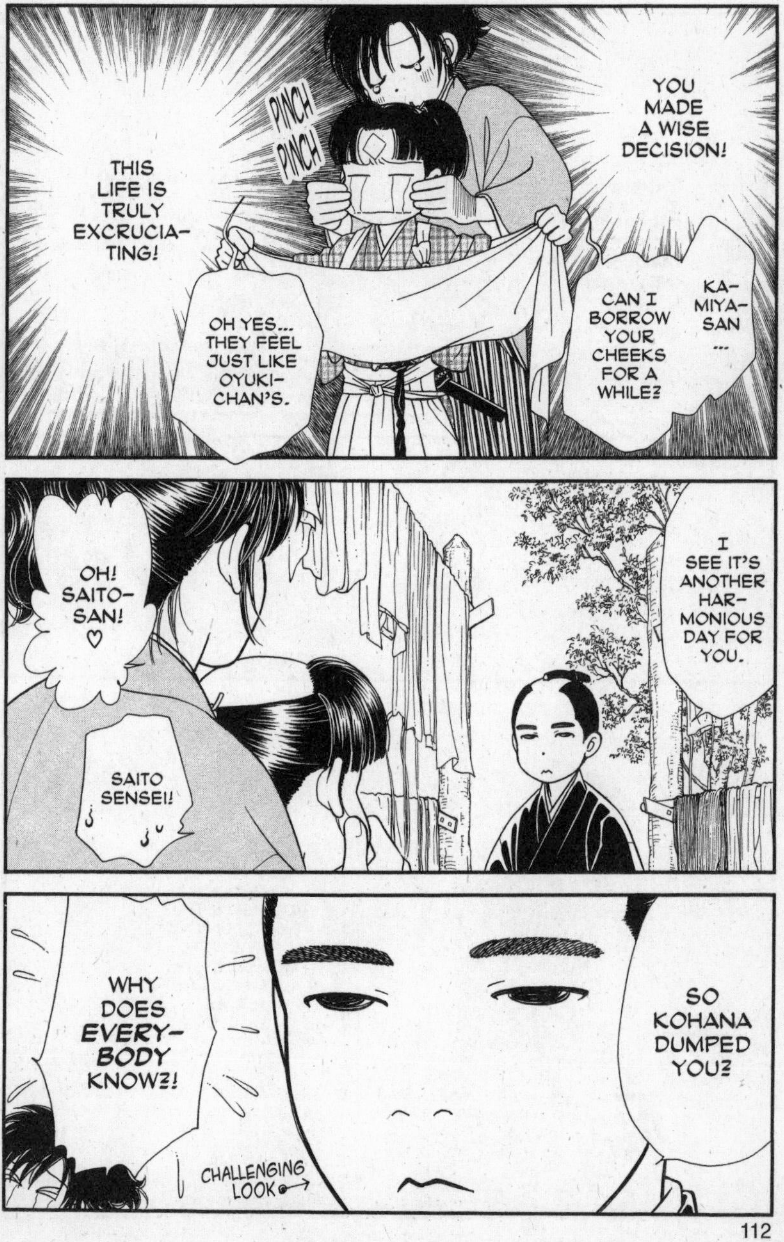
YOU MADE A WISE DECISION!
PINCH PINCH
THIS LIFE IS TRULY EXCRUCIATING!
KAMIYA-SAN...
CAN I BORROW YOUR CHEEKS FOR A WHILE?
OH YES... THEY FEEL JUST LIKE OYUKI-CHAN'S.
I SEE IT'S ANOTHER HARMONIOUS DAY FOR YOU.
OH! SAITO-SAN! ♡
SAITO SENSEI!
SO KOHANA DUMPED YOU?
WHY DOES EVERYBODY KNOW?!
CHALLENGING LOOK

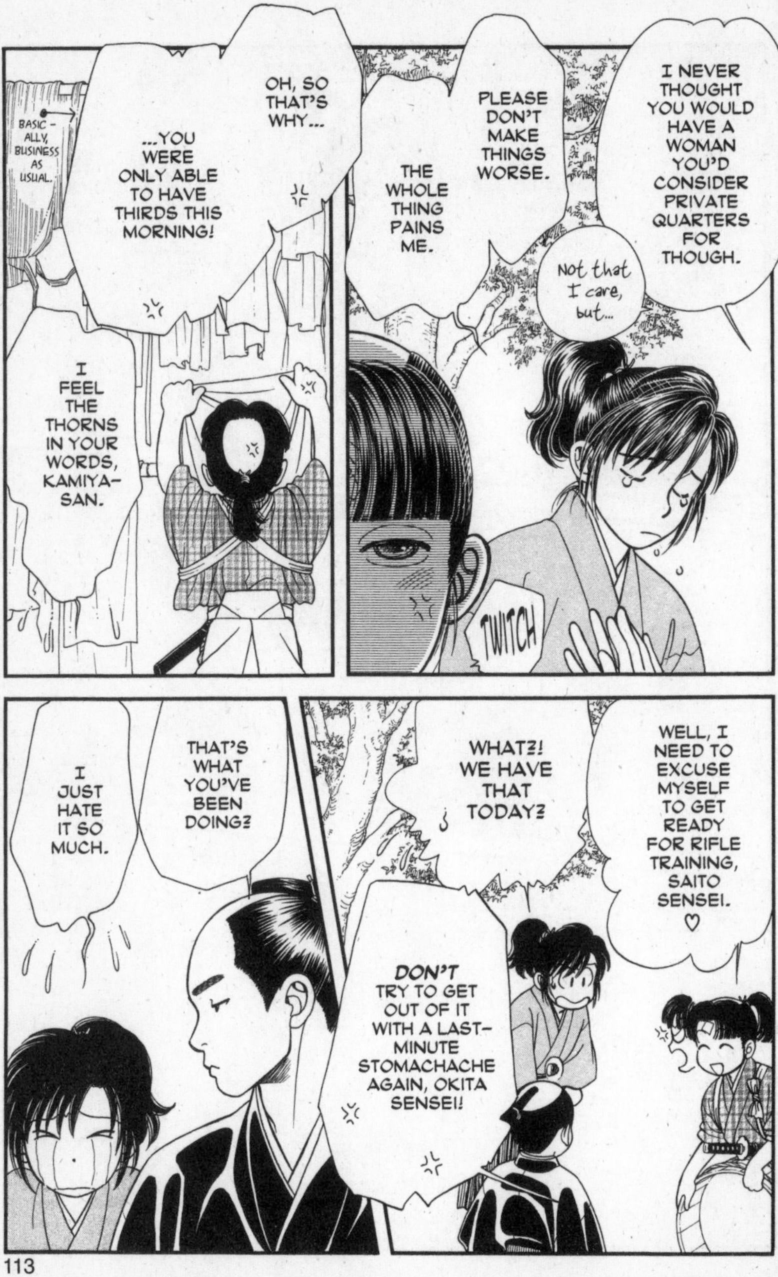
I NEVER THOUGHT YOU WOULD HAVE A WOMAN YOU'D CONSIDER PRIVATE QUARTERS FOR THOUGH.
Not that I care, but...
PLEASE DON'T MAKE THINGS WORSE.
THE WHOLE THING PAINS ME.
TWITCH
OH, SO THAT'S WHY...
...YOU WERE ONLY ABLE TO HAVE THIRDS THIS MORNING!
BASIC-ALLY, BUSINESS AS USUAL.
I FEEL THE THORNS IN YOUR WORDS, KAMIYA-SAN.
WELL, I NEED TO EXCUSE MYSELF TO GET READY FOR RIFLE TRAINING, SAITO SENSEI. ♡
WHAT?! WE HAVE THAT TODAY?
DON'T TRY TO GET OUT OF IT WITH A LAST-MINUTE STOMACHACHE AGAIN, OKITA SENSEI!
THAT'S WHAT YOU'VE BEEN DOING?
I JUST HATE IT SO MUCH.

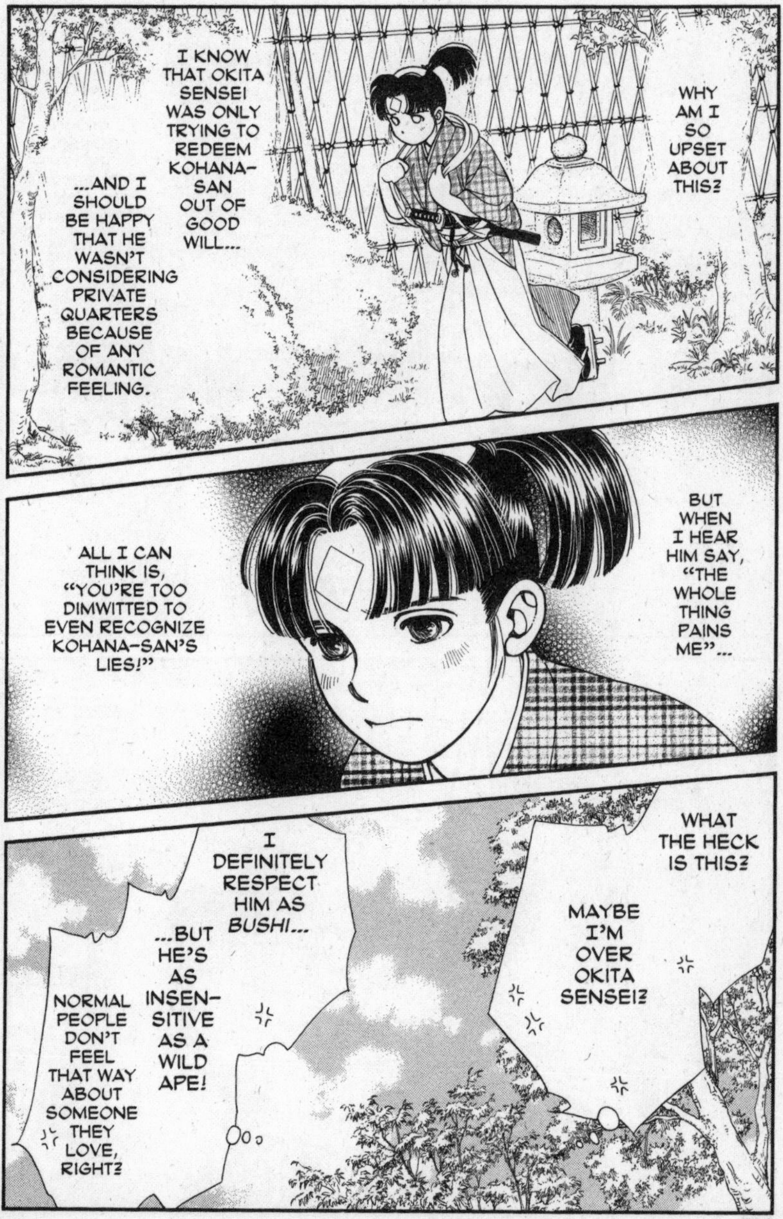
WHY AM I SO UPSET ABOUT THIS?
I KNOW THAT OKITA SENSEI WAS ONLY TRYING TO REDEEM KOHANA-SAN OUT OF GOOD WILL...
...AND I SHOULD BE HAPPY THAT HE WASN'T CONSIDERING PRIVATE QUARTERS BECAUSE OF ANY ROMANTIC FEELING.
BUT WHEN I HEAR HIM SAY, "THE WHOLE THING PAINS ME"...
ALL I CAN THINK IS, "YOU'RE TOO DIMWITTED TO EVEN RECOGNIZE KOHANA-SAN'S LIES!"
WHAT THE HECK IS THIS?
MAYBE I'M OVER OKITA SENSEI!?
I DEFINITELY RESPECT HIM AS *BUSHI*...
...BUT HE'S AS INSEN-SITIVE AS A WILD APE!
NORMAL PEOPLE DON'T FEEL THAT WAY ABOUT SOMEONE THEY LOVE, RIGHT?

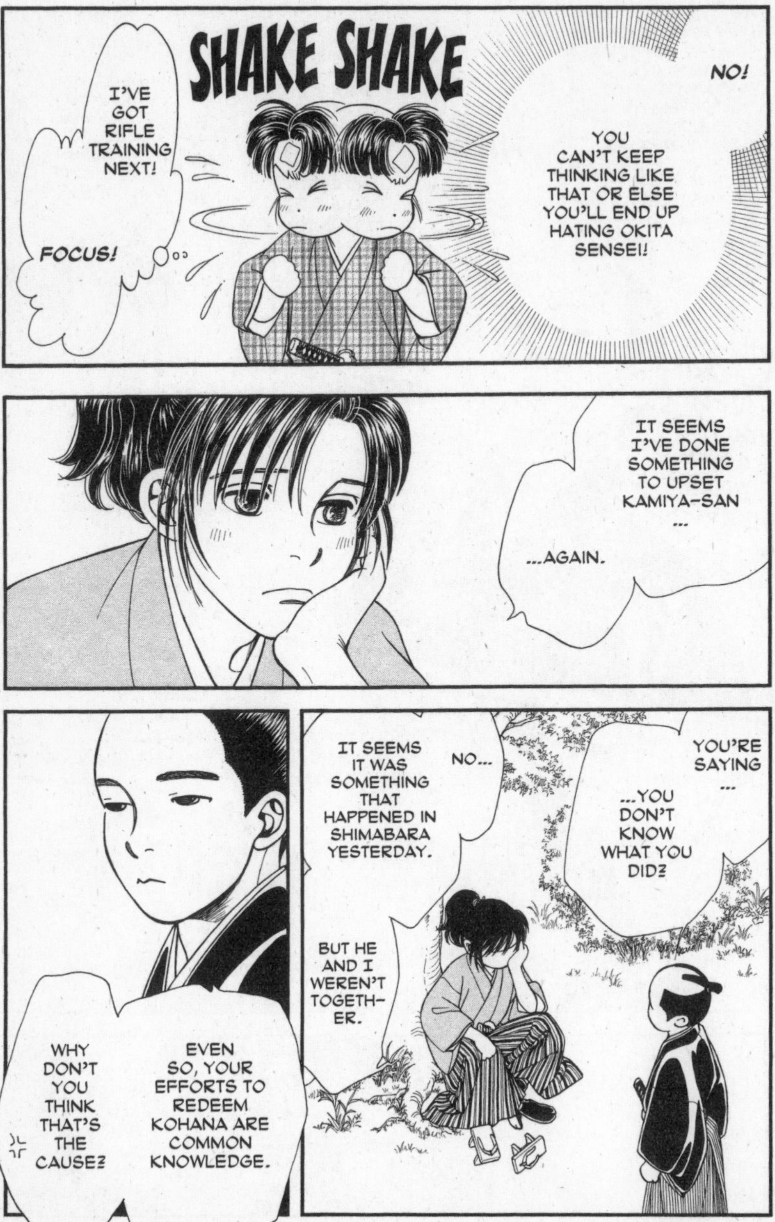
NO!
YOU CAN'T KEEP THINKING LIKE THAT OR ELSE YOU'LL END UP HATING OKITA SENSEI!
SHAKE SHAKE
I'VE GOT RIFLE TRAINING NEXT!
FOCUS!
IT SEEMS I'VE DONE SOMETHING TO UPSET KAMIYA-SAN ...
...AGAIN.
YOU'RE SAYING ...
...YOU DON'T KNOW WHAT YOU DID?
NO...
IT SEEMS IT WAS SOMETHING THAT HAPPENED IN SHIMABARA YESTERDAY.
BUT HE AND I WEREN'T TOGETH-ER.
EVEN SO, YOUR EFFORTS TO REDEEM KOHANA ARE COMMON KNOWLEDGE.
WHY DON'T YOU THINK THAT'S THE CAUSE?

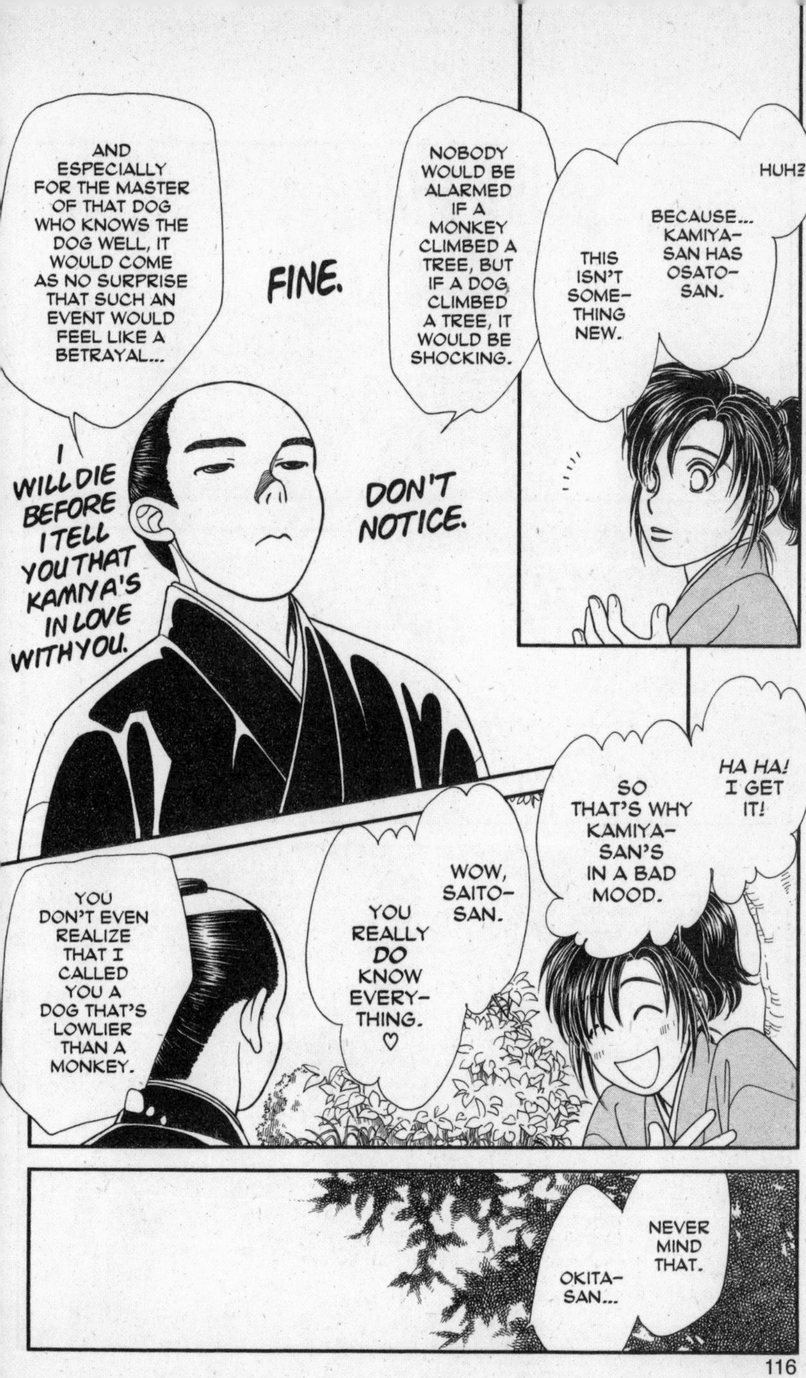
HUH?
BECAUSE... KAMIYA-SAN HAS OSATO-SAN.
THIS ISN'T SOMETHING NEW.
NOBODY WOULD BE ALARMED IF A MONKEY CLIMBED A TREE, BUT IF A DOG CLIMBED A TREE, IT WOULD BE SHOCKING.
FINE.
AND ESPECIALLY FOR THE MASTER OF THAT DOG WHO KNOWS THE DOG WELL, IT WOULD COME AS NO SURPRISE THAT SUCH AN EVENT WOULD FEEL LIKE A BETRAYAL...
DON'T NOTICE.
I WILL DIE BEFORE I TELL YOU THAT KAMIYA'S IN LOVE WITH YOU.
HA HA! I GET IT!
SO THAT'S WHY KAMIYA-SAN'S IN A BAD MOOD.
WOW, SAITO-SAN.
YOU REALLY DO KNOW EVERYTHING. ♡
YOU DON'T EVEN REALIZE THAT I CALLED YOU A DOG THAT'S LOWLIER THAN A MONKEY.
NEVER MIND THAT.
OKITA-SAN...

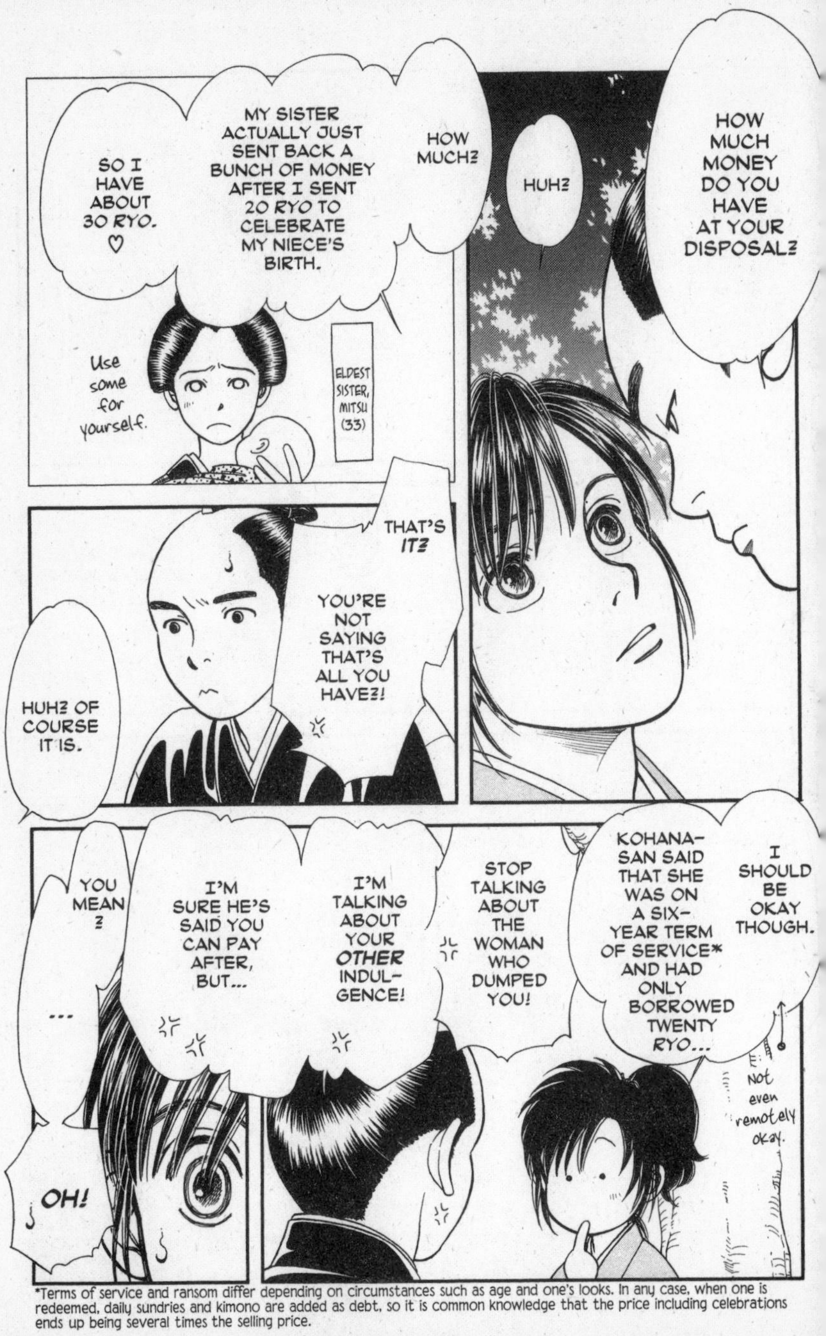
HOW MUCH MONEY DO YOU HAVE AT YOUR DISPOSAL?
HUH?
HOW MUCH?
MY SISTER ACTUALLY JUST SENT BACK A BUNCH OF MONEY AFTER I SENT 20 RYO TO CELEBRATE MY NIECE'S BIRTH.
SO I HAVE ABOUT 30 RYO. ♡
ELDEST SISTER, MITSU (33)
Use some for yourself.
THAT'S IT?
YOU'RE NOT SAYING THAT'S ALL YOU HAVE?!
HUH? OF COURSE IT IS.
I SHOULD BE OKAY THOUGH.
KOHANA-SAN SAID THAT SHE WAS ON A SIX-YEAR TERM OF SERVICE* AND HAD ONLY BORROWED TWENTY RYO...
Not even remotely okay.
STOP TALKING ABOUT THE WOMAN WHO DUMPED YOU!
I'M TALKING ABOUT YOUR OTHER INDULGENCE!
I'M SURE HE'S SAID YOU CAN PAY AFTER, BUT...
YOU MEAN?
...
OH!

*Terms of service and ransom differ depending on circumstances such as age and one's looks. In any case, when one is redeemed, daily sundries and kimono are added as debt, so it is common knowledge that the price including celebrations ends up being several times the selling price.

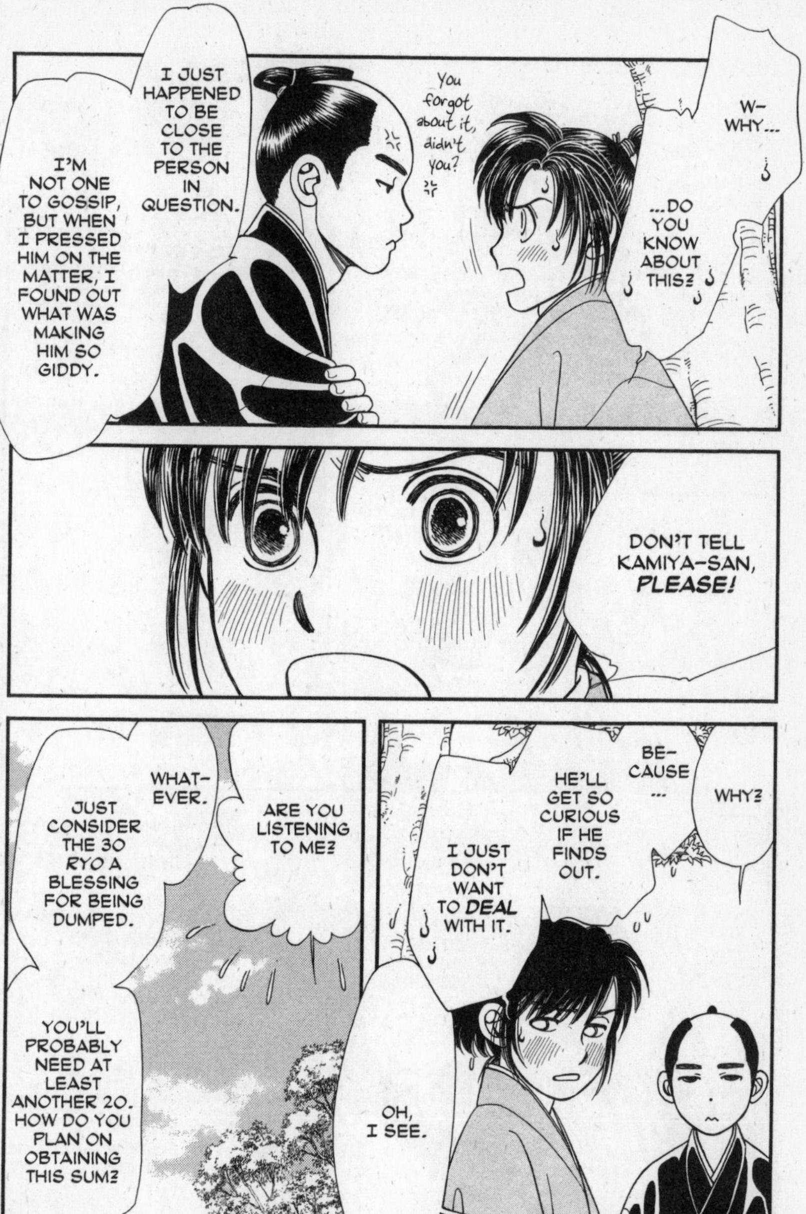
W–WHY...
...DO YOU KNOW ABOUT THIS?
You forgot about it, didn't you?
I JUST HAPPENED TO BE CLOSE TO THE PERSON IN QUESTION.
I'M NOT ONE TO GOSSIP, BUT WHEN I PRESSED HIM ON THE MATTER, I FOUND OUT WHAT WAS MAKING HIM SO GIDDY.
DON'T TELL KAMIYA-SAN, *PLEASE!*
WHY?
BE-CAUSE ...
HE'LL GET SO CURIOUS IF HE FINDS OUT.
I JUST DON'T WANT TO *DEAL* WITH IT.
OH, I SEE.
ARE YOU LISTENING TO ME?
WHAT-EVER.
JUST CONSIDER THE 30 *RYO* A BLESSING FOR BEING DUMPED.
YOU'LL PROBABLY NEED AT LEAST ANOTHER 20. HOW DO YOU PLAN ON OBTAINING THIS SUM?

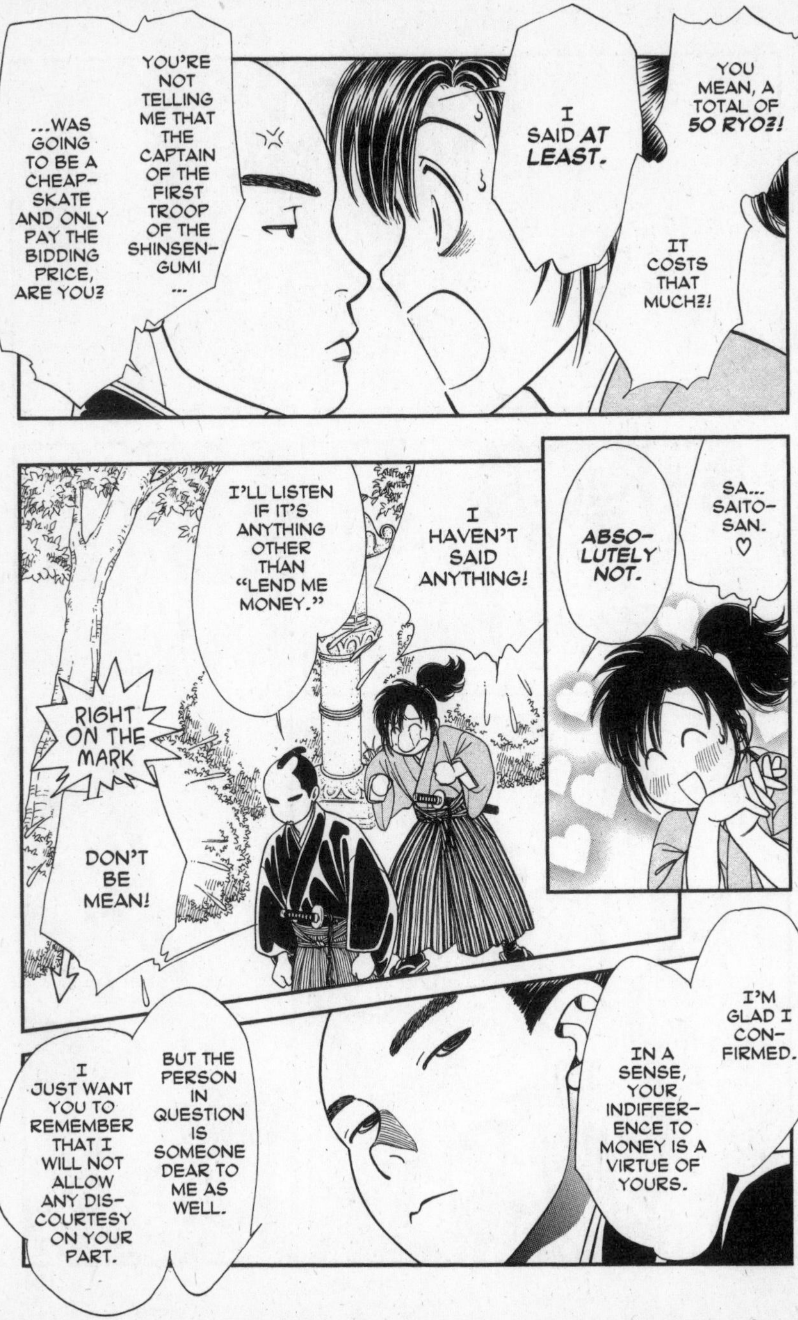
YOU MEAN, A TOTAL OF 50 RYO?!
I SAID AT LEAST.
IT COSTS THAT MUCH?!
YOU'RE NOT TELLING ME THAT THE CAPTAIN OF THE FIRST TROOP OF THE SHINSEN-GUMI ...
...WAS GOING TO BE A CHEAP-SKATE AND ONLY PAY THE BIDDING PRICE, ARE YOU?
SA... SAITO-SAN. ♡
ABSO-LUTELY NOT.
I'LL LISTEN IF IT'S ANYTHING OTHER THAN "LEND ME MONEY."
I HAVEN'T SAID ANYTHING!
RIGHT ON THE MARK
DON'T BE MEAN!
I'M GLAD I CON-FIRMED.
IN A SENSE, YOUR INDIFFER-ENCE TO MONEY IS A VIRTUE OF YOURS.
BUT THE PERSON IN QUESTION IS SOMEONE DEAR TO ME AS WELL.
I JUST WANT YOU TO REMEMBER THAT I WILL NOT ALLOW ANY DIS-COURTESY ON YOUR PART.

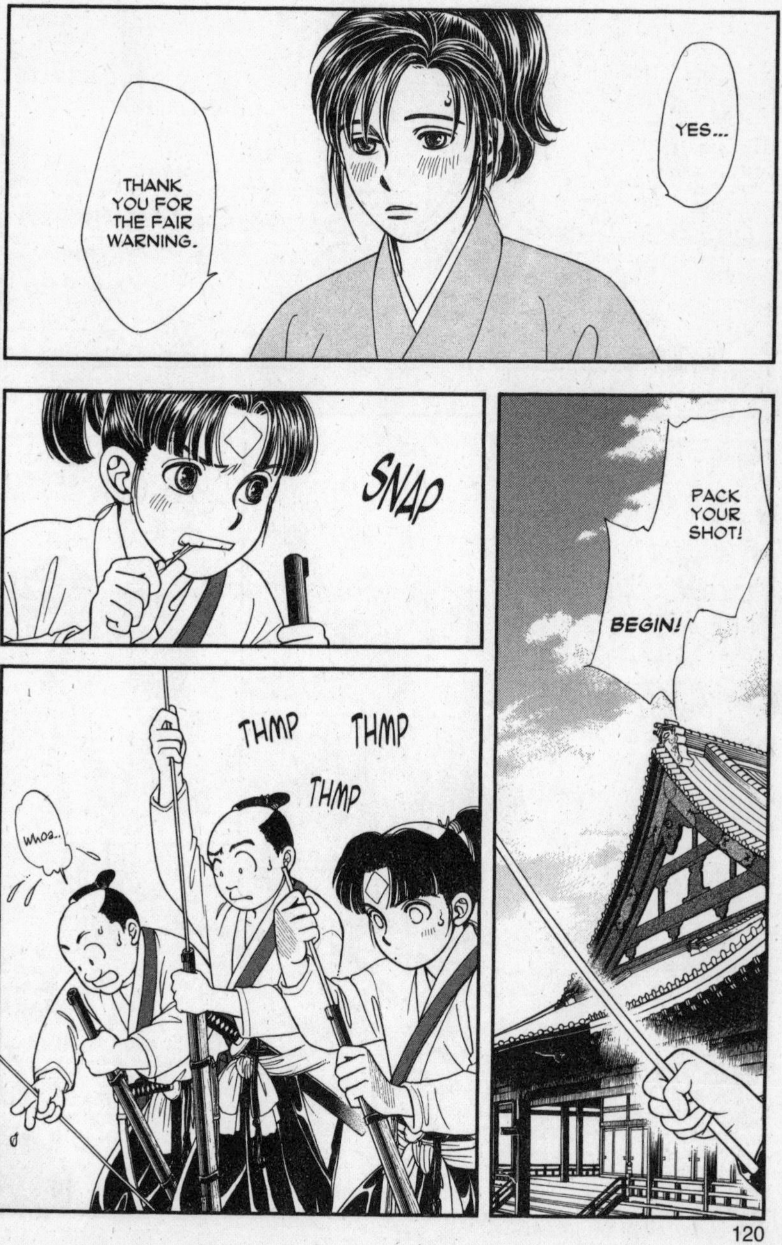
YES...
THANK YOU FOR THE FAIR WARNING.
PACK YOUR SHOT!
BEGIN!
SNAP
THMP
THMP
THMP
whoa..

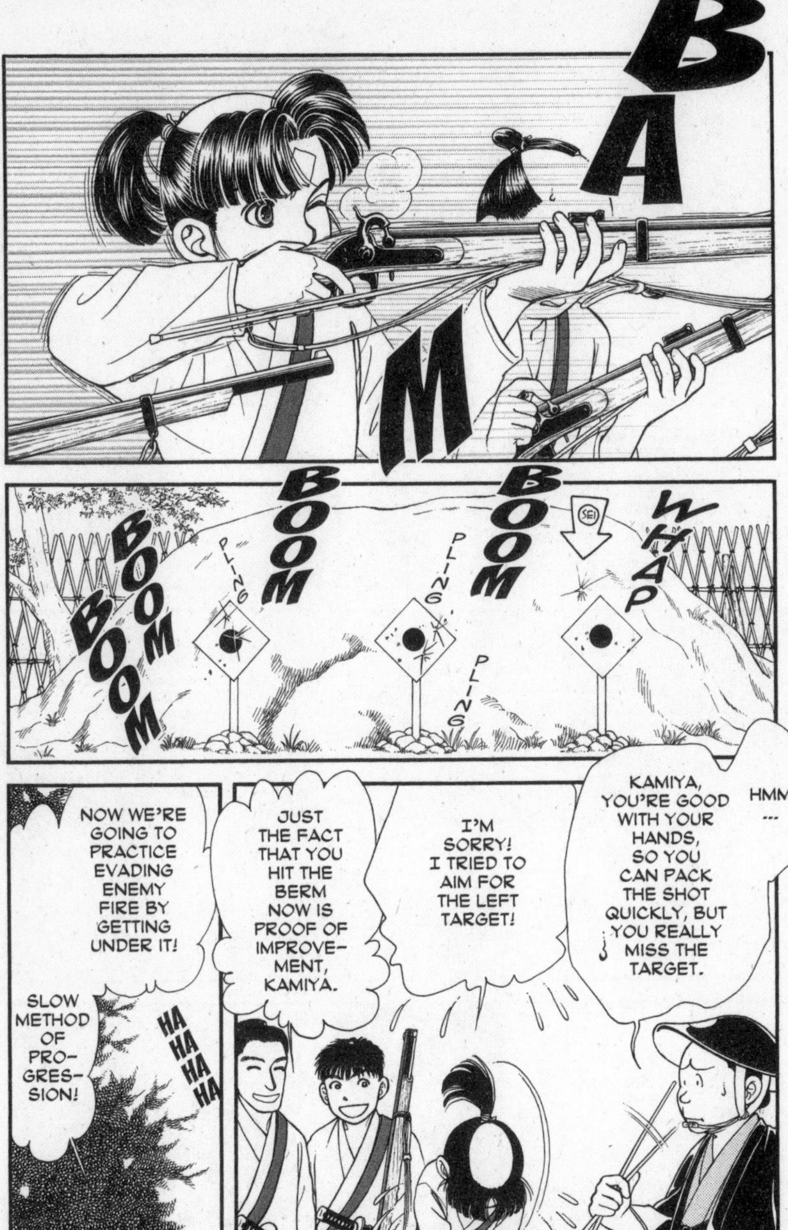
BAM
WHAP
SEI
BOOM
PLING
PLING
BOOM
PLING
BOOM
BOOM BOOM
HMM ...
KAMIYA, YOU'RE GOOD WITH YOUR HANDS, SO YOU CAN PACK THE SHOT QUICKLY, BUT YOU REALLY MISS THE TARGET.
I'M SORRY! I TRIED TO AIM FOR THE LEFT TARGET!
JUST THE FACT THAT YOU HIT THE BERM NOW IS PROOF OF IMPROVE-MENT, KAMIYA.
NOW WE'RE GOING TO PRACTICE EVADING ENEMY FIRE BY GETTING UNDER IT!
HA HA HA HA HA
SLOW METHOD OF PRO-GRES-SION!

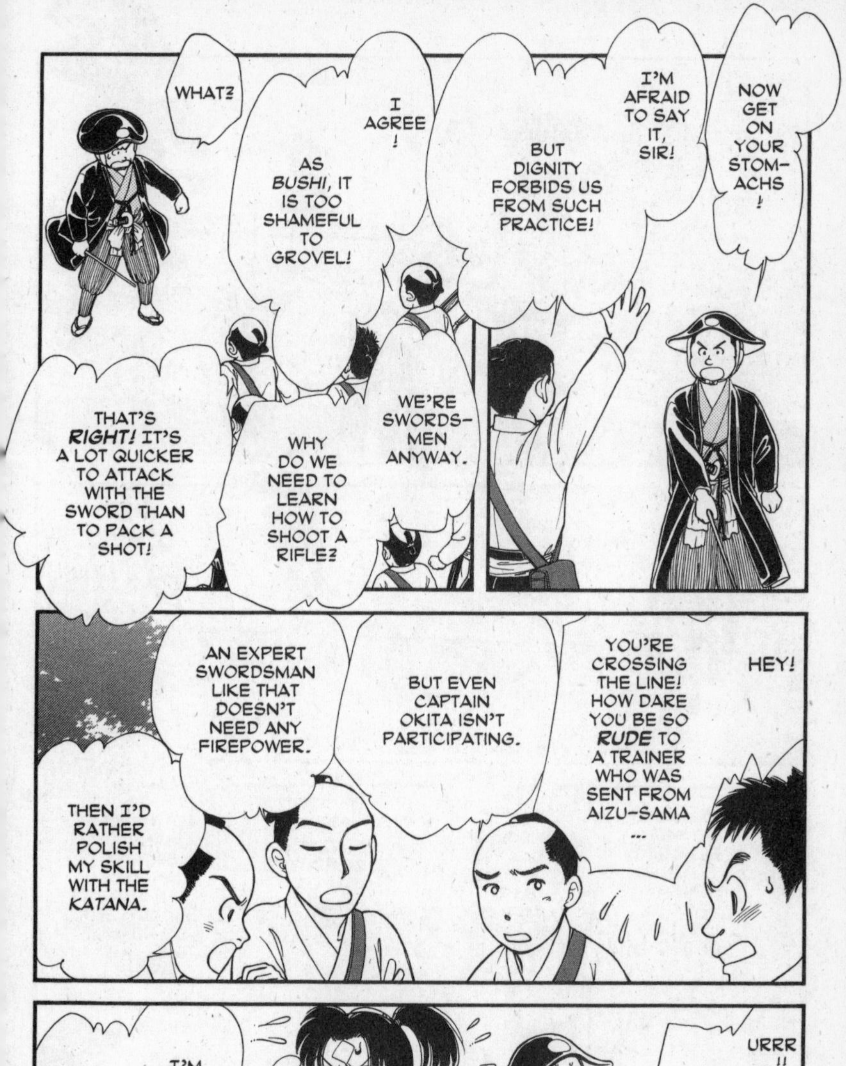
NOW GET ON YOUR STOMACHS!
I'M AFRAID TO SAY IT, SIR!
BUT DIGNITY FORBIDS US FROM SUCH PRACTICE!
I AGREE!
AS *BUSHI*, IT IS TOO SHAMEFUL TO GROVEL!
WHAT?
WE'RE SWORDSMEN ANYWAY.
WHY DO WE NEED TO LEARN HOW TO SHOOT A RIFLE?
THAT'S ***RIGHT!*** IT'S A LOT QUICKER TO ATTACK WITH THE SWORD THAN TO PACK A SHOT!
HEY!
YOU'RE CROSSING THE LINE! HOW DARE YOU BE SO ***RUDE*** TO A TRAINER WHO WAS SENT FROM AIZU-SAMA...
BUT EVEN CAPTAIN OKITA ISN'T PARTICIPATING.
AN EXPERT SWORDSMAN LIKE THAT DOESN'T NEED ANY FIREPOWER.
THEN I'D RATHER POLISH MY SKILL WITH THE *KATANA*.
URRR...!!
W-WHERE IS OKITA-DONO?!
I'M TERRIBLY SORRY!
I'LL GO AND FETCH HIM!

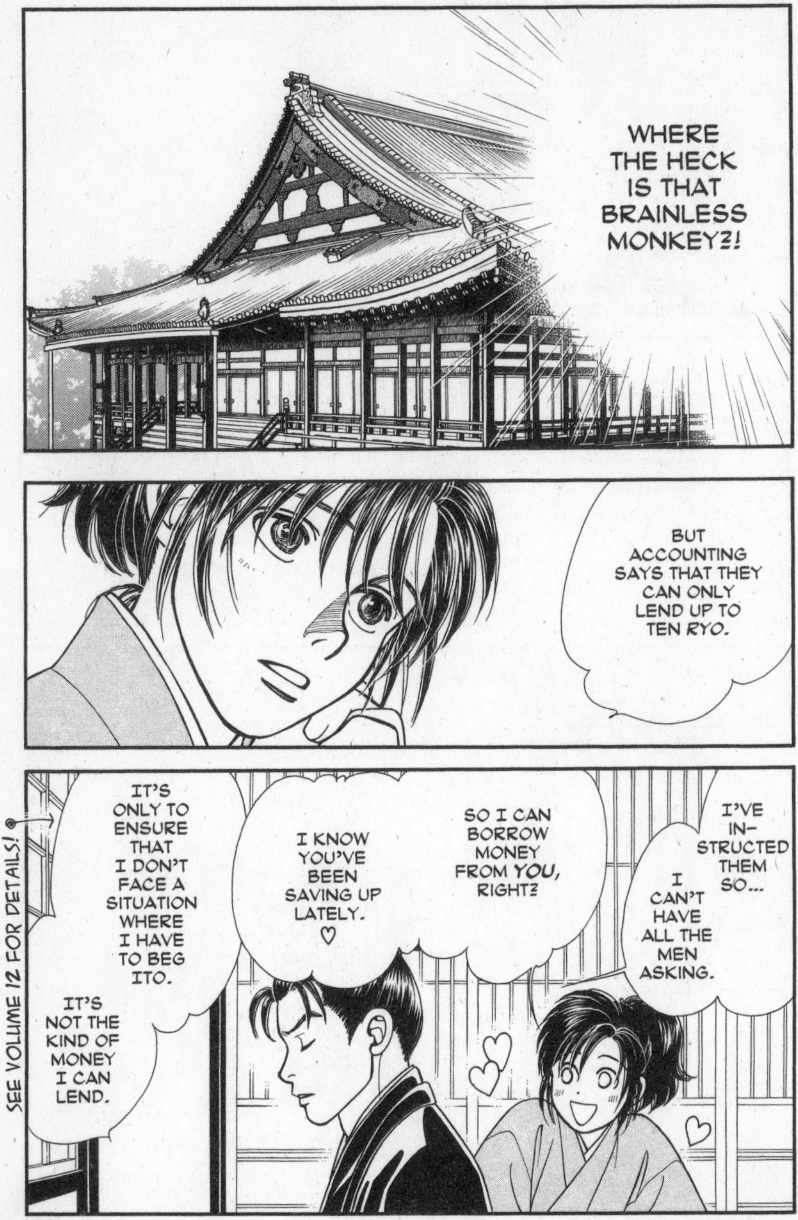

WHERE THE HECK IS THAT BRAINLESS MONKEY?!
BUT ACCOUNTING SAYS THAT THEY CAN ONLY LEND UP TO TEN *RYO*.
I'VE IN-STRUCTED THEM SO...
I CAN'T HAVE ALL THE MEN ASKING.
SO I CAN BORROW MONEY FROM *YOU*, RIGHT?
I KNOW YOU'VE BEEN SAVING UP LATELY. ♡
IT'S ONLY TO ENSURE THAT I DON'T FACE A SITUATION WHERE I HAVE TO BEG ITO.
IT'S NOT THE KIND OF MONEY I CAN LEND.
SEE VOLUME 12 FOR DETAILS!

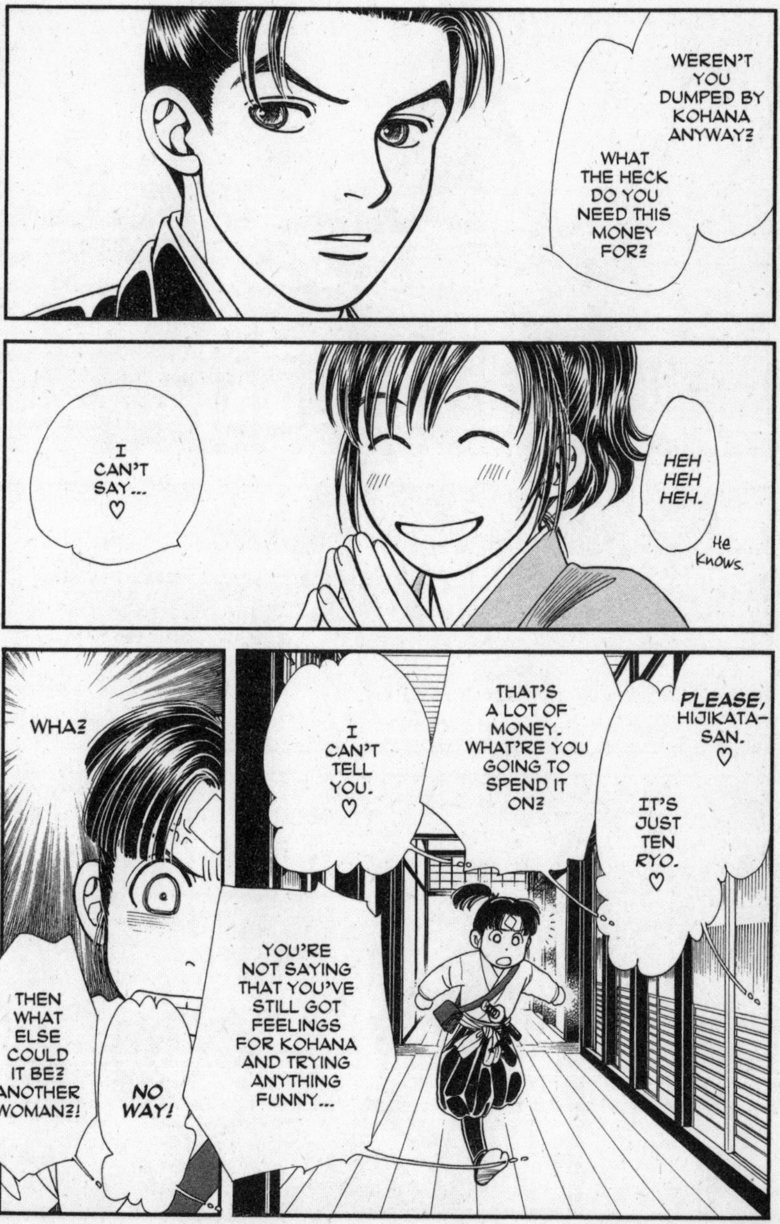
WEREN'T YOU DUMPED BY KOHANA ANYWAY?
WHAT THE HECK DO YOU NEED THIS MONEY FOR?
HEH HEH HEH.
He knows.
I CAN'T SAY... ♡
PLEASE, HIJIKATA-SAN. ♡
IT'S JUST TEN RYO. ♡
THAT'S A LOT OF MONEY. WHAT'RE YOU GOING TO SPEND IT ON?
I CAN'T TELL YOU. ♡
YOU'RE NOT SAYING THAT YOU'VE STILL GOT FEELINGS FOR KOHANA AND TRYING ANYTHING FUNNY...
WHA?
NO WAY!
THEN WHAT ELSE COULD IT BE? ANOTHER WOMAN?!

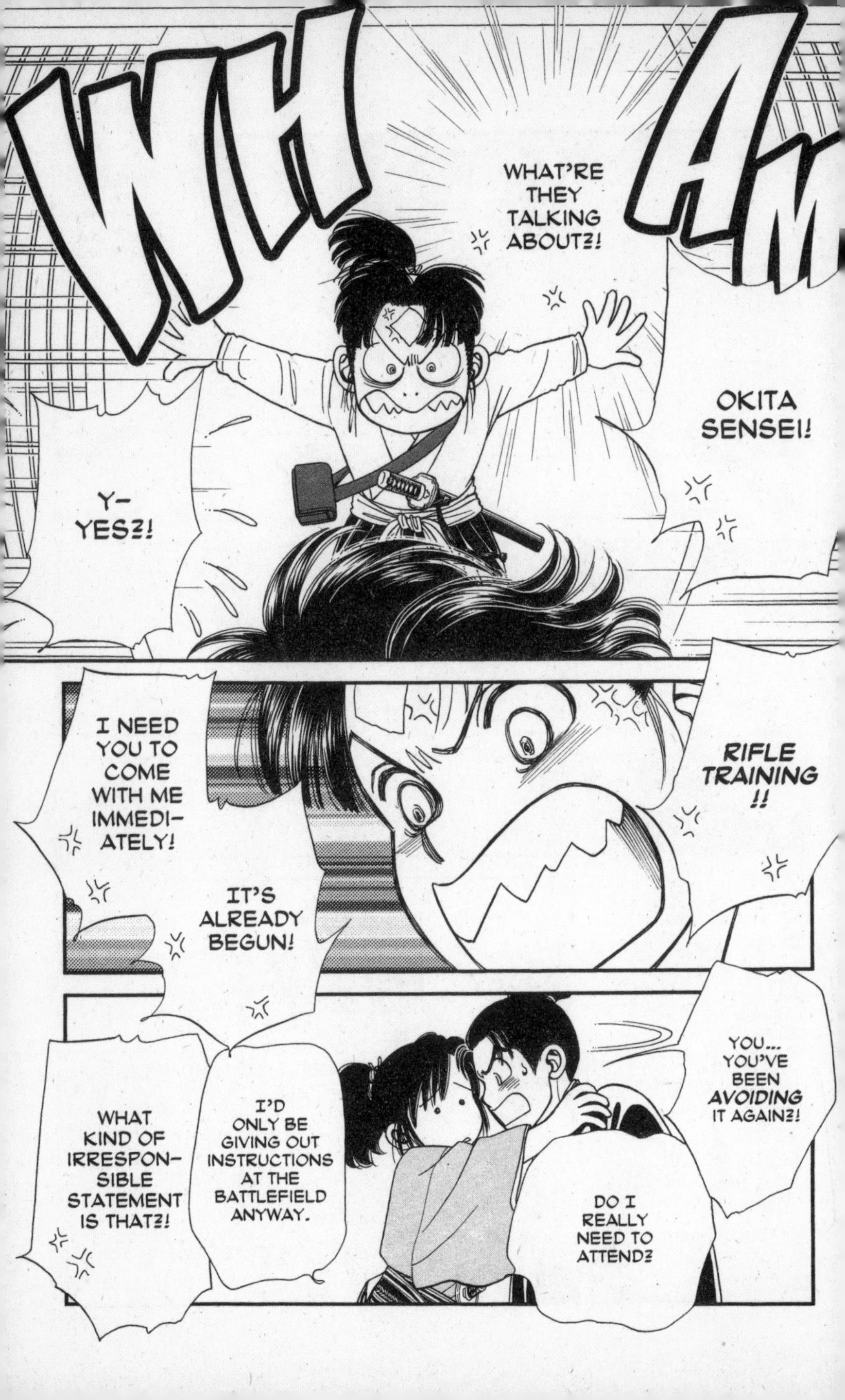
WHA
WHAT'RE THEY TALKING ABOUT?!
OKITA SENSEI!
Y-YES?!
RIFLE TRAINING !!
I NEED YOU TO COME WITH ME IMMEDI-ATELY!
IT'S ALREADY BEGUN!
YOU... YOU'VE BEEN AVOIDING IT AGAIN?!
DO I REALLY NEED TO ATTEND?
I'D ONLY BE GIVING OUT INSTRUCTIONS AT THE BATTLEFIELD ANYWAY.
WHAT KIND OF IRRESPON-SIBLE STATEMENT IS THAT?!

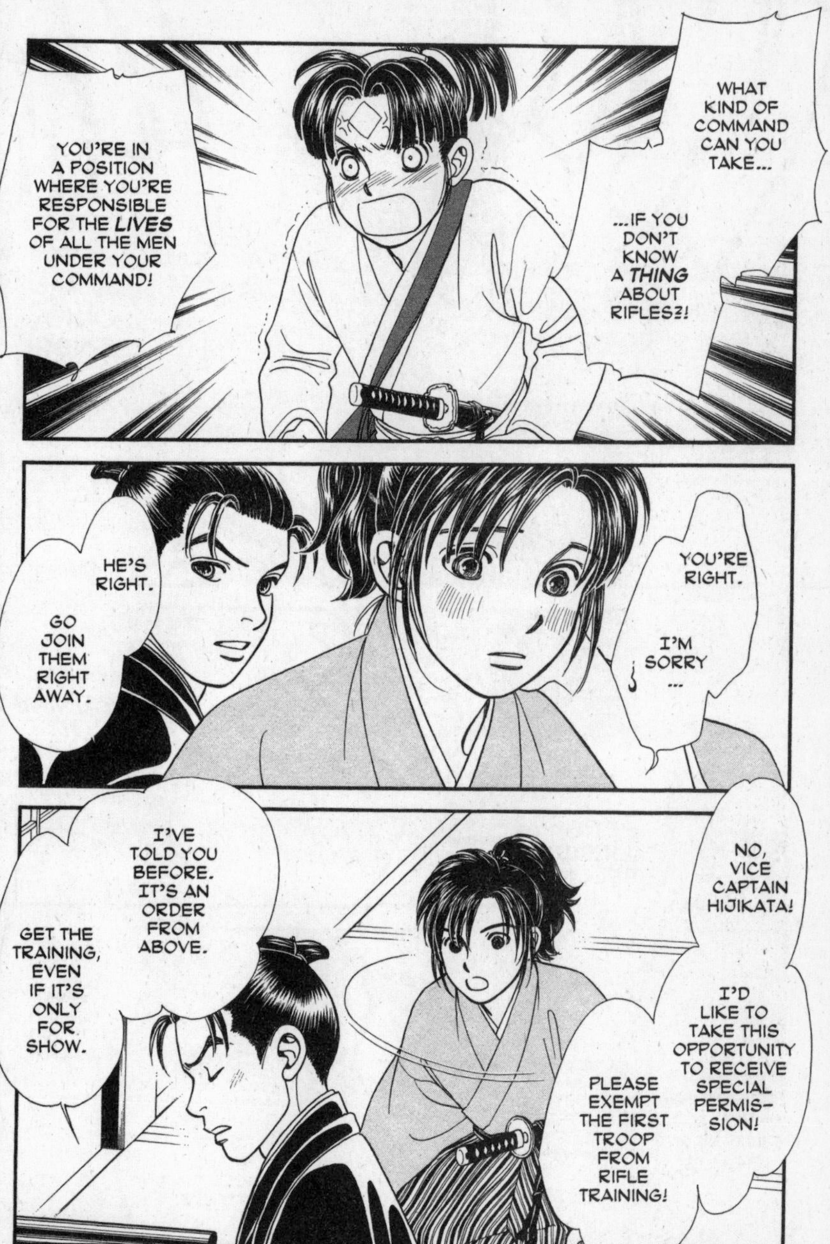
WHAT KIND OF COMMAND CAN YOU TAKE...
...IF YOU DON'T KNOW A *THING* ABOUT RIFLES?!
YOU'RE IN A POSITION WHERE YOU'RE RESPONSIBLE FOR THE *LIVES* OF ALL THE MEN UNDER YOUR COMMAND!
YOU'RE RIGHT.
I'M SORRY...
HE'S RIGHT.
GO JOIN THEM RIGHT AWAY.
NO, VICE CAPTAIN HIJIKATA!
I'D LIKE TO TAKE THIS OPPORTUNITY TO RECEIVE SPECIAL PERMIS-SION!
PLEASE EXEMPT THE FIRST TROOP FROM RIFLE TRAINING!
I'VE TOLD YOU BEFORE. IT'S AN ORDER FROM ABOVE.
GET THE TRAINING, EVEN IF IT'S ONLY FOR SHOW.

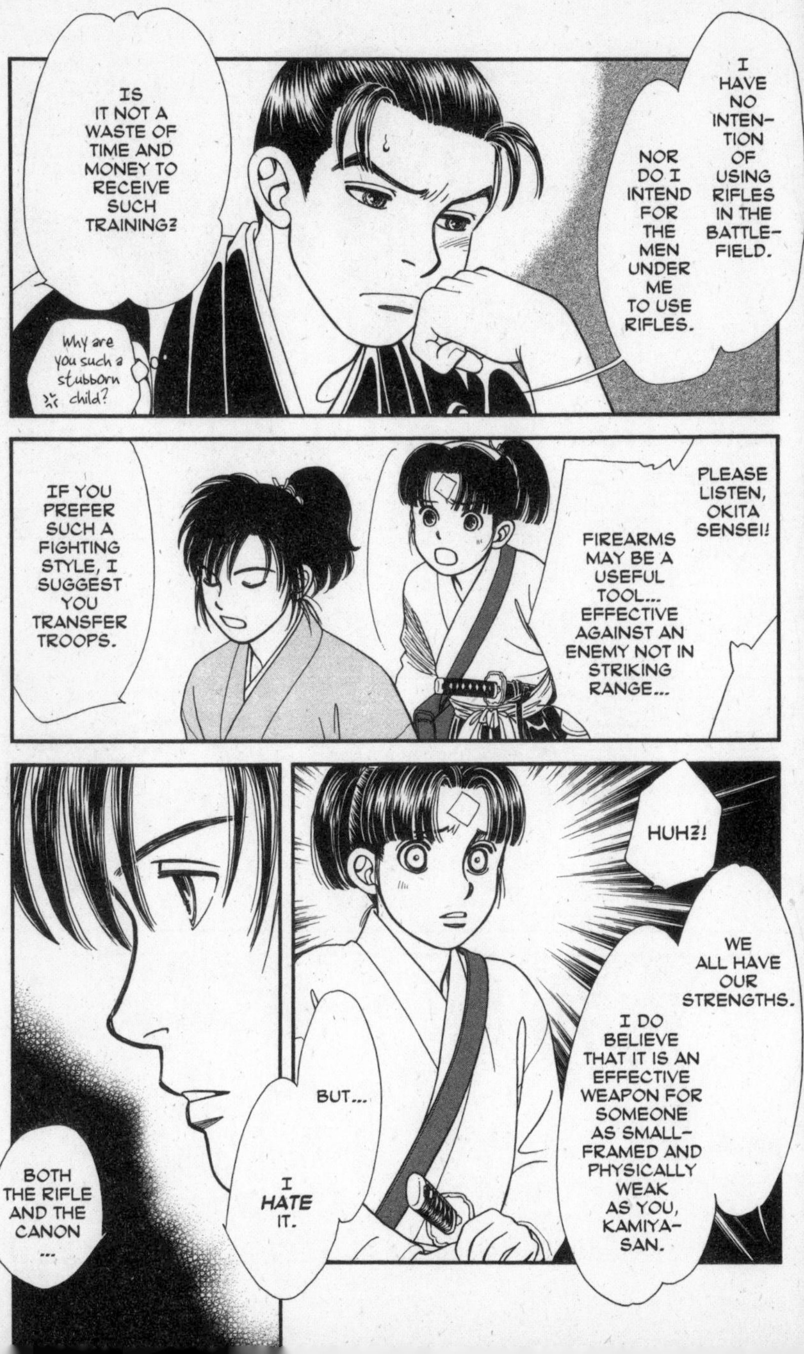
I HAVE NO INTENTION OF USING RIFLES IN THE BATTLEFIELD.
NOR DO I INTEND FOR THE MEN UNDER ME TO USE RIFLES.
IS IT NOT A WASTE OF TIME AND MONEY TO RECEIVE SUCH TRAINING?
Why are you such a stubborn child?
PLEASE LISTEN, OKITA SENSEI!
FIREARMS MAY BE A USEFUL TOOL... EFFECTIVE AGAINST AN ENEMY NOT IN STRIKING RANGE...
IF YOU PREFER SUCH A FIGHTING STYLE, I SUGGEST YOU TRANSFER TROOPS.
HUH?!
WE ALL HAVE OUR STRENGTHS.
I DO BELIEVE THAT IT IS AN EFFECTIVE WEAPON FOR SOMEONE AS SMALL-FRAMED AND PHYSICALLY WEAK AS YOU, KAMIYA-SAN.
BUT...
I *HATE* IT.
BOTH THE RIFLE AND THE CANON ...

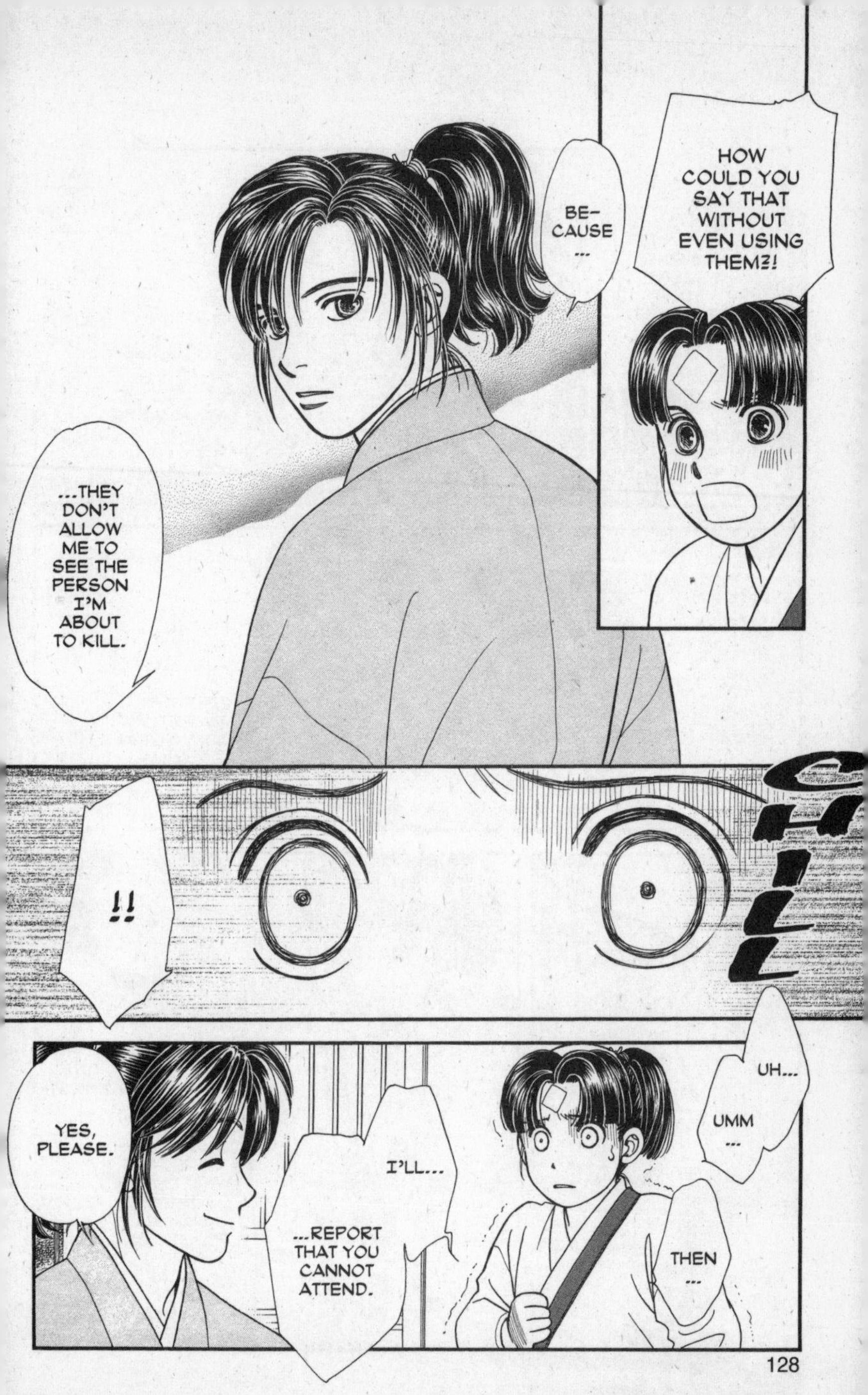
HOW COULD YOU SAY THAT WITHOUT EVEN USING THEM?!
BE-CAUSE...
...THEY DON'T ALLOW ME TO SEE THE PERSON I'M ABOUT TO KILL.
CHILL
!!
UH...
UMM...
THEN...
I'LL...
...REPORT THAT YOU CANNOT ATTEND.
YES, PLEASE.

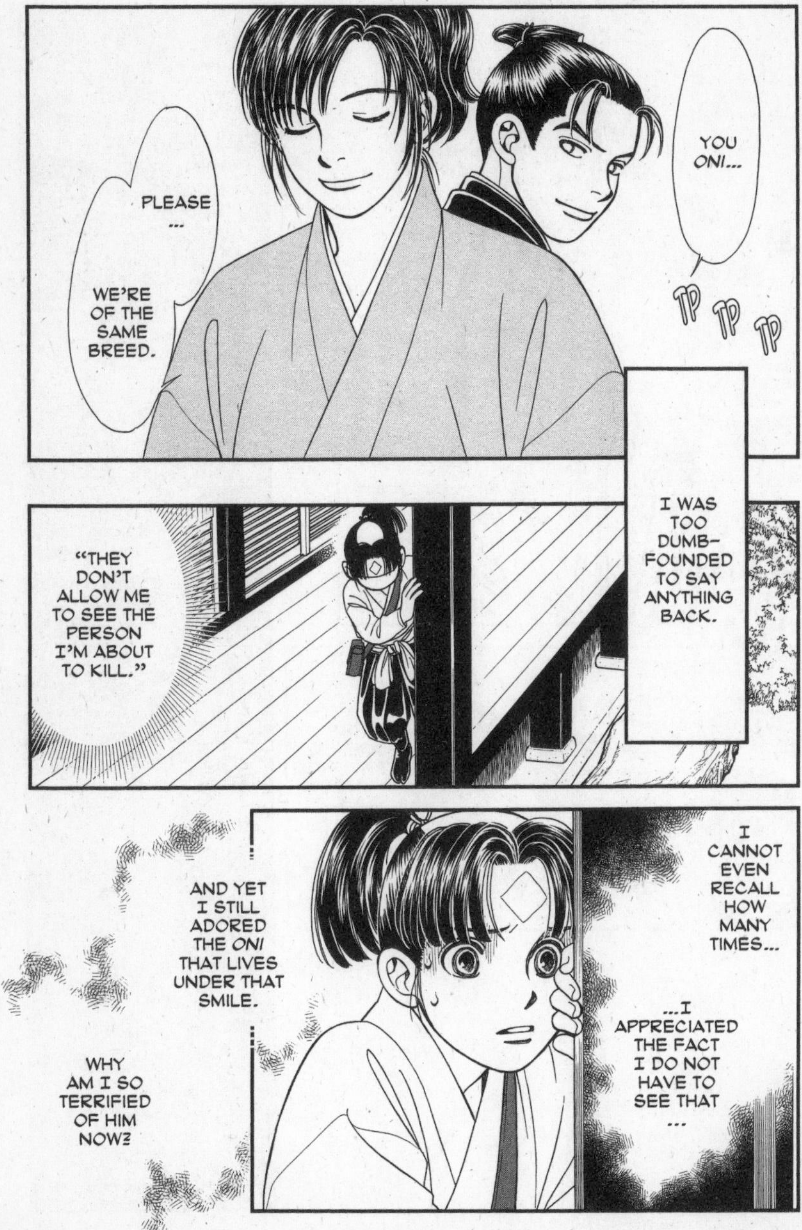
YOU *ONI*...
TP TP TP
PLEASE ...
WE'RE OF THE SAME BREED.
I WAS TOO DUMB-FOUNDED TO SAY ANYTHING BACK.
"THEY DON'T ALLOW ME TO SEE THE PERSON I'M ABOUT TO KILL."
I CANNOT EVEN RECALL HOW MANY TIMES...
...I APPRECIATED THE FACT I DO NOT HAVE TO SEE THAT ...
AND YET I STILL ADORED THE *ONI* THAT LIVES UNDER THAT SMILE.
WHY AM I SO TERRIFIED OF HIM NOW?

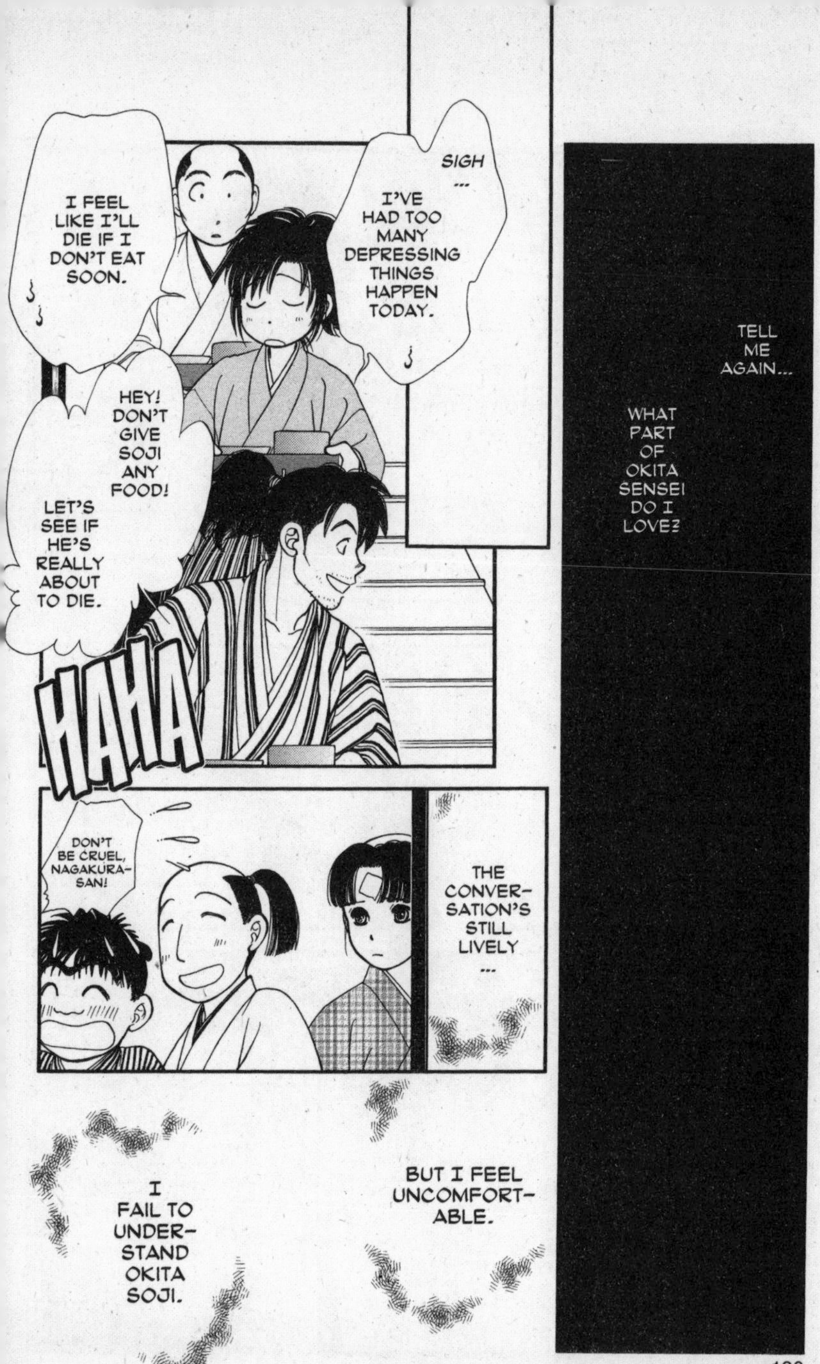
SIGH ... I'VE HAD TOO MANY DEPRESSING THINGS HAPPEN TODAY.
I FEEL LIKE I'LL DIE IF I DON'T EAT SOON.
HEY! DON'T GIVE SOJI ANY FOOD!
LET'S SEE IF HE'S REALLY ABOUT TO DIE.
HAHA
THE CONVERSATION'S STILL LIVELY ...
DON'T BE CRUEL, NAGAKURA-SAN!
BUT I FEEL UNCOMFORTABLE.
I FAIL TO UNDERSTAND OKITA SOJI.
TELL ME AGAIN...
WHAT PART OF OKITA SENSEI DO I LOVE?

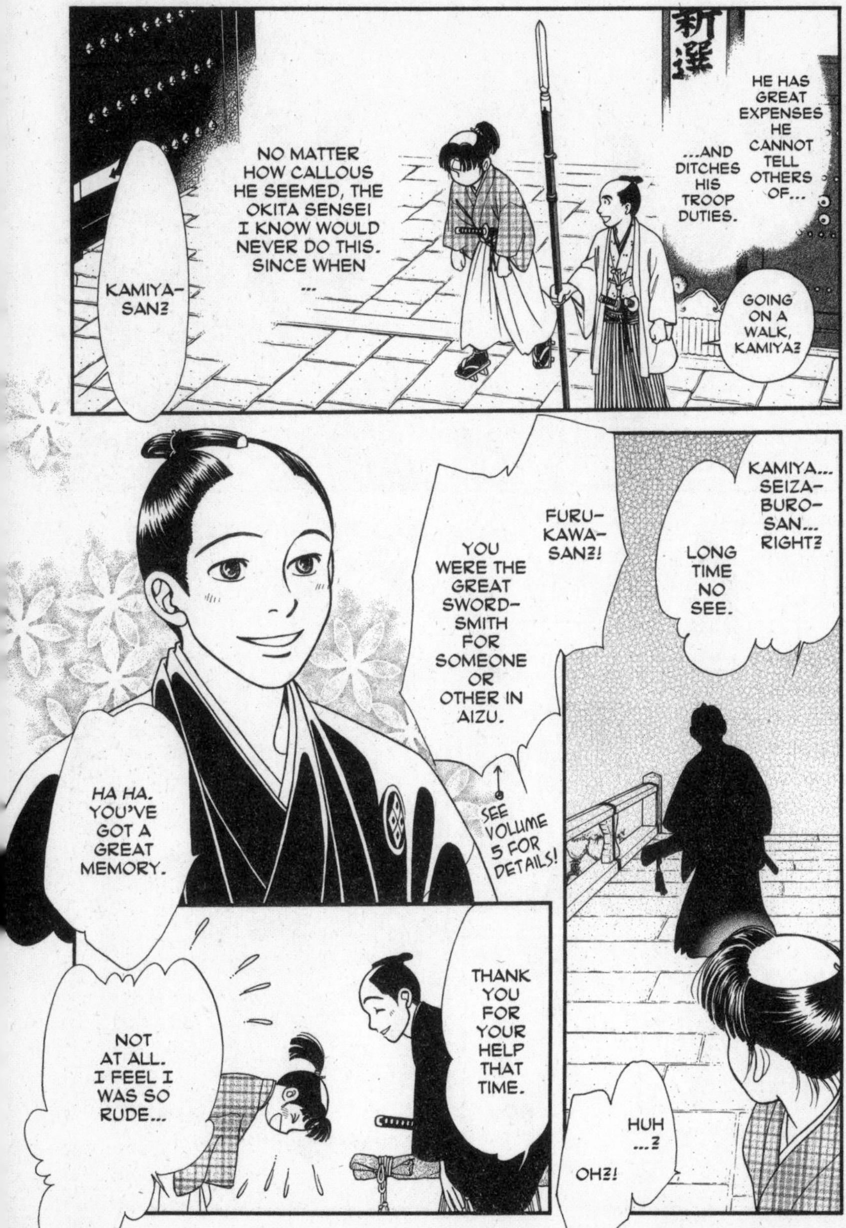
HE HAS GREAT EXPENSES HE CANNOT TELL OTHERS OF...
...AND DITCHES HIS TROOP DUTIES.
GOING ON A WALK, KAMIYA?
NO MATTER HOW CALLOUS HE SEEMED, THE OKITA SENSEI I KNOW WOULD NEVER DO THIS. SINCE WHEN ...
KAMIYA-SAN?
KAMIYA... SEIZA-BURO-SAN... RIGHT?
LONG TIME NO SEE.
HUH ...?
OH?!
FURU-KAWA-SAN?!
YOU WERE THE GREAT SWORD-SMITH FOR SOMEONE OR OTHER IN AIZU.
SEE VOLUME 5 FOR DETAILS!
HA HA. YOU'VE GOT A GREAT MEMORY.
THANK YOU FOR YOUR HELP THAT TIME.
NOT AT ALL. I FEEL I WAS SO RUDE...

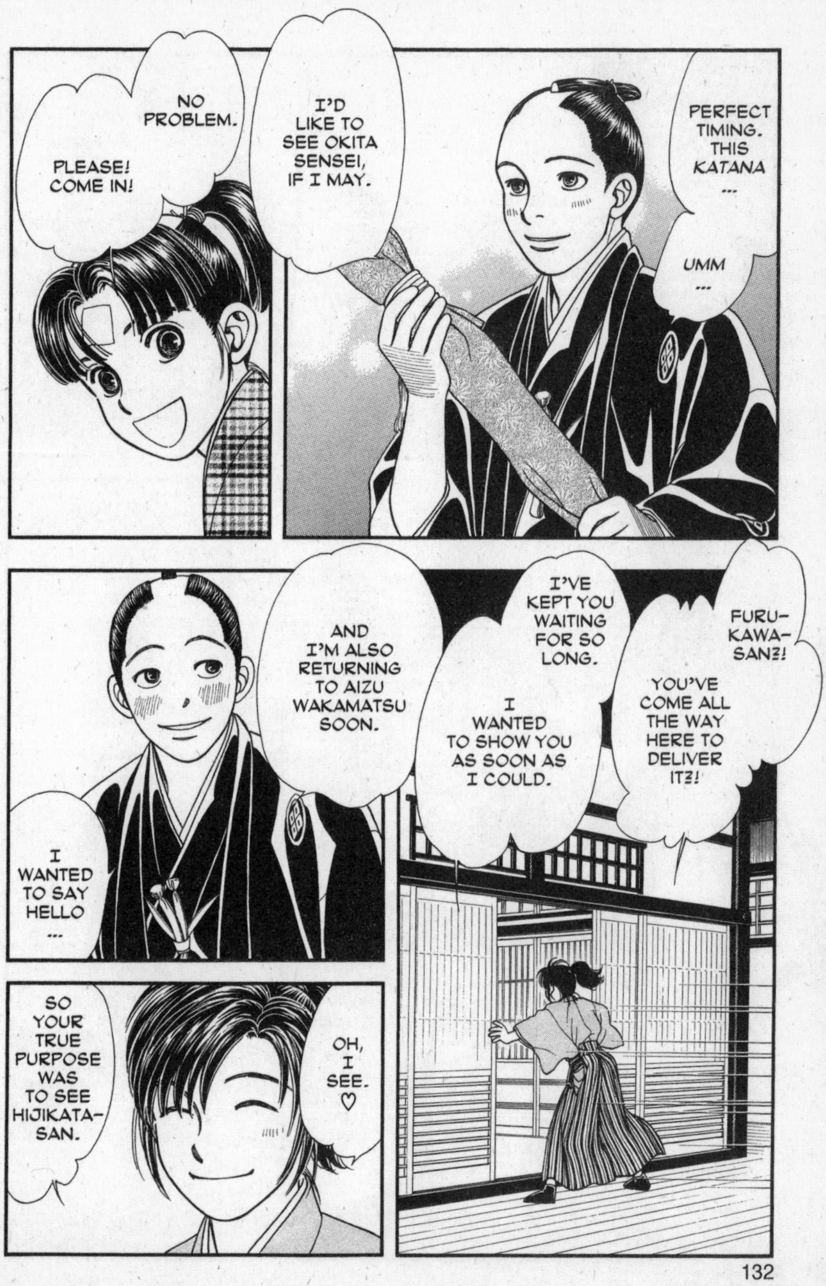
PERFECT TIMING. THIS KATANA ...
UMM ...
I'D LIKE TO SEE OKITA SENSEI, IF I MAY.
NO PROBLEM.
PLEASE! COME IN!
FURU-KAWA-SAN?!
YOU'VE COME ALL THE WAY HERE TO DELIVER IT?!
I'VE KEPT YOU WAITING FOR SO LONG.
I WANTED TO SHOW YOU AS SOON AS I COULD.
AND I'M ALSO RETURNING TO AIZU WAKAMATSU SOON.
I WANTED TO SAY HELLO ...
OH, I SEE. ♡
SO YOUR TRUE PURPOSE WAS TO SEE HIJIKATA-SAN.

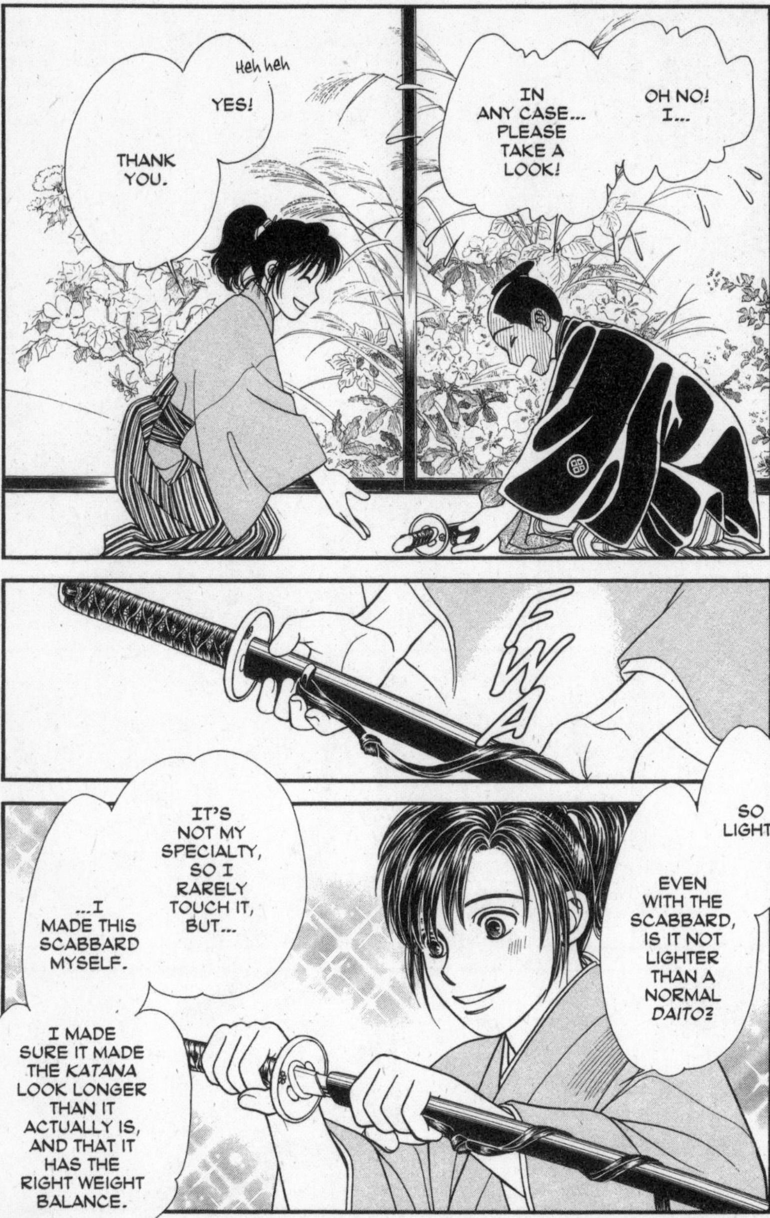
OH NO! I...
IN ANY CASE... PLEASE TAKE A LOOK!
Heh heh
YES!
THANK YOU.
FWA
SO LIGHT!
EVEN WITH THE SCABBARD, IS IT NOT LIGHTER THAN A NORMAL *DAITO*?
IT'S NOT MY SPECIALTY, SO I RARELY TOUCH IT, BUT...
...I MADE THIS SCABBARD MYSELF.
I MADE SURE IT MADE THE *KATANA* LOOK LONGER THAN IT ACTUALLY IS, AND THAT IT HAS THE RIGHT WEIGHT BALANCE.

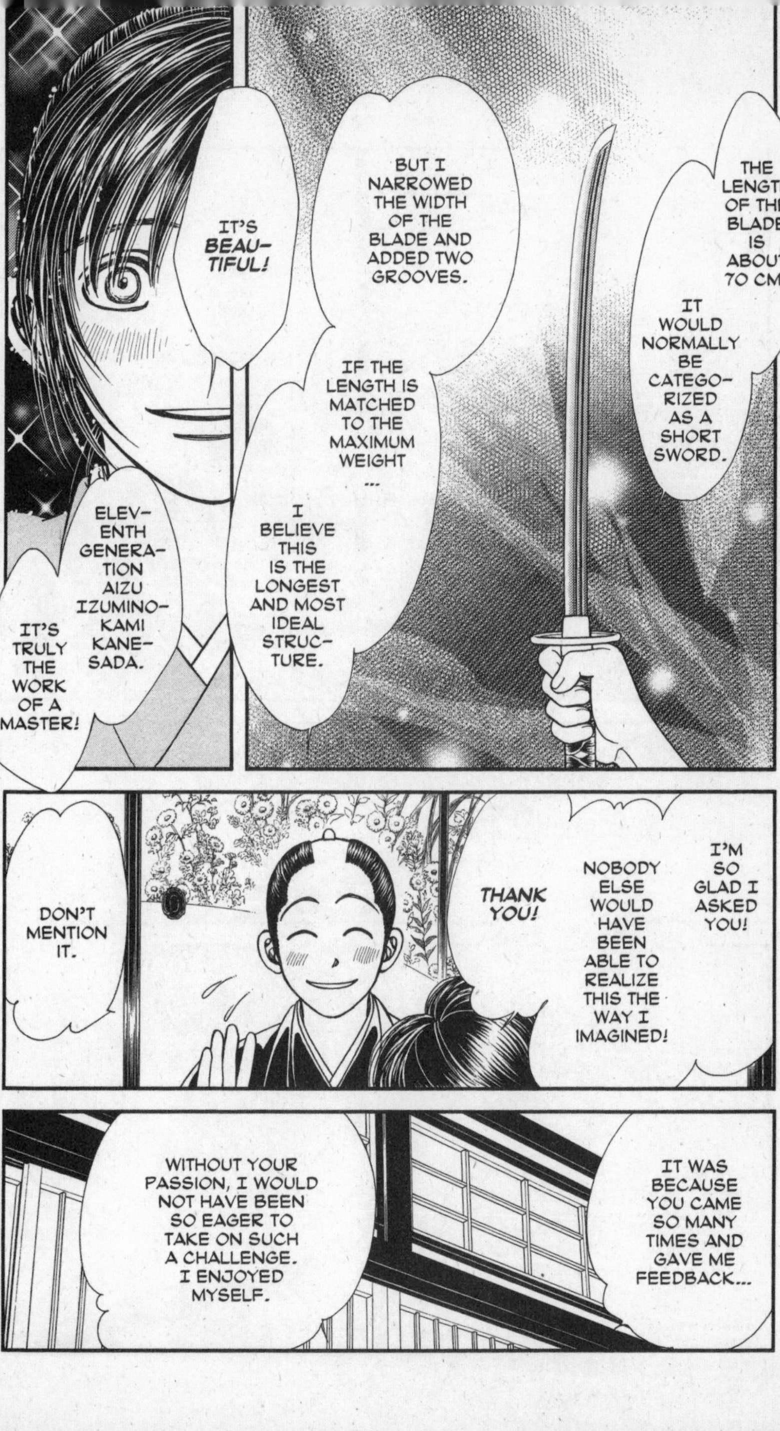
THE LENGTH OF THE BLADE IS ABOUT 70 CM.
IT WOULD NORMALLY BE CATEGO-RIZED AS A SHORT SWORD.
BUT I NARROWED THE WIDTH OF THE BLADE AND ADDED TWO GROOVES.
IF THE LENGTH IS MATCHED TO THE MAXIMUM WEIGHT ...
I BELIEVE THIS IS THE LONGEST AND MOST IDEAL STRUC-TURE.
IT'S BEAU-TIFUL!
ELEV-ENTH GENERA-TION AIZU IZUMINO-KAMI KANE-SADA.
IT'S TRULY THE WORK OF A MASTER!
I'M SO GLAD I ASKED YOU!
NOBODY ELSE WOULD HAVE BEEN ABLE TO REALIZE THIS THE WAY I IMAGINED!
THANK YOU!
DON'T MENTION IT.
IT WAS BECAUSE YOU CAME SO MANY TIMES AND GAVE ME FEEDBACK...
WITHOUT YOUR PASSION, I WOULD NOT HAVE BEEN SO EAGER TO TAKE ON SUCH A CHALLENGE. I ENJOYED MYSELF.

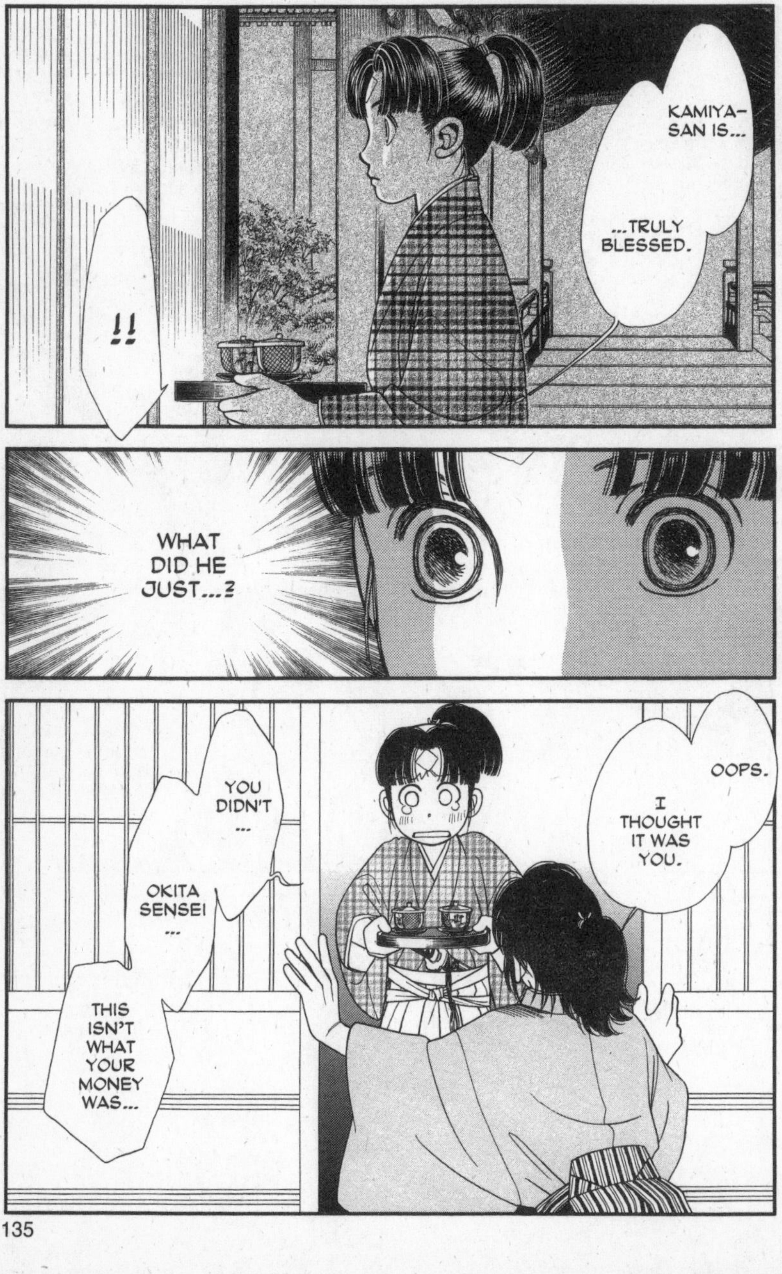
KAMIYA-SAN IS...
...TRULY BLESSED.
!!
WHAT DID HE JUST...?
OOPS.
I THOUGHT IT WAS YOU.
YOU DIDN'T ...
OKITA SENSEI ...
THIS ISN'T WHAT YOUR MONEY WAS...

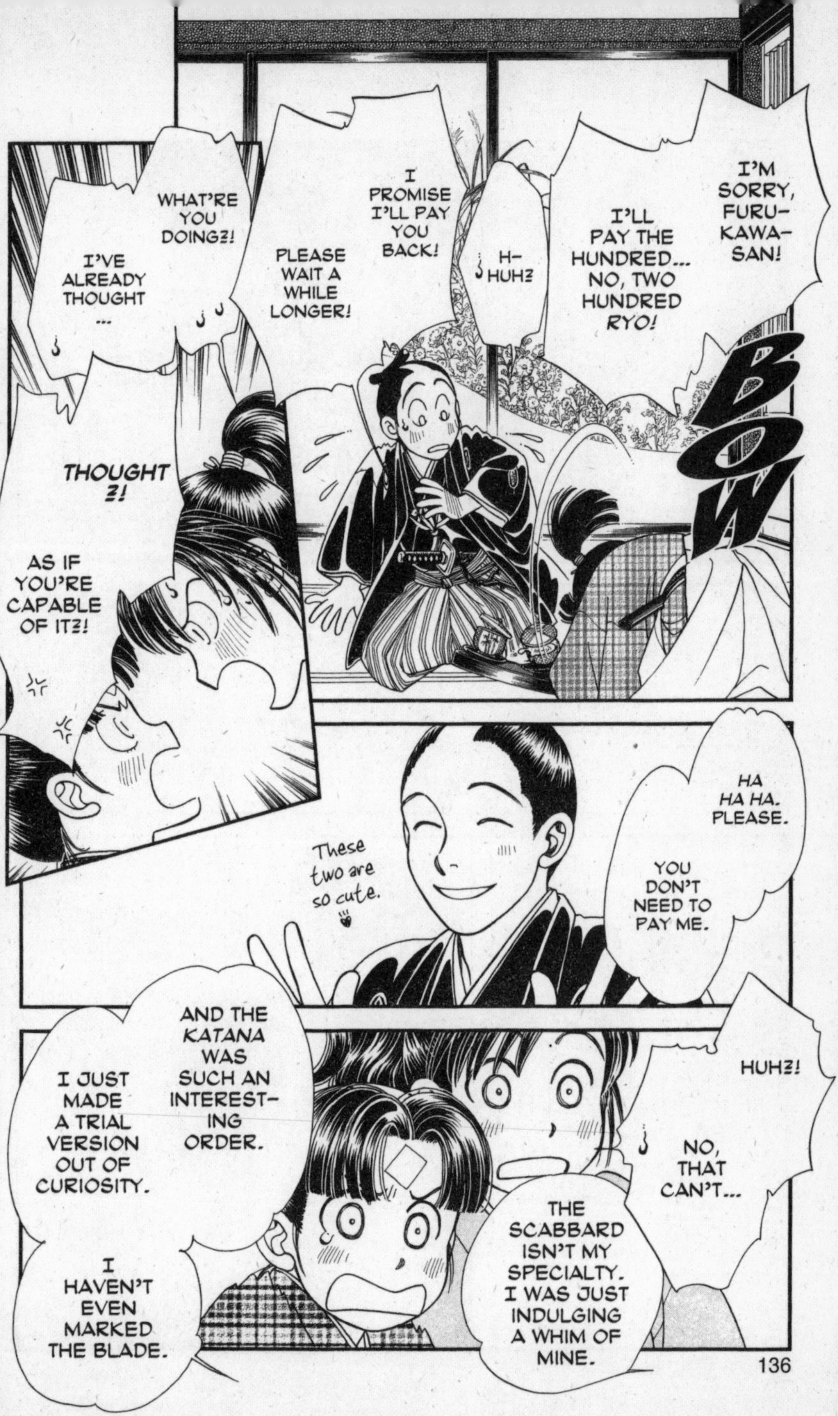
I'M SORRY, FURU-KAWA-SAN!
I'LL PAY THE HUNDRED... NO, TWO HUNDRED *RYO!*
BOW
H-HUH?
I PROMISE I'LL PAY YOU BACK!
PLEASE WAIT A WHILE LONGER!
WHAT'RE YOU DOING?!
I'VE ALREADY THOUGHT...
THOUGHT?!
AS IF YOU'RE CAPABLE OF IT?!
HA HA HA. PLEASE.
YOU DON'T NEED TO PAY ME.
These two are so cute.
HUH?!
NO, THAT CAN'T...
THE SCABBARD ISN'T MY SPECIALTY. I WAS JUST INDULGING A WHIM OF MINE.
AND THE *KATANA* WAS SUCH AN INTERESTING ORDER.
I JUST MADE A TRIAL VERSION OUT OF CURIOSITY.
I HAVEN'T EVEN MARKED THE BLADE.

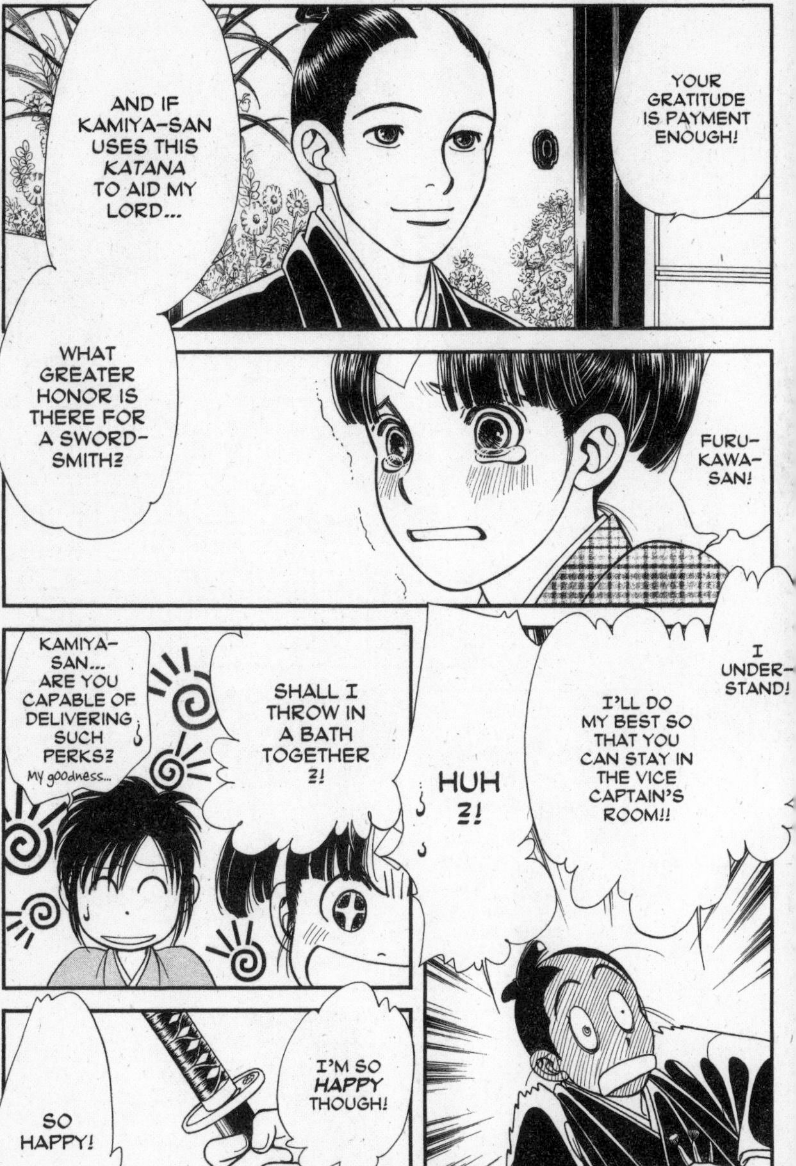
YOUR GRATITUDE IS PAYMENT ENOUGH!
AND IF KAMIYA-SAN USES THIS *KATANA* TO AID MY LORD...
WHAT GREATER HONOR IS THERE FOR A SWORD-SMITH?
FURU-KAWA-SAN!
I UNDER-STAND!
I'LL DO MY BEST SO THAT YOU CAN STAY IN THE VICE CAPTAIN'S ROOM!!
HUH ?!
SHALL I THROW IN A BATH TOGETHER ?!
KAMIYA-SAN... ARE YOU CAPABLE OF DELIVERING SUCH PERKS?
My goodness...
I'M SO *HAPPY* THOUGH!
SO HAPPY!

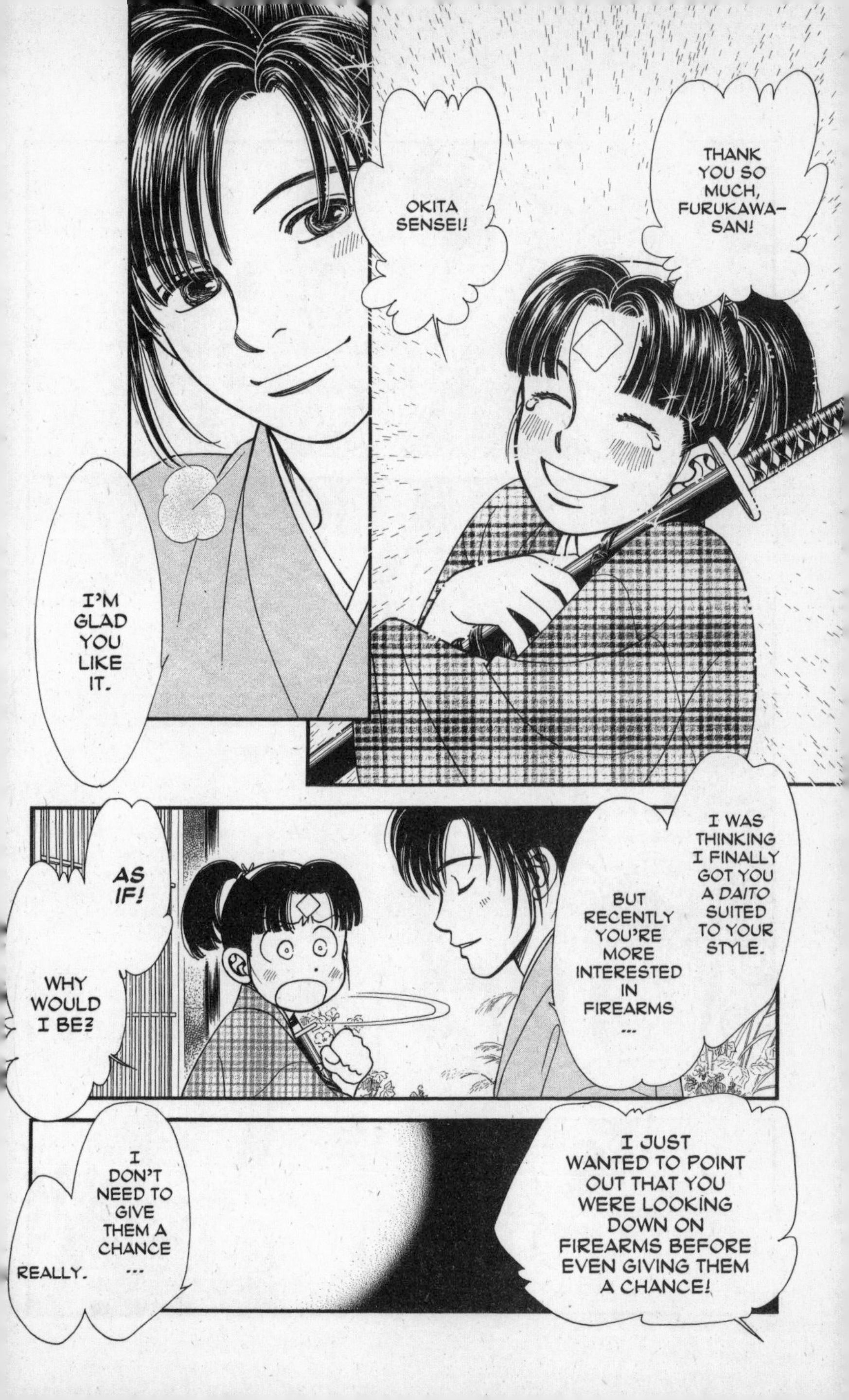
THANK YOU SO MUCH, FURUKAWA-SAN!
OKITA SENSEI!
I'M GLAD YOU LIKE IT.
I WAS THINKING I FINALLY GOT YOU A *DAITO* SUITED TO YOUR STYLE.
BUT RECENTLY YOU'RE MORE INTERESTED IN FIREARMS ...
AS IF!
WHY WOULD I BE?
I JUST WANTED TO POINT OUT THAT YOU WERE LOOKING DOWN ON FIREARMS BEFORE EVEN GIVING THEM A CHANCE!
I DON'T NEED TO GIVE THEM A CHANCE ... REALLY.

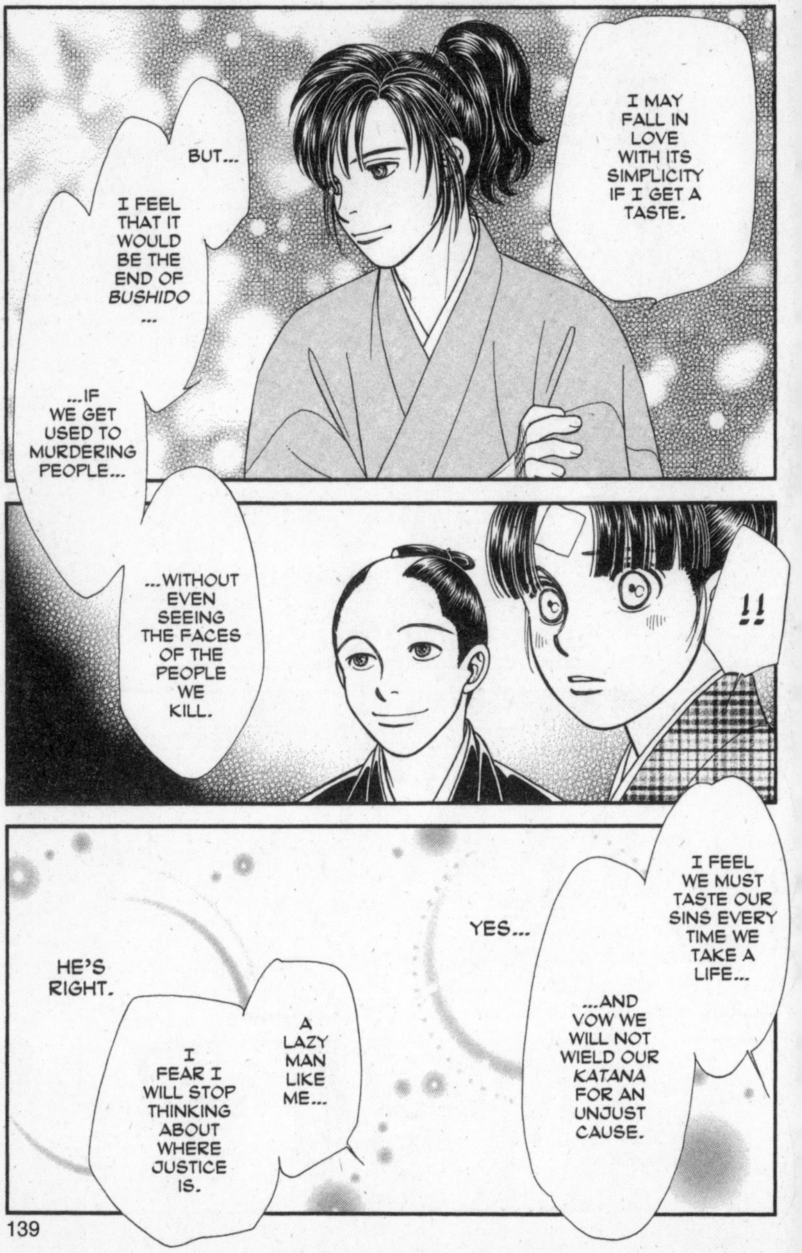
I MAY FALL IN LOVE WITH ITS SIMPLICITY IF I GET A TASTE.
BUT...
I FEEL THAT IT WOULD BE THE END OF *BUSHIDO* ...
...IF WE GET USED TO MURDERING PEOPLE...
!!
...WITHOUT EVEN SEEING THE FACES OF THE PEOPLE WE KILL.
I FEEL WE MUST TASTE OUR SINS EVERY TIME WE TAKE A LIFE...
...AND VOW WE WILL NOT WIELD OUR *KATANA* FOR AN UNJUST CAUSE.
YES...
A LAZY MAN LIKE ME...
I FEAR I WILL STOP THINKING ABOUT WHERE JUSTICE IS.
HE'S RIGHT.

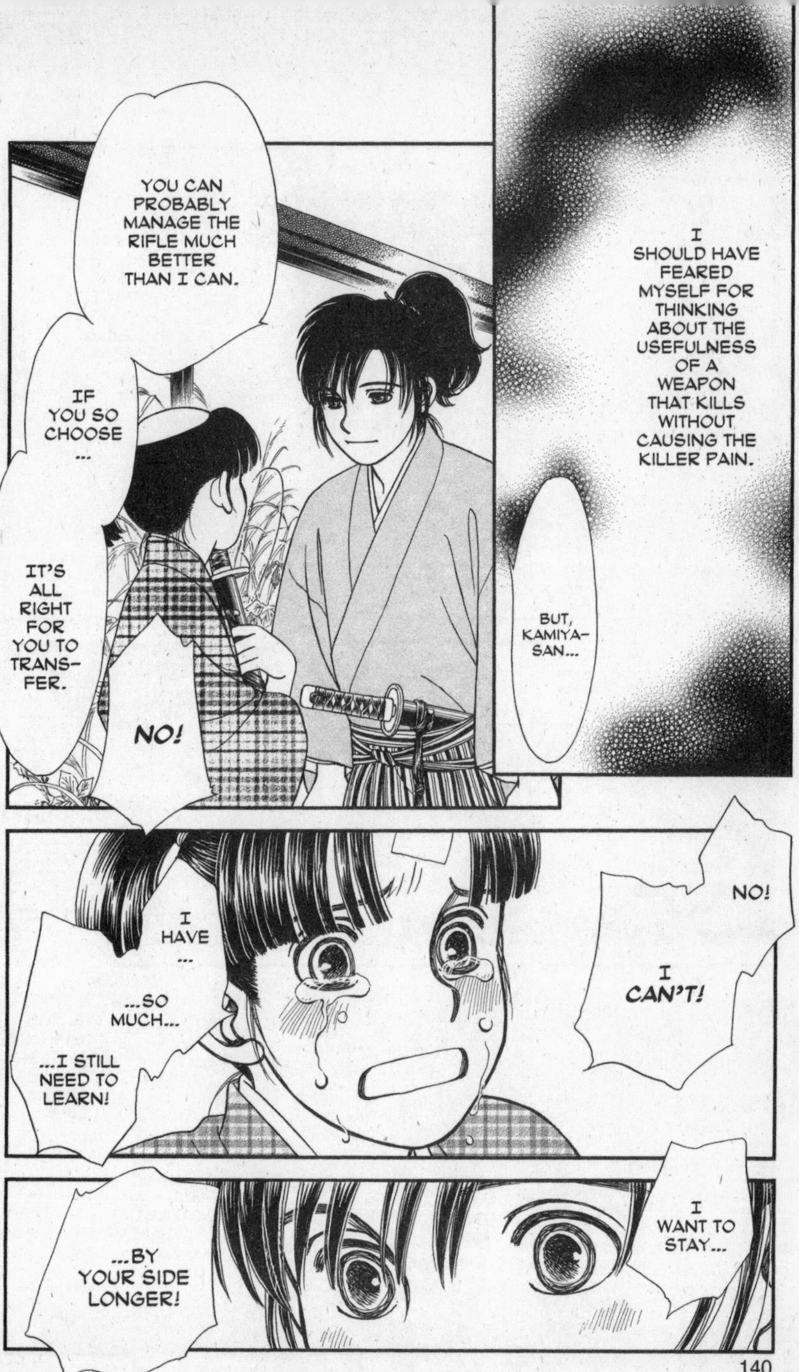
I SHOULD HAVE FEARED MYSELF FOR THINKING ABOUT THE USEFULNESS OF A WEAPON THAT KILLS WITHOUT CAUSING THE KILLER PAIN.
BUT, KAMIYA-SAN...
YOU CAN PROBABLY MANAGE THE RIFLE MUCH BETTER THAN I CAN.
IF YOU SO CHOOSE...
IT'S ALL RIGHT FOR YOU TO TRANS-FER.
NO!
NO! I CAN'T!
I HAVE... ...SO MUCH... ...I STILL NEED TO LEARN!
I WANT TO STAY...
...BY YOUR SIDE LONGER!

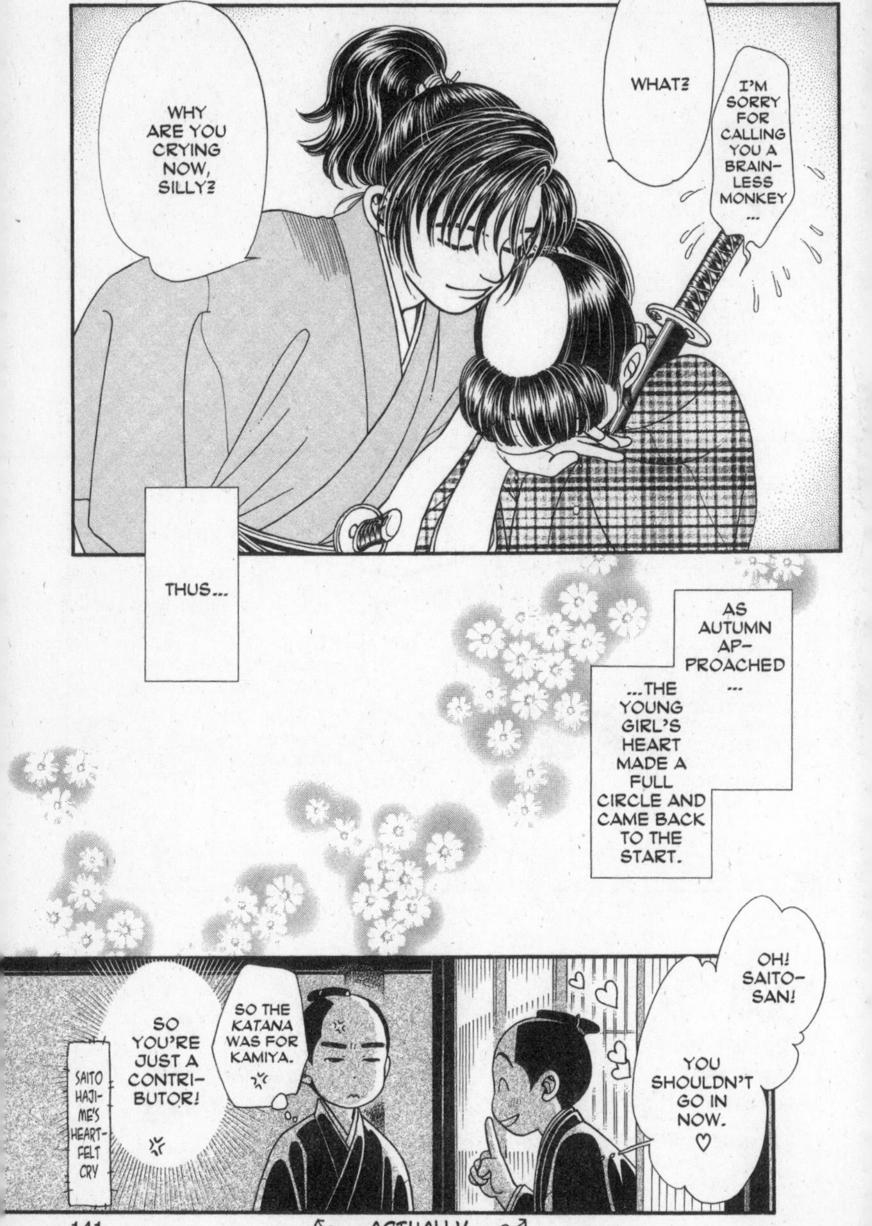

I'M SORRY FOR CALLING YOU A BRAIN-LESS MONKEY...
WHAT?
WHY ARE YOU CRYING NOW, SILLY?
THUS...
AS AUTUMN AP-PROACHED...
...THE YOUNG GIRL'S HEART MADE A FULL CIRCLE AND CAME BACK TO THE START.
OH! SAITO-SAN!
YOU SHOULDN'T GO IN NOW. ♡
SO THE KATANA WAS FOR KAMIYA.
SO YOU'RE JUST A CONTRI-BUTOR!
SAITO HAJIME'S HEART-FELT CRY

ACTUALLY KATANA BUDDIES

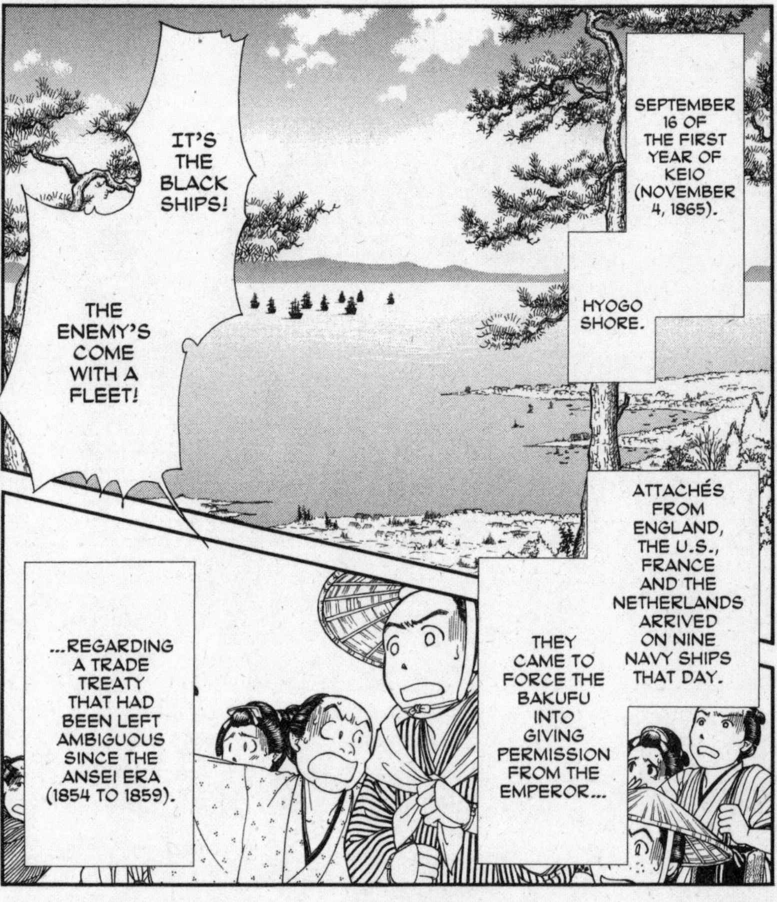
SEPTEMBER 16 OF THE FIRST YEAR OF KEIO (NOVEMBER 4, 1865).
HYOGO SHORE.
IT'S THE BLACK SHIPS!
THE ENEMY'S COME WITH A FLEET!
ATTACHÉS FROM ENGLAND, THE U.S., FRANCE AND THE NETHERLANDS ARRIVED ON NINE NAVY SHIPS THAT DAY.
THEY CAME TO FORCE THE BAKUFU INTO GIVING PERMISSION FROM THE EMPEROR...
...REGARDING A TRADE TREATY THAT HAD BEEN LEFT AMBIGUOUS SINCE THE ANSEI ERA (1854 TO 1859).

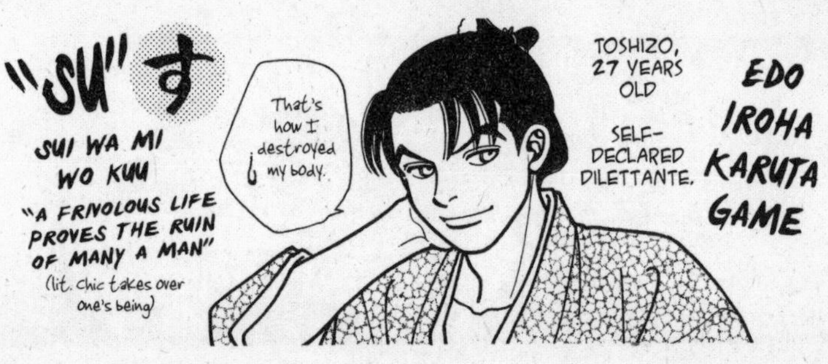
EDO IROHA KARUTA GAME
"SU" す
SUI WA MI WO KUU
"A FRIVOLOUS LIFE PROVES THE RUIN OF MANY A MAN"
(lit. chic takes over one's being)
TOSHIZO, 27 YEARS OLD
SELF-DECLARED DILETTANTE.
That's how I destroyed my body.

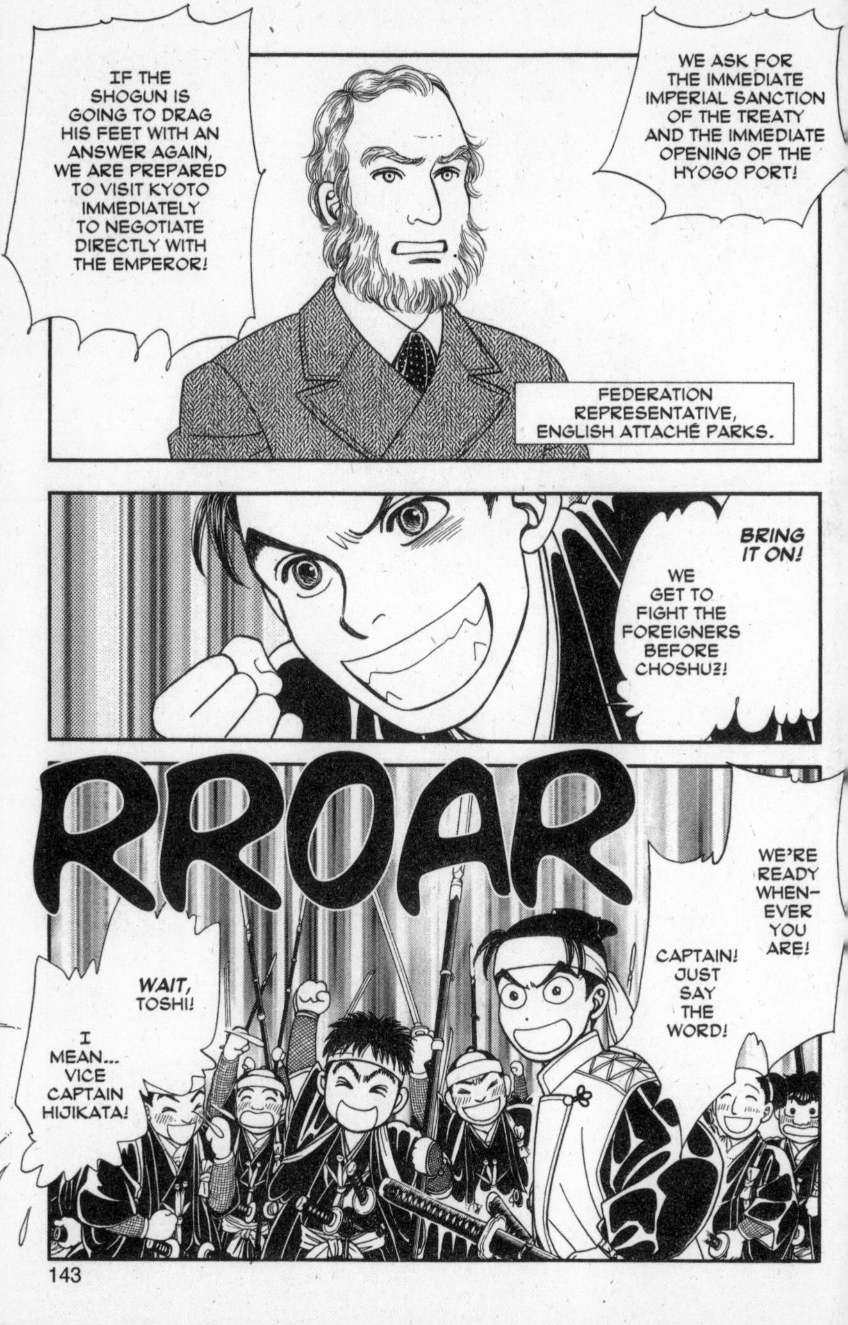
WE ASK FOR THE IMMEDIATE IMPERIAL SANCTION OF THE TREATY AND THE IMMEDIATE OPENING OF THE HYOGO PORT!
IF THE SHOGUN IS GOING TO DRAG HIS FEET WITH AN ANSWER AGAIN, WE ARE PREPARED TO VISIT KYOTO IMMEDIATELY TO NEGOTIATE DIRECTLY WITH THE EMPEROR!
FEDERATION REPRESENTATIVE, ENGLISH ATTACHÉ PARKS.
BRING IT ON!
WE GET TO FIGHT THE FOREIGNERS BEFORE CHOSHU?!
RROAR
WE'RE READY WHEN-EVER YOU ARE!
CAPTAIN! JUST SAY THE WORD!
WAIT, TOSHI!
I MEAN... VICE CAPTAIN HIJIKATA!

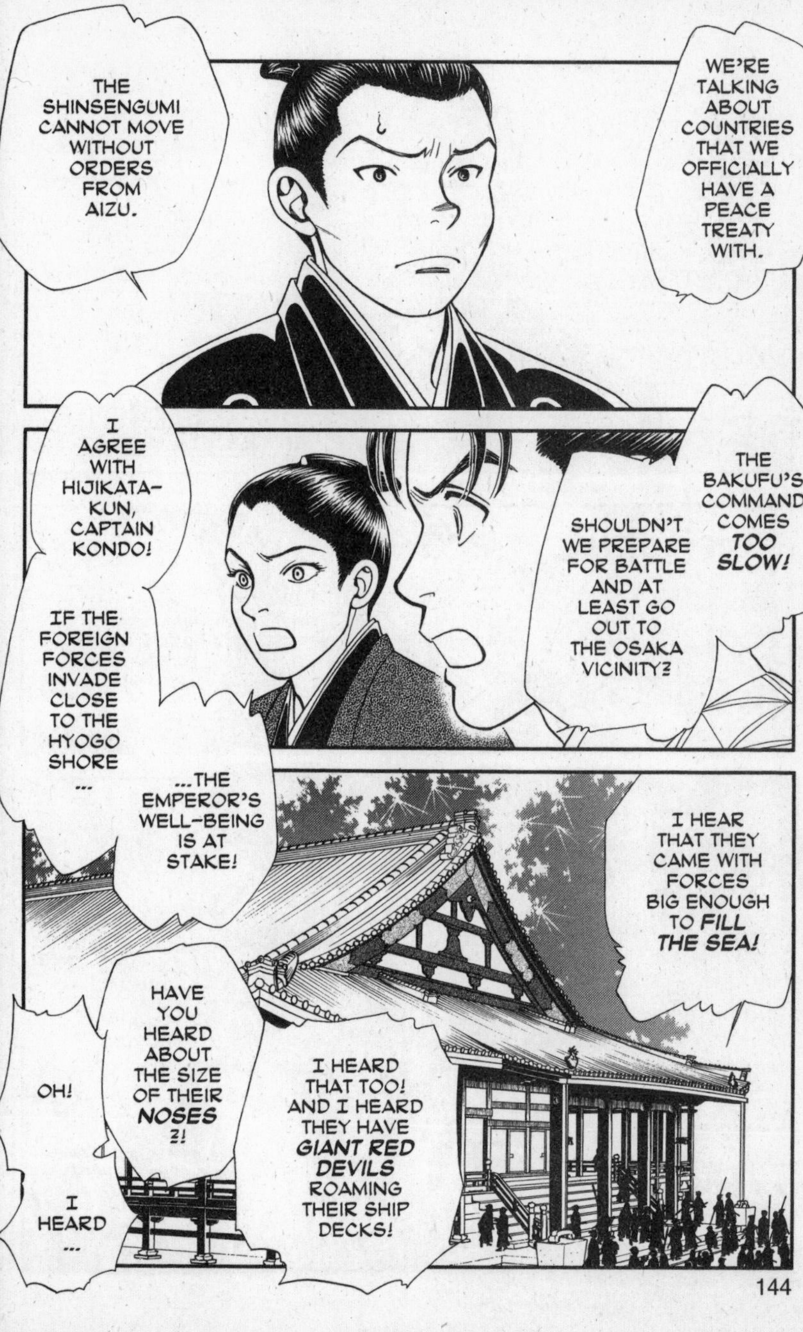
WE'RE TALKING ABOUT COUNTRIES THAT WE OFFICIALLY HAVE A PEACE TREATY WITH.
THE SHINSENGUMI CANNOT MOVE WITHOUT ORDERS FROM AIZU.
THE BAKUFU'S COMMAND COMES TOO SLOW!
SHOULDN'T WE PREPARE FOR BATTLE AND AT LEAST GO OUT TO THE OSAKA VICINITY?
I AGREE WITH HIJIKATA-KUN, CAPTAIN KONDO!
IF THE FOREIGN FORCES INVADE CLOSE TO THE HYOGO SHORE ...
...THE EMPEROR'S WELL-BEING IS AT STAKE!
I HEAR THAT THEY CAME WITH FORCES BIG ENOUGH TO FILL THE SEA!
I HEARD THAT TOO! AND I HEARD THEY HAVE GIANT RED DEVILS ROAMING THEIR SHIP DECKS!
HAVE YOU HEARD ABOUT THE SIZE OF THEIR NOSES ?!
OH!
I HEARD ...

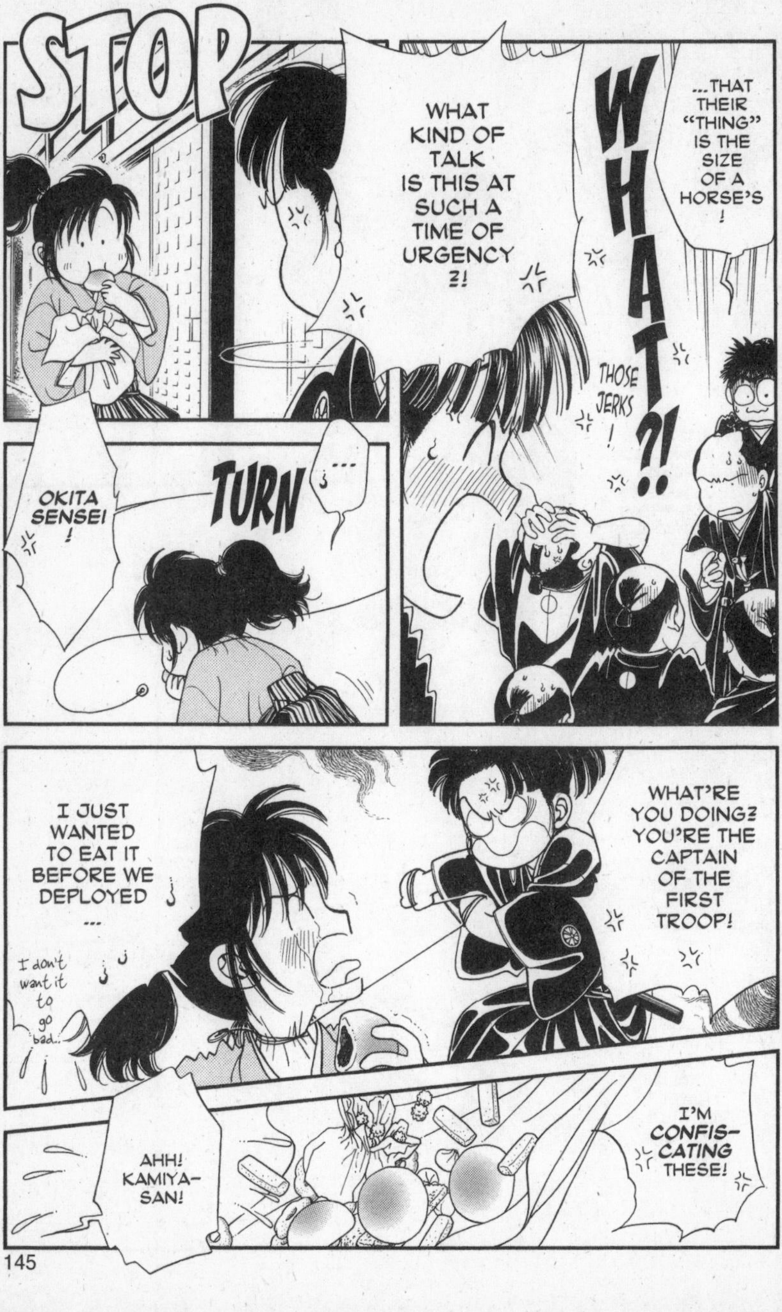
...THAT THEIR "THING" IS THE SIZE OF A HORSE'S!
WHAT?!
WHAT KIND OF TALK IS THIS AT SUCH A TIME OF URGENCY?!
STOP
THOSE JERKS!
...
TURN
OKITA SENSEI!
WHAT'RE YOU DOING? YOU'RE THE CAPTAIN OF THE FIRST TROOP!
I JUST WANTED TO EAT IT BEFORE WE DEPLOYED...
I don't want it to go bad...
I'M CONFISCATING THESE!
AHH! KAMIYA-SAN!

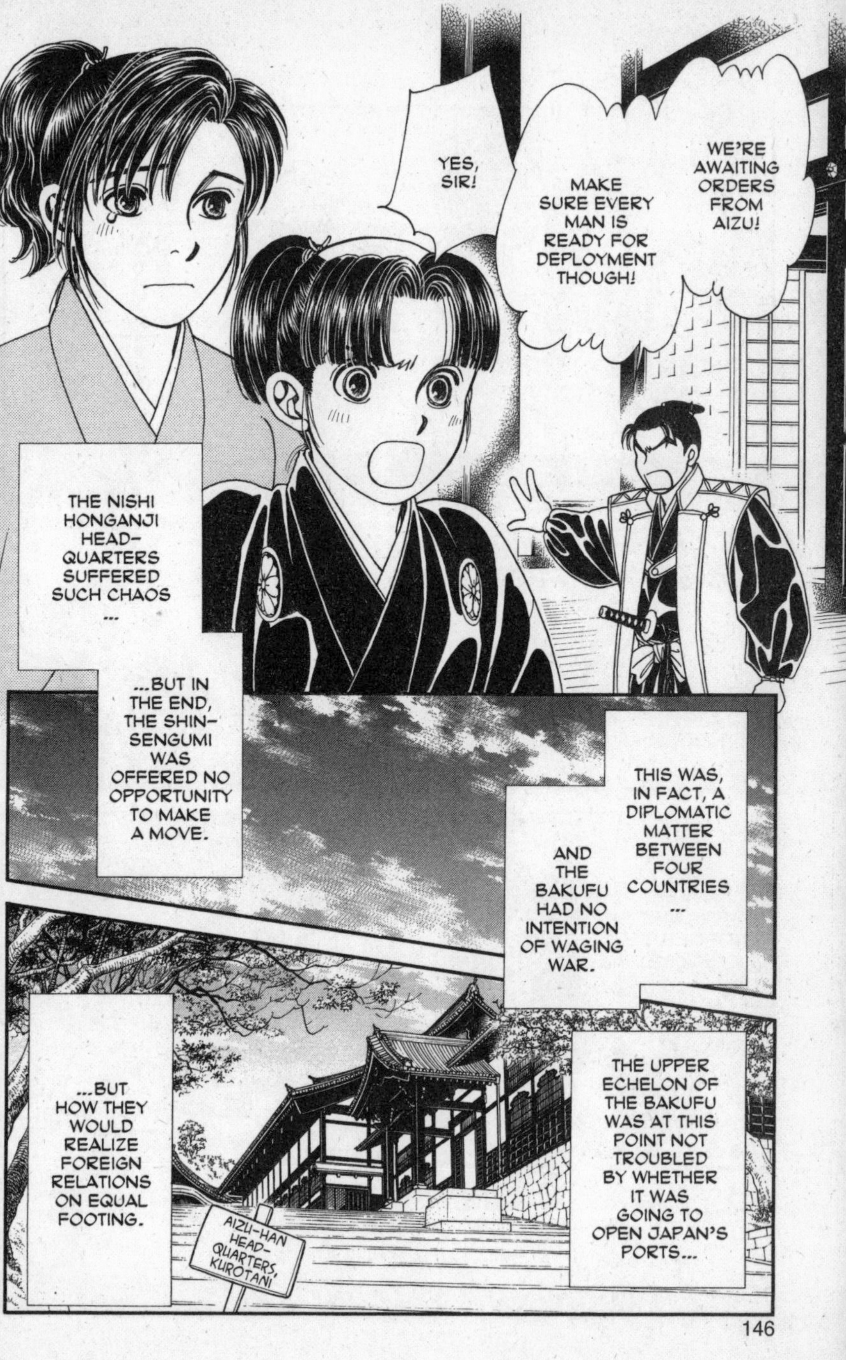
WE'RE AWAITING ORDERS FROM AIZU!
MAKE SURE EVERY MAN IS READY FOR DEPLOYMENT THOUGH!
YES, SIR!
THE NISHI HONGANJI HEAD-QUARTERS SUFFERED SUCH CHAOS ...
...BUT IN THE END, THE SHIN-SENGUMI WAS OFFERED NO OPPORTUNITY TO MAKE A MOVE.
THIS WAS, IN FACT, A DIPLOMATIC MATTER BETWEEN FOUR COUNTRIES ...
AND THE BAKUFU HAD NO INTENTION OF WAGING WAR.
THE UPPER ECHELON OF THE BAKUFU WAS AT THIS POINT NOT TROUBLED BY WHETHER IT WAS GOING TO OPEN JAPAN'S PORTS...
AIZU-HAN HEAD-QUARTERS, KUROTANI
...BUT HOW THEY WOULD REALIZE FOREIGN RELATIONS ON EQUAL FOOTING.

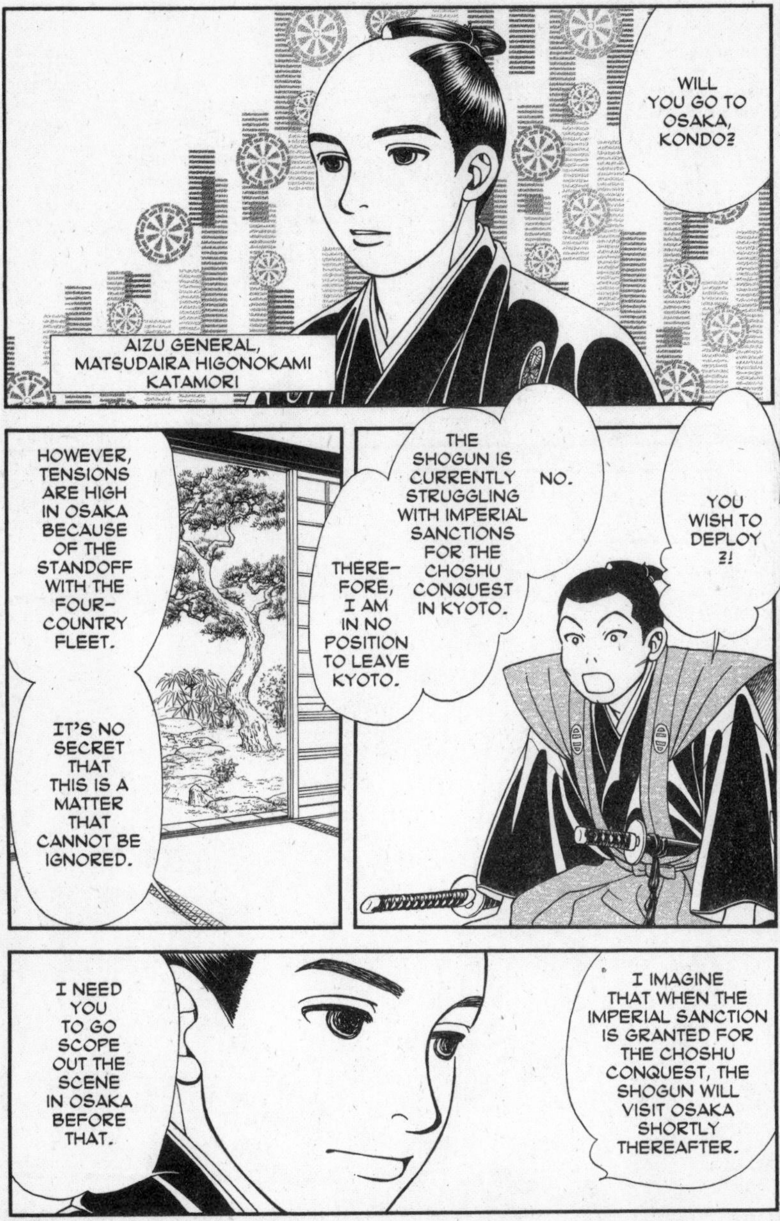
WILL YOU GO TO OSAKA, KONDO?
AIZU GENERAL, MATSUDAIRA HIGONOKAMI KATAMORI
YOU WISH TO DEPLOY?!
NO.
THE SHOGUN IS CURRENTLY STRUGGLING WITH IMPERIAL SANCTIONS FOR THE CHOSHU CONQUEST IN KYOTO.
THEREFORE, I AM IN NO POSITION TO LEAVE KYOTO.
HOWEVER, TENSIONS ARE HIGH IN OSAKA BECAUSE OF THE STANDOFF WITH THE FOUR-COUNTRY FLEET.
IT'S NO SECRET THAT THIS IS A MATTER THAT CANNOT BE IGNORED.
I IMAGINE THAT WHEN THE IMPERIAL SANCTION IS GRANTED FOR THE CHOSHU CONQUEST, THE SHOGUN WILL VISIT OSAKA SHORTLY THEREAFTER.
I NEED YOU TO GO SCOPE OUT THE SCENE IN OSAKA BEFORE THAT.

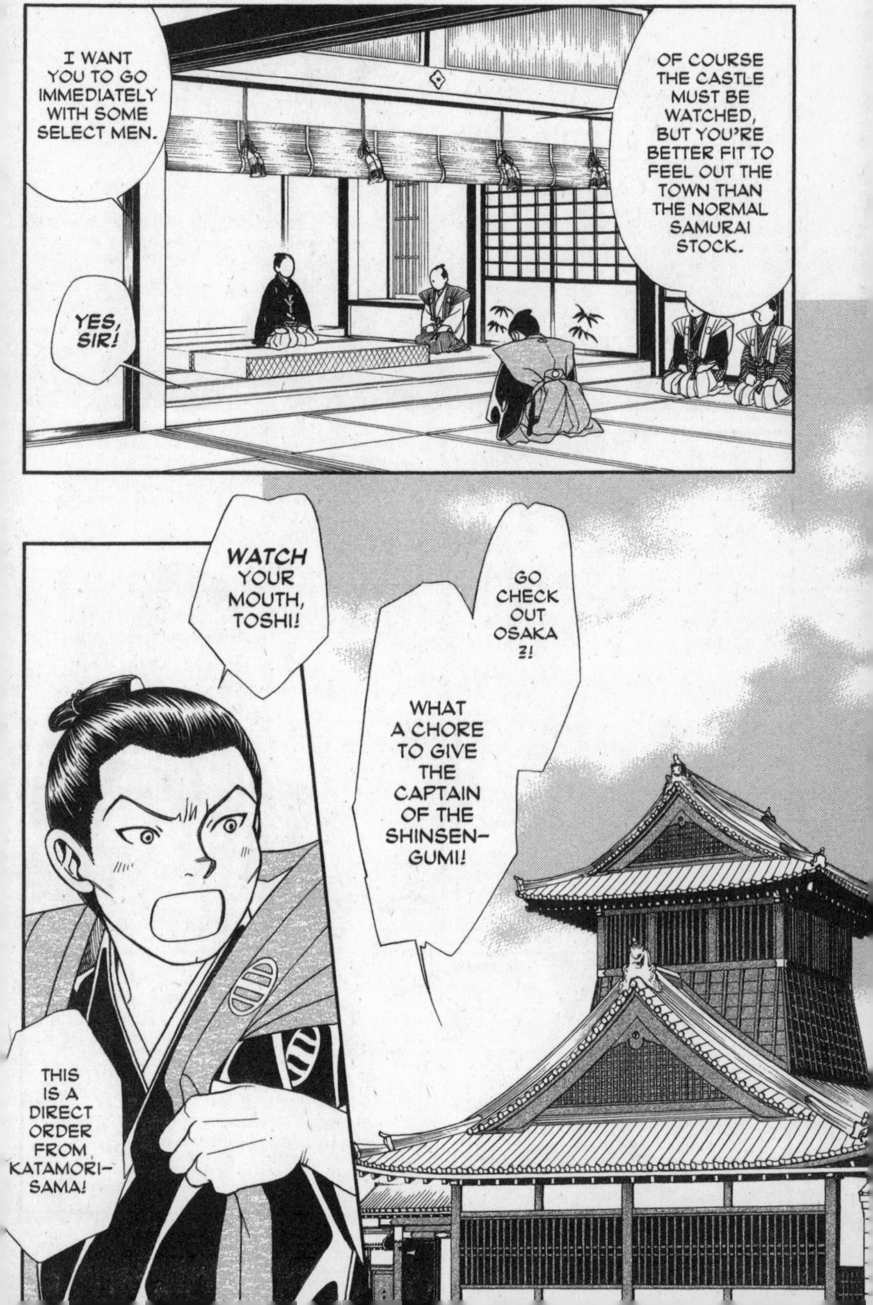
OF COURSE THE CASTLE MUST BE WATCHED, BUT YOU'RE BETTER FIT TO FEEL OUT THE TOWN THAN THE NORMAL SAMURAI STOCK.
I WANT YOU TO GO IMMEDIATELY WITH SOME SELECT MEN.
YES, SIR!
GO CHECK OUT OSAKA?!
WHAT A CHORE TO GIVE THE CAPTAIN OF THE SHINSEN-GUMI!
WATCH YOUR MOUTH, TOSHI!
THIS IS A DIRECT ORDER FROM KATAMORI-SAMA!

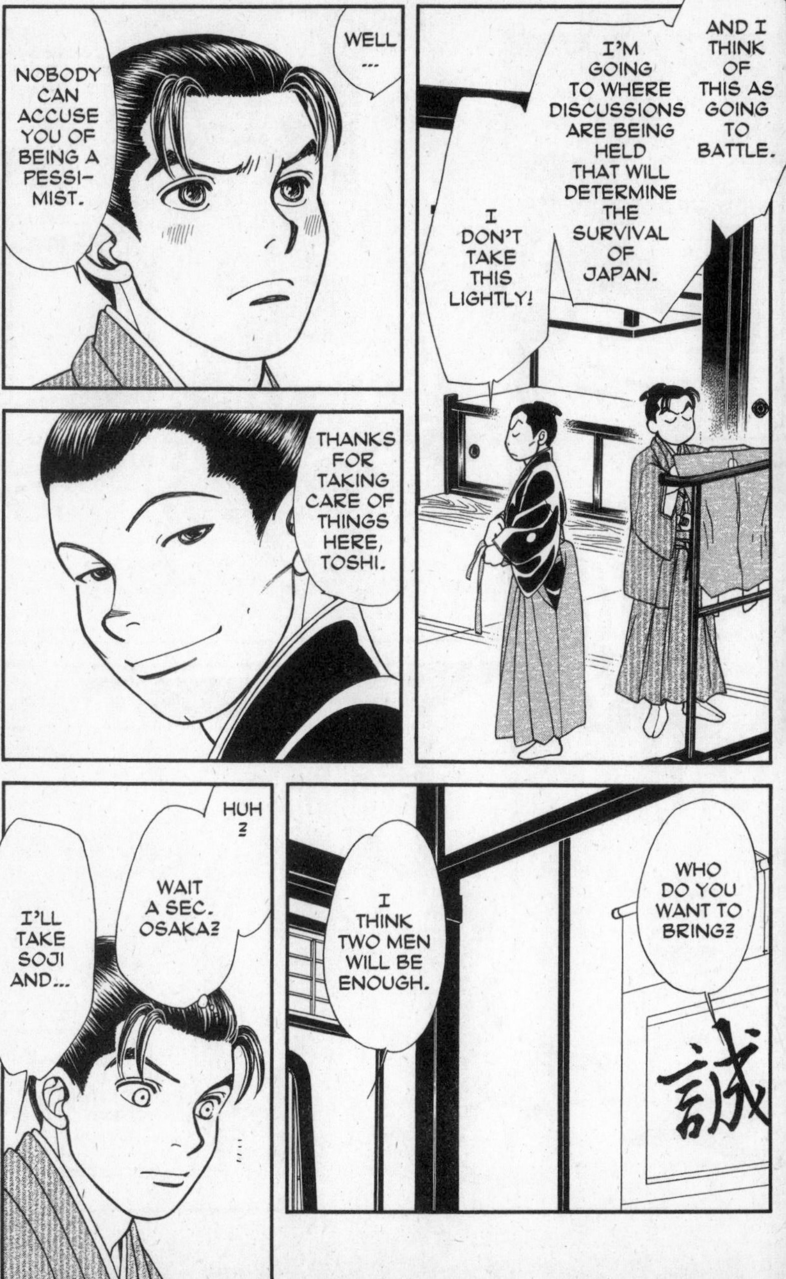
I'M GOING TO WHERE DISCUSSIONS ARE BEING HELD THAT WILL DETERMINE THE SURVIVAL OF JAPAN.
AND I THINK OF THIS AS GOING TO BATTLE.
I DON'T TAKE THIS LIGHTLY!
WELL ...
NOBODY CAN ACCUSE YOU OF BEING A PESSI-MIST.
THANKS FOR TAKING CARE OF THINGS HERE, TOSHI.
WHO DO YOU WANT TO BRING?
誠
I THINK TWO MEN WILL BE ENOUGH.
HUH?
WAIT A SEC. OSAKA?
I'LL TAKE SOJI AND...

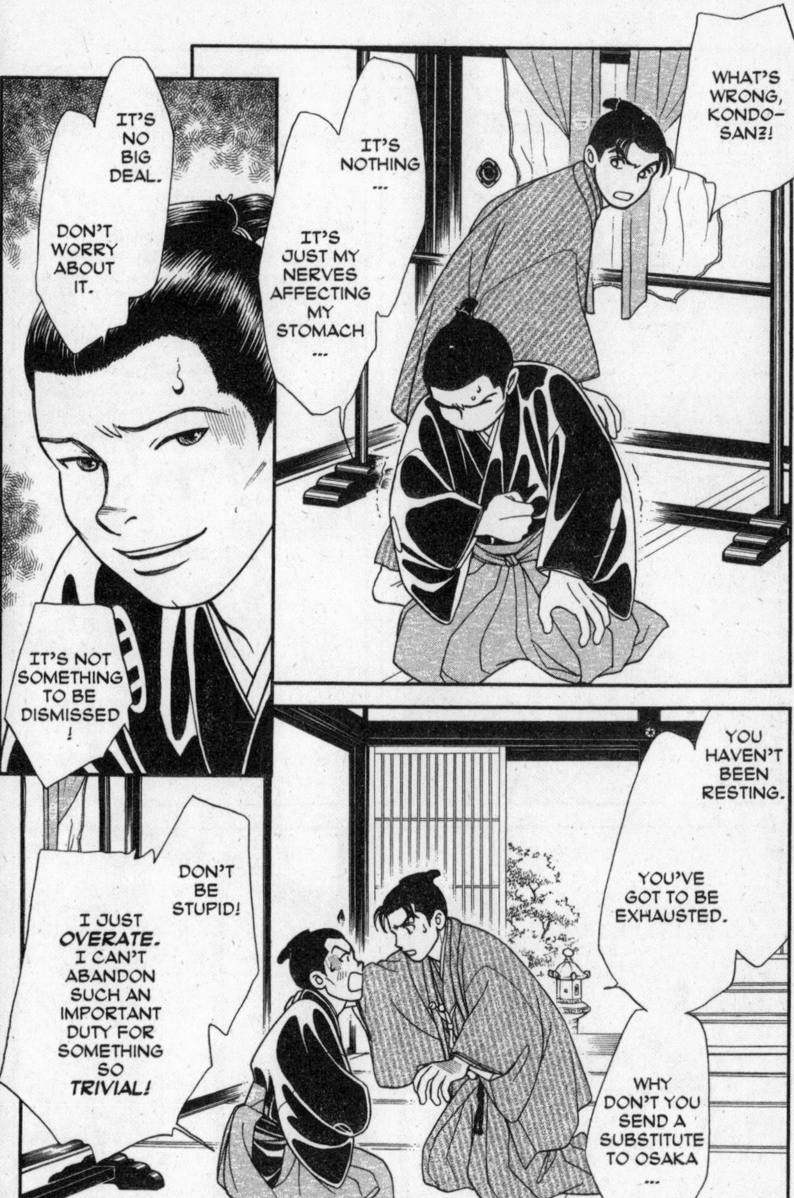
WHAT'S WRONG, KONDO-SAN?!
IT'S NOTHING ... IT'S JUST MY NERVES AFFECTING MY STOMACH ...
IT'S NO BIG DEAL.
DON'T WORRY ABOUT IT.
IT'S NOT SOMETHING TO BE DISMISSED!
YOU HAVEN'T BEEN RESTING.
YOU'VE GOT TO BE EXHAUSTED.
WHY DON'T YOU SEND A SUBSTITUTE TO OSAKA ...
DON'T BE STUPID!
I JUST *OVERATE.* I CAN'T ABANDON SUCH AN IMPORTANT DUTY FOR SOMETHING SO *TRIVIAL!*

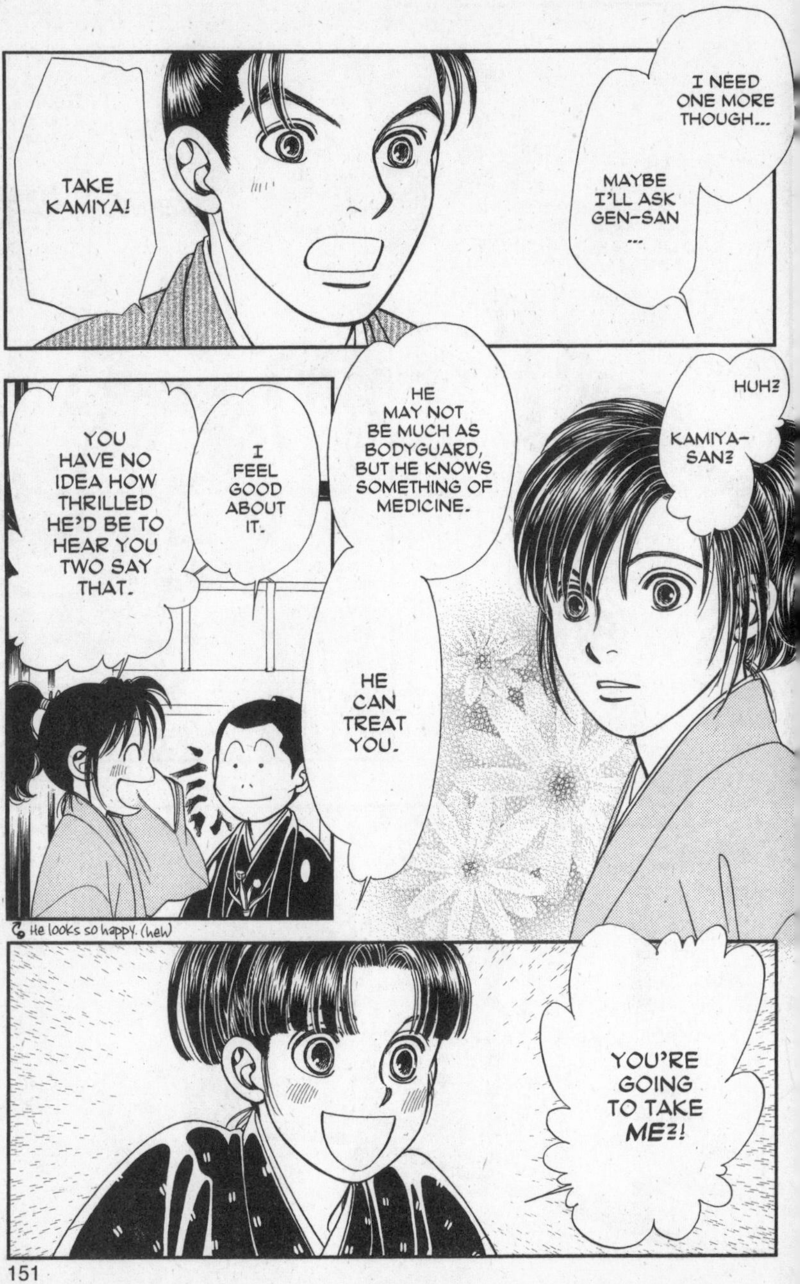
I NEED ONE MORE THOUGH...
MAYBE I'LL ASK GEN-SAN...
TAKE KAMIYA!
HUH?
KAMIYA-SAN?
HE MAY NOT BE MUCH AS BODYGUARD, BUT HE KNOWS SOMETHING OF MEDICINE.
HE CAN TREAT YOU.
I FEEL GOOD ABOUT IT.
YOU HAVE NO IDEA HOW THRILLED HE'D BE TO HEAR YOU TWO SAY THAT.
He looks so happy. (heh)
YOU'RE GOING TO TAKE *ME*?!

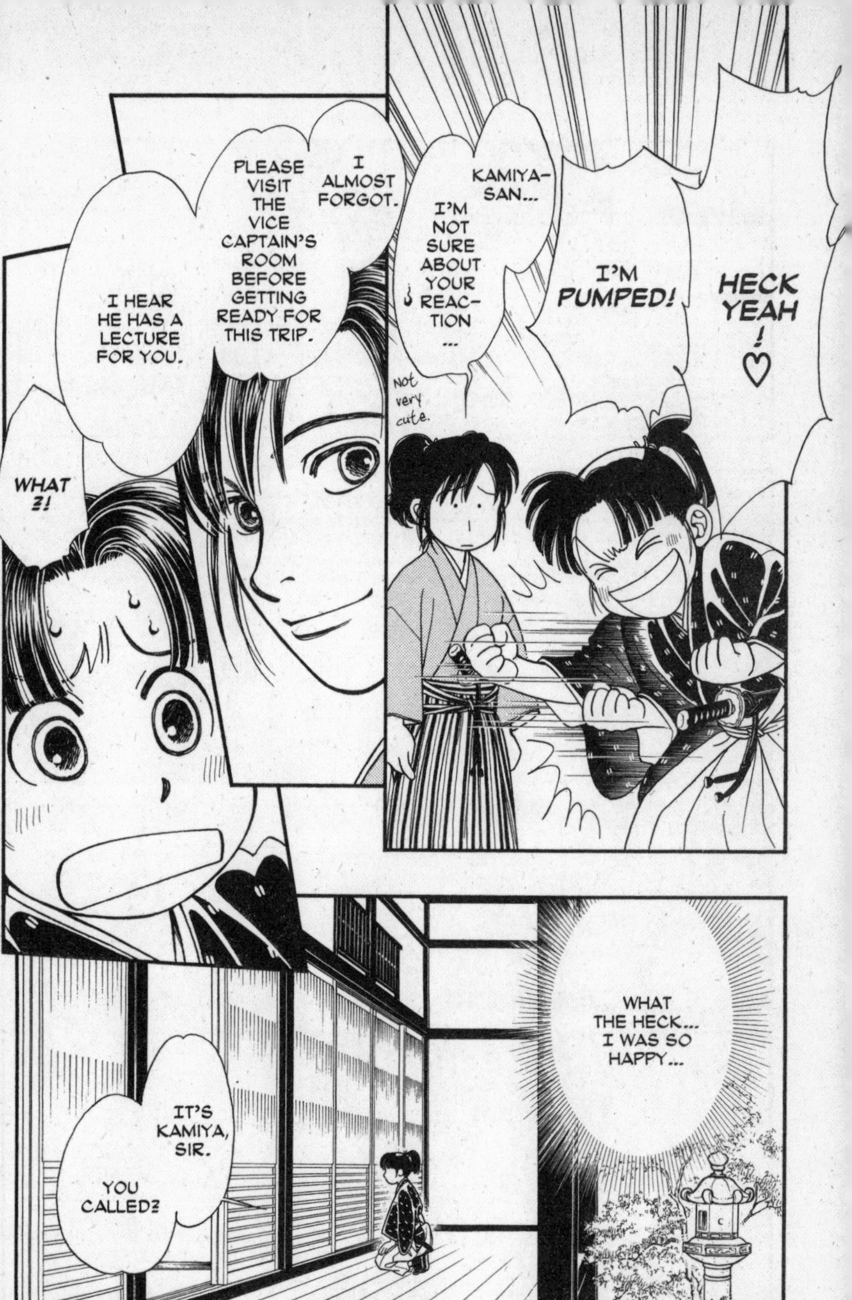
HECK YEAH! ♡
I'M PUMPED!
KAMIYA-SAN...
I'M NOT SURE ABOUT YOUR REAC-TION...
Not very cute.
I ALMOST FORGOT.
PLEASE VISIT THE VICE CAPTAIN'S ROOM BEFORE GETTING READY FOR THIS TRIP.
I HEAR HE HAS A LECTURE FOR YOU.
WHAT?!
WHAT THE HECK... I WAS SO HAPPY...
IT'S KAMIYA, SIR.
YOU CALLED?

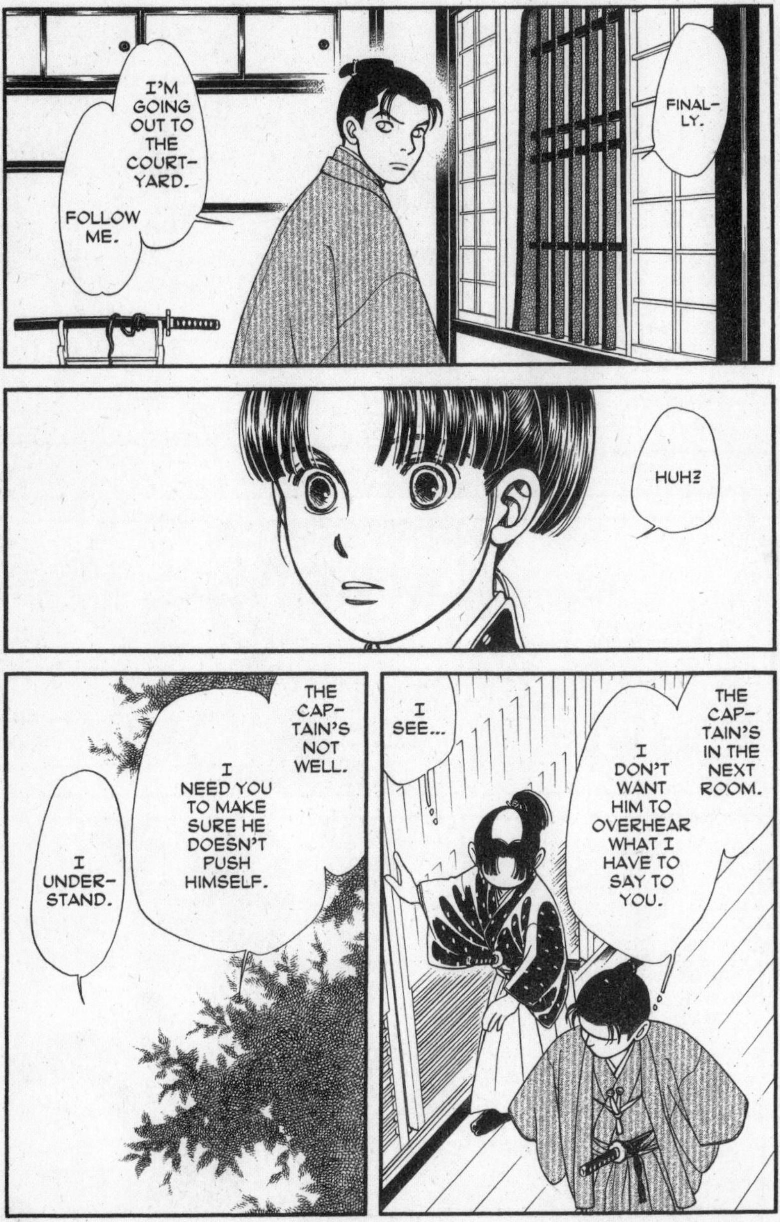
FINAL-LY.
I'M GOING OUT TO THE COURT-YARD.
FOLLOW ME.
HUH?
THE CAP-TAIN'S IN THE NEXT ROOM.
I DON'T WANT HIM TO OVERHEAR WHAT I HAVE TO SAY TO YOU.
I SEE...
THE CAP-TAIN'S NOT WELL.
I NEED YOU TO MAKE SURE HE DOESN'T PUSH HIMSELF.
I UNDER-STAND.

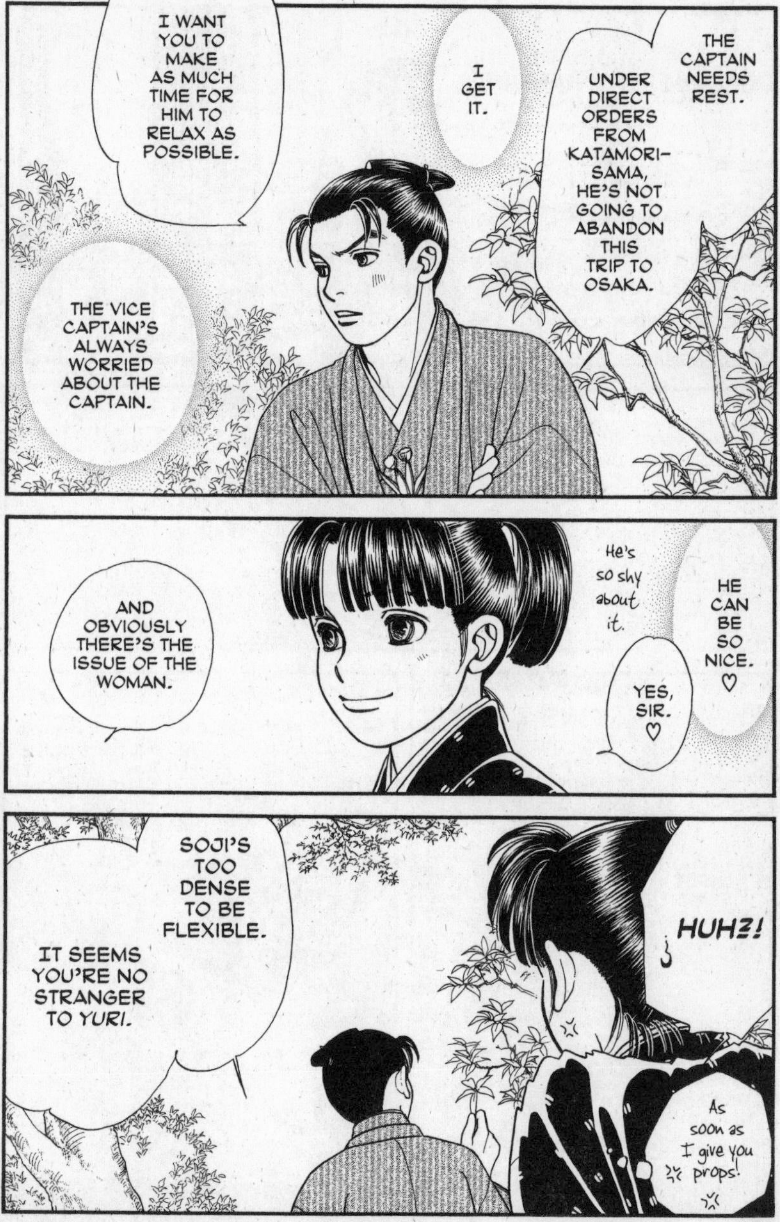
THE CAPTAIN NEEDS REST.
UNDER DIRECT ORDERS FROM KATAMORI-SAMA, HE'S NOT GOING TO ABANDON THIS TRIP TO OSAKA.
I GET IT.
I WANT YOU TO MAKE AS MUCH TIME FOR HIM TO RELAX AS POSSIBLE.
THE VICE CAPTAIN'S ALWAYS WORRIED ABOUT THE CAPTAIN.
HE CAN BE SO NICE. ♡
He's so shy about it.
YES, SIR. ♡
AND OBVIOUSLY THERE'S THE ISSUE OF THE WOMAN.
HUH?!
As soon as I give you props!
SOJI'S TOO DENSE TO BE FLEXIBLE.
IT SEEMS YOU'RE NO STRANGER TO YURI.

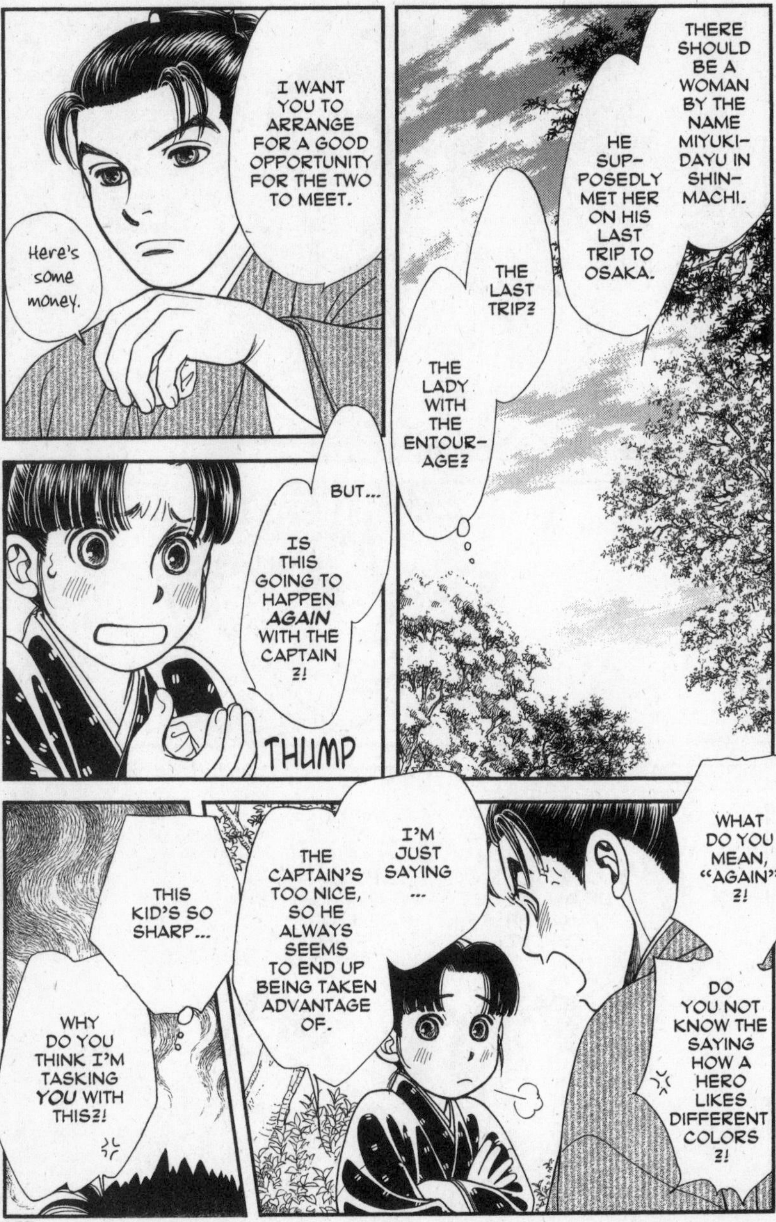
THERE SHOULD BE A WOMAN BY THE NAME MIYUKI-DAYU IN SHIN-MACHI.
HE SUPPOSEDLY MET HER ON HIS LAST TRIP TO OSAKA.
THE LAST TRIP?
THE LADY WITH THE ENTOURAGE?
I WANT YOU TO ARRANGE FOR A GOOD OPPORTUNITY FOR THE TWO TO MEET.
Here's some money.
BUT...
IS THIS GOING TO HAPPEN *AGAIN* WITH THE CAPTAIN?!
THUMP
WHAT DO YOU MEAN, "AGAIN"?!
DO YOU NOT KNOW THE SAYING HOW A HERO LIKES DIFFERENT COLORS?!
I'M JUST SAYING...
THE CAPTAIN'S TOO NICE, SO HE ALWAYS SEEMS TO END UP BEING TAKEN ADVANTAGE OF.
THIS KID'S SO SHARP...
WHY DO YOU THINK I'M TASKING *YOU* WITH THIS?!

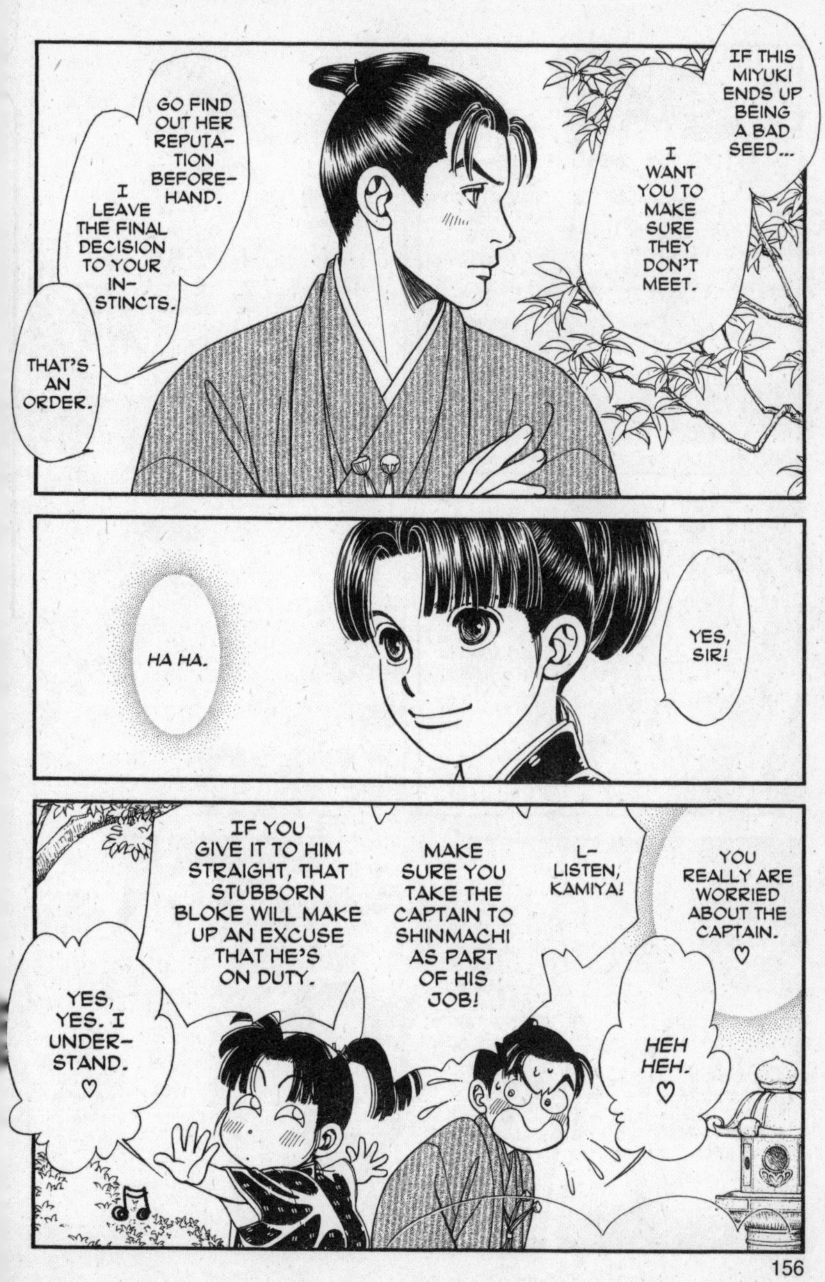
IF THIS MIYUKI ENDS UP BEING A BAD SEED...
I WANT YOU TO MAKE SURE THEY DON'T MEET.
GO FIND OUT HER REPUTATION BEFOREHAND.
I LEAVE THE FINAL DECISION TO YOUR INSTINCTS.
THAT'S AN ORDER.
YES, SIR!
HA HA.
YOU REALLY ARE WORRIED ABOUT THE CAPTAIN. ♡
HEH HEH. ♡
L-LISTEN, KAMIYA!
MAKE SURE YOU TAKE THE CAPTAIN TO SHINMACHI AS PART OF HIS JOB!
IF YOU GIVE IT TO HIM STRAIGHT, THAT STUBBORN BLOKE WILL MAKE UP AN EXCUSE THAT HE'S ON DUTY.
YES, YES. I UNDERSTAND. ♡

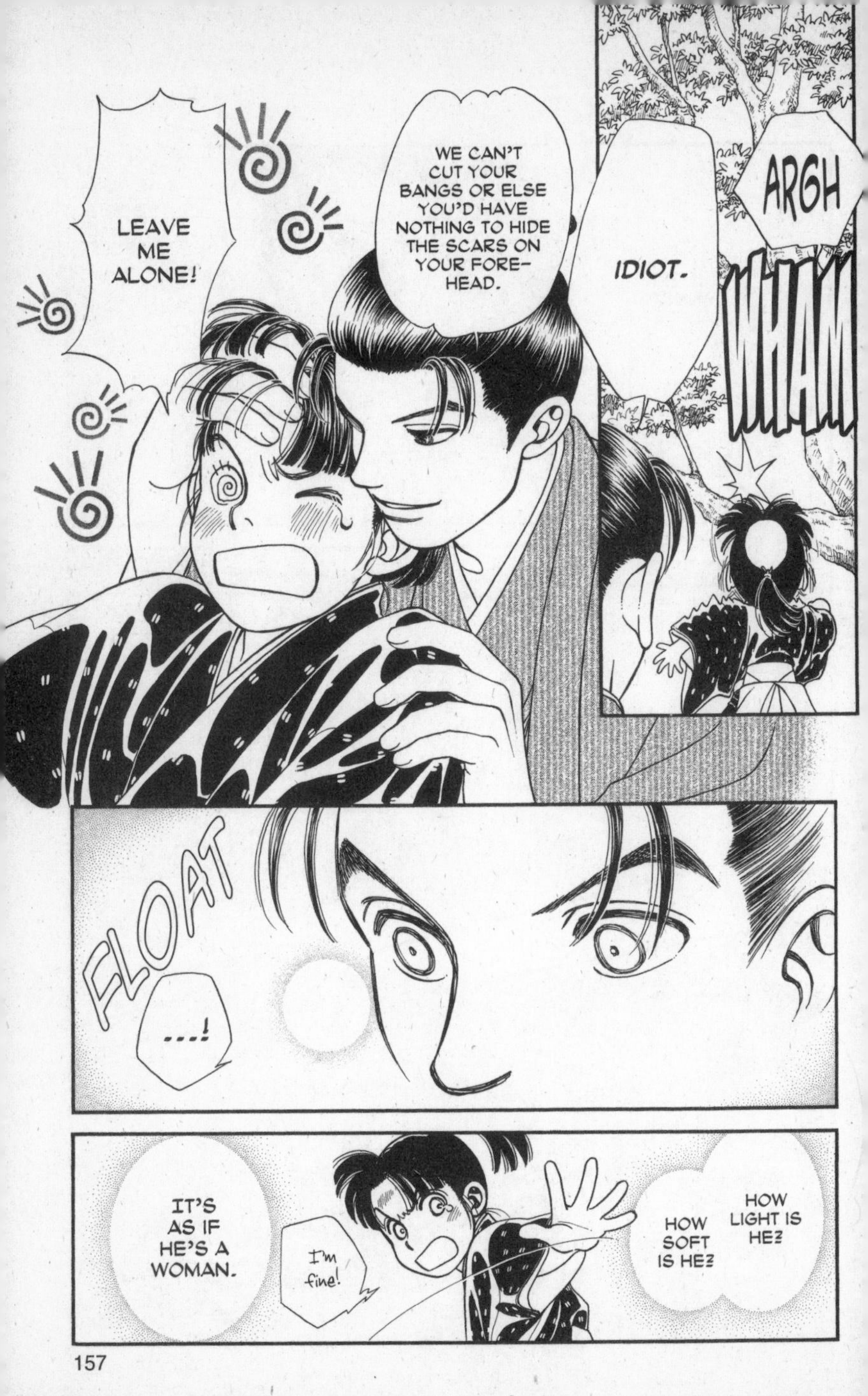
ARGH
WHAM
IDIOT.
WE CAN'T CUT YOUR BANGS OR ELSE YOU'D HAVE NOTHING TO HIDE THE SCARS ON YOUR FORE-HEAD.
LEAVE ME ALONE!
FLOAT
...!
HOW LIGHT IS HE?
HOW SOFT IS HE?
I'm fine!
IT'S AS IF HE'S A WOMAN.

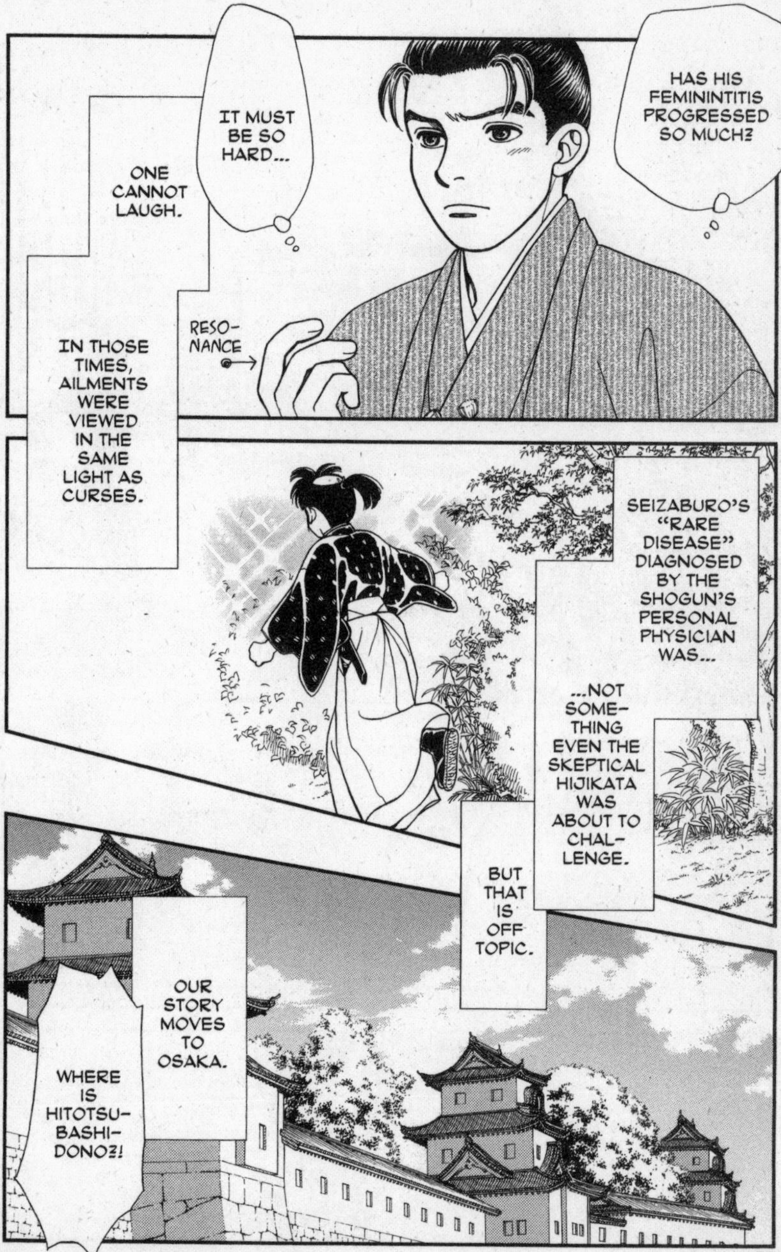
HAS HIS FEMININTITIS PROGRESSED SO MUCH?
IT MUST BE SO HARD...
ONE CANNOT LAUGH.
RESO-NANCE
IN THOSE TIMES, AILMENTS WERE VIEWED IN THE SAME LIGHT AS CURSES.
SEIZABURO'S "RARE DISEASE" DIAGNOSED BY THE SHOGUN'S PERSONAL PHYSICIAN WAS...
...NOT SOMETHING EVEN THE SKEPTICAL HIJIKATA WAS ABOUT TO CHALLENGE.
BUT THAT IS OFF TOPIC.
OUR STORY MOVES TO OSAKA.
WHERE IS HITOTSUBASHI-DONO?!

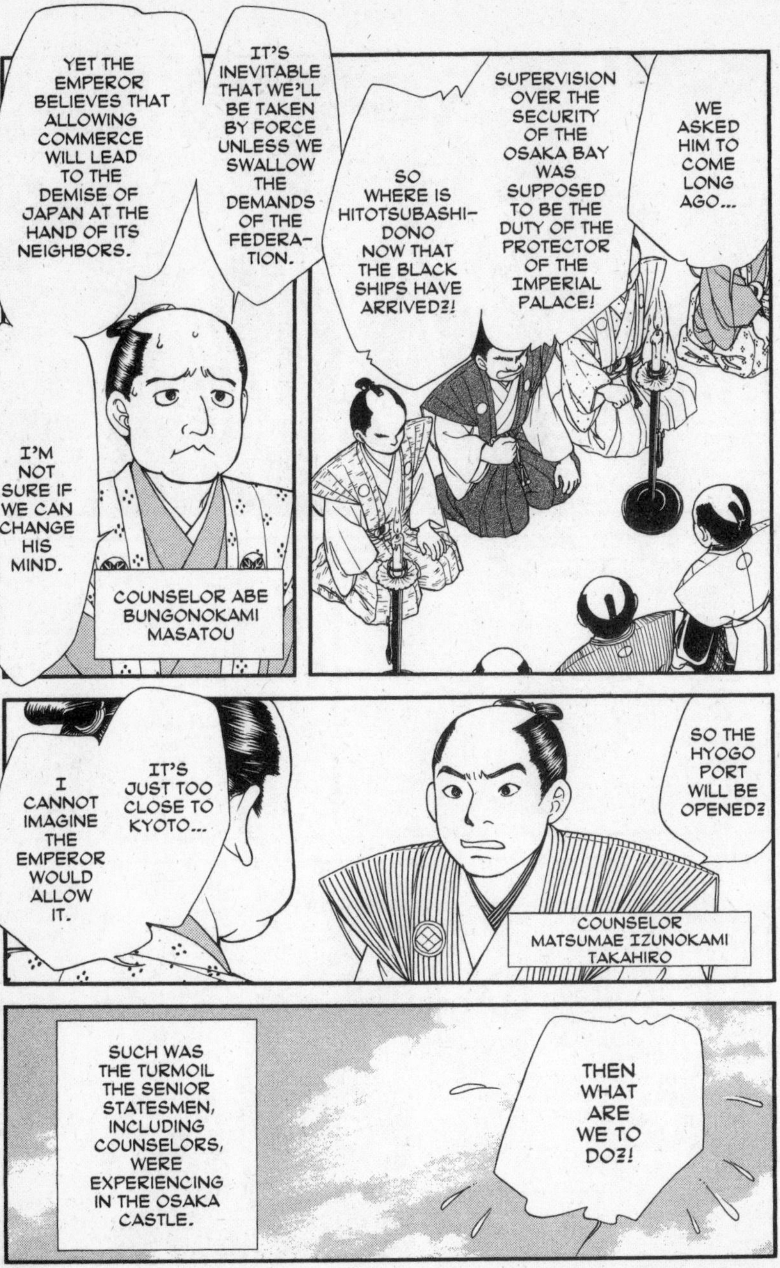
WE ASKED HIM TO COME LONG AGO...
SUPERVISION OVER THE SECURITY OF THE OSAKA BAY WAS SUPPOSED TO BE THE DUTY OF THE PROTECTOR OF THE IMPERIAL PALACE!
SO WHERE IS HITOTSUBASHI-DONO NOW THAT THE BLACK SHIPS HAVE ARRIVED?!
IT'S INEVITABLE THAT WE'LL BE TAKEN BY FORCE UNLESS WE SWALLOW THE DEMANDS OF THE FEDERATION.
YET THE EMPEROR BELIEVES THAT ALLOWING COMMERCE WILL LEAD TO THE DEMISE OF JAPAN AT THE HAND OF ITS NEIGHBORS.
I'M NOT SURE IF WE CAN CHANGE HIS MIND.
COUNSELOR ABE BUNGONOKAMI MASATOU
SO THE HYOGO PORT WILL BE OPENED?
COUNSELOR MATSUMAE IZUNOKAMI TAKAHIRO
IT'S JUST TOO CLOSE TO KYOTO...
I CANNOT IMAGINE THE EMPEROR WOULD ALLOW IT.
THEN WHAT ARE WE TO DO?!
SUCH WAS THE TURMOIL THE SENIOR STATESMEN, INCLUDING COUNSELORS, WERE EXPERIENCING IN THE OSAKA CASTLE.

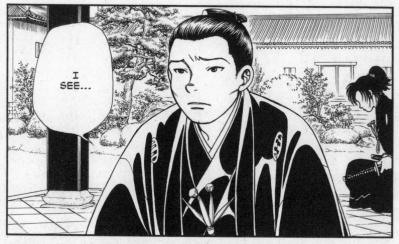

I SEE...
THERE IS NO PLACE FOR THE SHINSEN-GUMI.
I'M SORRY FOR THE LONG JOURNEY HERE, BUT WE'VE NO CHOICE BUT TO WAIT FOR THE SHOGUN.
PLEASE INFORM HIGO-DONO* OF THIS.
"THERE IS NO PLACE ?!"
CAN YOU BELIEVE THAT *RUDE* BASTARD ?!
Didn't even invite him in!
KAMIYA-SAN!
IT SEEMS THINGS AREN'T GOING WELL.
EVERYBODY HERE IS ON EDGE.

*Matsudaira Katamori, the Lord of Aizu.

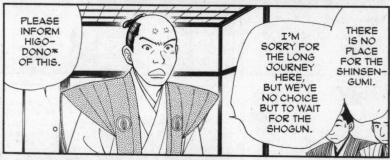

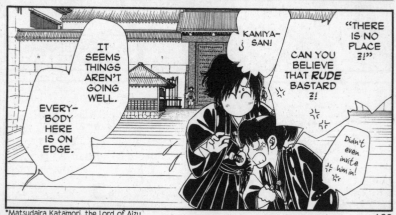

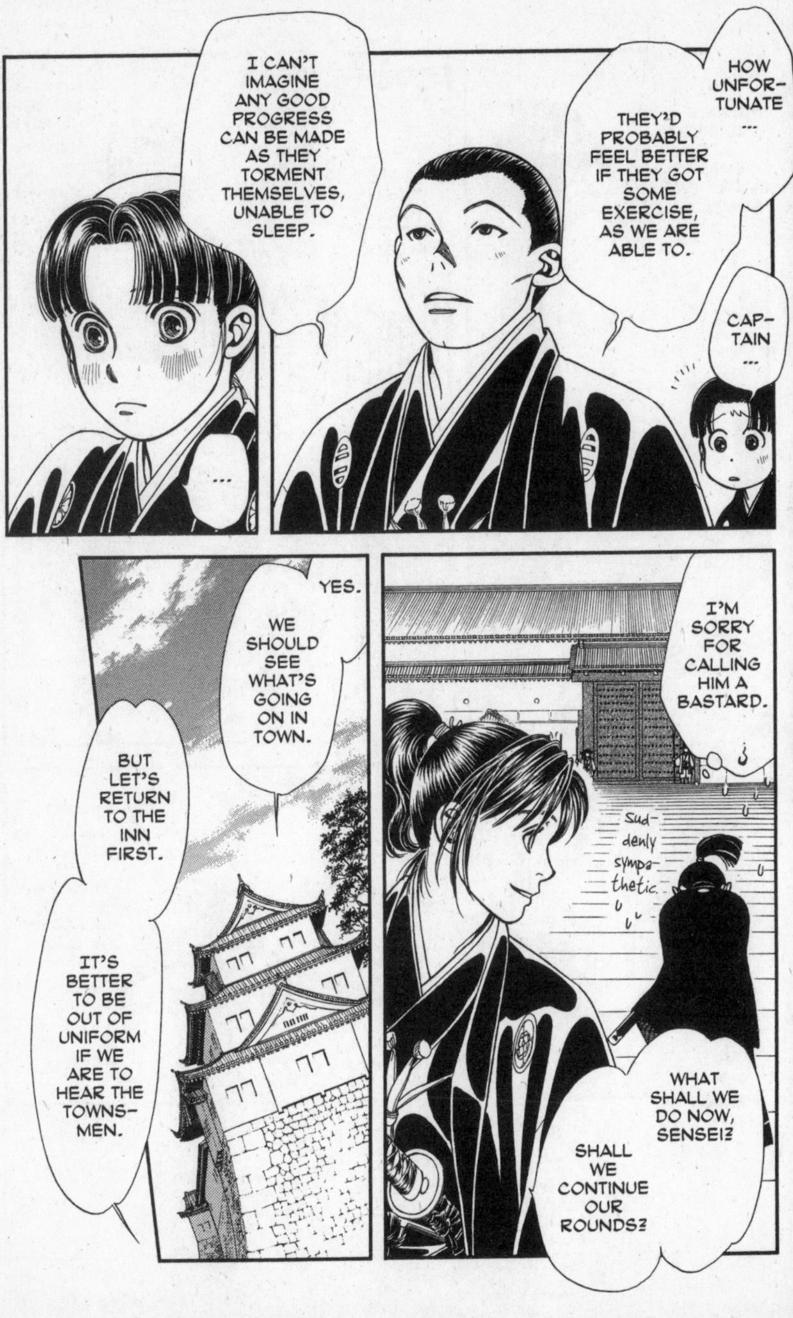
HOW UNFORTUNATE ...
THEY'D PROBABLY FEEL BETTER IF THEY GOT SOME EXERCISE, AS WE ARE ABLE TO.
CAPTAIN ...
I CAN'T IMAGINE ANY GOOD PROGRESS CAN BE MADE AS THEY TORMENT THEMSELVES, UNABLE TO SLEEP.
...
I'M SORRY FOR CALLING HIM A BASTARD.
Suddenly sympathetic.
WHAT SHALL WE DO NOW, SENSEI!?
SHALL WE CONTINUE OUR ROUNDS!?
YES.
WE SHOULD SEE WHAT'S GOING ON IN TOWN.
BUT LET'S RETURN TO THE INN FIRST.
IT'S BETTER TO BE OUT OF UNIFORM IF WE ARE TO HEAR THE TOWNSMEN.

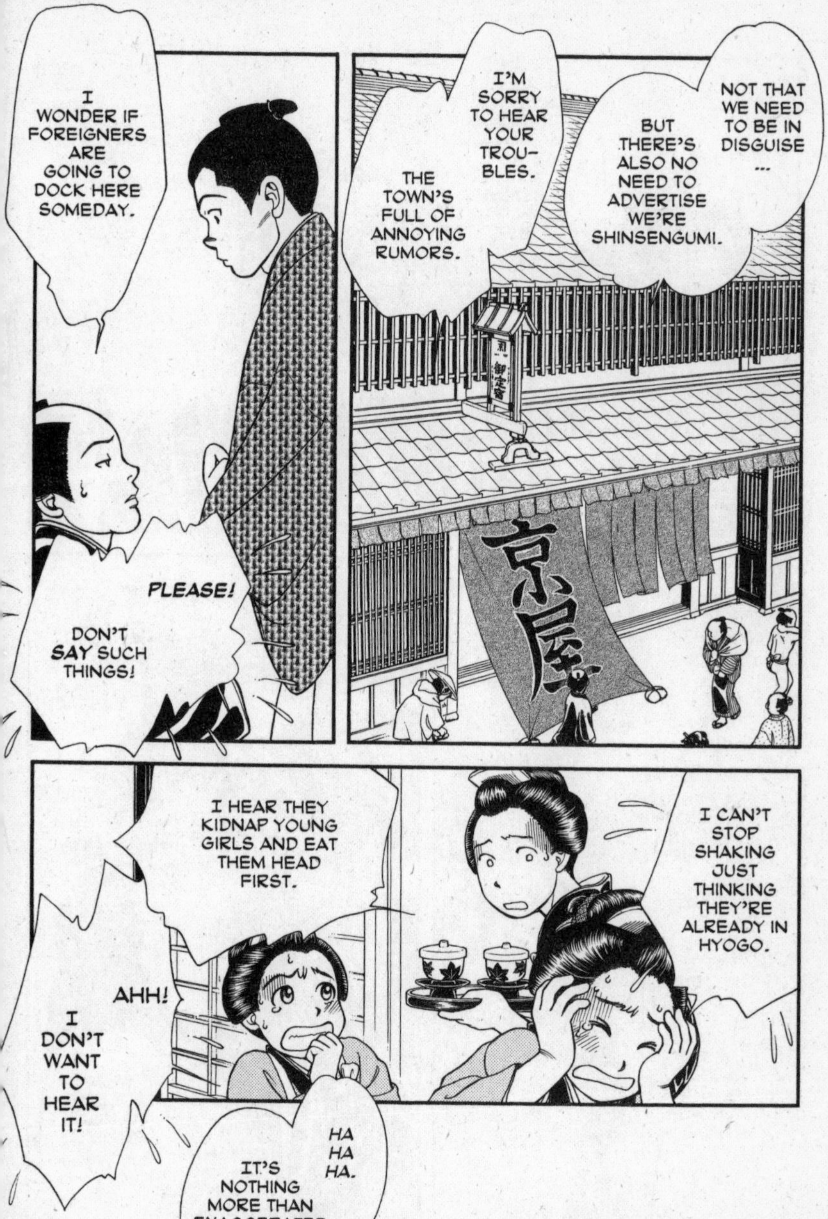

NOT THAT WE NEED TO BE IN DISGUISE ...
BUT THERE'S ALSO NO NEED TO ADVERTISE WE'RE SHINSENGUMI.
I'M SORRY TO HEAR YOUR TROUBLES.
THE TOWN'S FULL OF ANNOYING RUMORS.
京屋
I WONDER IF FOREIGNERS ARE GOING TO DOCK HERE SOMEDAY.
PLEASE!
DON'T SAY SUCH THINGS!
I CAN'T STOP SHAKING JUST THINKING THEY'RE ALREADY IN HYOGO.
I HEAR THEY KIDNAP YOUNG GIRLS AND EAT THEM HEAD FIRST.
AHH!
I DON'T WANT TO HEAR IT!
HA HA HA.
IT'S NOTHING MORE THAN EXAGGERATED RUMORS.

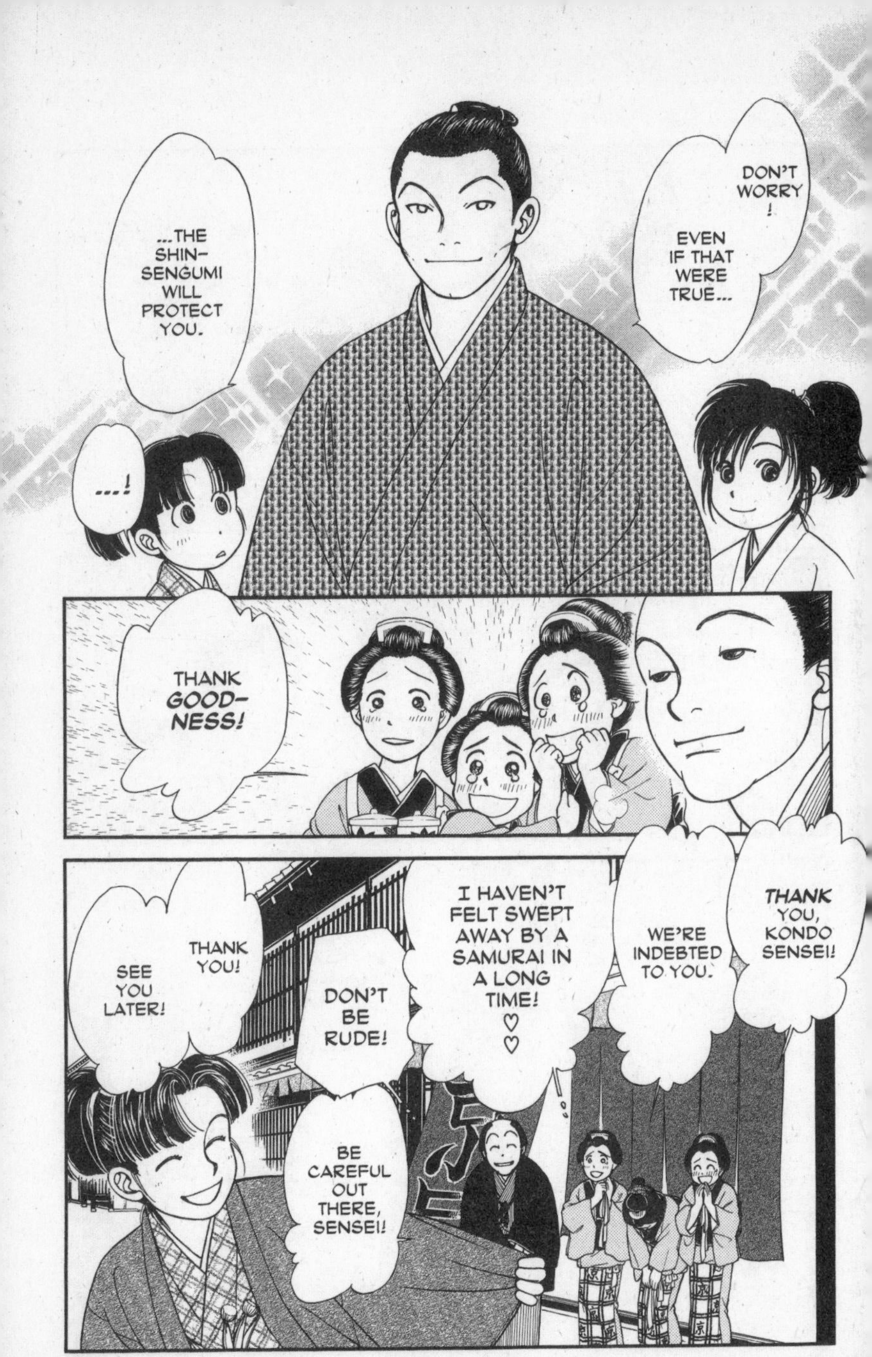
DON'T WORRY!
EVEN IF THAT WERE TRUE...
...THE SHIN-SENGUMI WILL PROTECT YOU.
...!
THANK GOODNESS!
THANK YOU, KONDO SENSEI!
WE'RE INDEBTED TO YOU.
I HAVEN'T FELT SWEPT AWAY BY A SAMURAI IN A LONG TIME! ♡ ♡
DON'T BE RUDE!
BE CAREFUL OUT THERE, SENSEI!
THANK YOU!
SEE YOU LATER!

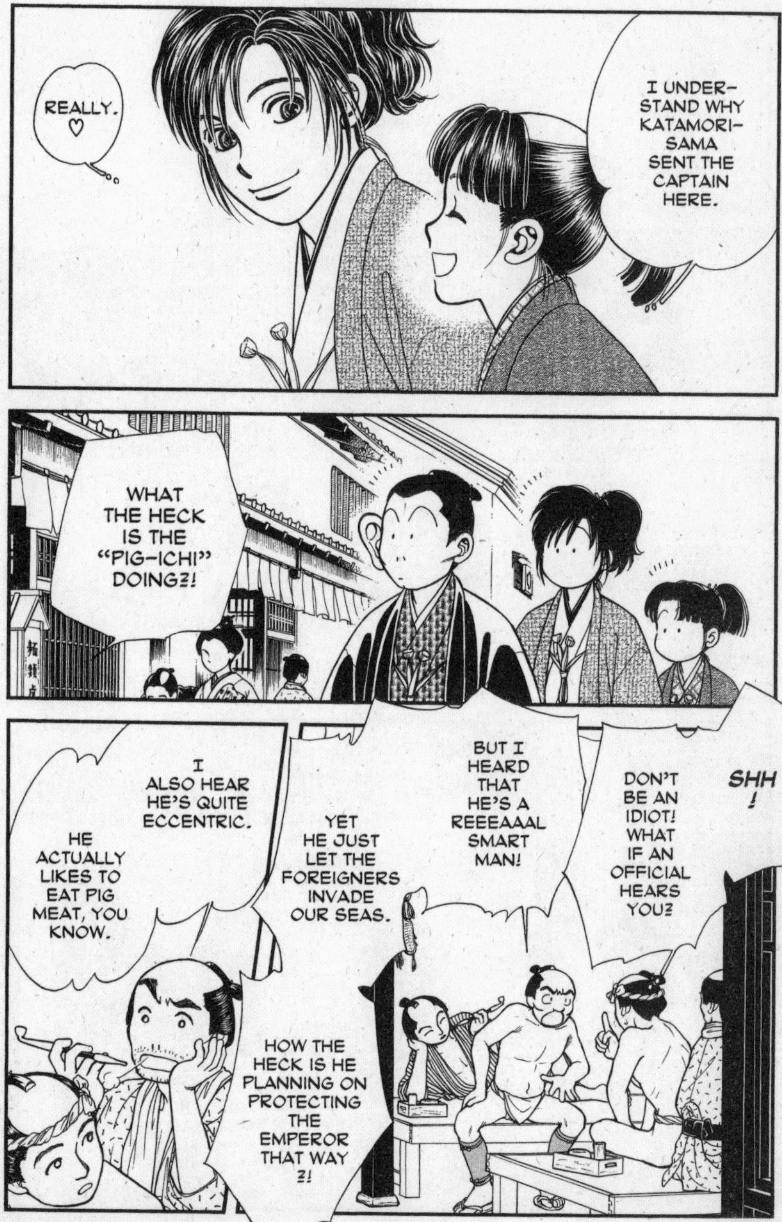
I UNDERSTAND WHY KATAMORI-SAMA SENT THE CAPTAIN HERE.
REALLY. ♡
WHAT THE HECK IS THE "PIG-ICHI" DOING?!
SHH!
DON'T BE AN IDIOT! WHAT IF AN OFFICIAL HEARS YOU?
BUT I HEARD THAT HE'S A REEEAAAL SMART MAN!
YET HE JUST LET THE FOREIGNERS INVADE OUR SEAS.
I ALSO HEAR HE'S QUITE ECCENTRIC.
HE ACTUALLY LIKES TO EAT PIG MEAT, YOU KNOW.
HOW THE HECK IS HE PLANNING ON PROTECTING THE EMPEROR THAT WAY?!

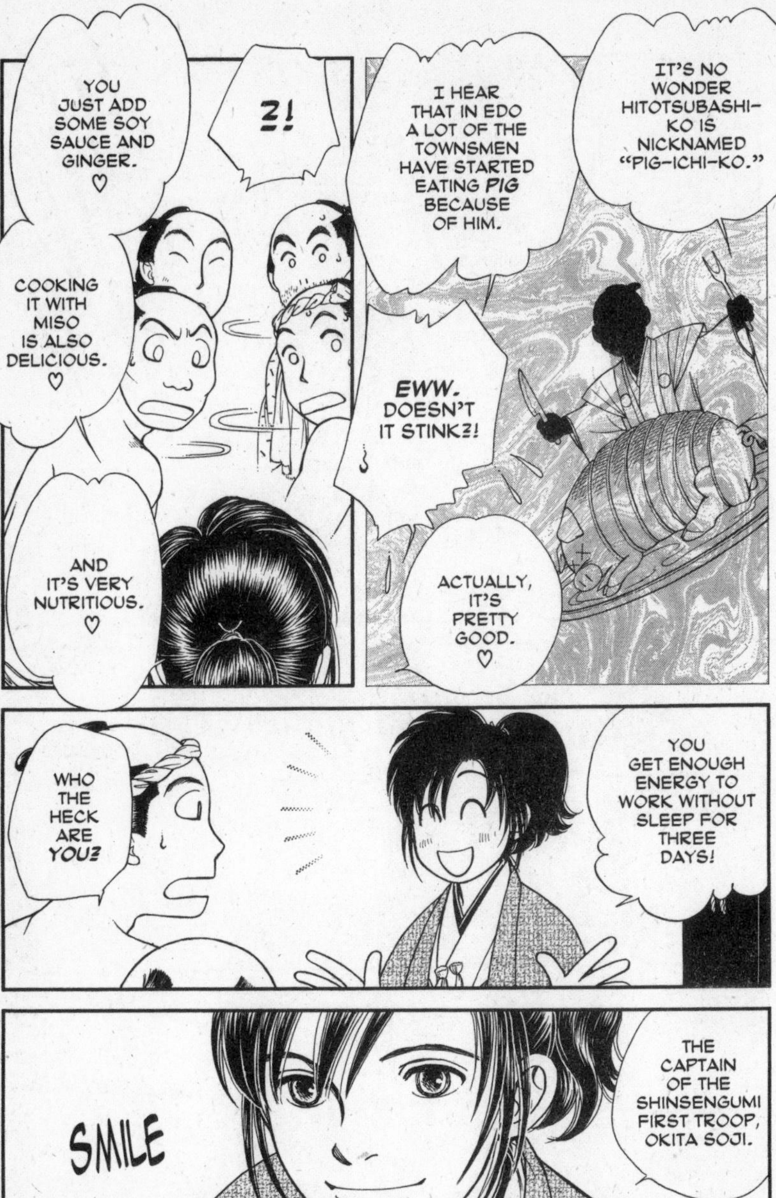
IT'S NO WONDER HITOTSUBASHI-KO IS NICKNAMED "PIG-ICHI-KO."
I HEAR THAT IN EDO A LOT OF THE TOWNSMEN HAVE STARTED EATING *PIG* BECAUSE OF HIM.
EWW. DOESN'T IT STINK?!
ACTUALLY, IT'S PRETTY GOOD. ♡
?!
YOU JUST ADD SOME SOY SAUCE AND GINGER. ♡
COOKING IT WITH MISO IS ALSO DELICIOUS. ♡
AND IT'S VERY NUTRITIOUS. ♡
YOU GET ENOUGH ENERGY TO WORK WITHOUT SLEEP FOR THREE DAYS!
WHO THE HECK ARE *YOU?*
THE CAPTAIN OF THE SHINSENGUMI FIRST TROOP, OKITA SOJI.
SMILE

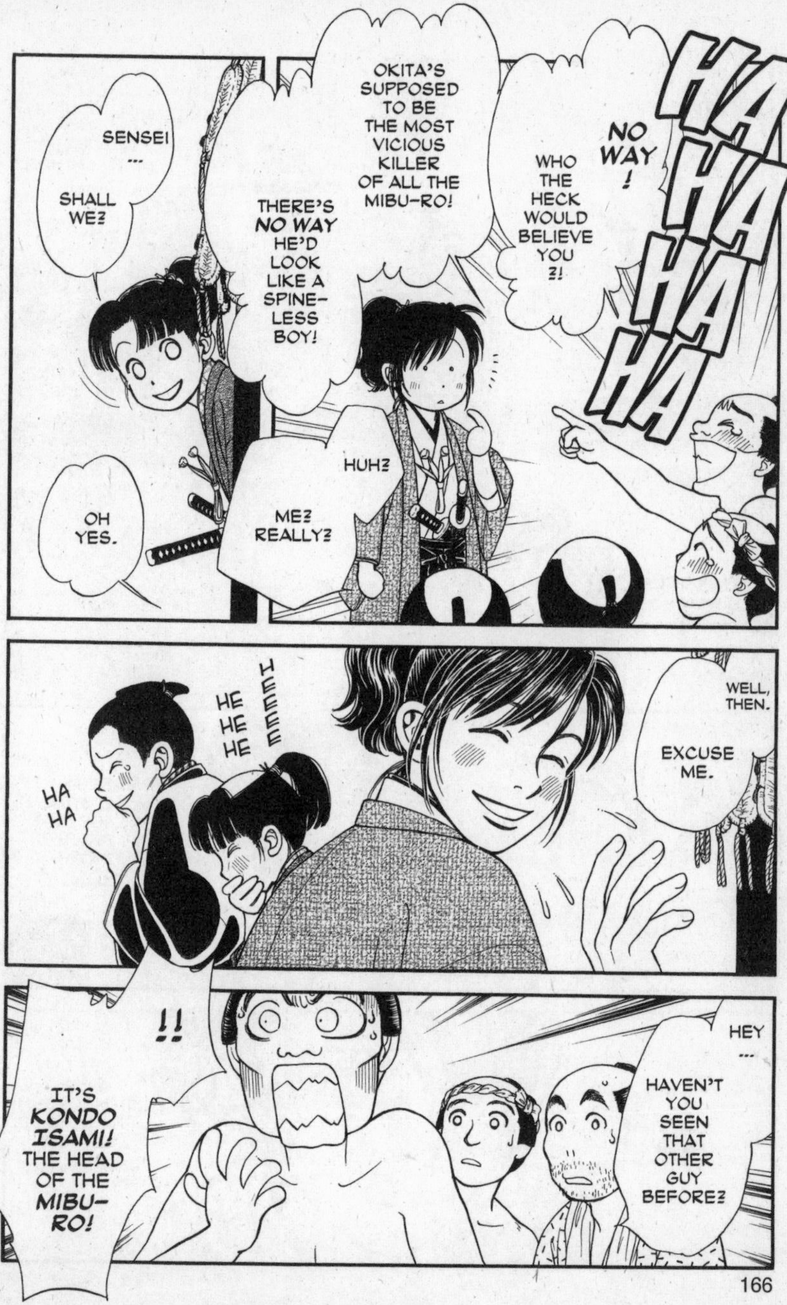
HA HA HA HA HA
NO WAY!
WHO THE HECK WOULD BELIEVE YOU?!
OKITA'S SUPPOSED TO BE THE MOST VICIOUS KILLER OF ALL THE MIBU-RO!
THERE'S NO WAY HE'D LOOK LIKE A SPINE-LESS BOY!
HUH?
ME? REALLY?
SENSEI... SHALL WE?
OH YES.
WELL, THEN.
EXCUSE ME.
HEEEE
HE HE HE
HA HA
HEY... HAVEN'T YOU SEEN THAT OTHER GUY BEFORE?
!!
IT'S KONDO ISAMI! THE HEAD OF THE MIBU-RO!

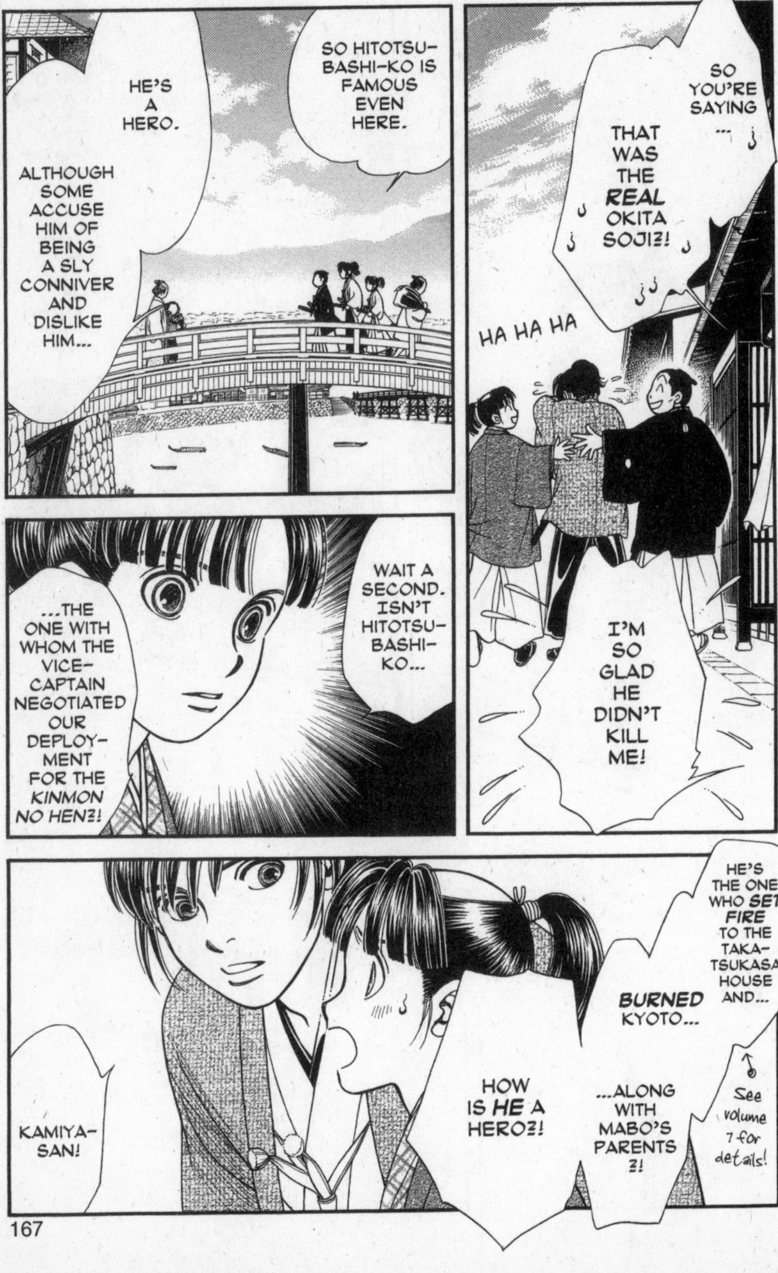
SO YOU'RE SAYING...
THAT WAS THE REAL OKITA SOJI?!
HA HA HA
I'M SO GLAD HE DIDN'T KILL ME!
SO HITOTSUBASHI-KO IS FAMOUS EVEN HERE.
HE'S A HERO.
ALTHOUGH SOME ACCUSE HIM OF BEING A SLY CONNIVER AND DISLIKE HIM...
WAIT A SECOND. ISN'T HITOTSUBASHI-KO...
...THE ONE WITH WHOM THE VICE-CAPTAIN NEGOTIATED OUR DEPLOYMENT FOR THE KINMON NO HEN?!
HE'S THE ONE WHO SET FIRE TO THE TAKATSUKASA HOUSE AND...
See volume 7 for details!
BURNED KYOTO...
...ALONG WITH MABO'S PARENTS?!
HOW IS HE A HERO?!
KAMIYA-SAN!

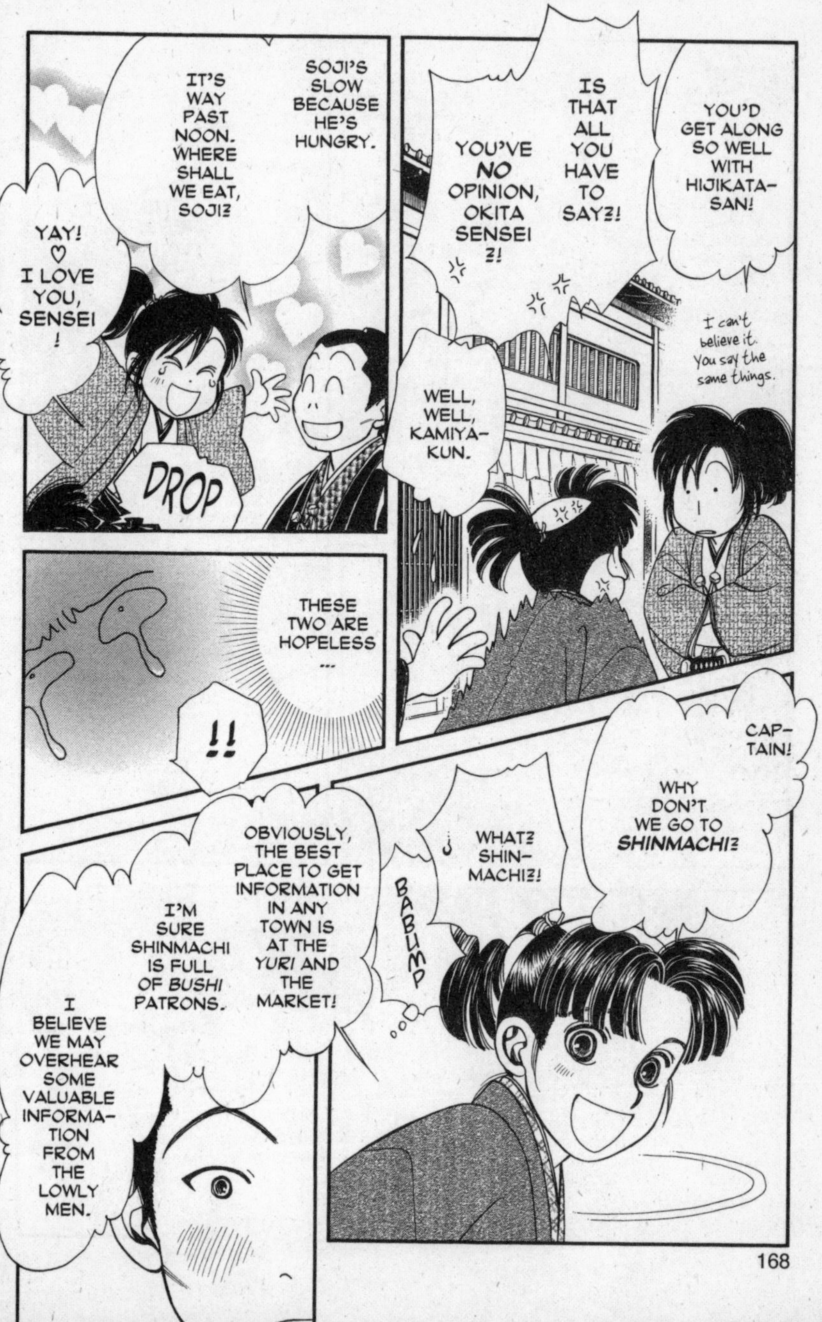

YOU'D GET ALONG SO WELL WITH HIJIKATA-SAN!
IS THAT ALL YOU HAVE TO SAY?!
YOU'VE NO OPINION, OKITA SENSEI ?!
I can't believe it. You say the same things.
WELL, WELL, KAMIYA-KUN.
SOJI'S SLOW BECAUSE HE'S HUNGRY.
IT'S WAY PAST NOON. WHERE SHALL WE EAT, SOJI?
YAY! ♡ I LOVE YOU, SENSEI !
DROP
THESE TWO ARE HOPELESS...
!!
CAP-TAIN!
WHY DON'T WE GO TO SHINMACHI?
WHAT? SHIN-MACHI?!
BABUMP
OBVIOUSLY, THE BEST PLACE TO GET INFORMATION IN ANY TOWN IS AT THE *YURI* AND THE MARKET!
I'M SURE SHINMACHI IS FULL OF *BUSHI* PATRONS.
I BELIEVE WE MAY OVERHEAR SOME VALUABLE INFORMA-TION FROM THE LOWLY MEN.

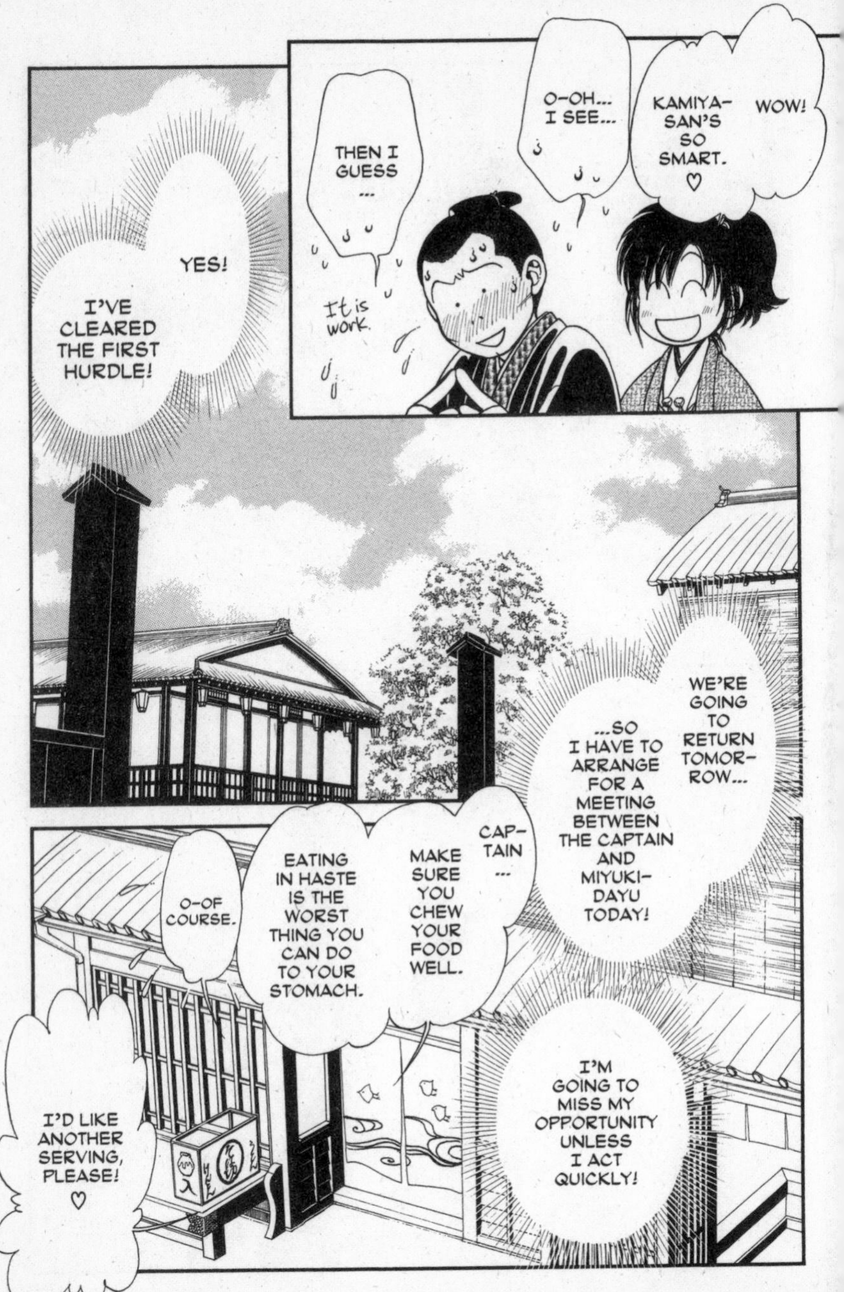
WOW!
KAMIYA-SAN'S SO SMART. ♡
O-OH... I SEE...
THEN I GUESS ...
It is work.
YES!
I'VE CLEARED THE FIRST HURDLE!
WE'RE GOING TO RETURN TOMOR-ROW...
...SO I HAVE TO ARRANGE FOR A MEETING BETWEEN THE CAPTAIN AND MIYUKI-DAYU TODAY!
I'M GOING TO MISS MY OPPORTUNITY UNLESS I ACT QUICKLY!
CAP-TAIN ...
MAKE SURE YOU CHEW YOUR FOOD WELL.
EATING IN HASTE IS THE WORST THING YOU CAN DO TO YOUR STOMACH.
O-OF COURSE.
I'D LIKE ANOTHER SERVING, PLEASE! ♡

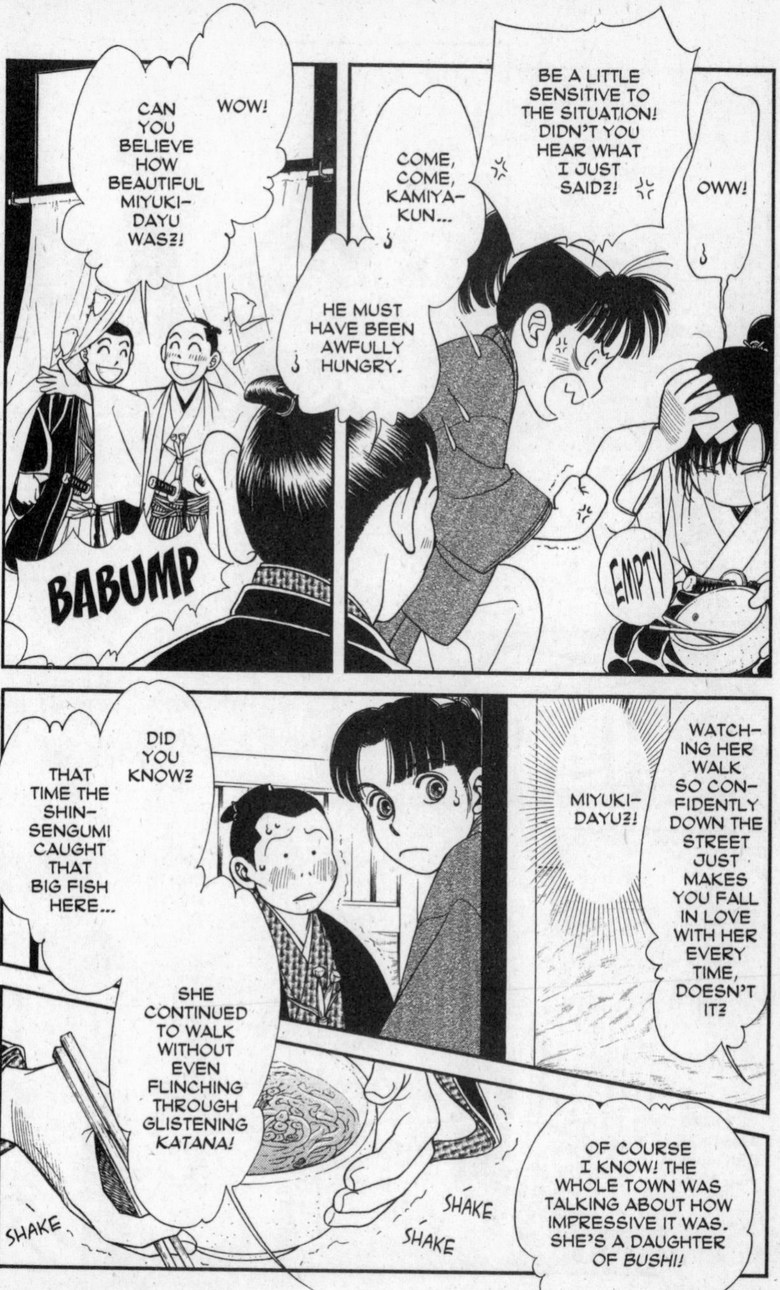
BE A LITTLE SENSITIVE TO THE SITUATION! DIDN'T YOU HEAR WHAT I JUST SAID?!
OWW!
COME, COME, KAMIYA-KUN...
HE MUST HAVE BEEN AWFULLY HUNGRY.
EMPTY
WOW!
CAN YOU BELIEVE HOW BEAUTIFUL MIYUKI-DAYU WAS?!
BABUMP
WATCHING HER WALK SO CONFIDENTLY DOWN THE STREET JUST MAKES YOU FALL IN LOVE WITH HER EVERY TIME, DOESN'T IT?
MIYUKI-DAYU?!
DID YOU KNOW?
THAT TIME THE SHINSENGUMI CAUGHT THAT BIG FISH HERE...
SHE CONTINUED TO WALK WITHOUT EVEN FLINCHING THROUGH GLISTENING KATANA!
OF COURSE I KNOW! THE WHOLE TOWN WAS TALKING ABOUT HOW IMPRESSIVE IT WAS. SHE'S A DAUGHTER OF BUSHI!
SHAKE
SHAKE
SHAKE

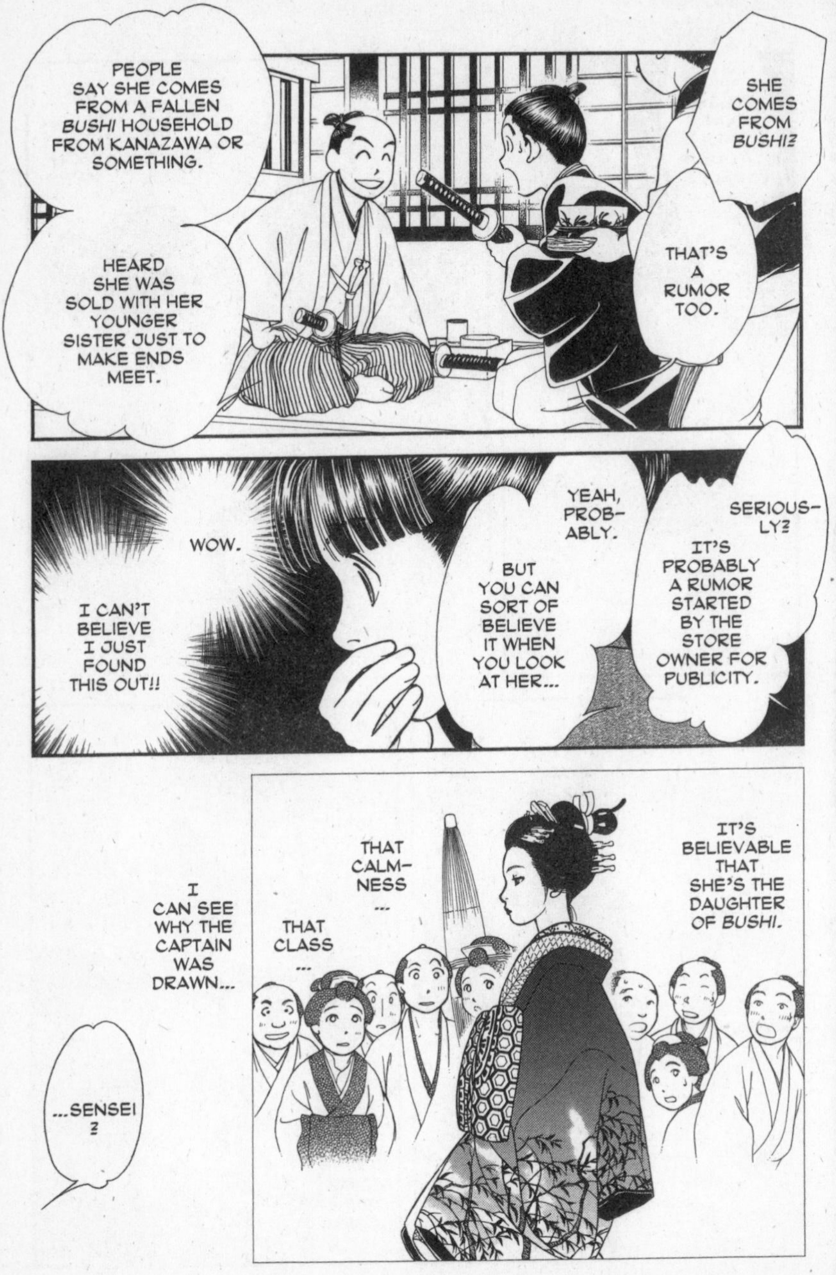
SHE COMES FROM *BUSHI*?
PEOPLE SAY SHE COMES FROM A FALLEN *BUSHI* HOUSEHOLD FROM KANAZAWA OR SOMETHING.
THAT'S A RUMOR TOO.
HEARD SHE WAS SOLD WITH HER YOUNGER SISTER JUST TO MAKE ENDS MEET.
SERIOUSLY?
IT'S PROBABLY A RUMOR STARTED BY THE STORE OWNER FOR PUBLICITY.
YEAH, PROBABLY.
BUT YOU CAN SORT OF BELIEVE IT WHEN YOU LOOK AT HER...
WOW.
I CAN'T BELIEVE I JUST FOUND THIS OUT!!
IT'S BELIEVABLE THAT SHE'S THE DAUGHTER OF *BUSHI*.
THAT CALMNESS...
THAT CLASS...
I CAN SEE WHY THE CAPTAIN WAS DRAWN...
...SENSEI?

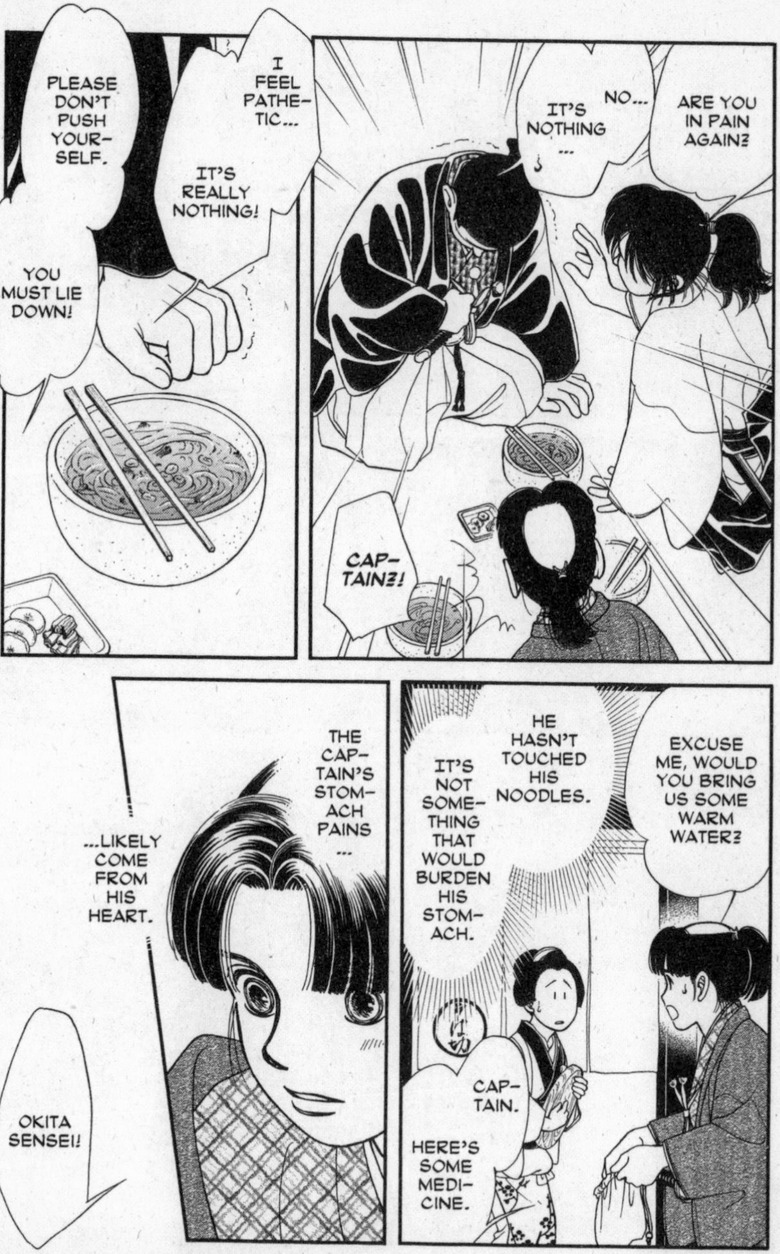
ARE YOU IN PAIN AGAIN?
NO...
IT'S NOTHING ...
CAP-TAIN?!
I FEEL PATHE-TIC...
IT'S REALLY NOTHING!
PLEASE DON'T PUSH YOUR-SELF.
YOU MUST LIE DOWN!
EXCUSE ME, WOULD YOU BRING US SOME WARM WATER?
HE HASN'T TOUCHED HIS NOODLES.
IT'S NOT SOME-THING THAT WOULD BURDEN HIS STOM-ACH.
CAP-TAIN.
HERE'S SOME MEDI-CINE.
THE CAP-TAIN'S STOM-ACH PAINS ...
...LIKELY COME FROM HIS HEART.
OKITA SENSEI!

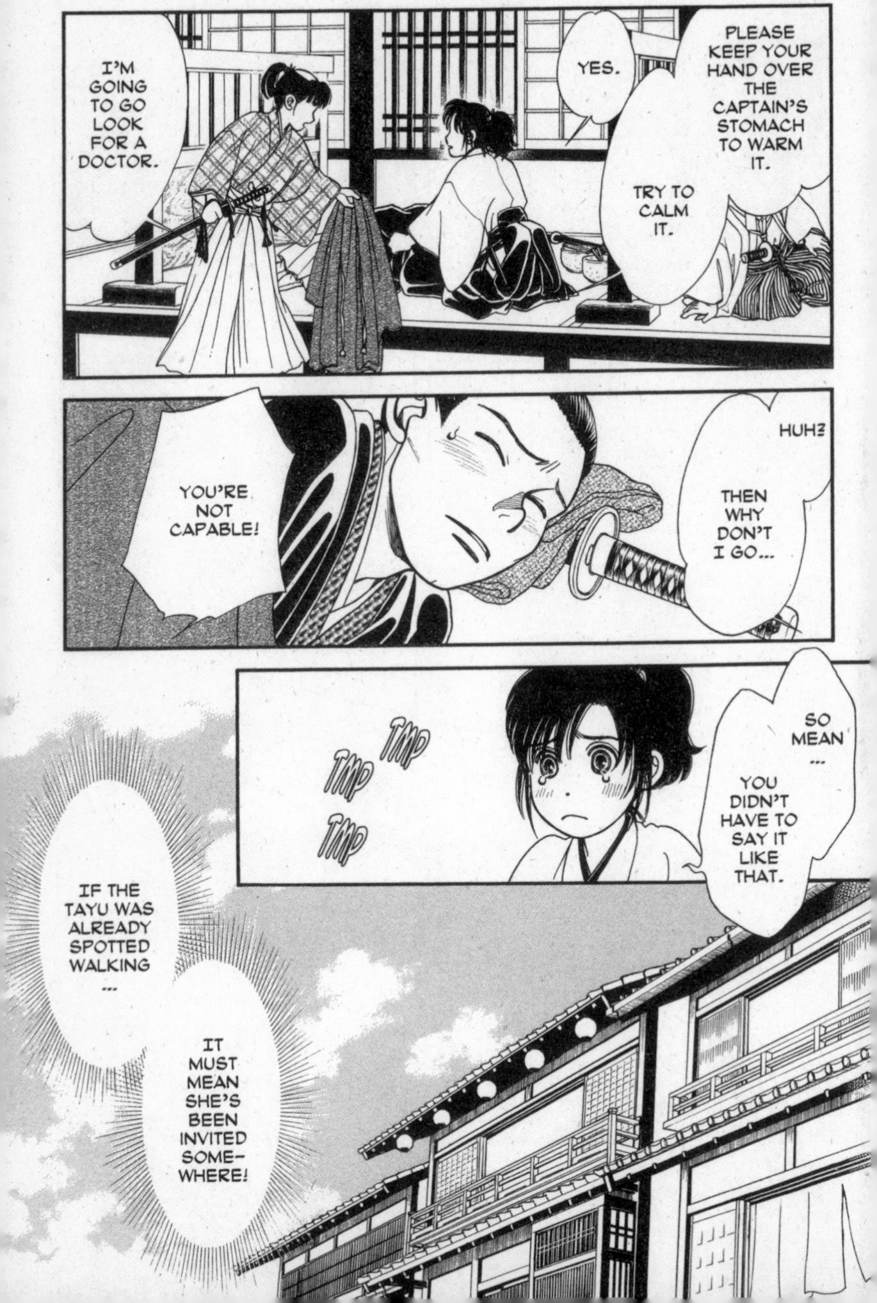
PLEASE KEEP YOUR HAND OVER THE CAPTAIN'S STOMACH TO WARM IT.
TRY TO CALM IT.
YES.
I'M GOING TO GO LOOK FOR A DOCTOR.
HUH?
THEN WHY DON'T I GO...
YOU'RE NOT CAPABLE!
SO MEAN...
YOU DIDN'T HAVE TO SAY IT LIKE THAT.
TMP
TMP
TMP
IF THE TAYU WAS ALREADY SPOTTED WALKING...
IT MUST MEAN SHE'S BEEN INVITED SOMEWHERE!

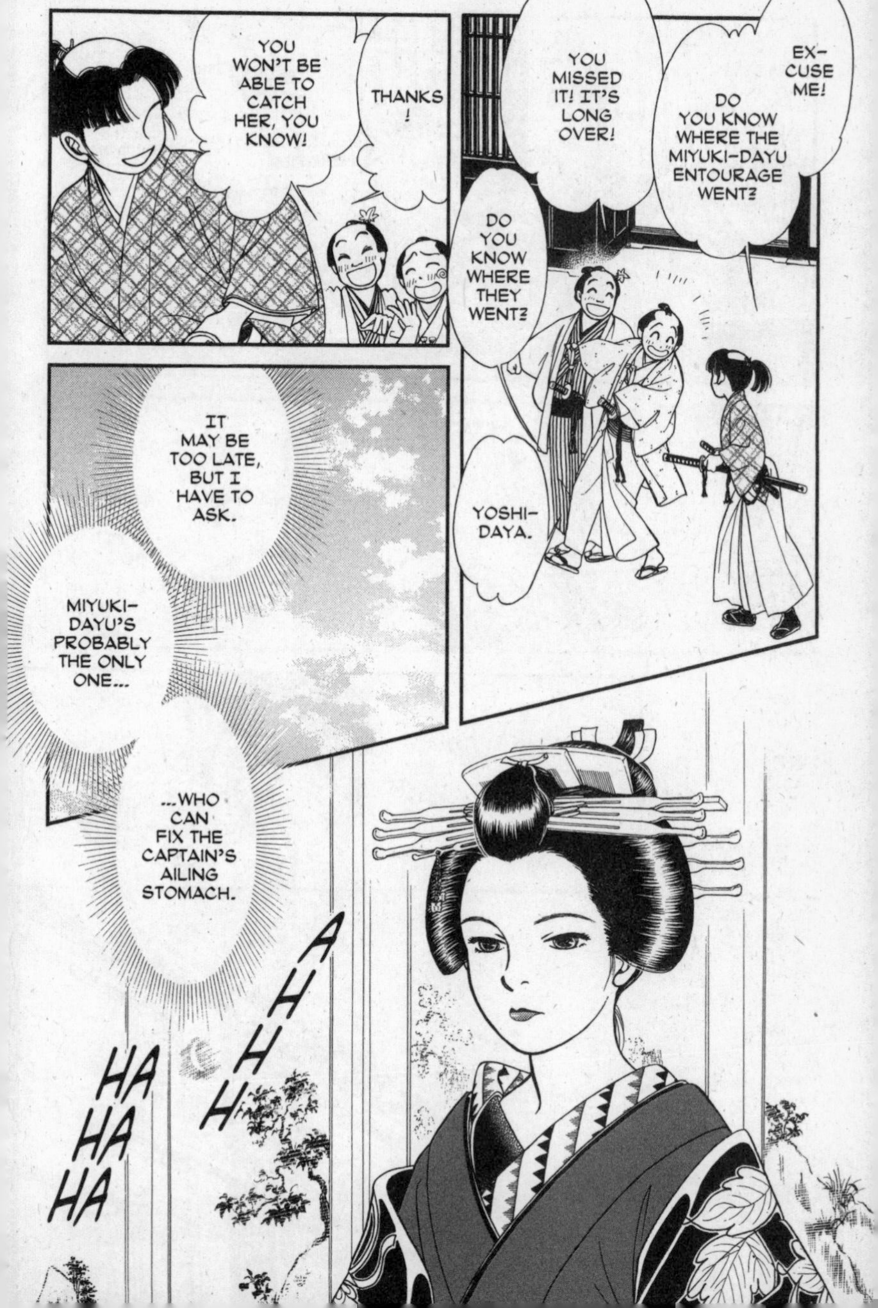
EX-CUSE ME!
DO YOU KNOW WHERE THE MIYUKI-DAYU ENTOURAGE WENT?
YOU MISSED IT! IT'S LONG OVER!
DO YOU KNOW WHERE THEY WENT?
YOSHI-DAYA.
THANKS!
YOU WON'T BE ABLE TO CATCH HER, YOU KNOW!
IT MAY BE TOO LATE, BUT I HAVE TO ASK.
MIYUKI-DAYU'S PROBABLY THE ONLY ONE...
...WHO CAN FIX THE CAPTAIN'S AILING STOMACH.
AHHHH
HAHAHAHA

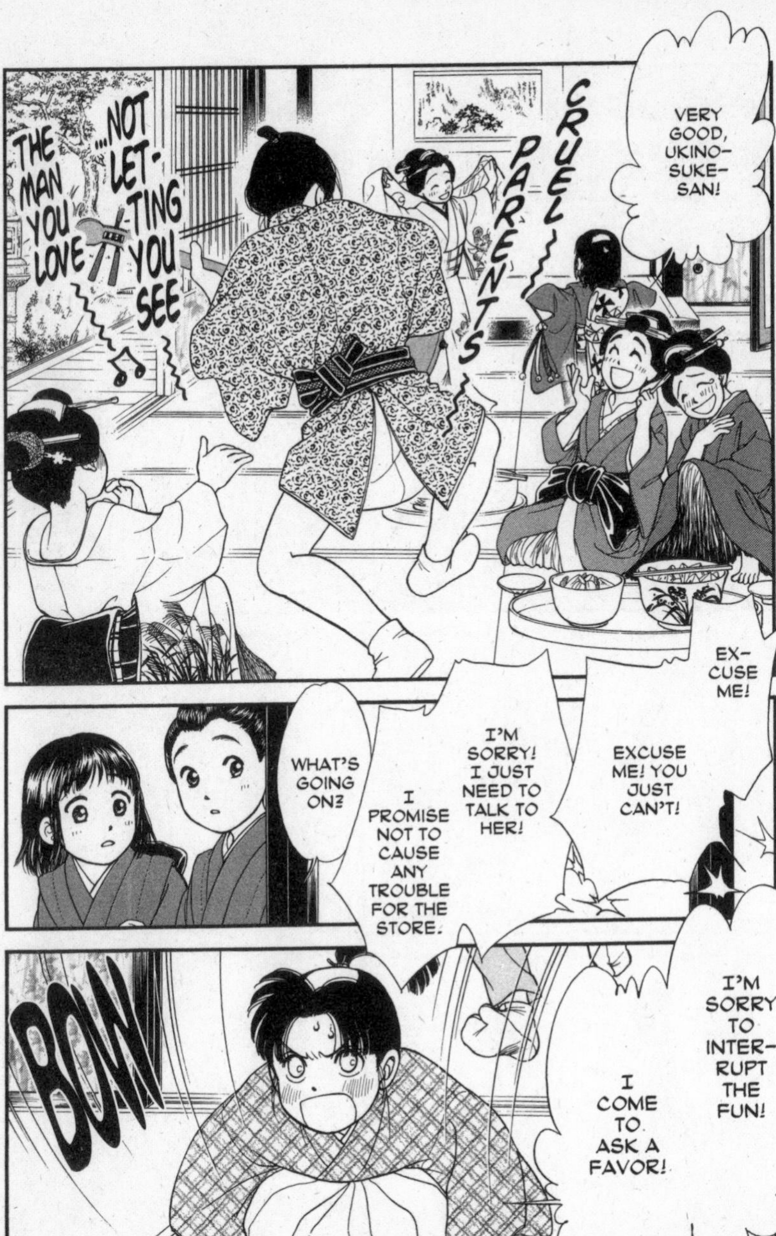
VERY GOOD, UKINO-SUKE-SAN!
CRUEL PARENTS
...NOT LETTING YOU SEE
THE MAN YOU LOVE
EX-CUSE ME!
EXCUSE ME! YOU JUST CAN'T!
I'M SORRY! I JUST NEED TO TALK TO HER!
I PROMISE NOT TO CAUSE ANY TROUBLE FOR THE STORE.
WHAT'S GOING ON?
I'M SORRY TO INTERRUPT THE FUN!
I COME TO ASK A FAVOR!
BOM

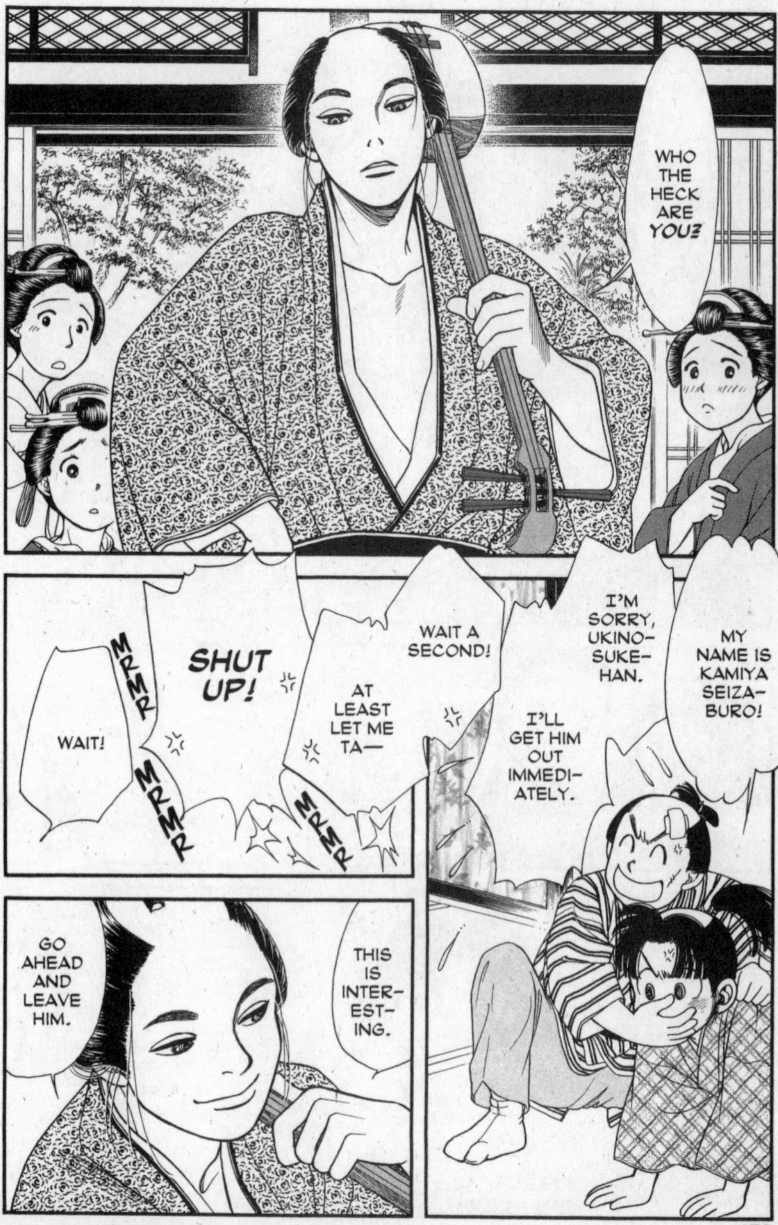
WHO THE HECK ARE YOU!?
MY NAME IS KAMIYA SEIZABURO!
I'M SORRY, UKINOSUKE-HAN.
I'LL GET HIM OUT IMMEDIATELY.
WAIT A SECOND!
AT LEAST LET ME TA—
MRMR
SHUT UP!
MRMR
MRMR
WAIT!
THIS IS INTERESTING.
GO AHEAD AND LEAVE HIM.

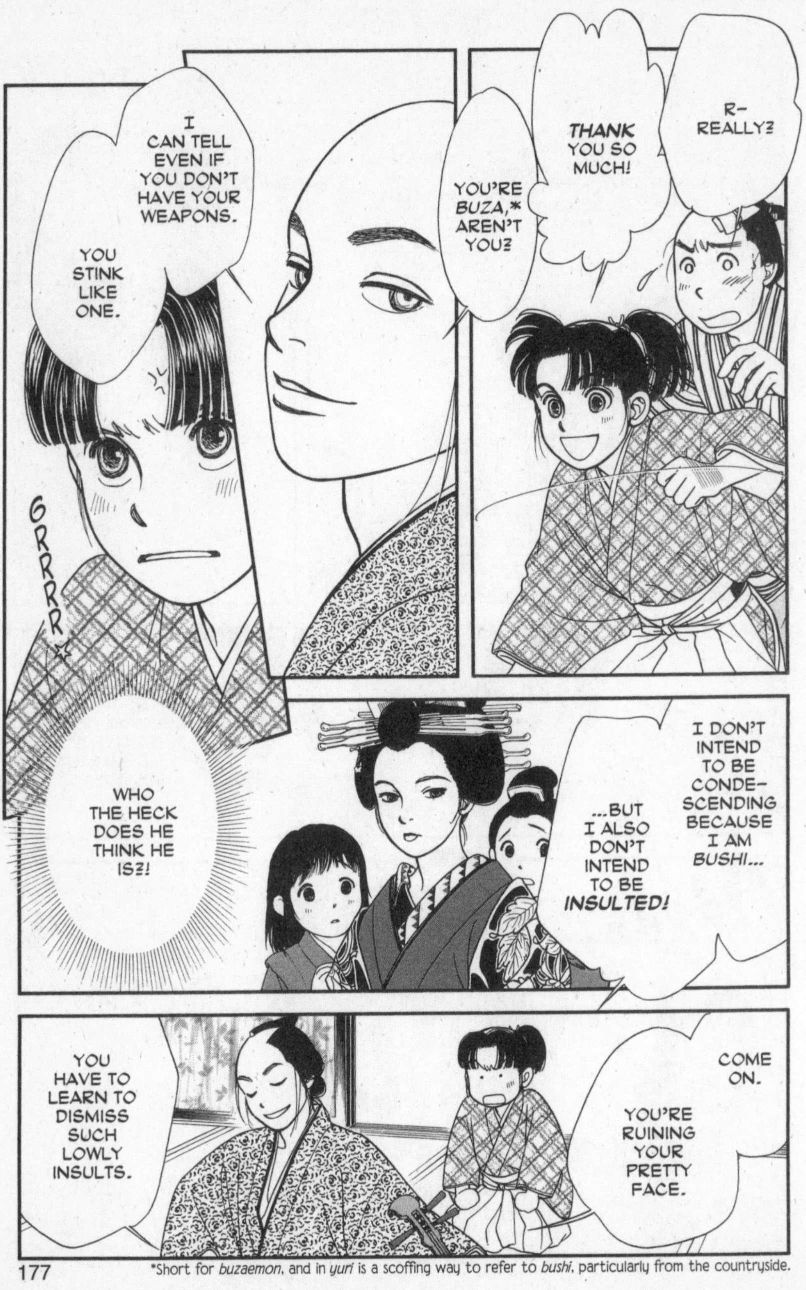
R-
REALLY?
THANK YOU SO MUCH!
YOU'RE BUZA,* AREN'T YOU?
I CAN TELL EVEN IF YOU DON'T HAVE YOUR WEAPONS.
YOU STINK LIKE ONE.
GRRRR
I DON'T INTEND TO BE CONDESCENDING BECAUSE I AM BUSHI...
...BUT I ALSO DON'T INTEND TO BE INSULTED!
WHO THE HECK DOES HE THINK HE IS?!
COME ON.
YOU'RE RUINING YOUR PRETTY FACE.
YOU HAVE TO LEARN TO DISMISS SUCH LOWLY INSULTS.

*Short for *buzaemon*, and in *yuri* is a scoffing way to refer to *bushi*, particularly from the countryside.

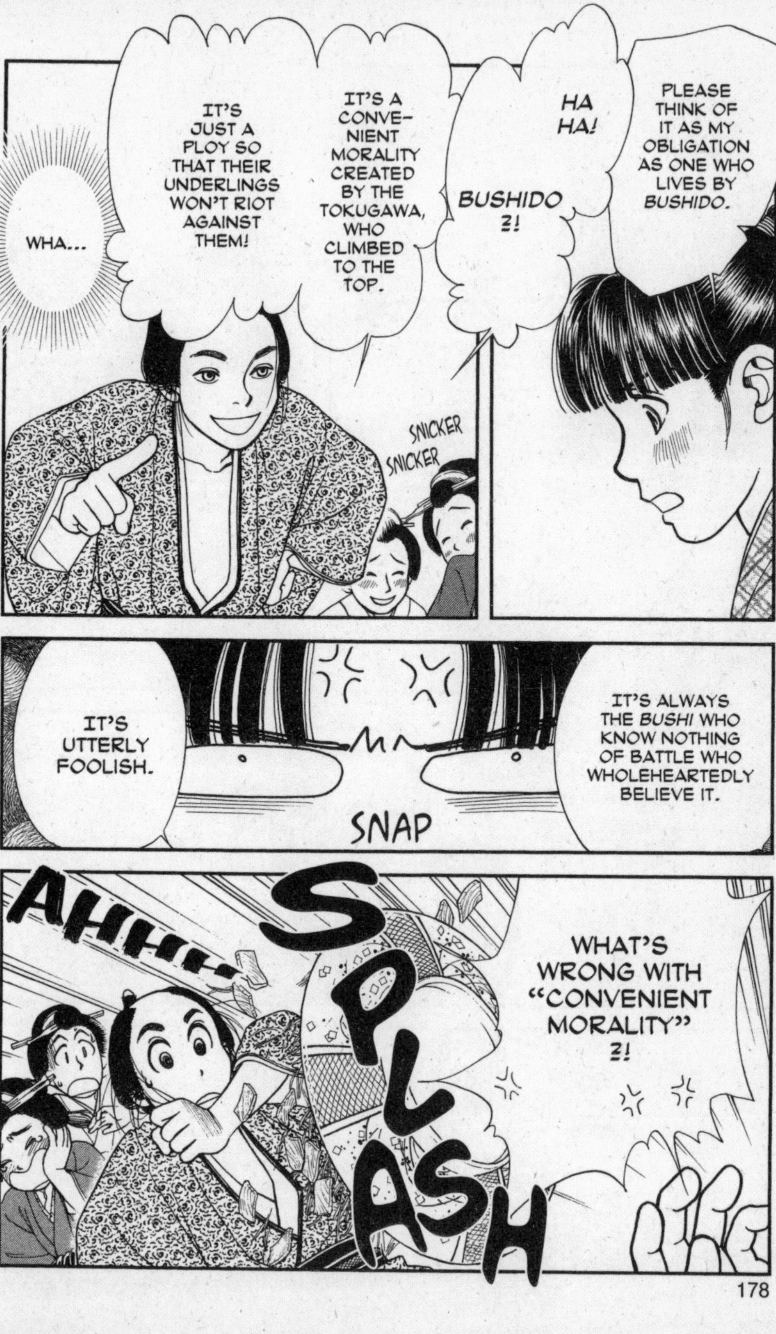
PLEASE THINK OF IT AS MY OBLIGATION AS ONE WHO LIVES BY *BUSHIDO*.
HA HA!
BUSHIDO ?!
IT'S A CONVENIENT MORALITY CREATED BY THE TOKUGAWA, WHO CLIMBED TO THE TOP.
IT'S JUST A PLOY SO THAT THEIR UNDERLINGS WON'T RIOT AGAINST THEM!
WHA...
SNICKER
SNICKER
IT'S ALWAYS THE *BUSHI* WHO KNOW NOTHING OF BATTLE WHO WHOLEHEARTEDLY BELIEVE IT.
SNAP
IT'S UTTERLY FOOLISH.
WHAT'S WRONG WITH "CONVENIENT MORALITY" ?!
SPLASH
AHHH

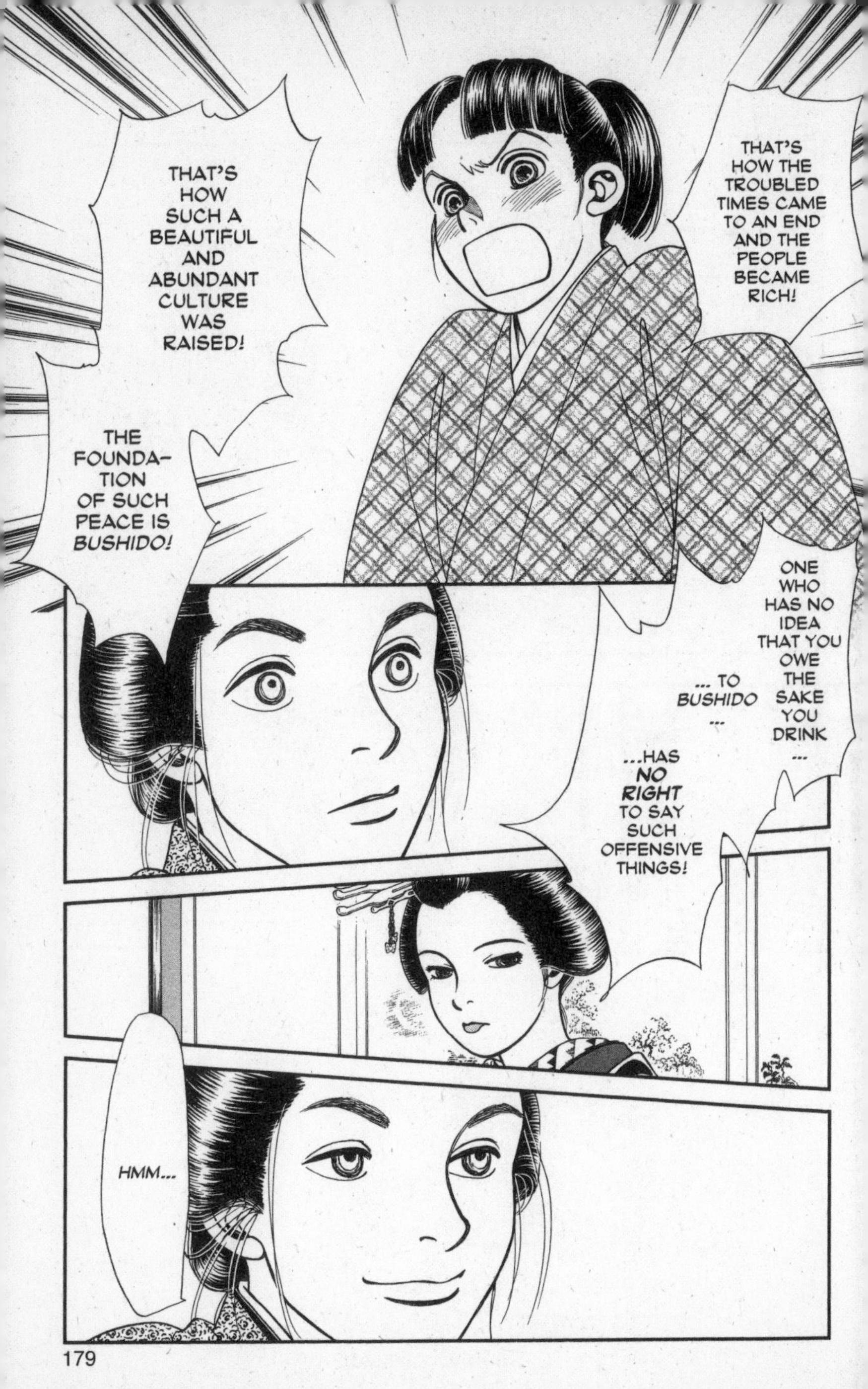
THAT'S HOW THE TROUBLED TIMES CAME TO AN END AND THE PEOPLE BECAME RICH!
THAT'S HOW SUCH A BEAUTIFUL AND ABUNDANT CULTURE WAS RAISED!
THE FOUNDATION OF SUCH PEACE IS *BUSHIDO*!
ONE WHO HAS NO IDEA THAT YOU OWE THE SAKE YOU DRINK ...
... TO *BUSHIDO* ...
...HAS ***NO RIGHT*** TO SAY SUCH OFFENSIVE THINGS!
HMM...

HEY.
DIDN'T YOU COME HERE TO ASK ME A FAVOR?
SMIRK
AGH!
CRAP!

KAMIYA-SAN...
I HOPE SHE'S NOT UP TO NO GOOD.
She's been gone awhile.
ZZZZ

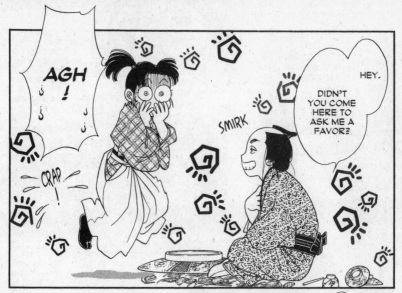

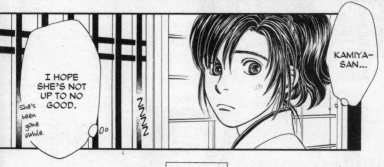

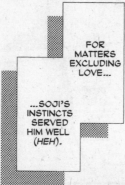

FOR MATTERS EXCLUDING LOVE...

...SOJI'S INSTINCTS SERVED HIM WELL (*HEH*).

To Be Continued!

TAEKO WATANABE PRESENTS

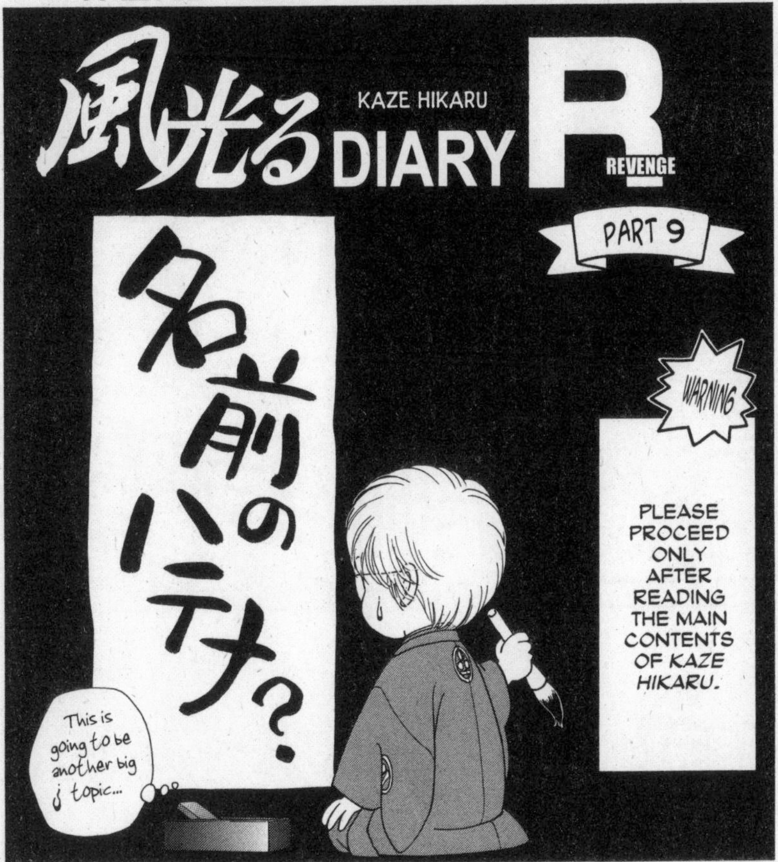
風光る KAZE HIKARU DIARY R REVENGE
PART 9
WARNING
PLEASE PROCEED ONLY AFTER READING THE MAIN CONTENTS OF KAZE HIKARU.
名前のハテナ？
This is going to be another big topic...

Sign: Questions involving names?

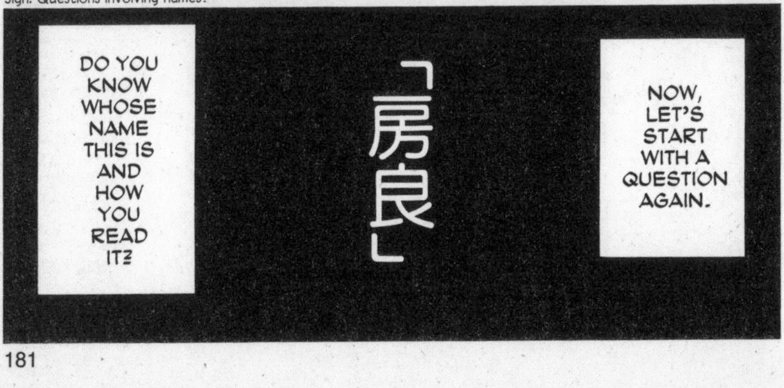
NOW, LET'S START WITH A QUESTION AGAIN.
「房良」
DO YOU KNOW WHOSE NAME THIS IS AND HOW YOU READ IT?

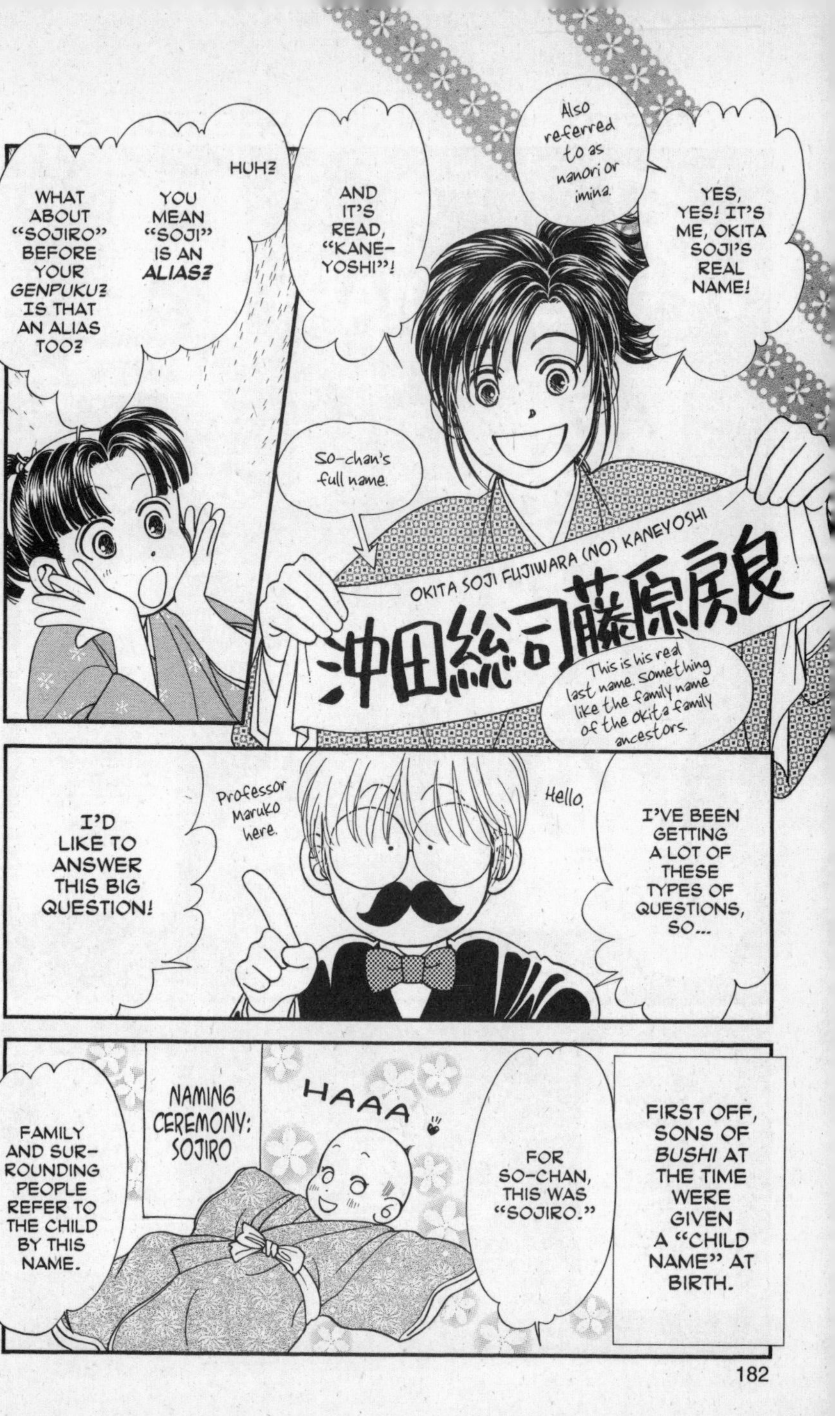
YES, YES! IT'S ME, OKITA SOJI'S REAL NAME!
Also referred to as nanori or imina.
AND IT'S READ, "KANE-YOSHI"!
So-chan's full name.
OKITA SOJI FUJIWARA (NO) KANEYOSHI
沖田総司藤原房良
This is his real last name. Something like the family name of the Okita family ancestors.
HUH?
YOU MEAN "SOJI" IS AN *ALIAS?*
WHAT ABOUT "SOJIRO" BEFORE YOUR *GENPUKU?* IS THAT AN ALIAS TOO?
Hello.
I'VE BEEN GETTING A LOT OF THESE TYPES OF QUESTIONS, SO...
Professor Maruko here.
I'D LIKE TO ANSWER THIS BIG QUESTION!
FIRST OFF, SONS OF *BUSHI* AT THE TIME WERE GIVEN A "CHILD NAME" AT BIRTH.
FOR SO-CHAN, THIS WAS "SOJIRO."
HAAA
NAMING CEREMONY: SOJIRO
FAMILY AND SUR-ROUNDING PEOPLE REFER TO THE CHILD BY THIS NAME.

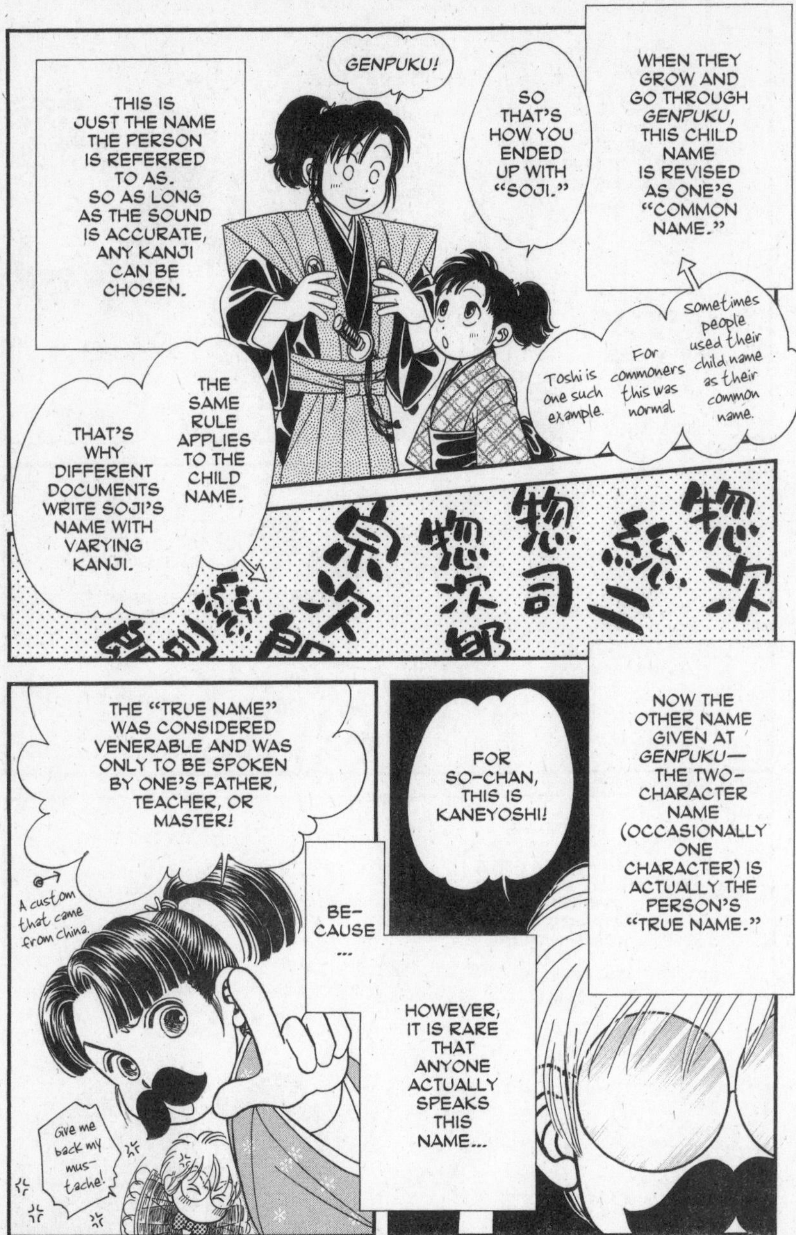
WHEN THEY GROW AND GO THROUGH GENPUKU, THIS CHILD NAME IS REVISED AS ONE'S "COMMON NAME."
SO THAT'S HOW YOU ENDED UP WITH "SOJI."
GENPUKU!
THIS IS JUST THE NAME THE PERSON IS REFERRED TO AS. SO AS LONG AS THE SOUND IS ACCURATE, ANY KANJI CAN BE CHOSEN.
Sometimes people used their child name as their common name.
For commoners this was normal.
Toshi is one such example.
THE SAME RULE APPLIES TO THE CHILD NAME.
THAT'S WHY DIFFERENT DOCUMENTS WRITE SOJI'S NAME WITH VARYING KANJI.
惣次
総三
惣司
惣次郎
宗次郎
NOW THE OTHER NAME GIVEN AT GENPUKU—THE TWO-CHARACTER NAME (OCCASIONALLY ONE CHARACTER) IS ACTUALLY THE PERSON'S "TRUE NAME."
FOR SO-CHAN, THIS IS KANEYOSHI!
HOWEVER, IT IS RARE THAT ANYONE ACTUALLY SPEAKS THIS NAME...
BE-CAUSE ...
THE "TRUE NAME" WAS CONSIDERED VENERABLE AND WAS ONLY TO BE SPOKEN BY ONE'S FATHER, TEACHER, OR MASTER!
A custom that came from China.
Give me back my mus-tache!

*Although this was omitted in the story, Soji actually had the true name, Harumasa, before his *genpuku*, and changed it after his *genpuku* to Kaneyoshi. There were such cases as well.

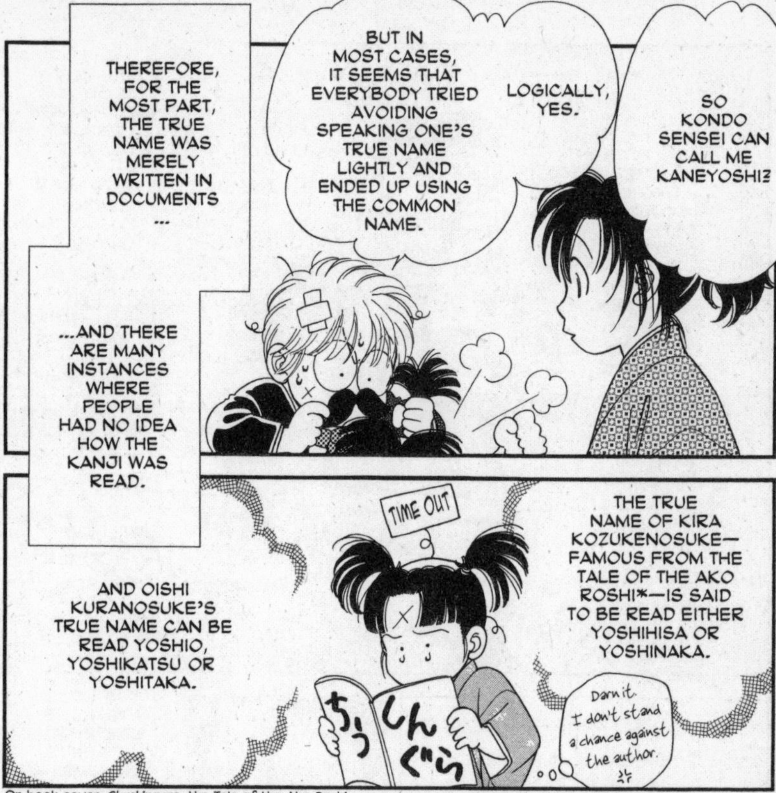
SO KONDO SENSEI CAN CALL ME KANEYOSHI?
LOGICALLY, YES.
BUT IN MOST CASES, IT SEEMS THAT EVERYBODY TRIED AVOIDING SPEAKING ONE'S TRUE NAME LIGHTLY AND ENDED UP USING THE COMMON NAME.
THEREFORE, FOR THE MOST PART, THE TRUE NAME WAS MERELY WRITTEN IN DOCUMENTS ...
...AND THERE ARE MANY INSTANCES WHERE PEOPLE HAD NO IDEA HOW THE KANJI WAS READ.
THE TRUE NAME OF KIRA KOZUKENOSUKE—FAMOUS FROM THE TALE OF THE AKO ROSHI*—IS SAID TO BE READ EITHER YOSHIHISA OR YOSHINAKA.
TIME OUT
AND OISHI KURANOSUKE'S TRUE NAME CAN BE READ YOSHIO, YOSHIKATSU OR YOSHITAKA.
ちゅうしんぐら
Darn it. I don't stand a chance against the author.

On book cover: *Chushingura*–the Tale of the Ako Roshi.

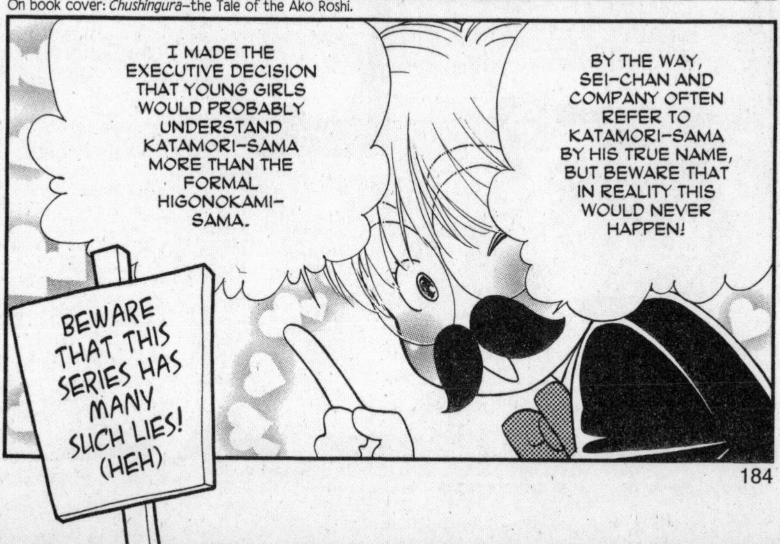
BY THE WAY, SEI-CHAN AND COMPANY OFTEN REFER TO KATAMORI-SAMA BY HIS TRUE NAME, BUT BEWARE THAT IN REALITY THIS WOULD NEVER HAPPEN!
I MADE THE EXECUTIVE DECISION THAT YOUNG GIRLS WOULD PROBABLY UNDERSTAND KATAMORI-SAMA MORE THAN THE FORMAL HIGONOKAMI-SAMA.
BEWARE THAT THIS SERIES HAS MANY SUCH LIES! (HEH)

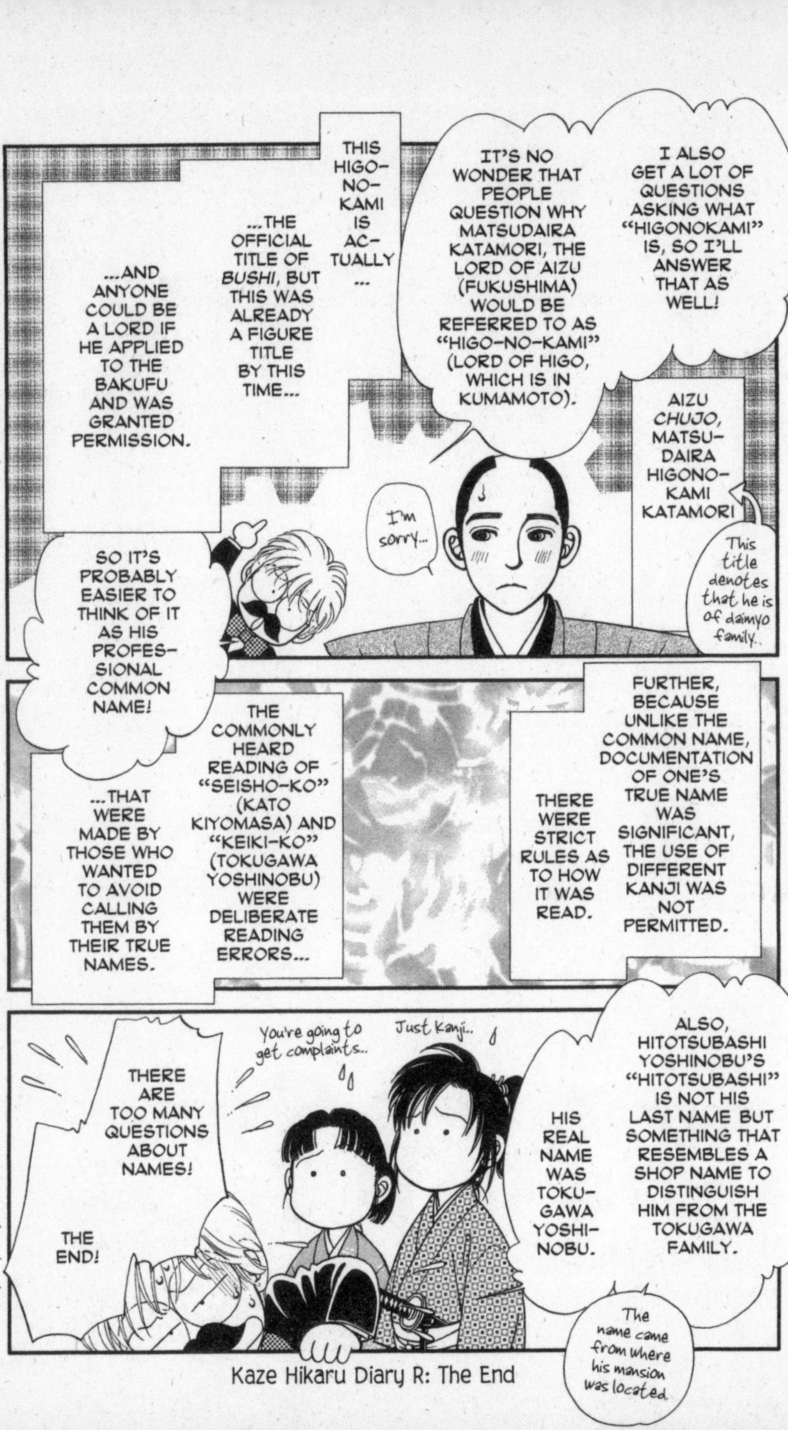
I ALSO GET A LOT OF QUESTIONS ASKING WHAT "HIGONOKAMI" IS, SO I'LL ANSWER THAT AS WELL!
IT'S NO WONDER THAT PEOPLE QUESTION WHY MATSUDAIRA KATAMORI, THE LORD OF AIZU (FUKUSHIMA) WOULD BE REFERRED TO AS "HIGO-NO-KAMI" (LORD OF HIGO, WHICH IS IN KUMAMOTO).
THIS HIGO-NO-KAMI IS ACTUALLY...
...THE OFFICIAL TITLE OF BUSHI, BUT THIS WAS ALREADY A FIGURE TITLE BY THIS TIME...
...AND ANYONE COULD BE A LORD IF HE APPLIED TO THE BAKUFU AND WAS GRANTED PERMISSION.
AIZU CHUJO, MATSUDAIRA HIGONOKAMI KATAMORI
This title denotes that he is of daimyo family..
I'm sorry...
SO IT'S PROBABLY EASIER TO THINK OF IT AS HIS PROFESSIONAL COMMON NAME!
FURTHER, BECAUSE UNLIKE THE COMMON NAME, DOCUMENTATION OF ONE'S TRUE NAME WAS SIGNIFICANT, THE USE OF DIFFERENT KANJI WAS NOT PERMITTED.
THERE WERE STRICT RULES AS TO HOW IT WAS READ.
THE COMMONLY HEARD READING OF "SEISHO-KO" (KATO KIYOMASA) AND "KEIKI-KO" (TOKUGAWA YOSHINOBU) WERE DELIBERATE READING ERRORS...
...THAT WERE MADE BY THOSE WHO WANTED TO AVOID CALLING THEM BY THEIR TRUE NAMES.
ALSO, HITOTSUBASHI YOSHINOBU'S "HITOTSUBASHI" IS NOT HIS LAST NAME BUT SOMETHING THAT RESEMBLES A SHOP NAME TO DISTINGUISH HIM FROM THE TOKUGAWA FAMILY.
HIS REAL NAME WAS TOKUGAWA YOSHINOBU.
The name came from where his mansion was located.
Just Kanji..
You're going to get complaints..
THERE ARE TOO MANY QUESTIONS ABOUT NAMES!
THE END!

Kaze Hikaru Diary R: The End

"KI" 京

KYO NO YUME,
OSAKA NO YUME

"IT IS THE THOUGHT
THAT COUNTS"

(lit. Dream of Kyoto,
dream of Osaka)

EDO
IROHA
KARUTA
GAME

Decoding Kaze Hikaru

Kaze Hikaru is a historical drama based in 19th century Japan and thus contains some fairly mystifying terminology. In this glossary we'll break down archaic phrases, terms and other linguistic curiosities for you so that you can move through life with the smug assurance that you are indeed a know-it-all.

First and foremost, because *Kaze Hikaru* is a period story, we kept all character names in their traditional Japanese form—that is, family name followed by first name. For example, the character Okita Soji's family name is Okita and his personal name is Soji.

AKO-ROSHI:
The *ronin* (samurai) of Ako; featured in the immortal Kabuki play *Chushingura* (Loyalty), aka *47 Samurai.*

ANI-UE:
Literally, "brother above"; an honorific for an elder male sibling.

BAKUFU:
Literally, "tent government." Shogunate; the feudal, military government that dominated Japan for more than 200 years.

BUSHI:
A samurai or warrior (part of the compound word *bushido*, which means "way of the warrior").

CHICHI-UE:
An honorific suffix meaning "father above."

DO:
In kendo (a Japanese fencing sport that uses bamboo swords), a short way of describing the offensive single-hit strike *shikake waza ippon uchi.*

-HAN:

The same as the honorific *-san*, pronounced in the dialect of southern Japan.

-KUN:

An honorific suffix that indicates a difference in rank and title. The use of *-kun* is also a way of indicating familiarity and friendliness between students or compatriots.

MEN:

In the context of *Kaze Hikaru*, *men* refers to one of the "points" in kendo. It is a strike to the forehead and is considered a basic move.

MIBU-ROSHI:

A group of warriors that supports the Bakufu.

NE'E-SAN:

Can mean "older sister," "ma'am" or "miss."

NI'I-CHAN:

Short for *oni'i-san* or *oni'i-chan*, meaning older brother.

OKU-SAMA:

This is a polite way to refer to someone's wife. *Oku* means "deep" or "further back" and comes from the fact that wives (in affluent families) stayed hidden away in the back rooms of the house.

ONI:

Literally "ogre," this is Sei's nickname for Vice Captain Hijikata.

RANPO:

Medical science derived from the Dutch.

RONIN:
Masterless samurai.

RYO:
At the time, one *ryo* and two *bu* (four bu equaled roughly one ryo) were enough currency to support a family of five for an entire month.

-SAN:
An honorific suffix that carries the meaning of "Mr." or "Ms."

SENSEI:
A teacher, master or instructor.

SEPPUKU:
A ritualistic suicide that was considered a privilege of the nobility and samurai elite.

SONJO-HA:
Those loyal to the emperor and dedicated to the expulsion of foreigners from the country.

KAZE HIKARU
VOL. 18
Shojo Beat Edition

STORY AND ART BY
TAEKO WATANABE

© 1997 Taeko WATANABE/Shogakukan
All rights reserved.
Original Japanese edition "KAZE HIKARU" published by SHOGAKUKAN Inc.

Translation & English Adaptation/Mai Ihara
Touch-up Art & Lettering/Rina Mapa
Design/Julie Behn
Editor/Jonathan Tarbox

VP, Production/Alvin Lu
VP, Sales & Product Marketing/Gonzalo Ferreyra
VP, Creative/Linda Espinosa
Publisher/Hyoe Narita

Printed in Canada

Published by VIZ Media, LLC
P.O. Box 77010
San Francisco, CA 94107

10 9 8 7 6 5 4 3 2 1
First printing, August 2010

www.viz.com

www.shojobeat.com